Radio Mystery
and Adventure
and Its Appearances
in Film, Television
and Other Media

Radio Mystery and Adventure and Its Appearances in Film, Television and Other Media

by
Jim Harmon

McFarland & Company, Inc., Publishers
Jefferson, North Carolina, and London

The present work is a reprint of the library bound edition of Radio Mystery and Adventure: And Its Appearances in Film, Television and Other Media, *first published in 1992 by McFarland.*

LIBRARY OF CONGRESS CATALOGUING-IN-PUBLICATION DATA

Harmon, Jim.
   Radio mystery and adventure : and its appearances in film, television and other media / by Jim Harmon.
      p.   cm.
   Includes index.

   ISBN 0-7864-1810-9 (softcover : 50# alkaline paper)

   1. Radio serials. 2. Motion picture serials. 3. Television serials. I. Title.
PN1991.8.S4H3   2003
791.44'655—dc20   92-54086

British Library cataloguing data are available

©1992 Jim Harmon. All rights reserved

No part of this book may be reproduced or transmitted in any form or by any means, electronic or mechanical, including photocopying or recording, or by any information storage and retrieval system, without permission in writing from the publisher.

Cover photograph ©1997 PhotoDisc

Manufactured in the United States of America

McFarland & Company, Inc., Publishers
  Box 611, Jefferson, North Carolina 28640
    www.mcfarlandpub.com

To
Carlton E. Morse,
*as before, whose mastery of radio drama gave me great
pleasure as a boy, and who was first to welcome me into his
home and share his memories and memorabilia with me,*

*And to the memory of
Curley Bradley,
idol of my youth as "Tom Mix," and in mid-life, pal, mentor,
partner, and "unofficial" adoptive father, who more than
fulfilled the typical fan's fantasy of "coming to know"
his hero,*

*And to the memories of
John and Valeria Harmon,
my own father and mother, who started it all by giving me my
own radio at age three and then supplying boxes of Ralston,
largely uneaten, for box-top premiums,*

*And to
Barbara Gratz Harmon
and Dawn Kovner,
my wife and step-daughter who have put up with the clutter
of many cereal boxes, tapes and scripts, and who have
assisted me in everything possible,*

*And to
Redd Boggs,
analyst of science fiction and of life, who has assisted me
on this project as he has in various ways for over thirty years,*

*And to the memory of
Ron Haydock,
who in a short life filled with creating music, books and
films assisted me in every way possible on my projects,*

*And to all my friends,
living and deceased, whom I have mentioned in the
"acknowledgments" or whom I may have forgotten to mention
under the pressure of events.*

ACKNOWLEDGMENTS

I owe a great deal to everyone who worked in the world of "old time radio" or who only listened and imagined, and joined the participants in sharing their memories with me. Thanks, too, to all those who shared memorabilia with me, tapes, pictures, artifacts, who helped me with the physical aspects of storing material, and preparing manuscripts for publication. Thanks to the friends and family who provided me with encouragements and inspiration. Thanks to every one of you:

ABC, Forrest J Ackerman, Kirk Alyn, Dave Amaral, Mr. and Mrs. Slim Andrews, Boris Aplon, Gene Autry, Redd Boggs, Ray Bradbury, Eddie Brandt, Bobbie Bresee, Frank Bresee, CBS, Tony Clay, Ed Corcoran, Margaret Courtney, Helen Crosby, Serge Darrigrand, Eddie Dean, Judge Douglas R. Due, Harlan Ellison, Charles Flynn, Fred Foy, John & Larry Gassman, Donald F. Glut, Ken Greenwald, Monte Hale, Martin Halperin, Ray Harryhausen, Art Hern, Jay Hickerson, Jonathan Hole, Dave Holland, Bill Kaufman, Steve Kendall, John Milton Kennedy, Fred King, Chris Lembesis, Jack Lesser, Bobb Lines, Don Maris, Steve Markham, Paul Mix, George Montgomery, Clayton Moore, Carlton E. Morse, Millie Morse, Mutual network, NBC, the Rev. Bob Neily, Lloyd Nesbitt, Lil Neville, M. G. "Bud" Norris, Richard O'Brien, Pacific Pioneer Broadcasters, Ed Prentiss, Ralston-Purina, Roy Rogers, Lee Sapiro, Richard Seiverling; SPERDVAC (Society for Preservation and Encouragement of Radio Drama, Variety and Comedy), Jeremy Tarcher, Roy Thomas, Dann Thomas, Anthony Tollin, Les Tremayne, Barbara Watkins, William Witney, Joe Young and John Zinewitcz.

And to the memory of these unforgettable people: John Andrews, Roy Barcroft, Blackstone, Jim Boles, Curley Bradley, Yakima Canutt, Howard Culver, George DeNormand, Walter Gibson, Bob Greenberg, Richard Gulla, Forrest Lewis, Col. Tim McCoy, Ken Maynard, Kris Neville, Jay Novello, Betsy King Ross, and Glenn Strange.

CONTENTS

Acknowledgments vii

Forewords xi
(Carlton E. Morse, Jack Lester, Les Tremayne)

Preface xv

The Air Adventures of Jimmie Allen 1

Captain Midnight 7

Challenge of the Yukon (Sergeant Preston of the Yukon) 18

Dick Tracy 26

Green Hornet 41

I Love a Mystery 50

Jack Armstrong 79

Little Orphan Annie 99

The Lone Ranger 106

The Shadow 149

Sherlock Holmes 169

Sky King 183

Superman 197

Tom Mix 219

Appendix 257

Annotated Bibliography 267

Index 271

FOREWORDS

There has never been anything to stimulate the young mind the way radio affected the imagination in the heyday of audio entertainment. Listening alone made it possible for children to build their own illusions, make their minds wander into far places. What the eyes see limits the mind to what TV places on the screen. Radio opened the imagination to wonders beyond everyday living into new, vivid adventure and excitement.

Fantasy? Yes, I suppose so, but in my private thinking we're all figments of each other's imagination! A man thinks a neighbor hates him! The neighbor is unaware, but the man thinks he is an ugly, disagreeable, dangerous person. Actually, the neighbor is a decent man completely unaware and in *his* imagination wonders about the strange man next door and *he* fabricates *his* image, just as absurd as the first, and so the world goes on and actually it's all Fantasy and mostly completely untrue. We're just bits of fuzz floating in the Never Never.

Just looking over your *Great Radio Heroes*... My copy says October 3, 1967, with your signature 20 years ago! Love it! Love it!

Whether I deserve such ardent enthusiasm or not, I want you to know you have won a high place in my world of friendships.

I am dedicating our first *I Love a Mystery* novel, *Stuff the Lady's Hatbox*, to you for all your good efforts.

> Carlton E. Morse
> Woodside, Calif.
> *1988*

Radio! What a magical word to me when at the age of thirteen I first sang into a carbon microphone in my hometown of Enid, Oklahoma. Later, pursuing an acting career at the University of Oklahoma, I wrote and acted in many dramas and variety shows at the college station, WNAD. At the same time, at the fine arts building, we built our own sets and performed the best of 1930s Broadway. What a delight!

After announcing and acting stints, leads in local soaps and adventure series, and singing in Oklahoma and around the country, I went to Chicago in 1941 and joined AFRA – American Federation of *Radio* Artists – so I could appear in the many network soap operas and adventure serials originating in Chicago – like *Sky King* where I played the lead for some years.

Then with Jim Ameche on *The Silver Eagle* I played his faithful companion, the French-Canadian Joe Bidot. My name credit on this show was "Jacques Listaire," which writer-producer Jim Jewell thought more appropriate. "What's in a name?" I said.

What a wonderful 17 years in radio they were for me and my family, where I was doing what I loved and earning a good living. My announcing duties covered many years on ABC and NBC, where I had the pleasure of working with Garry Moore, Durwood Kirby, Curley Bradley (all of them on *Club Matinee*, for instance).

Curley Bradley – my dear friend. To me he was a real cowboy and really *was* Tom Mix. His abilities showed to good advantage, making *Tom Mix* perhaps the most popular Western kid show on the air.

Jim Harmon was probably as close to Curley as anyone could be, and can tell many stories of this famous cowboy who once rode horseback from one side of the United States to the other.

Thanks, Jim, for helping us remember.

The AFRA became AFTRA with the accent on "T" for Television. Now we watch cars explode, earthquakes earthquake, and people jump in and out of beds. The special effects people have taken over, and real actors are at a premium.

We had a great group of performers in those radio days. I'll never forget them. Too many have slipped off the raft and gone to the "Big Broadcast in the Sky." Someday I'll join them and we'll all have a ball!

Jack Lester
Canoga Park, Calif.
1988

How I was able to attain whatever status I enjoy, with meager education and no powerful or influential friends to assist me, remains a mystery to me. Stubborn perseverance, I guess. However, I must state that the climate has changed so in show-biz that even this no longer seems to apply – at least for me. The public remembers – the powers that be, whoever they are, do not. It is comforting, confusing and sad to be "a Legend in one's own time." I am grateful for the good things I have been given in my lifetime. Were it possible to live it over I would change very little. I've been privileged to work in radio in the golden days . . . Nothing can top that. I've had a good time in my work . . . I have simply not attained what I should have. As opposed to, say, Great Britain, where I was born, where they honor their veterans, there are few redeeming features to growing old in our society. I feel I can say this for, no matter where I was born, I am an American, thanks to my father. Thanks to my blessed mother's dogged determination, I have enjoyed an exciting, ever-changing life in her profession. She introduced me, at the age of three in England, to motion pictures, her chosen field, and encouraged me ever after, until she left us at age 99 last June. She was beautiful as a young girl . . . she was still beautiful when she passed away. I am eternally grateful to her for she bestowed upon me the same tough stubbornness which was so much a part of her being. And, in retrospect, everything that went before was like a funnel that aimed me right at radio broadcasting.

For those of you who are too young to remember dramatic radio, I wish to stress that when I say radio I refer to the dramatic portion of it more than any other. I have said this many times before in interviews and lectures but it bears repeating. In the profession, actors are a necessary evil. The business can't do without them and goodness knows they've tried. Except in the hearts of the audience, actors have always been low man on the totem pole . . . and it's a tough fight! I won't repeat a lot of well known facts but throwing your trunk out of a hotel window and then going out after it in order to skip your bill, because the manager of your company had gone before, absconding with what little money there was, was never fun. It was degrading as hell . . . and even worse if they caught up with you. *Then came radio!* The greatest thing that ever happened to performers. Low as the pay was, if any at the beginning, it was more or less steady. An actor was able to stay in one town, eventually buy a home or lease a fine apartment or perhaps even a penthouse, get married, raise children, have a bank account, earn a triple-A credit rating and become "somebody." End up with friends all over the world, having had a helluva good time all your life. We were blessed. What more could we ask? How many people can make such a claim?

We really had the best of it. No learning lines, no makeup, wardrobe, props, etc., ad infinitum. Really none of the pressure and stress that is part and parcel of working in television! Not even when I was doing forty-five shows a week for three years solid did I experience the kind of pressure I did on the latest TV show I did, "One Life to Live," where we did ten one-hour shows in four days. And the saddest part of all is that they didn't have to kill radio drama. They thought they had to in order to promote TV. No other nation I know of did that to radio . . . and I've traveled all over the world. Radio was too dominant when TV began. The men who controlled it are the same men who nurtured TV. When they pulled the plug, and, let's face it, everything is "economics," which was the main reason the plug was pulled, they left vast audiences stranded, such as convalescents, the aged, the blind, particularly, who still get starry-eyed when they talk to you about "those days" and can tell you more about you and your career than *you* know about yourself.

Les Tremayne
Los Angeles, Calif.
May 30, 1988

PREFACE

This book attempts to give the reader a detailed analysis of the more important radio programs in the category of mystery and adventure. It does not attempt to list every such program that ever existed. There is really nothing to say about many such radio programs other than they existed, who played what, and the general subject matter. Other programs are rich in content and varied in history. Some programs might be of interest, but not enough has survived of the recordings, scripts, or personal memory to make more than a few lines.

The volume at hand is not designed to help play "trivia" games by coming up with the name of the Lone Ranger's nephew's horse (although that information can be found here; in fact the now often used question was first made up by this writer). Those games are no longer so popular, and I never regarded the subject matter of dramatic radio as trivial. The creative content of old radio drama and serials was higher by far than that offered by television and most movies and novels appearing today. It was a precise treasure, nearly lost except for the efforts of a number of dedicated enthusiasts, including myself.

When I wrote my first book on the subject, *The Great Radio Heroes* (Doubleday, 1967), not a single episode of many famous old radio shows was known to exist on recording. For my chapter on *Tom Mix* I had to rely only on my memory and a juvenile novel based on the show by the radio scripter, George Lowther. Not that the world has become flooded with recordings now, but there are more than twenty episodes of *Tom Mix* in circulation among collectors, and reports of others waiting to be released. There are long runs of over a hundred episodes each of *Jack Armstrong* and *Captain Midnight*. The story on *Superman* is beyond what most enthusiasts could have dreamed in 1967 with well over a thousand episodes, the majority of the total number made, in existence.

The complete runs, from the beginning of the time they were transcribed, of *The Lone Ranger* and *Sergeant Preston of the Yukon* are in the warehouse of the Society for the Preservation and Encouragement of Radio Drama, Variety and Comedy (SPERDVAC) in the Los Angeles area.

Not that the story of preservation is all rosy. Since 1967, only a handful more episodes of radio's greatest adventure series, Carlton E. Morse's *I*

Love a Mystery, have surfaced. There are rumors of more somewhere but they are not available to fans, collectors or researchers.

Moreover, on some series, such as one of the better early science fiction–horror dramas, *Peter Quill,* not a single recorded episode has yet been found.

In this book, I have told everything I know or can find out about the programs being covered, not one-paragraph descriptions trying to convey the creative work of dozens of people over a score of years.

I originally planned one book about "old time radio" as it has come to be known, but the size got out of hand. A series of books would be required.

In this book, I have covered the primary adventure shows and those involving "mystery," which for my purposes is a program with an atmosphere of the sinister, the unknown, sometimes the supernatural. I am leaving the police detective and private eye for later volumes. Nor am I dealing with shows without continuing characters. Programs such as *Suspense, Lights Out,* and *Quiet Please* I will leave to a volume on anthology series in general.

The guidelines may not be perfect but they had to be drawn somewhere.

Depending on the reception to this book, and on my time, energy and life expectancy (I am 58 at this writing) I plan books with the tentative titles *Radio Detectives and Science Fiction* and *Radio Anthology Drama and Comedy,* and perhaps others.

The full title of the present volume is *Radio Mystery and Adventure and Its Appearances in Film, Television and Other Media.* The way these famous characters were handled before and after their radio appearances is a part of their history, I feel. I haven't attempted to list every film, every book, every bit of merchandising on these characters, but since it is a part of radio in my mind I have tried to document all the premiums and giveaways offered by each program.

Either through my own efforts, or the hand of Fate (as I believe) I not only got a chance to write about radio drama but to revive one of my favorites of that genre, *Tom Mix,* to write and produce it, and appear as the second lead, Pecos. The die has been cast. Some are called to greater duties, but my lot in life is to chronicle the world of radio drama. I am doing my best.

Jim Harmon
Burbank, Calif.
Summer 1992

The Air Adventures of Jimmie Allen

Syndicated by World Broadcasting. Two seasons were recorded in 1933-34 and 1935-36 and repeated for many years on many stations around the country. In 1946, a new cast (unidentified at this writing) performed new productions of the only slightly revised old scripts for another recorded, syndicated series that played into the fifties. The revision on the old scripts was often inappropriate, with "loose wing fabric" being found on all-metal jet planes. Sponsors: various.

Production: World Broadcasting **Writer-Directors:** Robert M. Burtt, Willfred Moore, others **Jimmie Allen:** Murray McLean **Speed Robertson:** Robert Fiske **Announcer:** Ed Prentiss, others.

The air itself was an important concept of the world of early radio. The electronic waves that brought all the thrills and laughter and contact with history and other parts of the world came over the air. "Bad" air brought only static. The princes of the air were the pilots—Charles Lindbergh, the first man to fly the Atlantic solo... Commander Byrd, conqueror of the South Pole, who broadcast from his base there regularly to America.

Fictional pilots flew in their shadow. Over the history of dramatic radio the patrol would be joined by Captain Midnight, Sky King, Hop Harrigan and Tailspin Tommy. While they were not full-time pilots, Dick Tracy and Tom Mix in his adventures in the modern West often took the controls, as did Jack Packard of *I Love a Mystery*. Some flew without a plane—Buck Rogers with his rocket belt, and Superman with only his red cloak. One of the first of these airmen was really only a boy.

The Air Adventures of Jimmie Allen was created by Robert M. Burtt and Willfred G. Moore, who wrote most of the other aviation series on radio in the 1930s, including *Captain Midnight* and the other programs already mentioned. Jimmie Allen, though never quite as popular as these other characters, was the first of the breed. In the early thirties Jimmie and his pal, former World War I pilot Speed Robertson, flew many dangerous missions to battle foreign spies, air bandits, kidnappers, and even a mad scientist or two. Other regular characters in the stories were Flash, the aircraft mechanic who kept Jimmie's plane, the *Blue Bird Special,* in perfect flying condition, and Barbara Croft, an airline stewardess and Jimmie's devoted girlfriend.

When the series began Jimmie was only an apprentice pilot of National Airways, learning to fly under the tutelage of veteran airman Speed Robertson, but he soon won his wings, and was off on more exciting adventures. The longest and most thrilling sequence during the first year was the transcontinental airplane race in which both Jimmie and Speed were entered, flying different planes. One reason the story took so long to tell, aside from the usual villainy and intrigue that was involved, was that the race was not nonstop coast to coast, but in short flights from city to city across the country. That was long ago when such races were really air adventures, involving fast planes whose range was not great. As befitted his status as hero of the series, Jimmie won the race, thus besting his tutor and best friend, Speed. Luckily their friendship was so strong that Speed evidently didn't suffer the least pang of jealousy.

Another sequence of adventures concerned the filming of an airwar epic in Hollywood, something on the order of "Wings" or "Dawn Patrol" – the 1930 version, that is, for the later Errol Flynn version had not yet been made. In the making of this movie Jimmie and Speed flew World War I planes to provide the aerial footage, along with an old wartime buddy of Speed's who had become an alcoholic failure in the intervening years. The man's alcoholism was never spelled out, of course, but even a kid could tell what ailed him. This pilot, whose life ended in a plane crash during the filming, was one of the few tragic characters ever depicted in a kid's radio show.

After such interludes, life as an airline pilot didn't seem too exciting, and Jimmie and Speed were soon chasing off toward the far horizons. One of their most memorable air adventures took them to China, where, like Charles A. Lindbergh, they mapped air routes for future airlines. Unlike Lindbergh, however, they got involved in a shooting conflict between rival warlords in one of the far provinces of pre-Red China.

Each program began with theme music that was a march tune that sounded as low-fidelity as anything ever heard on the air. Even old phonograph records played on a wind-up Victrola sounded better. The announcer's voice was distinctive, but not at all mellow and commanding, like Pierre André's or Truman Bradley's. His opening words, "The Air Adventures of

Radio's Jimmie Allen (actor Murray McLean) in flying togs for his 1936 movie, *Sky Parade.*

Jimmie Allen," were spoken in such a tense, shaky voice that one might think he was being forced to say them at gunpoint. They were followed by the buzz of an airplane, sounding suspiciously like an electric fan being passed in front of the microphone.

The theme music's lack of resonance probably derived from the fact that it was played from a phonograph record being rerecorded on a transcription, because *The Air Adventures of Jimmie Allen* was one of the few shows that was distributed by electrical transcription rather than broadcast on a radio network. The show was credited to the World Broadcasting System, not one of the famous names in Golden Age Radio, and originated first from Cleveland, later from Chicago. Jimmie was played by Murray McLean, Speed by Robert Fiske.

Because it was transcribed, *Jimmie Allen* had different sponsors in different parts of the country. In the Midwest it advertised the Skelly Oil Company, offering a challenge to its young listeners. You might be able to coax your mom to buy Wheaties or Ralston cereal—after all, you were going to eat the stuff, weren't you?—but would you be able to urge your dad to patronize a Skelly gas station just because Skelly was Jimmie Allen's sponsor? Dad was more likely to fill the tank at the nearest gas station regardless of the brand name, or—in those Depression days—at the station where gas sold at the cheapest price. Skelly tried on at least two occasions in the mid-1930s to put the pressure on its listeners to convince their fathers to drive in to one of their stations by offering premiums that, unlike those from *Jack Armstrong* or *Little Orphan Annie*, weren't available by mail. The *Jimmie Allen* ones had to be picked up at a Skelly station. Fortunately, at least in the author's town, the friendly Skelly service man would hand out the premium to any kid who came walking in and asked for it politely.

The first premium offer was a *Jimmie Allen* adventure, badly printed on rough newsprint, that continued for twelve or fifteen weekly installments over the spring and early summer, about the time school let out for the year. The story involved a secret invention that a mad scientist had developed: a little capsule that would unleash a smothering fog, thick and pervasive enough to hide an entire city. In those pre-radar days, this was a grave concern of Jimmie, Speed and other pilots who couldn't land their planes under such conditions, but was also of interest to foreign powers, even then gearing up for the war that came in only a few more years. How could they bomb a city if they couldn't even find it under all that eerie fog?

A second premium offer came a year later, and by then, the mushrooming comic-book phenomenon had already influenced the creators of the *Jimmie Allen* story. Instead of a story told entirely in words, as in the previous year, they now told a story in comic-book form, once again in weekly installments published on bad newsprint. The artwork was poorly done, and only minimally in color. The story concerned a mysterious flying wing (as in the original *Dick Tracy* movie serial) or perhaps it was a flying saucer or UFO, although such things were at least a dozen years in the future.

Despite such futuristic adventures, Jimmie Allen always seemed to belong to the bygone era of Flying Jennies and Spads. He must have been right at home at the joystick of those World War I aircraft he flew for the air-war movie. His creators, Burtt and Moore, must have felt the same way about Jimmie, for in 1940 they went on to create *Captain Midnight,* and in the mid-1940s to create *Sky King.* The last *Jimmie Allen* show was done in 1938, but by the magic of electrical transcription, rerun episodes continued to appear here and there on the dial until sometime in the 1950s.

Films

Jimmie Allen was never a popular enough hero to make it to the movie screen as a serial star, but there was a single feature movie about him. It appeared in 1934 and was called *Jimmie Allen in Sky Parade*. Murray McLean and Robert Fiske went to Hollywood to recreate their original roles as Jimmie and Speed, but for some reason Fiske, a veteran radio actor who had appeared on many other shows, including *The Story of Mary Marlin*, did not strike the movie producers as the sort of personality to play a hero's sidekick. McLean erroneously remembered Fiske being assigned a villain's role. Actually, Bob Fiske was given a fairly decent part as Jimmie's tragic father, Scotty Allen, and he played it well.

Genial, Irish William Gargan was the screen Speed Robertson. The film was directed by workmanlike Arthur Lovering, adapted from Burtt and Moore's scripts. It opened in France in 1917, just early enough to show Speed completing one of his air war victories. On the ground, he watched his pal, Scotty Allen, get the news of the birth of his son and the death of his wife.

The two stuck together in the development of aviation, raising Jimmy Allen with the help of Gerry Croft (Katherine DeMille). The two men tried a transatlantic flight to Paris in 1927, but the plane crashed on takeoff, killing the elder Allen. Lindbergh made it.

Another war buddy, Casey (Grant Withers), came back into their lives, along with gangster Gat Billings. The shady pair determined to steal Speed's airline project, an automatic pilot.

Jimmie (McLean, very believable) had grown into an eager teenager, and was in training to be a pilot. He found himself on the plane with the autopilot Casey and Billings stole. When the gangster accidentally shot Casey, it was up to the inexperienced Jimmie to land the plane. With Speed's help by radio, he did it, saving the invention and the day. Though predictable, the film was very well made for its day, almost reaching "A" level.

Books

There was a Big Little Book about Jimmie, with the story credited to creators Burtt and Moore. The highlight of this book was an illustration that supposedly showed Jimmie and Speed "loosening their belts" (that is, their seatbelts in the plane) as stated in the text. The drawing, done by an amazingly ignorant artist, depicted Jimmie and Speed standing alongside the plane yanking manfully at the belts that held up their pants. What happened then went unpictured, but the scene was set for one of Jimmie Allen's most amazing adventures. The story followed the events of Jimmie's earliest radio adventures at Kansas City Air Terminal.

Premiums

The premiums offered were as follows, listed alphabetically with sponsor, date and approximate value in 1992 (assuming average condition).

Album (Skelly, 1935, $30), Blotter (?, ?, $5), Book of Air Battles (?, 1934, $25), Bracelet, I.D. (Richfield, 1935, $25), Bracelet, I.D. (Weather Bird, 1935, $25), Bracelet, Kansas City Air Races (?, 1935, $15), Chart, Flying Maneuvers (?, 1934, $10), Club Newspapers, 12 Issues (?, 1935, $10 ea), Flight Wings, Flying Cadet (Town Talk Bread, 1934, $10), Flight Wings, Flying Cadet, Type I (Skelly, 1934, $15), Flight Wings, Flying Cadet, Type II (Skelly, 1934, $15), Flight Wings, Flying Cadet, Type III (Hi-Speed, 1934, $15), Flight Wings, Flying Cadet, Type III (Blue Flash, 1934, $15), Flight Wings, Flying Cadet, Type IV (Richfield, 1934, $15), Flight Wings, Flying Cadet, Type V (Richfield, 1934, $15), Flight Wings, Flying Cadet, Type V (Colonial, 1934, $10), Flight Wings, Flying Cadet, Type V (Log Cabin, 1934, $10), Flight Wings, Flying Cadet, Type V (Certified, 1934, $10), Flight Wings, Flying Cadet, Type V (Debus, 1934, $10), Flight Wings, Flying Cadet, Type V (Cleo Cole, 1934, $10), Flight Wings, Flying Cadet, Type V (Rainbo Gas, 1934, $10), Flight Wings, Flying Cadet, Type V (Duplex, 1934, $10), Flight Wings, Flying Cadet, Type V (Weather Bird, 1934, $10), Flight Wings, Flying Cadet, Type V (Sawyer, 1934, $15), Flight Wings, Flying Cadet, Type V (Certified, 1934, $15), Flight Wings, Flying Cadet, Type V (Butter Nut, 1934, $15), Flying Lessons, 5 total (?, 1934, $10 ea), Knife (?, 1936, $35), Manual, Weather Bird (Weather Bird, 1936, $20), Membership Card (?, 1934, $10), Monoplane, Blue Flash Paper (?, 1934, $25), Patch, Weather Bird (Weather Bird, 1936, $20), Photo, Jimmie Allen (Synd-various, 1934, $10), Photo, Jimmie Allen (?, 1934, $10), Photo, Jimmie Allen (?, 1934, $10), Photo, Speed Robertson (?, 1934, $10), Pilot's Creed (?, 1934, $15), Pin, Airplane (Skelly, 1934, $15), Road Maps, Various States (Various sponsors and dates, $10), Stamp Album (?, 1934, $25), Whistle, Brass (?, 1936, $25).

Captain Midnight

Afternoon adventure series, Monday–Friday, syndicated fall 1938–spring 1940. Sponsor: Skelly Gasoline (only three times a week in the beginning). Network broadcast: Mutual, September 1940 to late December 1949. Sponsor: Ovaltine.

Writers: Robert M. Burtt, Willfred G. Moore, others **Producer-Directors:** Kirby Hawkes, Russ Young, Alan Wallace **Captain Midnight:** Ed Prentiss (1938–39, 1940–49), Bill Bouchey (1939–40), Paul Barnes (1949) **Chuck Ramsey:** Bill Rose, Jack Bivens, Johnny Coons **Joyce Ryan:** Angeline Orr, Marilou Neumayer **Ichy Mudd:** Hugh Studebaker, Sherman Marks, Art Hern **Ivan Shark:** Boris Aplon **Fury Shark** (Ivan's daughter): Rene Rodier, Sharon Grainer **Gardo** (Ivan's chief henchman): Earl George, Art Hern **SS-11:** Olan Soule **Announcers:** Don Gordon, Tom Moore, Pierre Andre **Others in the Cast:** Marvin Miller, Maurice Copeland, Harry Elders, Jess Pugh.

The legend went like this. An American air corps captain was given a world-shaking assignment on which the whole outcome of World War I depended. He had to succeed in his task before twelve that night. The hours dragged by. The room full of staff officers began to lose hope. Then ... faintly ... now clearer, they heard the drone of a lone returning plane. "And it is just midnight," one officer observed. "Yes," Major Steele said, "And to me, he will always be ... *Captain Midnight!*"

Captain Midnight had the most colorful name of a long line of aviation heroes on radio. The roar of airplane engines lifting into the sky, the shriek of wind through wing struts as planes dove in defiance of mundane earth and sudden death–these were part of the warp and woof of radio drama in the thirties.

It was in the fall of 1938 that *Captain Midnight* first appeared, originally on only a scattering of Midwest stations, sponsored by a regional gasoline brand, Skelly. At first, Captain Midnight was not as colorful as his name.

He wore the tan flying togs of an ordinary pilot, transporting cargo and passengers. "Captain Midnight" was a code name, a secret designation only referred to in the opening of the show. He was working undercover to get the goods on a gang of criminals. Other characters referred to him by his real name, Jim Albright, or more often his nickname "Red."

But quickly the creators of the show realized there was more appeal in the mysterious Captain Midnight than in his civilian persona. As soon as the undercover work was over, everyone started to call him "Captain Midnight" and his real name was rarely used. Publicity photos now showed the man dressed in a solid black flying suit, mysteriously lit in shadow. A costumed, double-identity superhero had arrived on the scene, before Batman in the comics and approximately at the same time as Superman. Captain Midnight owed something to the pulp and radio character the Shadow, created in 1930, who was eventually revealed to have been a World War I fighter pilot.

The Midnight series was created by Robert M. Burtt and Willfred G. Moore. It was not their first aviation program for radio, and it wouldn't be their last. Their first important creation was *The Air Adventures of Jimmie Allen*, the story of a teenage student pilot, played by Murray McLean who, while eventually delivering the mail, took part in air races. Recently McLean remembered the man who would become Captain Midnight—actor Ed Prentiss—when he was the announcer on the *Allen* series.

Jimmie Allen had simply grown up to become Captain Midnight, it seemed. Nearly every, "leading man" type actor in Chicago tried out for the new aviation show in 1938. Prentiss was the first man to play Red Albright, Captain Midnight. The first series concluded in the spring of 1939, and the show vacationed for the summer. Prentiss read of new auditions in the fall for *Captain Midnight*. It didn't apply to him, he thought—he *was* Captain Midnight. He didn't show up for the tryout, and the part was given to Bill Bouchey.

Bouchey was a good actor who went on to Hollywood films, often as a gruff judge. But Ed Prentiss really was Captain Midnight, and in the 1939-40 season, he resumed the role after another audition. This was the last season sponsored by Skelly. The Wander company, makers of Ovaltine, bought the show for national sponsorship over the Mutual Broadcasting System beginning in 1940. Prentiss played the lead role through the end of the 1949 season. The quarter-hour serial format on radio was giving way to the complete thirty-minute story. *Midnight* was tried out with a half-hour format during 1949, but it didn't seem to adapt well. Paul Barnes replaced Prentiss for these final six months.

Midnight's recurring mission was to thwart the plans of Eurasian master spy Ivan Shark, played by Boris Aplon over the entire twelve-year run. He was not only the longest running villain in radio but also the vilest. His only spark of humanity was devotion to his daughter, Fury (Rene Rodier,

Captain Midnight director Kirby Hawkes makes a point to actors Jack Bivans ("Chuck Ramsey," center) and Ed Prentiss ("Captain Midnight," right at microphone), circa 1942. (Courtesy Boris Aplon)

others). He would cheerfully threaten to reward failure with death to henchman like Gardo (Art Hern, who would switch sides to be one of several to play Ichabod Mudd, Midnight's mechanic and sidekick). Both Aplon and Hern worked with this writer on a recent radio project and still have that Midnight timing.

About every second serial would concern Ivan Shark, and the alternate ones weren't much different with villains also usually played by Aplon (with a slightly less raspy voice). He blew up hangars and planes trying to wipe out Captain Midnight and his Secret Squadron members—Ikky and the two teens, Chuck Ramsey (Johnny Coons, then Jack Bivans) and Joyce Ryan (Marilou Neumeyer, others). They escaped to crush his espionage plots. In the final broadcast Shark tried to escape Midnight across the Arctic ice and was killed by a polar bear. It was a chilling climax for Captain Midnight's radio exploits.

The episode and the series ended with Midnight and his Secret Squadron members singing their rather new theme song. (Only in the final few years had any music at all been added to the show.) Pierre Andre asked listeners all to remember always, even when they grew up, Captain Midnight and his healthful beverage, Ovaltine.

Captain Midnight as a name and general concept does seem to have become a part of the national memory, along with Jack Armstrong, Gangbusters and a very few other radio immortals.

Films

When Columbia Pictues brought Captain Midnight to the screen, he remained a career military flier named Jim Albright who earned his famous code name on a daring secret mission during World War I. In 1942, he would have to have been around 42 years of age to have been even a teenage flier in 1918. The actor who had the part didn't look that old. An older performer like Jack Holt might have been more appropriate. Not that the likeable Dave O'Brien wasn't suitable as the Secret Squadron leader. O'Brien seemed to do well whatever he was called upon to do. He was a stuntman and a writer as well as a B Western cowboy hero beside Tex Ritter, the pair and their comic sidekick making up the trio. O'Brien was also a funny comic in the *Pete Smith Specialties*. He died of a heart attack in the fifties as a comedy writer on *The Red Skelton Show*. He was showing someone how he used to do a backflip, and it proved too much for him.

The *Captain Midnight* screen cast also included the same characters from the radio series, mechanic Ichabod Mudd (played by Guy Wilkerson, the aforementioned comic relief to Dave "Tex" O'Brien and Tex Ritter); young assistant Chuck (Sam Edwards, a radio actor who played parts similar to Chuck on the air, but from Hollywood, not from Chicago, Midnight's radio base); and finally the evil Ivan Shark (James Craven, whose screen specialty was treason). Joyce (Dorothy Short) also was on hand, but her identity had been altered from Joyce Ryan of the Secret Squadron to Joyce Edwards, daughter of eccentric inventor John Edwards (Bryant Washburn).

The *Captain Midnight* movie serial offered Dave O'Brien in the title role.

The change in Joyce's identity was minor, compared to what most movie serial versions did to famous creations.

Columbia did follow the established format of the celebrated characters they brought to film life better than many other film producers. For example, Republic's version of *Captain America*, was a great action chapterplay but one where all that is left of Jack Kirby's comic strip creation is the name and part of the costume.

The outfit for Midnight had never been clearly nailed down. In early Dell comic books he wore a pretty ordinary leather jacketed flying outfit with a winged clock over his heart. The publicity pictures from the radio show were much the same. A newspaper comic strip gave him a blue uniform. He wore red superhero tights in Fawcett comics publications. In an illustrated novel for Whitman, publishers of Big Little Books, he wore an all-black suit that was probably the most effective. His screen image, a black leather flying outfit with the winged clock in place of military campaign ribbons, came close to this image. In some scenes Midnight wore a black mask below the already disguising goggles to keep his identity of Captain Midnight separate from Jim Albright. For film, it was a good touch, making the hero live up to the title of the opening chapter, "The Mysterious Pilot."

Columbia Studios managed to acquire screen rights to some of the greatest characters of all time, and sometimes they did not do them justice, especially in the later days when Sam Katzman produced all the serials at that studio. *Captain Midnight* fared somewhat better than most Columbia chapterplays, according to critic Alan Barbour, but it lacked the polished action famous at Republic. Still, for faithful radio Secret Squadron members, it was an exciting experience.

One of the problems with Columbia serials was director James V. Horne, who was in charge of many Laurel and Hardy's best comedies. He could be a good action director, as he proved in *The Spider's Web*, one of the best serials ever made. But Horne got bored with serial action quickly and failed badly in *The Spider Returns* which he turned into a farce with horrendously overacting master villain, et al. In *Captain Midnight*, he steered nearer the wind.

For 15 chapters, the Secret Squadron chief protects the secret of inventor Edwards' Range finder, a gadget to make aerial bombing more deadly accurate, from Ivan Shark and his spies. For doing his duty, Midnight receives a series of death traps. Shark has his pilots bomb Midnight in a deserted cabin. He escaped with only split seconds to spare (in next week's Chapter Two, naturally).

In the fourth chapter, the mysterious aviator encounters one of the prototypical cliffhangers, notorious from the silent epics of Pearl White in *Perils of Pauline*. The famous ace is on a conveyer belt, headed straight into the teeth of a buzz saw, when the chapter ends. The following week the old inventor finds the switch on the devilish machine with no time to squander.

The eighth episode, "Shells of Evil," pits Captain Midnight against his nemesis, Ivan Shark, in a dogfight in the skies. Since no living man was a better pilot than Captain Midnight, one realized his plane is older and less airworthy than Shark's, because the criminal mastermind does manage to empty his guns into Midnight's ship and send it down to flaming disaster. Chuck and Ikky pull the famous ace from wreckage. Perhaps only Captain Midnight could survive such a crash, thanks to his body being fortified by drinking Ovaltine.

There were more gunshots and scything propellors to be dodged by Midnight, more crashes into the earth and in the clouds, but finally Chapter 15 came. The Secret Squadron commander and a squad of police close in on Shark's hideout, where he has plans against the lives of Joyce, her father, and Midnight's commanding officer, Major Steele (Joe Girard). Retreating from the heroic figure of Captain Midnight, Shark draws back his weapon, a crowbar, makes contact with some electrical wiring and, in a Frankenstein-like finale, destroys himself by his own monstrous device.

In the final sense, the serial succeeded in giving an acceptable image to one of the great unseen characters of radio.

Television

The first flight for Captain Midnight on television was a short one, but then so was the Wright Brothers' first hop. In 1951, a little more than a year after his final radio show, Captain Midnight landed a jet plane on screen and opened *Captain Midnight's Adventure Theatre*. The body of the show did not feature the Secret Squadron leader; it consisted of slightly edited chapters of various old Republic serials including *Mysterious Dr. Satan* and *Zorro's Fighting Legion*. The handsome actor playing a youthful Midnight (identity not known today) returned to deliver commericals for Ovaltine and at various times to offer as premiums both a Shake-Up Mug and a drinking cup. The bits with Midnight were on film and rerun to the point of desperate boredom.

In 1955, Captain Midnight really came to TV in the person of deep-voiced, angular-faced Richard Webb, who is still a striking, impressive man, though recovering from several bouts of serious illness. He told the author Ovaltine contacted him about use of his image in a modest revival of Midnight, with a few new premiums and TV commercials (not complete episodes) in 1988. They offered him a fee and he said "Double it!" Apparently they did because the commercials ran.

Midnight's sidekick was Sid Melton, sometimes described as a low comic, perhaps for both the level of his material and the level of his height. Melton has hung around long enough to play Estelle Getty's husband in flashbacks on *Golden Girls*. He wasn't the tall, raw-boned, Lincolnesque Ichabod Mudd described on radio and depicted in comics, but Ikky he was to the TV generation. (Actually, one of the radio actors to play Ikky, Art Hern, may be shorter than Melton). The final regular cast member was Olan Soule as Tut (short for Aristotle), a scientific genius. Soule told me once that he thought he was the only TV cast member to repeat his role from radio. But while Soule came in and out of the radio cast, sometimes playing a lieutenant in the Secret Squadron, at other times a plane manufacturer threatened by enemy agents and so forth, there doesn't seem to be any evidence the character Tut was ever in the radio series. Olan Soule may have appeared as a similar brilliant scientist at one time.

For a time the series was hugely popular, and a new generation of kids made *Captain Midnight* their favorite hero. He was the hero for the fifties, a stern, unbending foe of communism and anything that threatened America.

In "Top Secret Weapon" Midnight takes under his wing a boy refugee from behind the Iron Curtain, one corrupted by communists even at that early age into being a spy, to learn the secret of that weapon, a wireless controlled robot car such as could be bought in any toy store within a few years. But thanks to Captain Midnight's demonstrating American virtures to the boy, he is saved for democracy, and the robot car is saved—perhaps for the Mattel Toy Company.

The philosophy may have been simplistic, but the action sequences were good. Webb was good at movie serial style stunt fighting, convincing even with the odds three to one against him. The aerial sequences were too brief, mainly stock footage of the Navy Silver Dart Jet. The dramatics? The show followed the advice of that great movie serial director, Spencer Bennet, given to action star Kirk Alyn: "Just say the words and get into the fight."

Other episodes had Midnight saving plans for America's space station, which was in danger of becoming "The Lost Moon." A missing nuclear scientist was rescued from an Arctic location in "The Frozen Man." Other stories turned to that staple of early television, the western, and Webb changed his flying helmet for a Stetson, briefly entering the air space of his contemporary, Sky King.

All the episodes met with great acceptance, but surprisingly Ovaltine opted out after only two seasons. Planning ahead, they had had every actor who spoke the name of Captain Midnight also record the words "Jet Jackson." These words were dubbed into the shows (not very adroitly) and the series reran for a time under that title.

The Wander Company, makers of Ovaltine, wanted to reserve the name Captain Midnight for possible future use. There has been very little use made. Occasionally, a minor premium has appeared to keep the name alive, with the modest revival in the late 1980s the most significant reappearance to date.

There has been talk of a major film being made of *Captain Midnight*, following the examples of *Superman, Batman,* and *Dick Tracy,* but so far none of these plans have gone the distance.

The name is still known, even to those too young to have heard his radio show or seen his television series. The deeds of Captain Midnight are the stuff of legend. But perhaps it is only a distant, half-remembered legend that will remain.

Comics

The first issue of the *Captain Midnight* comic magazine shows the aviation hero, dressed in a red jacket and riding-type britches, standing next to the massively muscular superhero, Captain Marvel, who introduces him to the public. Speculation has it that Fawcett obtained the rights to Captain Midnight so that there would not be another heroic Captain M – giving competition on the stands to their Marvel.

Midnight had appeared in comics before his 1942 debut in his own magazine. Dressed in a brown leather flying jacket, he was one feature among many appearing in Dell's *The Funnies*, starting in 1940. These short episodes were slavishly adapted from the radio scripts, even using much the same dialogue as the broadcasts. But at Fawcett, there were changes. Midnight now wore a red costume like Captain Marvel. Eventually it would become a skin-tight regulation superhero uniform, and Midnight would fly on his own power – or at least only with the aid of his "gliderchute" – winglike webbing from his sleeves to his body.

It is too bad the great C. C. Beck, co-creator of Captain Marvel, did not have more time from that famous creation to devote to the comics of Midnight, to give them some humor and charm. One of his partners, Otto Bender, did some of the scripts. Artist Mac Raboy contributed some beautiful covers to the magazine, but mostly the stories were routine, with plenty of wartime propaganda against the Japanese and Nazis.

Only a year or so earlier a newspaper strip by Erwin Hess had begun, featuring Midnight in a striking *blue* uniform. (Probably no other comic character was ever given such a succession of different colored outfits. The hugely successful ones got it right to begin with and stuck to it). The color went out of the tales in more ways than one. Captain Midnight became dressed in khaki, like so many fighting men in reality and comics, undistinguished from many others. The strip faded away, but the Fawcett comic magazines persisted into the fifties. Comic strip style advertisements have appeared virtually to the present writing.

Some of the newspaper strips were adapted into the famous Big Little Books, one page of text for each page of illustration. There were some originals of Russ Winterbothom, who remembered that he just "knocked them out," like the tons of pulp and comics material that he produced in a lifetime.

Whitman, publisher of Big Little Books, also offered a full-size novel with only a handful of illustrations (what once they would have called a Big Big Book) called *Joyce of the Secret Squadron*, obviously aimed at the girls' market. But it presented in those few illustrations what was probably Captain Midnight's best and most appropriate costume – solid black, so black that not even crease lines showed. This was the only place this costume appeared. It might have been to somber for the young comics readers back then, but this was a uniform that fit.

Premiums

During the syndication period, Skelly gasoline offered a number of "get them from your Skelly dealer" items. There was a Flight Patrol badge, a riddle book, a Heroes of the Air stamp album, maps of airline routes and photographs of Captain Midnight, Chuck and Patsy Donovan.

When the network series for Ovaltine came along, the primary premium became the annual Codeograph badge and Secret Manual. These were issues for 1941, 1942 and 1945 through 1949 (there were none for the deepest of the war years because of rationing). Besides being badges these instruments sported code dials, and in the second year there was space for a photograph of Midnight, which could be replaced with one of your own. Later versions added mirrors, magnifying glasses, secret compartments, a police whistle and, for the last one, a secret key needed to activate the code dial. The manuals were handsome booklets with reproductions of full color paintings of the radio heroes and villians. The one for 1942 contains the most pages and color portraits, and is considered the best. The codeographs sell today for $50 to $75, and the manuals are worth $75 to $100.

There were a few other premiums besides this annual membership set, such as the Mystic Sun God ring, with its simulated ruby stone and strange inscriptions. This is one of the rarest of all premiums from any character and has sold for $500 in mint condition.

During the last couple of years, Ovaltine has run some Midnight television commercials and offered premium T-shirts, watches, and iron-on patches. As of now, these are worth only $10 to $20 to collectors (the watch, $75). So far, this advertising activity has generated no new radio or TV adventure episodes, no new flights for the Secret Squadron.

The premiums offered were as follows, listed alphabetically with sponsor, date and approximate value in 1992 (assuming average condition).

Aerial Torpedo Bombers (Ovaltine, 1940–41, $45), Aviation Wings, Pilot's Badge (Ovaltine, 1940–41, $15), Blackout Lite-Ups (Magic) (Ovaltine, 1942, $40), Book of Tricks and Riddles (Skelly Oil, 1939, $25), Certificate, Flight Commander (TV) (Ovaltine, 1955–56, $5), Code-O-Graph, Key-O-Matic (Ovaltine, 1949, $25), Code-O-Graph, Magni-Matic (Ovaltine, 1945, $45), Code-O-Graph, Mirro-Flash (Ovaltine, 1946, $35), Code-O-Graph, Mirro-Magic, w/red plastic back (Ovaltine, 1948, $30), Code-O-Graph, Mystery Dial (Ovaltine, 1940–41, $25), Code-O-Graph, Photomatic, W/ C.M. photo (Ovaltine, 1942, $45), Code-O-Graph, Photomatic, W/O C.M. photo (Ovaltine, 1942, $15), Code-O-Graph, Whistling, plastic (Ovaltine, 1947, $30), Decoder,

Silver Dart Sq., plastic (TV) (Ovaltine, 1957, $90), Decoder, Sq. plane puzzle, plastic (TV) (Ovaltine, 1955–56, $100), Detect-O-Scope, Five-way w/metal insert (Ovaltine, 1940–41, $35), *Flight Patrol Reporter* newspaper, Vol. 1, No. 1 (Skelly Oil, 1939, $30), *Flight Patrol Reporter* newspaper, Vol 1, No. 2 (Skelly Oil, 1939, $25), *Flight Patrol Reporter* newspaper, Vol. 1, No. 3 (Skelly Oil, 1939, $25), *Flight Patrol Reporter* newspaper, Vol. 1, No. 4 (Skelly Oil, 1939, $25), *Flight Patrol Reporter* newspaper, Vol. 1, No. 5 (Skelly Oil, 1940, $25), *Flight Patrol Reporter* newspaper, Vol. 1, No. 6 (Skelly Oil, 1940, $25), Flight Wings, Mystic Magic Weather Forecasting (Skelly Oil, 1939, $9), Flying Cross, Flight Commander (Ovaltine, 1942, $85), Folder, Insignia (Ovaltine, 1943, $50), Folder, Service Ribbon (Ovaltine, 1944, $30), Game, Jumping Bean, Ringo Jumpo (Skelly Oil, 1940–41, $40), Handbook, Flight Commander (Ovaltine, 1942, $55), Handbook, Flight Commander (TV) (Ovaltine, 1957, $100), Handbook, Secret, Flight Commander (TV) (Ovaltine, 1955–56, $40), Insignia Transfer (Ovaltine, 1949, $20), Letter from Chuck's Dad (Skelly Oil, 1939, $35), Manual (Ovaltine, 1940–41, $100), Manual (Ovaltine, 1942, $85), Manual (Ovaltine, 1945, $85), Manual (Ovaltine, 1946, $75), Manual (Ovaltine, 1948, $75), Manual, (Ovaltine, 1949, $65), Manual (TV) (Ovaltine, 1955–56, $150), Manual (TV) (Ovaltine, 1957, $90), Manual, First Smaller Size (Ovaltine, 1947, $75), Map, Airline, of America (Skelly Oil, 1940–41, $175), Map, Chuck's Treasure (Skelly Oil, 1939, $65), Membership Card (Skelly Oil, 1939, $40), Membership Card (Skelly Oil, 1940–41, $40), Membership Card (Skelly Oil, 1940–41, $40), Membership Card (TV) (Ovaltine, 1955–56, $25), Membership Token, Brass Spinner (Skelly Oil, 1940–41, $10), Membership Token, Pewter Spinner (Repro) (Skelly Oil, 1940–41, $2), Membership Token, Reproduction (Skelly Oil, 1940–41, $2), Model Kit, Spartan Bomber (Skelly Oil, 1939, $100), Mug, Embossed Shakeup, ivory w/orange top (Ovaltine, 1947, $55), Mug, Hot Ovaltine (TV) (Ovaltine, 1953, $15), Mug, Shake-Up, 15th Anniversary, Red w/blue top (Ovaltine, 1957, $25), Patch, Cloth, Sq., 15th Anniversary (TV) (Ovaltine, 1957, $20), Patch, Sq. Cloth (TV) (Ovaltine, 1955–56, $30), Photo (TV) General Mills, 1955–56, $30), Photo, Chuck Ramsey (Skelly Oil, 1939, $11), Photo, C.M. Wearing Secret Ring (Skelly Oil, 1939, $23), Photo, C.M. With Treasure Hunt Rules Reverse Side (Skelly Oil, 1939, $30), Photo, C.M., Chuck and Patsy (Skelly Oil), Pin, American Flag Loyalty, w/paper (Ovaltine, 1940–41, $50), Pin, American Flag Loyalty, W/O paper (Ovaltine, 1940–41, $45), Pin, Flight Commander's (Skelly Oil, 1939, $350), Pin, School (Ovaltine, 1942, $25), Pin, Service Ribbon, Unmarked (Ovaltine, 1944, $25), Plane Detector, Complete w/Plane Inserts (Ovaltine, 1942, $110), Radio Recordings: Longines Symphonette Soc Pkg (Ovaltine, '60s–'70s, $40), Radio Recordings: Ovaltine Record (Also Stores) (Ovaltine, '60s–'70s, $20), Ring, Flight Commander (Ovaltine, 1940–41, $75), Ring, Flight Commander Signet, Plastic (TV) (Ovaltine, 1957, $120), Ring, Initial Print, w/Top (Ovaltine, 1948, $70), Ring, Marine Corps (Ovaltine, 1942, $120), Ring, Mystic Sun God (Ovaltine, 1946, $300), Ring, Sliding Secret Compartment (Ovaltine, 1942, $70), Ring, Whirlwind Whistling (Ovaltine, 1940–41, $125), Shoulder Patch, Insignia (Ovaltine, 1943, $45), Shoulder Patch, Insignia (Ovaltine, 1944, $45), Sky Scope (Ovaltine, 1947, $40), Stamp Album of Air Heroes w/16 Stamps (Skelly Oil, 1939, $25), "Story of U.S. Marines" by C.M. (Ovaltine, 1942, $50), T-Shirt (Ovaltine, 1987, $15), Transfer Patch, Iron-On (Ovaltine, 1948, $40), Watch (Ovaltine, 1987, $75).

Challenge of the Yukon (Sergeant Preston of the Yukon)

Began Jan. 3, 1939, as local Detroit-area show (some 15 min.) through 1940s, then ran as a half-hour complete story as follows: 1946–Oct. 1947, Sustaining, ABC, Thursday; Nov. 1, 1947–July 24, 1948, Sustaining, ABC, Sunday; July 28, 1948–Sept. 1, 1948, Sustaining, ABC, Wednesday night; Sept. 6, 1948–June 10, 1949, Quaker Oats, ABC, 3x/week; June 15, 1949–Sept. 7, 1949, Quaker Oats, ABC, Wednesday night; Sept. 12, 1949–Dec. 8, 1950, Quaker Oats, ABC, 3x/week; Jan. 20, 1951–July 8, 1951, Sustaining, Mutual, Saturday & Sunday; July, 10, 1951–June 9, 1955, Quaker Oats, Mutual, 5x/week.

Writers: Fran Striker, others **Directors:** Al Hodge, Charles D. Livingston, Fred Floweraday **Producer-Creator:** George W. Trendle **Sergeant Preston:** Brace Beemer (1941, 1953-54), Jay Michael (1941-46), Paul Sutton (1947-53) **Inspector:** John Todd **Announcers:** Bob Hite, Jay Michael, Fred Foy.

Busy as he was, week after week, bringing to justice another gang of cattle rustlers or stagecoach bandits, then galloping away in search of more deeds of derring-do, the Lone Ranger couldn't be everywhere. He was known in seven states, according to the narrator in the early days of the radio show, but to fight lawlessness north of the border he had to depend upon Sergeant William Preston of the Northwest Mounted Police.

The program featuring this radio hero and his dog Yukon King came out of the same shop that created *The Lone Ranger*—the production crew at WXYZ in Detroit—and featured most of the same cast. Even the theme music of the show, the "Donna Diana Overture" by von Reznicek, was part of the background and between-scenes music regularly heard on *The Lone Ranger*. The program was called the *Challenge of the Yukon*, but everyone seemed to call it "Sergeant Preston."

Perhaps it ought to have been called "Yukon King" after the Sergeant's Alaskan husky, who seemed to own most of the brains of the outfit. As listeners learned in a flashback, the young Mountie had rescued the dog from harm when Yukon King was just a small pup. The animal had an unusual history, having been raised by Three Toes, an old wolf. Once on patrol, the Mountie witnessed a lynx attacking the wolf and her cub and arrived just in time to kill the lynx and save the dog but not its adoptive mother.

Gathering up the cub in his arms, Sergeant Preston announced, "I'm going to call you Yukon King. I'll teach you to respect good men and to hate evil ones. You'll learn to captain a team, and to pull your own weight. I'll teach you self-control, and how to best use your great strength. Youngster, we're going to be partners, and when you're grown, you are going to be the greatest dog in all the Yukon!"

That's a lot of responsibility to load on a small animal, but the puppy responded well. In fact, he learned to sniff out bad men much better than Sergeant Preston himself. Often he would growl warningly at a newcomer, and the Mountie wouldn't take the hint, only to be bashed over the head or held up at pistol-point later. If only he had listened to the dog's urgent "Rrruff! Bow-wow-wow!" The concept of Yukon King owed a great deal to Rin Tin Tin, the German police dog who became a major animal star of both large and small screen, and ultimately to Buck, the part Saint Bernard dog who is stolen from his home in California and taken to the Klondike during the Gold Rush in Jack London's *Call of the Wild*.

The daily adventures of the Sergeant and the husky were probably inspired by the robust novels and short stories of James Oliver Curwood, who had popularized the conventions of Jack London's fiction with such books as *The Valley of Silent Men* and *The Country Beyond*. At one time his stories of the Far North, which he called "God's Country," were almost as popular as Zane Grey's novels about the Old West.

Another inspiration was the poetry of Robert W. Service, author of "The Shooting of Dan McGrew" ("A bunch of the boys were whooping it up in the Malamute saloon"), whose most popular book bore the title *The Spell of the Yukon* and whose poem "The Law of the Yukon" contains some lines that might apply to Sergeant Preston himself: "This is the Law of the Yukon, that only the Strong shall thrive; That surely the Weak shall perish, and only the Fit survive." Preston proved that Darwinian "law" week by week.

Although Sergeant Preston came out of Jack London, Curwood and

Service, some of the scripts were rather obviously recycled from *Lone Ranger* programs heard months or years before. This was of course self-plagiarism, for the *Challenge of the Yukon* was conceived and produced by George W. Trendle and written by Fran Striker, the men responsible for the *Ranger* shows. If a plot worked once, it would work again.

In the great tradition of popular heroes, Preston joined the Mounties for a very personal reason: to find and capture the murderer of his father. Once he has the man in irons, Preston says sternly, "On your feet, Spike Wilson! I'm taking you to Mounted Police Headquarters. You're going to pay for the murder of my father, and for your other crimes." And Wilson snarls, "Beaten! Me – the toughest outlaw in the Yukon beaten by one kid constable!" Every great hero knows such a moment of triumph. In Preston's case his reward was comparatively modest: he was promoted to sergeant.

Preston usually traveled by dog sled – led of course by Yukon King – but sometimes, like the Ranger, he rode a horse. His was called Blackie but was later rechristened Rex – or perhaps it was a different horse. Mushing through the eternal snow, by one mode or another, Sergeant Preston rescued gold-seekers from bandits and blizzards, saved fur pelts from thieves, and brought serum to victims of epidemics in the frozen North.

So far as I remember, the Lone Ranger never bothered to cross the northern border, probably feeling that things were in good shape up there due to the strenuous activities of Preston and Yukon King. At least once, though, the Sergeant ranged far south of the border to San Francisco, where he pursued smugglers in an automobile. He soon went back to the Yukon to take up the fight against renegades and Indians. Yukon King, usually called King for short, carried countless messages for help from trading posts under siege and prospectors' shacks being menaced by avalanches and floods. Sometimes he must have gotten footsore, and his throat must have been raw from barking unheeded messages.

The original Sergeant Preston was Brace Beemer, but he moved to *The Lone Ranger*, to become the voice of the Masked Rider after the death of Earle Graser. In 1954, when *The Lone Ranger* ended its "live" broadcasts, Beemer returned to play Preston on *Challenge of the Yukon*. Fred Foy, who had narrated *The Lone Ranger*, took over from Jay Michael as narrator of the *Preston* series during the final season. The senior members of the WXYZ stock company kept working through the end. The most familiar voice of Sergeant Preston belonged to Paul Sutton. His superior, the Inspector, was played by John Todd, "Tonto" of *The Lone Ranger*, in a neat reversal of roles.

It's lucky that the Yukon is such a vast territory (over 200,000 square miles) and the rest of Canada's northern frontier is so spacious. Otherwise it would have been a very competitive neighborhood for the cops. Even in the worst of times there might not have been enough bandits, killers, fur thieves, and swindlers to go around. Some of the Mounties might have been laid off or reduced to issuing bicycle licenses in Whitehorse. Operating at the same time as Sergeant Preston were a couple of other red-coated policemen who were just as rough and ready and just as sure of getting their man.

One was King of the Royal Mounted, in the newspaper strip of the name under Zane Grey's byline. King appeared briefly on radio, but had greater fame in two Republic movie serials in 1940 and 1942. There were other "Mounties" serials as well about other heroes less well remembered, including Sergeant Gray of *Perils of the Wilderness*, released by Columbia in 1956, the next-to-last serial ever made.

Far more memorable was *Renfrew of the Mounted*, a radio adventure story that offered strong competition to *Challenge of the Yukon* from its beginning in 1936. The show was written by Laurie York Erskine, and featured House Jameson – a busy radio actor best remembered for his role as the father of Henry Aldrich on *The Aldrich Family* – as Inspector Douglas Renfrew. *Renfrew* grew out of a series of stories by Erskine, and as a radio show was famous for its opening, which included the howl of a Northern gale, the howl of a wolf, and the voice of the announcer, almost a howl in itself, intoning "Ren-Frew! Renfrew – of the Mounted!" Kids of the late 1930s who did amateur impressions loved to imitate that voice.

Perhaps in a misguided attempt to give a small documentary touch to the *Sergeant Preston* stories, the programs, no matter how melodramatic, ended with the Sergeant announcing solemnly "This case is closed." At the same instant, in similar circumstances, the Lone Ranger would be heading for the far horizon with a clatter of hooves (courtesy of the WXYZ sound man) and somebody would be asking in wonder, "Who was that masked man?" There wasn't any mystery about Sergeant Preston.

Despite occasional moments of happy exuberance – for despite everything that conspired against him, Fran Striker was an artist – the stories of *Challenge of the Yukon* were often too mechanically proficient: exactly what was needed and nothing more. This charge cannot be made, at least in the large sense, against *The Lone Ranger*, which had a verve that the *Yukon* series lacked.

Although third among WXYZ's major productions, Sergeant Preston was still a Medal winner. And perhaps King should have gotten a special "Oscar."

Television

While there were plenty of movies with other radio-related Mounties, such as *Renfrew of the Mounted* and *King of the Mounted*, as well as other non-radio character members of the RCMP portrayed by Jim Bannon and

Bob Steele, among others, there were no feature-length movies of Sergeant Preston, only the television series.

The series began as *Sergeant Preston of the Yukon* (it was never known by the earlier radio title of *Challenge of the Yukon)* in 1955 and ran until 1958 with new episodes – the first seventy-eight in black and white, the final twenty-six in color. The color episodes are only occasionally seen in reruns, and the black and whites have been languishing in the vaults, unwanted in the age of color for many years. Today, any series that goes over 100 episodes is considered a fantastic success, but in earlier days of television when more episodes per year were routinely made, such success was not considered remarkable.

The lead actor in the television series was a splendid choice. Richard Simmons was a real outdoorsman and man of action. He was a professional pilot, broke wild horses as a hobby and engaged in many athletic activities. No doubt he could have met the requirements to be a real-life member of the Royal Mounted.

Something other commentators such as critic Gary H. Grossman have not noticed in their otherwise excellent commentaries is that Simmons also had a voice as good as – perhaps even better than – the radio Sergeant Preston, Paul Sutton. Simmons' voice was deep and commanding, yet friendly and sympathetic – perfect for the hero Mountie. During the filming of the premier show, Simmons was thrown from his black horse, Rex, when the animal was spooked by a badger, and the star's wrist was broken. He completed the episode and several more with a hidden wrist cast.

An apocryphal story that has been seen in print is that after this accident, Simmons refused to ride a horse again and all the subsequent episodes had to utilize dog teams in the snow country. Of course, there were other horseback episodes filmed, including a number in color made several years later. Simmons was not that type of Hollywood actor.

Some executive decision apparently was made that since there were so many horseback Westerns on television at that time, there would be a concentration on snow country locales and dog teams to offer variety. The stories of Preston in his scarlet tunic against the green trees of the high country, with the great dog King running alongside, were perhaps more colorful and exciting.

As on the radio, King was always an important part of the story. The dog chosen as King seemed a fine and intelligent animal, but some of the other dogs in the team were not so well behaved. Actor Richard Simmons, an expert at working with animals, was called from a dinner party to help the dog wranglers calm down the team, which was cranky and nervous after being flown up to a mountain location near Big Bear, California. The dogs were snapping at handlers, but Simmons soothed and reassured them and returned to dinner.

A typical episode concerned an embittered old man who had come to distrust all human beings and loved only dogs. Since he was shooting at anyone who came near, shutting off a pass, Preston got to him by having King do his lame dog act and distract the old man long enough for the Mountie to disarm him. But King only did it for the old man's own good, of course. Preston got enough information from the dog lover to track down the two thieves who had cheated the old fellow out of his life savings and disillusioned him.

The radio version of this story is among the fifty-two episodes of the broadcast series currently in syndication. So out of the hundreds of radio shows, and over 100 television shows, this episode alone is currently available in both versions. It is a good one, representative of the values exemplified by Sergeant Preston and King in both media. The program said that if a man loved and respected animals and nature, he would be on better terms with his fellow man as well. The justice of the Royal Mounted and all men of good will was only imposed on those who violated the rights of man and the environment.

The spirit of Sergeant Preston lives on in many grownup followers who can only wish Preston and King were present today to take on the polluters and despoilers of a post-frontier world.

Premiums

The premiums offered were as follows, listed alphabetically with sponsor (when known), date and approximate value in 1992 (assuming average condition).

Button, Membership (1956, $325), Card, Picture, Yukon Adventure, 36-pc. set (1950, $1 ea), Cards, Dog, Series 1 (1949, $5 ea), Cards, Dog, Series 2 (1949, $5 ea), Cards, Yukon Adventure Story, 36-pc. set (1956, $15 ea), Cards, Antique, 5 pcs. (1954, $25), Collection, Western Gun, 5 pcs. (1952, $20 ea), Deed, Yukon Square Inch Land (1955, $25), Detector, Gold Ore (1952, $55), Distance Finder (1955, $45), Flashlight, Signal (1949, $35), Goggles, Trail, Complete Cereal Box (1952, $150), Goggles, Trail, Package Back (1952, $20), Land Pouch, Klondike (1955, $45), Map, Yukon Territory, Color (1955, $25), Package Back, Adventure Game: Dog Sled Race (1949, $20), Package Back, Adventure Game: Great Yukon River Race (1949, $20), Package Box, Complete, Adventure Game: Dog Sled Race (1949, $150), Package Back, Adventure Game: Sgt. Preston Gets His Man (1949, $20), Package Box, Complete, Adventure Game: Great Yukon River Race (1949, $150), Package Box, Complete, Adventure Game: Sgt. Preston Gets His Man (1949, $150) Pedometer (1952, $25), Photo, 8½ x 11, B&W (1949, $20), Photo, Postcard Size, B&W (1949, $15), Photo, Richard Simmons, Color (1956, $15), Pictures to Color Package, 3 ea. (1952, $20), Pocket Comics: "How He Became a Sergeant" (1956, $15), Pocket Comics: "How He Found Yukon

Sergeant Preston of the Yukon advertisement for his 1950s "10-in-1" Electric Trail-Kit, one of the most elaborate premiums ever offered.

King" (1956, $15), Pocket Comics: "How Yukon King Saved Him from the Wolves" (1956, $15), Postcard, Contest (1950, $20), Poster, Contest Winner (1950, $250), Record: "Case of the Indian Rebellion" (1954, $20), Record: "Case of the Orphan Dog (1954, $20), Record: "Challenge of Yukon"/"Maple Leaf Forever" (1952, $20), Record: "How Preston Became a Sergeant" (1952, $20), Records: Totem Pole Collection, 78 or 45 RPM (1952, $85/set), Stove, Prospector's Camp, Unmarked (1954, $90), T-shirt (1956, $45), Tent, Prospector's Camp, Unmarked (1954, $90), Trail Kit, "10-in-1'" Electric (1956, $200), Trophy, North America Big Game, Set (1954, $15), Viewer, Movie (1954, $20), Western Wagons, 5 pcs. (1954, $40), Whistle, Mounted Police w/Cord (1950, $25), Yukon Trail Package, Complete Cereal Boxes (Quaker PR&W, 1949, $290 ea.), Yukon Trail Package Backs (Quaker PR&W, 1949, $30 ea.), Yukon Trail, Cardboard Models (Quaker PR&W, 1949; all 59 from 8 Boxes; $475).

Dick Tracy

Juvenile serial NBC, 1935–39, 15 min. One season, 1939, as half-hour nightime series. Returned on ABC as 15 min. daily series, 1944–49. Also heard in separate, concurrent half-hour complete story series, Saturday night, 1948–49.

Writers: George Lowther, Sidney Slon, John Wray **Producers-Directors:** Mitchell Grayson, Charles Powers **Dick Tracy:** Ned Wever (1938-42), Matt Crowley (1945-46), Barry Thomson (1947) **Junior:** Andy Donnelly, Jackie Kelk **Pat Patton:** Walter Kinsella **Chief Brandon:** Howard Smith **Tess Trueheart:** Helen Lewis **Announcers:** Don Gardiner, George Gunn, Dan Seymour, Ed Herlihy **Others:** Mandell Kramer, John Griggs, Mercedes McCambridge, Craig McDonnell, Gil Mack, Ralph Bell.

So many famous heroes, from Buck Rogers to Skippy, made the jump from the newspaper comic section to the airwaves in Radio's Golden Age that it was almost inevitable that Dick Tracy would make the jump too. Chester Gould's adventure story about cops in a big city (the locale was never specified) first hit the newspapers in 1931, and quickly became one of the premier cartoon strips in the country. The stories always moved fast, and even though they were fantastic in plot and character, they also had a gritty realism that lifted them a notch or two above the other comics of the day. In that long-ago era the commercializing of a successful product like a popular comic strip hadn't yet reached the proportions that are common today, but you had to suppose that *Dick Tracy* would sooner or later make the transition to movies and radio.

If you were a kid with an ear glued to the loudspeaker of the family radio one afternoon in 1935, you discovered *Dick Tracy* coming to life. You conjured him up out of the exciting noises you heard coming from your Mutual station in a far-off city. You heard the roar of a police car and the scream of sirens and a rasping voice on the police radio: "Calling Dick Tracy...Calling Dick Tracy!" and you heard a confident, resonant voice respond, "This is Dick Tracy – ready for action!"

Although the *Dick Tracy* of radio didn't last as long as the comic strip itself—which is still going, drawn by Chester Gould's former assistant Dick Locher and written by novelist Max Allen Collins—it did continue for more than a decade and is fondly remembered by people who were kids in the 1930s. Perhaps it is also remembered by a few old radio fans who were grownups back then, for some fictional heroes like Dick Tracy appeal to adults as well as children. Most of the time the show was a children's serial that ran five days a week on the NBC Blue Network. Though aimed at kids of school age, and broadcast in the late afternoon after school, the radio version, like the comic strip original, was a well-written and well-produced adventure story, capable of standing up under the critical scrutiny of adults. At times it must have had as many grownup fans as such programs as *The Lone Ranger* and *The Green Hornet*, and it was almost as well-done.

Much of the credit for the radio show's popularity belongs to the scriptwriter through most of its best years: George Lowther. His is not a household name, but he was a major talent in the radio world of the 1930s and 1940s. After *Dick Tracy* he went on to write for the *Superman* series, and to act as announcer/narrator as well, before that job was taken over by the better-remembered Jackson Beck. Later he authored the first *Superman* novel, adding details to the canon that remain even today. He was also hired to write the *Tom Mix* cowboy adventure series. All of these shows earned high marks for originality in a medium that often hovered not far above the dull and routine.

Early in the comics career of *Dick Tracy*, creator Chester Gould began to capitalize on his talent for creating bizarre and grotesque villains. Some of them are so memorable that they reappeared, decades later, in the Warren Beatty movie about Tracy, released in 1990. The radio series was never a close copy of the strip, although characters besides Tracy himself that were created by Gould appeared in the regular cast: Junior Tracy, Pat Patton, Chief Brandon, and Tess Trueheart. Its villains, though memorable, were not like those in the strip—by necessity, because those created by Gould usually depended upon their visual impact. Lowther and the other writers of the radio version worked in a far different medium, depending upon voices and sound effects, and calculated their effects from a far different perspective.

Chester Gould was renowned for his interest in police science, and his gadgetry in the comic strip verged on science fiction even in the early days, long before Tracy's famous trip to the moon in the 1950s. Dick Tracy's wrist-radio (later wrist-TV) was pictured in the strip starting in 1946, years before it was technologically possible. The transistor (invented in 1948) and other microelectronic devices that were necessary for its development were still in the future.

In contrast, writing the radio version, Lowther relied less on science fiction and more on what might be termed "atmospheric fantasy." He liked to write supernatural and ghostly stories which, though given logical explanation at the end, must have expanded the imagination of the youthful listeners of the show, who were often offered the opportunity of believing either the logical or the illogical solution to the situation that had been presented.

Lowther was also skillful in condensing a lot of action into the fifteen-minute episodes. There were always exciting and unexpected developments that kept the story moving from minute to minute and then suspended it in midair till the next episode. The kids who listened regularly must have hurried home every afternoon, eager to learn how the cliff-hanger of the previous day would be resolved. There was a lot of "story" in the Dick Tracy serial, and the action was fast-paced. Better than most writers Lowther knew how to dramatize an unusual situation and evolve its consequences without losing his listeners in a confused web of plot and counterplot.

One of the oddities of radio serials in the 1930s was that the characters became globe-trotters. Perhaps these plots were compensation on the part of the writers and actors of the radio serials, who – unlike the famous and affluent movie stars of the time – were poorly rewarded for their services, and could hardly travel to Europe and the Orient except in their imaginations. Such stories, however unreal in detail, must also have widened the horizons of the listeners, who were stuck in the insular, provincial America of the Depression era.

For whatever reason, radio heroes traveled a lot to the far corners of the globe. Jack Armstrong and Billy and Betty Fairfield, were high school students but spent much of their time flying off in Uncle Jim's amphibian plane, *The Silver Albatross*, to parts of the world far beyond the walls of Hudson High. Jimmie Allen and Speed Robertson were pilots of a transcontinental airline, but traveled to China, where they got involved in an armed conflict between rival warlords. Even Little Orphan Annie traveled to the South Seas in Daddy Warbuck's yacht.

Dick Tracy was no exception. As a plainclothes police officer in a big city he would presumably have enough to do battling gangsters and racketters close to home. On the contrary, during one long sequence in 1938 he visited Scotland Yard in London and became involved in the case – as the script called it – of "the Baron and the sub-stratosphere plans."

This led to a new mystery, that of "The Man with the Yellow Face." The name suggests an adventure of Tracy's distinguished predecessor, who also worked with Scotland yard on some occasions: Sherlock Holmes. He too, we remember, once had a case in which a "yellow livid face" was watching from an upper window. ("The Yellow Face" is collected in Conan Doyle's *Memoirs of Sherlock Holmes*.)

Ned Wever, radio's Dick Tracy, in an atmospheric publicity shot.

In the *Dick Tracy* adventure, Dick is hired to protect Driden Small, "the well-known Egyptologist," who is returning to America with treasures found in the "ancient tomb" of Tutominal. Small is being followed by a strange man who, he fears, is trying to kill him. Sailing with him on the ship – in those days you traveled across the Atlantic by ocean liner rather than by jet plane – Dick and Pat Patton soon have reason to suspect that Small is right about the danger, for while sitting in his cabin they see peering in at them "an awful face at the window" – the Man with the Yellow Face. Small tells them that he saw the strange man in Cairo before he sailed, and each time that he encountered him, a scarab was left as a warning.

There are many developments and plot twists. When Tracy and Patton return to Small's cabin after an unsuccessful search for the man, they see a message being written out on the wall: "You hour is at hand. Your end is near. The Black Pearl of Osiris must shine again." It looks like it is being scrawled right before their eyes by a ghostly unseen hand, but Dick shows that it was written earlier in invisible ink that was brought forth by the heat of the lamp. The yellow-faced man pushes Pat Patton overboard to be rescued by Dick—just one of those everyday heroics performed by the leading characters of radio dramas.

It finally turns out that Yellow Face is the High Priest of Osiris and seeks the return of the Black Pearl that Small has stolen from the mummy's tomb. Tracy becomes sympathetic to this quest, and the gem is given to the yellow-faced man, who isn't a villain after all. It is explained, a little offhandedly, that he suffers from a disease that gave him the evil jaundiced visage. His motives are pure.

In the wake of the blockbuster Warren Beatty movie *Dick Tracy*, the old movie-serial versions of *Tracy* were reshown on television, and the 1961 cartoon series was revived by Disney to coincide with the release of the new movie. These old versions of *Tracy* soon ran into trouble, being criticized, often vehemently, by Asians and Hispanics for the ethnic stereotypes that were depicted in them. The cartoon version, scheduled for a 13-week run on KCAL, Los Angeles, was hastily cancelled under pressure from minority groups. *Dick Tracy* originated before audiences generally were sensitive to racial slurs, and many decades before the establishment of the "Miranda warning," familiar in more recent times to viewers of such TV police dramas as *Hill Street Blues* and *Cagney and Lacey*. (The "Miranda" originated as recently as 1966 in the decision of the U.S. Supreme Court in the case of *Miranda vs. Arizona*).

Thus the radio serial is not free of racial slurs and often portrays the violation of a defendant's rights in a criminal case. But the radio *Dick Tracy* was at least marginally superior in this regard to the early movie versions. Tracy's sympathy for the claim of the yellow-faced High Priest of Osiris—after all, a man from a Third World country!—is only one example of the relatively enlightened attitude that prevailed on the radio show.

Another memorable sequence depicted a mysterious, somber figure who called himself the Unknown. Involving himself for a while in Tracy's adventures, moving in and out of the plots spun by friend and foe on either side of the law, he closely resembled the Shadow, the cloaked personage with the sinister laugh who knew "what evil lurks in the hearts of men." The creators of *Dick Tracy*, too, knew about at least one evil: that of plagiarism, and however close the resemblance of the two, they carefully avoided identifying the spectral figure with the Shadow, a character owned by Street & Smith. (After all, " the weed of crime bears bitter fruit.") Unfortunately, the man's real identity is lost to memory, and remains even more mysterious than that of the Shadow. He was then, and always will remain, the Unknown.

While the "Yellow Face" sequence was being heard, *Dick Tracy* became one of the many kids' shows that offered a radio "premium": in this case a Dick Tracy Secret Ring, described as "big, handsome" and "plated with 14-karat gold," which had Tracy's familiar profile (from the comic strip) imprinted upon it. The ring also had a "secret compartment for carrying secret messages," and all this was offered to kids who sent in five boxtops from packages of Quaker Puffed Wheat and Quaker Puffed Rice. Radio premium offers originated in the early 1930s when the Orphan Annie shakeup mug was sent to listeners in exchange for the inner seal of an Ovaltine jar. The offer occasioned a deluge of response. Kids were listening avidly all over the country, as the sponsor was gratified to learn. The inner seal of an Ovaltine jar had to be removed before using the product anyway, but the boxtop of a cereal box usually remains in place till the box is emptied. Therefore, the instructions given to listeners of *Dick Tracy* carefully stipulated that they should tear off the tops only when the boxes were empty.

Most radio premium offers requested only one boxtop; occasionally two were required. Five boxtops were unusual. We must suspect that the Quaker Oats company had a warehouse overstocked with cases of Puffed Wheat and Puffed Rice that they wanted to move in a hurry. Probably they succeeded, although the necessity of eating five packages of cereal in time to take advantage of the offer couldn't have been easy, except in large families.

The boxtops were sent to "Dick Tracy, Box L, Chicago"–those were simple, uncomplicated days a quarter century before the advent of ZIP codes–and we can imagine how stuffed the post office box must have gotten with grubby envelopes, lumpy with the tops of five cereal boxes, addressed in pencil in a childish scrawl.

The actor who played Dick Tracy on radio during the show's best days was Ned Wever. Others who took the part at various times were Matt Crowley and Barry Thomson. Wever appeared on other shows concurrently, including the popular soap opera *Young Widder Brown* (beginning in the late 1930s), in which he had the role of Ellen Brown's perennial romantic interest, Dr. Anthony Loring. He once described in an interview, with tongue in cheek, how he had to "get right off Young Widder Brown and rush over to do Dick Tracy." His most famous role, perhaps, was the lead in *Bulldog Drummond*, the detective who appeared "Out of the fog, out of the night" on prime time radio beginning in 1941. In later years he appeared in films and on television, though not in starring roles. He died in the mid–1960s.

In 1939, after its success as a serial adventure, *Dick Tracy* made the big switch to prime time, appearing as a half-hour drama every Saturday evening. Each episode was complete in itself, and most were well-done. One memorable story in this new version involved Tracy's dangerous trip by handcar over a railroad bridge that had been sabotaged to blow up at any moment. Luckily Tracy was brave and clever enough to discover the explosive device in the nick of time and avoid disaster.

The evening version of the show didn't last long. Almost a decade later, in 1947, another half-hour prime time *Dick Tracy* was offered. A new era was beginning, and not long afterward – in the fifties – other popular adventure heroes ventured into the evening hours. *Superman* was tried as a prime time radio show, and *Jack Armstrong, the All-American Boy* was retooled to become *Armstrong of the S.B.I.* (Those initials stood for the "Scientific Bureau of Investigation.") Neither of these attempts succeeded resoundingly. Jack Armstrong surely had had time to grow up and choose a profession, but the adult audience never admired him like the kids did who had loyally followed his adventures in earlier times. *Dick Tracy* didn't quite make it as a nighttime radio play, either, although it lasted just a little longer than one season.

Perhaps *Tracy* would have succeeded as a serious drama similar to the unforgettable *Gangbusters*. Instead, it was played as a comedy, in the "camp" fashion that – two decades later, in another era entirely – made it a hit of the *Batman* TV series. Familiar characters from the Chester Gould strip made their appearances, including the comic figures of Vitamin Flintheart and Gravel Gertie, more appropriate, perhaps, for Fred Allen's "Alley" or for *Fibber McGee and Molly* than for a police drama. There was a studio audience that could be heard laughing and cheering as in an ordinary comedy show.

The half-hour show was sponsored by Tootsie Rolls, and in one episode, "The Firebug Murders," Tracy, Vitamin and Gertie are left tied in Gertie's junk shop, which has been torched by the villain. Tracy breaks his bonds and saves the day with his great strength and energy, presumably from eating Tootsie Rolls, although this isn't spelled out. Truth in advertising, after all, wasn't a popular commodity in the media of that era.

While the weekly series appeared Saturday evenings, the afternoon version continued every weekday. George Lowther was no longer writing the scripts, however, and in this later incarnation the *Dick Tracy* show devolved into a rather routine series, earnest in its endeavors – Dick was on the trail of ration-book counterfeiters during World War II, showing his true patriotism although he didn't join the armed forces – but not very imaginative. It was never as popular as the earlier and greatly superior series.

Films

Dick Tracy never had it so good as in the summer of 1990. The big-budget movie starring Warren Beatty as Tracy opened to mostly rave reviews – although *New Yorker* critic Terrence Rafferty thought it was "less *Dick Tracy* than *Classics Illustrated*" – and garnered golden gobs of money.

It had been more than forty years since Chester Gould's famous detective had cashed in on the Hollywood bonanza. Most of the customers flocking to see the Beatty film had never seen Tracy's earlier exploits on the big screen. Probably they had never even heard of them, but the release of the blockbuster film brought some of those earlier movies back to mind for those old enough to remember the great movie serials, and into view for those too young. Those old films were seen on television and released on video in anticipation of the Beatty film.

Fifty years ago Republic Pictures – a newly organized studio at the time – put Dick Tracy into four movie serials that proved to be the most popular chapterplays ever made about a fictional detective. The first serial, fifteen chapters long, was made in 1937 on a small budget (less than $200,000, according to report), and to the surprise of many was a box office smash. Like the 1990 film, the serial was called simply *Dick Tracy*. The name alone was enough to sell it to the fans of the comic strip, which by the mid-1930s had become one of the most popular cartoon features in the world.

No actor of course quite resembles Chester Gould's hero, but the casting office located a copy that was close enough. The actor they chose was a young man named Ralph Byrd, who had recently appeared in a feature film, *Chinatown Squad*, for Universal. He had a squarish jaw and a dapper, dashing appearance, looking as if he could chase crooks and trade gunfire with the nastiest of evildoers. In black and white you couldn't tell whether his fedora was yellow, like Tracy's in the Sunday comic section, but in any case Byrd was a convincing personification of the comic strip hero.

In the Republic serials none of the other characters in the strip made the transition to the screen with the sole exception of Junior Tracy, played by Lee Van Atta. The script provided Dick with an attractive secretary, Gwen, played by the very young Kay Hughes, and a sidekick played by Smiley Burnette, who made a career of playing sidekicks, most memorably in the Gene Autry films. The latter's name was Mike McGurk, for some reason, rather that Pat Patton. The rest of the cast included Byron Foulger and Francis X. Bushman, one of the stars of the silent screen. The serial was directed by Ray Taylor, a longtime director of serials going back to the silent era, and Alan James.

There was another big change from the *Dick Tracy* comic strip. On screen Tracy was no longer a member of the city police force. As Chester Gould later commented, rather bemusedly, "In the four serial films about [Tracy], curiously enough, he is portrayed as a member of the Federal Bureau of Investigation." But the film producers knew what they were doing, obviously taking advantage of the fame of the FBI, often in the headlines for bringing to justice John Dillinger and other gangsters of the thirties. It was of little importance to the plot, for the chapterplay was nothing more nor less than a standard cops-and-robbers story.

The *Dick Tracy* strip began with the kidnapping of Dick's fiancée and the murder of her father. As a movie serial, *Dick Tracy* opened with the abduction of Dick's brother Gordon – it's tough to be a relative or an associate of a popular hero – who is subjected to a "gland-change" operation by one of the serial's heavies, Dr. Moloch. The operation prevents Gordon from distinguishing "evil from good," a flaw that many of us suffer from even with our glands in the right place. To accentuate the Jekyll-Hyde difference between Gordon pre-operation and post-operation the producers cast two different actors in the role: Richard Beach, before, and Carleton Young, after.

The hapless Gordon becomes a tool of Tracy's chief adversary in the serial, the Lame One (also referred to as the Spider), and is placed in charge of the Flying Wing, a futuristic airplane that looks like something from the cover of *Popular Mechanics* in the thirties, armed with a deadly sonic generator with which the bad guys attempt to destroy the newly completed Bay Bridge (the film is set in San Francisco). After fifteen chapters Gordon dies in a spectacular car crash, after showing a flash of his original self by swerving off the road to avoid running down Junior and Gwen. In between, there are of course scores of subplots and a cliffhanger at the end of each chapter except the last.

With the success of the original *Dick Tracy*, a sequel was inevitable, and *Dick Tracy Returns* appeared the following year. It was another Republic serial starring Ralph Byrd, this time directed by the veteran team of William Witney and John English. In this followup film Junior was played by Jerry Tucker, Tracy's secretary Gwen by Lynn Roberts, and McGurk by Lee Ford.

A well-crafted film for the genre, *Dick Tracy Returns* became the source of numerous action scenes that could be recycled in the later *Tracy* serials. One of the favorite scenes for this purpose is the cliffhanger at the end of Chapter Three in which Tracy boards a runaway freight car to save a colleague, Steve, played by Michael Kent. He attempts to stop the wildly careening car with the handbrake, but despite his frantic efforts the car runs off track and plunges into a ravine below. Other Republic serials later used the same footage, as in *Dick Tracy vs Crime, Inc.*

Dick Tracy Returns was marred by the presence of two "economy chapters." Most serials used one such chapter, the function of which was to save money on stuntwork and expensive car chases, but seldom two. In such a chapter the main characters sit around discussing what has already happened, these events graphically illustrated by flashbacks from the earlier chapters. Television sitcoms and dramas use the same technique even up to the present time.

The plot of *Dick Tracy Returns* was nothing more or less than a rewriting of the familiar real-life story of Ma Barker and her gangster family.

In the hands of the scriptwriters Ma was cleverly transformed into Pa Stark, played by Charles Middleton, easily the most sinister of chapterplay villians. In the final chapter Pa Stark dies in a spectacular plane crash after Tracy bails out to avoid the same fate.

In the third Tracy serial, *Dick Tracy's G-Men,* released in 1939, Ralph Byrd's cohorts from the previous serials are absent. Police officer or G-Man, Tracy always had a worthy adversary – this time a bearded master spy, Zarnoff, portrayed by Irving Pichel, a famous actor who later became a famous movie director. In the opening chapter Zarnoff, convicted of numerous crimes, apparently dies in the gas chamber, but secret drugs bring him back to life to bedevil Tracy for another fourteen chapters.

At the end, Zarnoff proves himself no smarter than most movie villains. Having captured Tracy he stops to gloat over his triumph instead of murdering him right off. Even Tracy could have told him, if he had asked, that this was a fatal mistake. Tracy is rescued, and Zarnoff dies of drinking poisoned water.

Nineteen forty-one was a vintage year for Republic serials. *Adventures of Captain Marvel* and *Spy Smasher,* two of the all-time best, were released that year, and the fourth *Tracy* adventure, *Dick Tracy vs. Crime, Inc.,* rates near the top of any list. Surely it is the finest film of the four Republic serials about the great detective. Its script was better written than most, and it had an excellent musical score composed by Cy Feuer. Once again Witney and English directed, and Ralph Byrd was back as Tracy for the fourth time. This time he confronts a mysterious villain known as the Ghost, who wears a skull mask and can make himself invisible. The best feature of this serial was that it was partly composed of the best action sequences from the previous three Republic serials as well as other sources. In the first chapter New York City is swept away by hugh waves in a spectacular inundation that Republic salvaged from scenes in an old RKO feature, *Deluge.* The serial was so popular that it was later rereleased under the title of *Dick Tracy vs. Phantom Empire.*

That was the last Republic serial about Dick Tracy, but RKO acquired rights to the character and in 1945 released a feature film about Gould's great detective. Once again the title was simply *Dick Tracy,* although it was later called *Dick Tracy, Detective.* This time the lead role was played by Morgan Conway, who unfortunately was never convincing as Tracy and was never accepted by Tracy fans. Though well done, neither this film nor its sequel the following year, *Dick Tracy vs Cueball,* was as popular with audiences as the serials. An effort was made, however, to capture more of the flavor of the comic strip, and characters from the strip – Junior, Tess, Pat Patton and Chief Brandon – were depicted by an excellent cast which included Mickey Kuhn, Anne Jeffreys, Lyle Latell and Joseph Crehan.

In 1947 two more *Tracy* feature films were released by RKO. This time they brought back Ralph Byrd for his last two appearances on the big screen in the title role. *Dick Tracy's Dilemma* and *Dick Tracy Meets Gruesome* were minor contributions to the canon at best, notable mostly for the return of Byrd and, in the case of the latter film, the presence of Boris Karloff. As Gruesome, Karloff assumed a role that after many years in horror movies he could play in his sleep, and at times this almost seemed what he was doing. The RKO features relied more on the solution of crimes than did the Republic serials, where the stuntmen were center stage most of the time.

Byrd made his last bow as Tracy only a few years later. In 1951–52 Byrd starred in the *Dick Tracy* television series, with Joe Devlin as Sam Catchem and villains borrowed from the comic strips: Diet Smith, Flattop, Breathless Mahoney, and the Mole. By that time Byrd must have felt like a one-trick pony. Typecast as Tracy, he never quite made it in other roles. He died of a heart attack in 1952 at the age of forty-three. The television shows were intended for syndication and never reached a big audience, which is just as well, for they were shabby contributions to the *Tracy* canon.

There was a poorly done series of *Dick Tracy* animated cartoons in 1961, with lots of talking animals and similar nonsense and very little of Tracy, and an unsold television pilot in 1966, which was intended to ride the wave of the *Batman* craze of that year. Aside from that, Tracy did not appear on the screen again till the release of the Warren Beatty film in the summer of 1990.

The comic-book-come-to-life concept of the latest *Dick Tracy* film was pleasant, but it was perhaps a too respectful treatment of what is, after all, a comic strip, not Dostoyevski. Beatty was too old to play Tracy (who remains a fairly young man even after fifty years in the strip), and looked too soft and sensual to be a tough police detective. Many Tracy aficionados thought there was too much singing by Madonna, who sang even over the action scenes. Enough, enough! As Breathless Mahoney she did a creditable impresonation of Marilyn Monroe, except that Marilyn was innocently sexy, not calculatingly raunchy. Of all the *Tracy* villains that appeared in the picture – Flattop, Mumbles, 88 Keys, and Pruneface among them – the most amusing was Al Pacino as a Capone figure named Big Boy Caprice.

The advent of the Beatty *Dick Tracy* brought back the old movie serials, both on television and in video versions. The four Republic serials are available, at this writing, on video, both full-length and abridged to avoid overlaps between chapters, and the RKO feature films are available as well. Two *Tracy* documentaries were released in the wake of the Beatty picture: *Dick Tracy – America's #1 Crimestopper* and *Dick Tracy – Saga of a Crime Fighter*. The latter has an excerpt from one of the 1951 television episodes with Ralph Byrd in the title role, one last glimpse of the real, authentic Tracy of the silver screen.

Despite the success of the Beatty–Madonna film, which was released by a division of Disney after years of delay and internal hassles, Dick Tracy may never again return to the screen. Yet his history in the movies is rich enough to keep his memory alive in the minds of movie buffs as it lives in the minds of *Dick Tracy* fans of the comics and of Golden Age radio.

The 1990 movie made a mostly successful attempt to recapture the flavor of the comic-strip world in which Tracy's first exploits battling crooks and foreign agents were chronicled by Chester Gould. But even in the loud and often overblown billows of hype for the movie, fans of Golden Age Radio could still hear, in the back of their minds, the mellow voice of another Dick Tracy of long ago, answering the police radio call for help with the calm, reassuring message, "This is Dick Tracy – ready for action!"

Comics

Who is "the logical successor to Sherlock"? According to mystery writer and critic Anthony Boucher, who occasionally wrote scripts for the *Sherlock Holmes* radio series, it was Ellery Queen. If you can picture Holmes as a slender, bookish young man wearing an "oxford gray" suit, carrying a walking stick, and – most oddly – adorned with a pair of rimless pince-nez glasses, perhaps he was. That's the way Ellery first appeared in the mystery novels written by Lee and Dannay under the Queen pseudonym, and that's the way many of his fans still picture him.

Comic strip artist Chester Gould, during the same period in which Queen made his first appearance (the late 1920s and early 1930s), had another answer. His own successor to Holmes looked more like the original, perhaps; at least that was the intention. Facially his detective had – as Gould himself described him – a "straight aquiline nose, square chin, generally sharp features." Instead of the deerstalker cap which we always picture Holmes as wearing (although in the original illustrations he more often wore a bowler) Gould's hero looked dapper in a snap brim fedora, and instead of a walking stick such as Ellery Queen affected, he carried a police .38. Gould's successor to Conan Doyle's immortal creation is named Dick Tracy.

The *Dick Tracy* strip had a long and difficult beginning, but having gotten under way, it has continued to depict the hero's career of fighting crime over a span of nearly six decades so far. Somewhat crippled with arthritis, Holmes had by the same age retired to a life of "leisured ease," raising bees on a small farm five miles from Eastbourne. We don't foresee Tracy retiring anytime in the near future – not when there are crooks to battle and murders to solve.

A native of Oklahoma, where he was born in the small town of Pawnee in 1900, Chester Gould attended Northwestern University in Chicago during the 1920s when, as he later remarked, that city was "the very heartland of gangsterdom." That fact eventually led to the creation of Tracy, but for ten years, 1921 to 1931, as an aspiring cartoonist, Gould tried countless other comic strip ideas, submitting them one by one to Captain Joseph Medill Patterson of the Chicago Tribune-New York News Syndicate, meanwhile supporting himself by cartooning freelance and doing artwork for ads in the *Chicago Tribune*. He also drew a few minor comic strips for the Hearst *Chicago American*, the best known being *Radio Cats*. None of this pleased him or was very promising.

Finally he decided to try an idea novel for those times. "Most cartoon strips," as he noted later, "were comic—that is, they were funny, or tried to be, anyway." It was the era of *Barney Google*, *Tillie the Toiler*, and *Gasoline Alley*. He determined to create a strip that would deal more realistically with life in the Depression era, and sent to Patterson six samples of a strip that featured a "hard-hitting, tough detective" who would battle the hoodlums and the underworld mobs and help bring back law and order to America. He was called "Plainclothes Tracy."

Patterson immediately recognized the potential appeal of the strip, primitive as it was in concept and execution, but he didn't like the title. It was too long, he thought, and in a moment of happy inspiration suggested "Dick Tracy" as the name of both strip and character. In those days the underworld called detectives "dicks," and the name was a natural.

Once the strip was accepted, Gould was given an early deadline for preparing the first two weeks of the strip. But Patterson helpfully provided the story line. Few fans of *Dick Tracy* realize that originally Tracy was a private citizen who volunteered his services to the police department after his fiancée, Tess Trueheart, was kidnapped and her father was murdered. After a monthlong pursuit Tracy finally brought the crooks and their leader, "Mr. Big," to justice, and as a reward he was appointed to the plainclothes squad of the police. He has been fighting the bad guys ever since.

Much has changed in the strip during its long history, but Tracy still looks much the same as he did at the beginning when he was the young man who got mixed up in police work by merest chance. The crime against his sweetheart must have been traumatic, however, for he didn't marry Tess till Christmas Day 1949, more than eighteen years after he made his fateful proposal of marriage on the night she was kidnapped. Two years later he became the father of Bonnie Braids, a cute little blonde girl.

Meantime his adopted son, Junior Tracy, was allowed to mature, growing up and getting married and having a child of his own. Other members of the *Tracy* cast changed as well. Dick's old partner, Pat Patton, took over as chief of police after Chief Brandon retired, and Dick's new partner became Sam Catchem. Gravel Gertie and B. O. Plenty, two of the more grotesque characters in the strip, got married and had a child, Sparkle Plenty, who grew up too and married. Lots can happen in a strip that goes on for sixty years. By the way, B. O. stands for Bob Oscar, although the usual connotation referring to the Lifebuoy soap ads of that era was not lost on followers of the strip.

Dick Tracy, from early in its existence, was famous for its "extraordinary rogue's gallery, "as Gould called it, of bizarre and misshapen villains, and they became more grotesque story by story, year by year. "All murderers are ugly, regardless of their visage," he explained in rationalizing this aspect of the strip. "But when someone reads a *Dick Tracy* comic strip, there is never a question or doubt about who the bad guy is. The villains are vicious, cruel, and ugly people, and neither Tracy nor I (nor readers) feels the slightest remorse when they get what's coming to them."

Among the most memorable of these macabre rogues are Pruneface, whose name says it all; the Mole, who lives underground in a sewer, like the much-later protagonist of the television series *Beauty and the Beast*, but with different motives and aspirations; B. B. Eyes, who squints out of two tiny dots for eyes; the Brow, a particularly sinister Nazi spy; Flattop, with a head that supposedly resembles the deck of an aircraft carrier; and Mumbles, who of course mumbles when he talks, one of the few *Tracy* villains famous for something other than a repulsive physique. A popular song with the refrain "What did he say?" became a hit at the time this villain was dominating the story. Other famous characters in the comic strip included Diet Smith, Breathless Mahoney, and Stooge Viller.

Balancing off this element of grotesquerie, Tracy used modern science and technology to fight crime. As Gould proudly pointed out, Tracy utilized "microscopes, lie detectors, X-ray and telescopic cameras, and other electronic equipment," and had a "good working knowledge of chemistry, ballistics, fingerprinting" and other sciences. If a device hadn't been developed yet, he used it anyway, as with the "atom-powered two-way wrist-radio," which was pictured in the strip years before it became feasible.

Gould was, perhaps, a science fiction writer at heart, for in the fifties he depicted Dick Tracy visiting the moon and encountering the Moon Maid, perhaps on the inspiration of Edgar Rice Burroughs. "Some people thought this was pretty far-fetched," Gould later observed, in a notable understatement. In the oddest development of all Junior Tracy finally married the Moon Maid. The space fantasy appeared long before the first trip to the moon was made by real-life astronauts, who disappointingly did not find a Moon Maid anywhere in sight.

Though its popularity has diminished in recent years, the *Dick Tracy* strip has continued since Chester Gould's retirement, which took place on Christmas Day 1977. Gould himself drew the strip until he was in his late

70s, though an assistant, Rick Fletcher, did the backgrounds. For many years Gould's brother Ray did the lettering. In recent times the strip was taken over by crime novelist Max Allan Collins and the cartoonist Dick Locher. Gould died on May 11, 1985, at his home in Woodstock, Illinois.

At one time the strip appeared in more than 800 newspapers and had a potential readership of 100 million. With an audience of that size it is no wonder that *Dick Tracy* crossed over into radio and the movies on many occasions and in many guises. Even the celebrated tenant of 221B Baker Street would have been proud to play to such an audience, and probably Ellery Queen was secretly green with envy. Surely, more than any other fictional detective, Dick Tracy is the "logical successor of Sherlock Holmes."

Premiums

The premiums offered were as follows, listed alphabetically with sponsor, date and approximate value in 1992 (assuming average condition).

Aviation Wings (Quaker, 1938, $30), Badge, Air Detective's (Quaker, 1938, $25), Badge, Belt, Detective Club, leather back pouch (Quaker P R/W, ?, $30), Badge, Brass Member (Quaker, 1939, $20), Badge, Captain's (Quaker, 1938, $80), Badge, Detective Club Shield (Quaker, ?, $30), Badge, Girls' Division (Quaker, 1939, $25), Badge, Inspector General's (Quaker, 1938, $100), Badge, Lieutenant's (Quaker, 1938, $50), Badge, Paper, from Detective Kit (Quaker, 1944, $15), Badge, Second Year Member's (Quaker, 1939, $25), Badge, Sergeant's (Quaker, 1938, $35), Book, Family Fun (Quaker, ?, $10), Book, Manual and Code (Quaker, 1939, $55), Bracelet, Lucky Bangle (Quaker, 1938, $75), Bracelet, Wing (Quaker, 1938, $45), Cap, Air Detective's (Quaker, 1938, $40), Cards, Decoder, Red & Green (Post Cereal, ?, $10), Certificate for Posting Promotion Stickers (Quaker, 1938, $20), Code Book, Secret, Secret Service Patrol (Quaker, 1938, $45), Decoder (Quaker, 1942, $35), Dial, Secret Code from Detective Kit (Quaker, 1944, $65), File Cards from Detective Kit (Quaker, 1944, $5), Flashlight, Pocket (Quaker, 1939, $30), Folio, Detective Club Tab Crime Detection (Quaker, 1942, $30), Gun, Paper Pop (Quaker, 1942, $20), Gun, Rubber Band (Quaker, ?, $30), Kit, Detective (Quaker, 1944, $200), Kit, Detective, w/Wood Decoder, Pot Metal Badge (?, 1961, $20), Kit, Secret Detecto (Quaker, 1938, $60), Manual and Code Book (Quaker, 1939, $55), Manual, from Detective Kit (Quaker, 1944, $35), Manual, Secret Detective Methods & Magic Tricks (Quaker, 1939, $25), Membership, Certificate from Detective Kit (Quaker, 1944, $15), Notebook (Quaker, 1942, $10), Pencil, Siren Code (Quaker, 1939, $30), Pin, Bar, Patrol Leader's (Quaker, 1938, $20), Pinback, Member's (Quaker, 1938, $20), Plane, Flagship Rocket (Quaker, 1939, $55), Plane, Siren (Quaker, 1938, $70), Puzzle (Quaker, 1942, $25), Radio Script: Vol. I, "The Invisible Man" (Quaker, 1939, $45), Radio Script: Vol. II, "Ghost Ship" (Quaker, (1939, $45), Ring, Air Detective (Quaker, 1938, $80), Ring, Enameled Hat (Quaker, ?, $50), Ring, Secret Compartment (Quaker, 1938, $80), Sheets, Mystery, Set of 3 (Quaker, 1942, $20), Suspect Wall Chart from Detective Kit (Quaker, 1944, $10), Tape Measure from Detective Kit (Quaker, 1944, $5), Telephones, Private (Quaker, 1939, $40).

The Green Hornet

Half-hour mystery-adventure. Began Jan. 31, 1936, and ran until Dec. 5, 1952, as follows: 1/31/36–1938, WXYZ, Detroit; 4/12/38–1939, Sustaining, Mutual, 2x/week; 1939–10/10/40, Sustaining, Mutual, first 2x/week, later Tues.; 12/28/40–11/28/42, Sustaining, Sat. 8 PM; 12/06/42–9/11/43, Sustaining, ABC, Sun. 4:30 PM; 4/20/43–8/24/43, Sustaining, ABC, Tues. 7 PM; 3/21/44– 1/23/45, Sustaining, ABC, Tues. 7:30 PM; 2/1/45–12/20/45, Sustaining, ABC, Thurs. 7:30 PM; 12/25/45–10/8/46, Sustaining, ABC, Tues. 7:30 PM; 10/13/46– 12/30/47, Sustaining, ABC, Sun. 4:30 PM; 1/6/48–12/30/47, General Mills, ABC, Sun. 4:30 PM; 9/14/48–6/9/49, Sustaining, ABC, 2x/ week; 6/13/49–9/12/49, Sustaining, Mutual, Mon., then Thurs., then Mon., then Tues.; 9/20/49–6/6/50, Sustaining, Mutual, Tues. night; 6/9/50–4/8/51, Sustaining, Mutual, Fri. night; 9/10/52–12/5/52, Orange Crush, Mutual, 2x/week.

Writer: Fran Striker **Producer:** James Jewell **Director:** Charles Livingston **The Green Hornet** (Britt Reid, publisher of the *Daily Sentinel*): Al Hodge (1936–43), Donovan Fause (1943), Bob Hall (1943–46), Jack McCarthy (1946–52) **Kato** (Reid's valet): Raymond Hayashi, Rollon Parker, Mickey Tolan **Dan Reid** (Britt's father): John Todd **Lenore Case** (Casey, Miss Case, Reid's secretary): Lee Allman **Michael Axford** (Reporter or Body Guard): Jim Irwin, Gil Shea **Ed Lowry** (Reporter): Jack Petruzzi **Newsboy:** Rollon Parker **Announcers:** Charles Woods, Mike Wallace, Feilden Farrington, Bob Hite, Hal Neal.

Many shows in the Golden Age of Radio were famous for their noisily dramatic openings that featured sound effects, mysterious theme music and darkly toned voices speaking through filter mikes. *I Love a Mystery, The Shadow, Grand Central Station,* and most memorably of all, *Gangbusters,* come instantly to mind. Their echoes still revereberate after fifty years and more. Once heard, they were almost unforgettable. The shows that came from the WXYZ shop in Detroit were not lacking in this regard, either. Few radio programs could equal *The Lone Ranger,* whose famous opening was known to every schoolkid in the land: hoofbeats, gunshots, "William Tell

Overture," and the narrator's "fiery horse with the speed of light." But another show produced by WXYZ, *The Green Hornet*, was almost as memorable for its opening.

Instead of "William Tell Overture" – still inexorably linked with the Masked Rider of the Plains after all these years – *The Green Hornet* had to be content with Rimsky-Korsakov's "Flight of the Bumble Bee," a less memorable piece of music, and of course a wrong identification. Hornets are wasps, not bees, but there probably isn't any familiar music referring to hornets, green or otherwise. (The green kind are supposed to be the angriest and most likely to sting anybody in their way.) Augmented with menacing hornet buzzes, the sound of a powerful car roaring away through two gear changes and the narrator intoning, "The Green Hornet! He hunts the biggest of all game – public enemies who would destroy our America!" it made a very effective opening one was not likely to forget.

The Green Hornet was a direct descendant of the Lone Ranger in more ways than one. The show was developed by George W. Trendle of WXYZ, who had made such a big success with the Masked Rider of the Plains. He conceived the idea of creating a modern Lone Ranger who, like the Ranger, wore a mask, hid his real identity – that of "Britt Reid, daring young publisher" – behind a mask and a fanciful name, the Green Hornet, and pursued evildoers with unsurpassed velocity: in this case, a faster car than anybody else's, "the sleek super-powered Black Beauty," instead of the fastest steed in the West, "the great horse Silver." (Perhaps it is significant that Black Beauty was the name of a horse almost as famous as Silver in the classic story by Anna Sewell.) The Lone Ranger toted a six-shooter loaded with silver bullets (but he never shot to kill), while the Green Hornet wielded a gas gun that instantly put criminals to sleep without killing them.

The Lone Ranger had his faithful Indian companion, Tonto, and the Hornet had Kato, his equally faithful houseboy, who accompanied the Hornet on his dangerous adventures and knew a thing or two about using a Bowie knife. In the past he had occasionally neglected his work in wardrobe and pantry to develop the Hornet's gas gun and to soup up the Hornet's streamlined automobile. Not too many rich playboys, as Britt Reid was supposed to be, are as fortunate in thier choice of servants, but then, not too many millionaires spend their evenings matching wits with the underworld either.

The parallels between the Lone Ranger and the Green Hornet were spelled out in a famous episode of the latter show in which the Hornet, in his everyday guise of Britt Reid, learns from his father, Dan, that the Masked Man was his ancestor, in fact his great-uncle John Reid. Although he has had a painting of the Lone Ranger on the wall for years, Britt had not known before of the connection between them. "Then I'm – I'm carrying on in his tradition, bringing to justice those he would fight if he were here today," Britt says in dawning amazement, while in the background the "William Tell Overture" plays faintly. "Yes, Britt," his father replies. "He would be as proud of you as I am." That was one of the all-time great scenes of radio adventure drama.

Trendle was inspired to create the Green Hornet in imitation of the Jimmy Dale stories by Frank Packard, in which Jimmy had the secret identity of the Gray Seal, which was also his signature, marked by such a symbol that was left behind at the scene wherever he appeared. The Hornet, in his turn, left his own seal, the semblance of a green hornet, which was discovered by the police when they arrived just too late to apprehend him. But the Green Hornet was not too far removed in concept from other superheroes who had taken up the cause of justice at about the same time: the Shadow, Doc Savage, and the Spider, though only the first-mentioned fought criminals and racketeers on the radio. Later examples of the hero with a secret identity were Captain Marvel, Batman and of course Superman. One of the great breed, the Green Hornet was one of the earliest and one of the hardiest.

In his public identity as the publisher of a big city newspaper, the *Daily Sentinel*, Britt Reid would learn of a racket that the law was powerless to touch and decide that it looked like a job not for Superman, who was employed by another newspaper, but for the Green Hornet. "Stepping through a secret panel in the rear of the closet in his bedroom," as the announcer described it, Britt Reid and Kato would hurry through "a narrow passage built within the walls of the apartment itself" and enter "a supposedly abandoned warehouse," where their car was concealed. Reid pressed a button, while Kato revved up the Black Beauty, and as "a section of the wall in front raised automatically" the car sped into the night. Luckily nobody ever saw the wall raise, then lower behind them, and nobody ever noticed the roar of that supercharged engine. It must have been a strange neighborhood: a posh apartment building in a warehouse district, or was it a deserted warehouse in an affluent part of town?

Britt Reid's father Dan was at first disapproving of his son's supposed jet-set existence and – perhaps in emulation of California Senator George Hearst, who had put his wayward son William Randolph Hearst in charge of the *San Francisco Examiner* – he had turned the *Daily Sentinel* over to Britt to give him a sense of responsibility and turn him into a proper businessman.

The elder Reid had hired an ex-policeman named Michael Axford to keep his wastrel son in line. Unaware of Britt's secret existence, Axford hated the Hornet, whom he believed to be a criminal. His greatest ambition, at least to hear him talk in his broad Irish brogue, was to capture the "Harnut." Reid's personal secretary at the newspaper was nicknamed Casey, although she didn't have an accent. She was presumably not Irish, either; her nickname derived from her surname, Case. Her first name was Lenore. She was one of the few people smart enough to suspect Reid of being the Green Hornet, and ultimately – and anticlimactically – he admitted his identity to her. Another character was Ed Lowery, ace reporter on the *Daily Sentinel* who hated politicians and crooks but sometimes confessed a grudging admiration for the Hornet.

The Green Hornet himself was played for the first seven years by Al Hodge, who was the director of another WXYZ program, *Challenge of the Yukon*, and later became Captain Video on television. Seventeen-year-old Bob Hall assumed the part during the war years when actors were in short supply due to the draft. In the postwar era the role was played for another six years by Jack McCarthy.

The role of Dan Reid was taken by John Todd, that of Axford by Jim Irwin and later by Gil Shea. Casey was played by Lee Allman, and Lowery by Jack Petruzzi. Kato, though Oriental according to the script, was played most of the time by Roland Parker. One of the enduring myths about *The Green Hornet*, by the way, is that Kato was called a Japanese houseboy till the day after the attack on Pearl Harbor on December 7, 1941, after which he abruptly became Filipino. It makes a good story, but unfortunately it is not true. Part of the time his ancestry is not specified at all, and on other occasions, at least as far back as 1940, he was described as Filipino.

The scripts were written by Fran Striker, who had come to WXYZ to write *The Lone Ranger* scripts. Unfortunately, even with all the melodramatic trappings and sound effects that could be crammed into half an hour, the *Green Hornet* stories were too seldom any more than the usual cops-and-robbers adventure. Perhaps the urban locale didn't offer him the limitless scope of the Wild West. At least it didn't fire Striker's imagination.

A representative example is one of the earlier adventures, called "Charity Takes It on the Chin." In those days, incidentally, the Hornet was said to "hunt the biggest game of all – public enemies even the G-Men cannot reach." Apparently J. Edgar Hoover, then head of the FBI, objected to this slur on the Bureau, and the introduction was changed to a more general statement about hunting "public enemies who try to destroy our America." In any case, the Green Hornet usually hunted local racketeers that the police department, not the feds, would have the responsibility for. In this episode a couple of hoodlums named Tinker and Murdock are swindling a million dollars of city welfare money by padding the rolls with phony names and collecting the money themselves. Even though it was the Depression era Britt Reid solemnly announces that "For a city the size of ours, more money is being spent than conditions warrant," although we might suppose that a million dollars would be all too small an amount to use to alleviate suffering in those desparate times. As the Green Hornet he investigates, and manages

In 1964, revival of the old recorded *Green Hornet* radio shows took lead actor Bob Hall away from his disc jockey duties for personal appearances. (Photo by Don Glut)

to cause a rift between the thugs by planting the suspicion in each that the other one is conspiring with the Green Hornet to doublecross him. He uses his gas pistol to capture both of them. "You're shaking, Murdock!" he remarks before rendering Murdock unconscious, and you couldn't really blame the poor hoodlum. He causes the two crooks to confront each other in a lonely farmhouse, where hot accusations and recriminations fly fast and furious until the police arrive to capture them both. The Hornet escapes just in time, his job completed.

With the Lone Ranger we returned to the "thrilling days of yesteryear," the time of the Old West. With the Green Hornet we are back in the days – now almost as far beyond recall – of fierce competition among city newspapers (there seem to be numerous papers in town besides the *Daily Sentinel*), of frequent "Extra" editions and of papers sold on the streets with newsboys shouting "Extry! Extry! Charity graft smashed! Tinker and Murdock indicted! Green Hornet still at large!" One-newspaper cities and newspaper coin boxes on the street corner were still in the future.

Another episode of the *Green Hornet* – after that line about G-Men had been altered – was "Murder in the Dope Racket," in which a "respected wholesale druggist" named Eaton Waterbury is dispensing "dope pills" to doctors, one being a Dr. Spencer, who has been giving the pills to a patient

The Green Hornet movie serial in 1939 offered the Hornet (Gordon Jones) costumed after radio publicity pictures.

named Violet Hill. When his patient becomes suspicious, Spencer decides to "move out before the police start an investigation." Waterbury has his goons murder Spencer on the street with a machine gun and abduct Miss Hill.

The mystery is, what sort of "dope" is Waterbury pushing? And why? The only "addict" we know about is Violet Hill, who is unaware she is taking "dope" till another doctor tells her. Its only effect seems to be that it keeps her ill so that she visits her physician, Dr. Spencer, regularly. Those were sedate and astonishingly naïve times.

Only when the Green Hornet enters the case are the bad guys brought to justice, once again by the clever device of arranging that the gang members suppose that each is doublecrossing the other. When one of the gangsters agrees to help the Hornet, but asks for "dough" in payment for his services, Britt promises him, ambiguously, that "You will get your share of everything that's coming – you can count on that!" Of course what is coming to him is jail. The Hornet didn't believe in plea bargaining it would seem.

Once the crooks are taken care of, Britt Reid returns to his apartment and is sleeping the sleep of the just when Axford bursts in and wakens him with the news, "The cops got 'em, every last one of them! And they found the girl, safe and sound! Who? The dope peddlers who murdered Doc Spencer, that's who!" But – of course – "the Har-nut got away!" When Reid remarks, "I might have known," Axford complains, "You don't know what it is to be surprised about anything." To which Reid replies, "Life *is* boring, isn't it, Axford?"

If not exactly boring – to faithful radio listeners of the program – life wasn't quite as thrilling as it might have been with more exciting scripts. Even so, the Green Hornet kept chasing criminals – and escaping the cops – in his "streamlined car" for fourteen years on network radio, well into the post-World War II days. Considering the risks Britt Reid had to face, that's a long time. By now the *Daily Sentinel* must have been taken over by an Australian publisher. Britt is probably living it up in Acapulco, in well-deserved retirement. Surely he must have married Casey, and paid off Kato with a handsome pension. But we can't imagine the former valet staying idle for long. Since he must have been the mechanic who kept the Black Beauty in good condition all those years – you couldn't take a car like that to the local tune-up shop when it failed to perform properly – perhaps Kato has opened a Ferrari repair shop in Santa Monica.

Films

While the 1939 Universal serial *The Green Hornet* was scripted by George H. Plympton, Basil Dickey, Morrison C. Wood and Lyonel Margolies, and directed by veteran serial workers, Ford Beebe and Ray Taylor, Fran Striker acted as adviser on the film, which resembled the radio show more than any other such radio-to-film metamorphosis. Radio Hornet Al Hodge supplied the voice of the Hornet under the Hornet mask, while Gordon Jones was nominally Britt Reid, and George DeNormand and other stuntmen under the mask and hat punched and pursued. Charming Gordon Jones was an easy-going hero during an all-too-brief slender period, before he became a chubby comic, but radio actor Al Hodge, who later played Captain Video in serial television, could have done the screen role.

Anne Nagel was an attractive Miss Case and more informed than radio's Lee Allman. Wade Boteler fully executed the stereotyped dumb Irish assistant whose only real virtue is good intentions for the employer he fails to respect or serve well. Keye Luke, also Charlie Chan's number one son, was an inspired houseboy-inventor and real assistant.

The action of the serial is broken into several subplots involving various rackets broken up by the Green Hornet, with an ultimate solution of the identification of a chief villain from a group of candidates, a device often used by Plympton and associates.

The "Flight of the Bumble Bee" theme music was retained, making the serial seem familiar to the radio listener.

Having had one successful serial, Universal was determined to repeat. Unfortunately, they repeated too much with stock footage from the first serial, which was only a little over a year old and still fresh in the audience's mind. The 1944 *The Green Hornet Strikes Again* featured Warren Hull, always a first-rate serial hero, taking over mask, seal and gas. He was joined by the returning Anne Nagel and Keye Luke again as Lenore Case and Kato.

Television

A new Kato appeared many years later, in 1966, on a television series of *The Green Hornet* made possible by the success of the *Batman* TV show (although *Batman* was camp, and the Hornet was played straight). This Kato was Bruce Lee, who went on to become one of the top action stars of all time. He was joined by handsome, competent Van Williams as Reid, the Hornet. The stories were not completely unlike the radio series, but had much more violence and delved into science fiction. In all, it was kind of fun.

The pilot for the series was "The Silent Gun," from executive producer William Dozier, who also helmed television's *Batman*. The first episode was written by line producer Ken Pettus and directed by Leslie H. Martinson. In it, the Hornet's mask and a few other details were slightly different, but the story was all too usual.

It opened with a funeral (perhaps not a good omen for a new series) where the dead man's son also dies, shot with a silent gun. The overenthusiastic reporter, very Irish Mike Axford (Lloyd Gough), rushes into

Daily Sentinel publisher Britt Reid's office, and tells him they can buy the story of the silent gun for a few thousand.

Reid talks it over with his secretary, Lenore Case (Wende Wagner), and D.A. Frank Scanlon (Walter Brooke), who know his secret. At his apartment, Reid and Kato go to his garage and press a switch that turns a section of the floor upside down, with Reid's clamped-down convertible flipping over to bring up the Hornet's special car, the Black Beauty. Reid, now masked as the Green Hornet, and Kato, in the goggles and cap of the Hornet's driver, get in the car and drive along a passage whose exit is a "Candy Mints" signboard of two kissing lovers who part long enough to let the Black Beauty out into the night.

The daring young publisher arrives at the payoff scene to unceremoniously put Axford to sleep with the gas gun, and hear the story of the person trying for a payoff, the girlfriend of the murdered son. She wants to have enough money to get away from gangsters who killed both father and son over the silent gun they have seized for criminal purposes.

The Hornet goes after the pair of feuding crooks, who each want the gun. At the showdown, there is no use of Bruce Lee's fantastic martial arts; only a routine fistfight the Hornet wins.

Some of the episodes were two-parters, giving the series a bit more atmosphere of a feature film. One of the better ones was "The Corpse of the Year," two thirty-minute programs about a fake Green Hornet who is a killer. Reid thinks that behind it might be the rival publisher of the *Daily Express*, Simon Neal. But then Neal is killed "accidentally" during an attempt by the "the Green Hornet" to kill Britt Reid. Neal's managing editor, Sabrina Bradley (significant star Joanne Dru in a guest role), comes under suspicion. Kato takes on her security guards, three to one, without strain. But the fake hornet turns out to be disgruntled reporter Dan Scully (Tom Simcox). When he tries dueling with the real Black Beauty, the supercar's weapons send his car over a cliff in flames. Producer Pettus did better on this script, directed by James Komack.

Creator Trendle wrote me: "The series was not too successful."

The *Hornet* television series is still played on some smaller stations, as is the Hornet and Kato's two-part guest appearance on *Batman*.

Premiums

The premiums offered were as follows, listed alphabetically with sponsor and approximate value in 1992 (assuming average condition).

Membership Card ($15), Photo ($25), Photo Postcard ($30), Photo, Britt Reid, 8 x 10 ($25), Photo, Kato ($25), Photo, Lenore Case ($25), Photo, Mike Axford ($25), Postcard to order Michigan network photos ($15), Ring, Seal, Green & Orange, Plastic (1966, $25), Ring, Secret Compartment, Glow-in-the Dark Seal (General Mills, $350).

I Love a Mystery

Began 1939, NBC regional as quarter-hour Monday–Friday. Later in 1939, NBC national, half-hour weekly. Returned 1943, CBS, as quarter-hour Monday–Friday, to 1944. Returned 1948, ABC, retitled *"I Love Adventure"* as complete half-hour stories, not serial episodes. Moved from Hollywood to New York origination, Mutual, 1949-1952, Monday–Friday; new quarter-hour productions repeating serial scripts as *I Love a Mystery*.

Creator-Writer-Producer-Director: Carlton E. Morse **Assistant Writers:** Michael Raffetto, Barton Yarborough **Occasional Director:** (Hollywood, 1940s): Michael Raffetto **Director:** (New York, 1951-52): Mel Bailey **Organists:** Paul Carson, Rex Corey, others **Jack Packard** (leader of Jack, Doc and Reggie, and other combinations; soldier of fortune; head of A-1, later Triple A-1 Detective Agency; one-time medical student; pragmatic, idealistic, loyal, distrustful of women; superb athletic condition; appears in all stories): Michael Raffetto (1939-43, also 1948), Jay Novello (1943), John McIntire (1943-44), Russell Thorson (1949-52, also audition episodes, circa 1954), Robert Dryden (1952), Elliot Lewis (audition [pilot] episode, circa 1945) **Doc Long** (long-legged, red-haired Texan with wonderful accent; companion to Jack Packard in his best remembered exploits; chivalrous, loves all women; opens locks and safes easily; masterful poker-player; best loved character in series and one of best loved in all radio drama): Barton Yarborough (1939-44, also 1948), Jim Boles (1949-52), Jack Edwards (audition episode, 1945), Parley Baer (audition episode circa 1954) **Reggie York** (third member of the team with Jack and Doc; not in very many serial stories; a youthful Englishman with high ideals and remarkable physical strength): Walter Patterson (1939-41), Tom Collins (1948), Tony Randall (1949-51), Ben Wright (audition episodes, circa 1954) **Jerri Booker** (or "Jerry") beautiful A-1 Detective Agency secretary and companion in adventure; in love with the boss, Packard:

Gloria Blondell (1940-42), Athena Lord (1951-52) **Michael** (a Frenchman who sounded so much like movie star Peter Lorre that Lorre's studio insisted the actor be given name credit to establish it was not Lorre): Forrest Lewis (1944) **Sunny Richards:** Mercedes McCambridge (1950), **Hermie** (a little boy): Sarah Fussel (1950), **The Maestro:** Luis Van Rooten (1949), **Announcers:** Dresser Dahlsted (1939-44), Jim Bannon (commercials, 1944), Frank McCarthy (1949-52), **Others:** Les Tremayne, Elliot Lewis, Cathy Lewis, Barbara Jean Wong, Page Gillman, John Gibson, Don Douglas.

Three colorful adventures ... giant vampire bats flapping through the ruins of an ancient temple ... a maniacal fat man who claims to have control over a howling werewolf in the Southwestern twilight ... three beautiful girls in a stately old mansion menaced by a killer who signals each death with the cry of a baby. These were elements that made *I Love a Mystery* perhaps the best loved and best remembered of all radio drama series with recurring characters ever broadcast.

It was the creation of Carlton E. Morse, who was born in 1901 and had just entered the book publishing business and a new marriage at the time of this writing. It took a remarkable man to create such a remarkable series. Morse himself attributes the appeal of the show to the power of children's imagination. But the series also appealed to the mental imagery of adults of that time and even of today encountering the series for the first time on recording. *I Love a Mystery* has a timeless, universal appeal.

Morse's adventure series is a true classic, a work of art on the level of Conan Doyle's stories of Sherlock Holmes or Robert Louis Stevenson's *Treasure Island*. Children loved those books, and the young people of the forties loved *I Love a Mystery*. As with the books, this radio series continues to be cherished by its audience even in adulthood. As an adult one sees more in it than previously.

The program had both the strengths and flaws characteristic of the radio medium. Radio required repetition for comprehension. Listeners were told many times, for instance, that Doc Long was a long-legged, redheaded Texan. Within each episode and in the following chapter certain elements were repeated to make sure the listeners, with only their ears to guide them, could follow what was happening. The writer could also depend on the talents of the actors to supply characterization beyond the scripted speeches. As his own director, Morse had sound effects and music (such as the organ rendition of Sibelius' *Valse Triste* that has haunted memories for over thirty years) to enhance mood. The present writer first visited Morse over twenty years ago at his ranch near Redwood City in Northern California. For a decade the stories had floated around in my memory, and I had

longed to get scripts or recordings of them, to be able to experience those thrills and pleasures again. Locating the then retired writer-producer, I exchanged some letters and phone calls with him (a thrill in itself) and he told me I could visit him at his home.

Opposite: **Michael Refetto ("Jack Packard"), Barbara Jean Wong("Girl in the Gilded Cage"), Gloria Blondell ("Jerri Booker") and Barton Yarborough ("Doc Long") in a publicity shot for** *I Love a Mystery*, **circa 1943.** *Above:* **Writer-producer Carlton E. Morse gives instructions to an unidentified sound effects woman, August 1943.**

Past the chiseled marker for the Seven Stone estate, up a winding road, the main house loomed in front of a stand of redwood trees like some rustic castle.

The man who came out to meet us went with the house, wearing a khaki shirt and pants and a thoughtful expression.

Inside, Morse denied any greatness attributed to him. He theorized there is some "greatness" out there in the universe for which he was a receiver. It spoke through him, and if he did not create works to rival Shakespeare it was because he was not a sensitive enough receiver.

As a writer, Morse is comparable to Doyle or H. G. Wells; as a director, he is akin to such film directors as John Ford, Frank Capra, and Alfred Hitchcock and such memorable radio directors as William Spear and Elliot Lewis, as well as those proficient in both mediums, such as Orson Welles. Although he was a capable director of many television episodes of *One Man's Family*, Morse was at his zenith as a radio director.

Morse often got up at four in the morning and completed a script of perhaps three thousand words before noon, sometimes seven days a week. He had learned to work hard as a boy on a ranch in Oregon, getting up early to milk cows and pitch hay at the horses. To amuse himself, Morse began concocting many of the characters and plot elements that would serve him for years.

Later on, he would learn to write clearly and concisely as a newspaper man in California, doing stories on the murdered gangsters and exposed politicians of the twenties. And as a director, he knew the importance of placing the right actors in the right role, perhaps from seeing too many people in real life trying to live a role not suited to them. In the dramatic department at the University of California at Berkeley during the twenties he met many of the actors who would give life to his words for nearly three decades. Morse gave the actors dialogue; the actors in turn fed his imagination with their own personalities. Michael Raffetto, radio and screen actor and attorney, in many ways was the gruff, no-nonsense man of both thought and action who was Jack Packard, the leader of the adventurers on *I Love a Mystery*.

Barton Yarborough was a former resident of Texas. He could rid himself of his Southwestern drawl when he wanted to, as in playing an upper-class San Franciscan on *One Man's Family* or an Englishman on *Suspense*. But the dialect all came back when he wanted it to, thank goodness, as when he played Jack's sidekick, Doc Long. Doc's passion for the fairer sex was reportedly not something that demanded of Yarborough a great "stretch" as an actor.

Later Morse would encounter Walter Patterson, a former resident of South Africa who sounded like a well-schooled Briton, and the character of Reggie York became part of the original cast of *I Love a Mystery*.

Of course, the pool of professional actors on the West Coast provided many other cast members. One of the most professional was Mercedes McCambridge. In a burst of enthusiasm Orson Welles had once called her the finest actress in the world. She certainly tied with a handful of other women as the finest actress in radio. She could and did play everything from a wheelchair-bound spinster in Morse's story "Island of Skulls" to a middle European ballet dancer in his "Bury Your Dead, Arizona" to a whimpering beauty constantly pursued by the invisible, menacing 'They" in "The Thing that Cries in the Night." She was the only major cast member to perform in both the original series from California and, after winning an Academy award for her film work, the repeat series from New York.

The opportunity to first employ the cast came in 1939 when the advertising agency for Fleishmann's Yeast asked Morse to present a concept for a new mystery program they were interested in sponsoring. For seven years, the writer had been turning out the domestic saga *One Man's Family*, then sponsored by another Standard Brands product, Tenderleaf Tea. For seven years, Morse had had his head inside the Barbour family home in the Seacliff area of San Francisco, and he needed a change of pace.

Years before, as he was just getting started in radio, Morse had written some thrillers with titles like "The City of the Dead" and "The Cobra King Strikes Back" featuring a certain Captain Post. The elements of a new series were there, and would blossom into *I Love a Mystery* in 1939. (In 1945, Morse would go back to these scripts, writing about Captain Friday in a syndicated program, *Adventures by Morse*).

For the new show, Morse wrote down on a sheet of paper a number of possible titles for the potential sponsor. The one selected was *I Love a Mystery*. Morse can't recall the unused, alternate titles today. We know Conan Doyle decided against Sherringford Holmes, but we'll never know what *I Love a Mystery* might have been called.

The series began on a West Coast–only subnetwork of NBC on January 16, 1939, as a Monday-through-Friday fifteen-minute serial. It proved so popular that by 1941 it was on as a half-hour episode once a week in prime evening time, coast to coast.

The serial format was retained, hearkening back to an earlier period in radio when serials were quite common even in prime time (which was yet to be given that name, of course). Most nighttime dramas in the forties were told as a complete story in half an hour (only rarely in a full hour). But Carlton E. Morse was unique; he followed his own star, doing it the way he wanted and making a great success of it.

At this time, the *Mystery* series was presented in thirty minutes as two approximately fifteen-minute chapters, divided by a commercial. Sometimes, though, the first act might go on for about twenty minutes, building to a climax. "When we repeated the shows as fifteen-minute episodes, it took a lot of work rewriting the scripts to make them break exactly in quarter-hour units," Morse recalled.

Morse admits he likes running a "one man show." His responsibility was not only writing the scripts, but casting them and directing them, and supervising the music and sound effects. The arrangement was unlike that of any current film or television project; Morse was in charge of everything.

As the creator of the show, he was meticulous in the use of sound effects. In the twenties and early thirties, most sound effects were done live. But by the mid-thirties, it was more practical to use a recording of a steam locomotive and whistle than to try to recreate it in the studio. It nevertheless remained a possiblity to get a passable approximation of a train on its track with a long tube-like box being pushed across a corrugated "washboard" surface, faster and faster to suggest a steam train gathering speed. Some of these ingenious inventions of sound technicians have been saved in special collections, but others are lost even to memory. Although Morse did use some recordings, at least for the bigger budgeted nighttime show, he vastly preferred live sounds.

For certain effects, Morse had to devise his own equipment. The script for a scene in "The Secret Passage to Death" called for a man to be found hanging from a tree, "slowly twisting in the wind" (according to the contemporary cliche). The writer-director brought the trunk and main branch of a tree into the studio and had a sound effects man hang from a rope on the limb. Humanely, Morse had him hold on with both hands instead of having the noose around his neck. The rope rubbed and groaned against the wood and the limb creaked as only real hemp and a real branch could sound.

In the appropriately named "Battle of the Century," Morse staged a mammoth fistfight with Jack and Doc against seven weathered ranch hands. His script instruction: "Pound away until the fists of every sound effects man in the network hurt like the toothache."

At NBC and CBS Morse managed to get the sound patterns he wanted, but by the time he had the *Mystery* series on the Mutual Broadcasting System this fourth network offered a different perspective. Like most of radio, Mutual now relied almost exclusively on the use of recordings for sound effects. Only such things that had to be chorographed to match certain dialogue and action was done live any longer—footsteps, individual punches and the like. Always creative, Morse suggested in his directions the combining of certain recordings for special effects—overlaying the sound of a waterfall with the blast of a hurricane to suggest an immense cascade for "The Stairway to the Sun." Unfortunately, few of these suggestions were used—the tired old pros of the last days of radio drama generally just pulled standard sound effect B-Y-70 off the shelf and used it.

The cast of the New York repeat series, 1949–52, might not have been absolutely perfect – after all, these scripts had not been written especially for them – but they were among the best working actors in the business.

Russell Thorson was chosen for Jack. A decade before, he had played the cowboy hero Tom Mix, with Curley Bradley as his sidekick Pecos. (Curley would go on to play the title role of Tom Mix himself for a number of years.) Curley says that Thorson was rather shy, despite his commanding voice, and sensitive about an acne-marked complexion. No doubt he was more comfortable in radio behind the microphone, but after drama disappeared, he did go on to work extensively in television and movies. He could be seen in many early television Westerns such as *Gunsmoke* and *Cheyenne* as a wealthy rancher or an honest sheriff. He was one of the group of vigilantes who strung up Clint Eastwood in the 1970s fiilm *Hang 'Em High*.

Morse saw Thorson as the best available replacement for his chosen leading man, Michael Raffetto. Raffetto had health problems including recurring attacks of tuberculosis, and his voice was affected from time to time – a bad condition for a radio actor. When *One Man's Family* went to television, Raffetto was already having this trouble. Morse was also doing the show on television, live from New York, the point of origin of all television at that primitive time in its development. The California-based and ailing Raffetto did not go to New York for the television series, nor did any of the other regulars. (For years, he directed the radio series of *One Man's Family* for Morse.) Another factor was that the writer was going back to the beginning of his scripts and starting the story all over, so the actors had to be some twenty years younger than the radio cast. Thorson became the eldest son, Paul. Eva Marie Saint was his sister, Claudia, and so on. And even as Raffetto had played both Paul and Jack Packard, Thorson took the role of Jack on the radio series of *I Love a Mystery* and that of Paul on television (and would eventually take it over on radio). Despite his fellow actor's assertion of his basic shyness, Thorson was a no-nonsense guy (like his character, Packard). The first Mrs. Morse, Patricia, told a story of Thorson's returning home to find his wife having prepared an elaborate meal of epicurean proportions. He pushed it all aside and told her to bring him meat and potatoes. Thorson was not so much a male chauvinist as a Thorson chauvinist – he was used to getting his way. On the *Tom Mix* show, he had a lot of say on the production in its entirety. However, surviving sample recordings of rehearsals on the Morse series show that he deferred to Morse. It is doubtful that anyone who did not would have worked for Morse so consistently. His fellow actor on the *Mix* program, Curley Bradley, felt that Thorson learned a greater range and sensitivity working for Morse. Bradley himself has been named one of the two or three finest radio actors by a number of people in the business, including Frank Bresee – who has done everything in broadcasting from playing Little Beaver on *Red Ryder* as a child to hosting and producing the longest running current radio vari-

In the 1949 revival of *I Love a Mystery* on Mutual, Tony Randall ("Reggie York") and Russell Thorson ("Jack") watch Jim Boles ("Doc") going all out for the microphone.

ety program, *Golden Days of Radio*, now more than twenty-five years on AFRTA.

In New York, Jim Boles was not the only actor to try out for the role of Doc Long. A young actor who was working in both radio and television in 1949, playing the second lead on *Mr. Peepers* on television and doing some parts in radio soap operas, auditioned for Doc. An Oklahoma native, he thought he could get the accent back. But for him it did not return as effortlessly as it did for Yarborough. He would not do for Doc. But there was something in his rather cultivated natural speech pattern than must have suggested the British to Morse. The director suggested he try for Reggie, and he got the part. He was Tony Randall, who went on to a long career in movies and television, perhaps best known as the prissy half of television's *Odd Couple*.

Jim Boles had been playing western characters on such New York–based series as *Tennessee Jed* and *Bobby Benson's B Bar B Riders*. A serious stage actor who had played Abraham Lincoln and a number of television roles, Boles brought a lot of professionalism to the part of the red-headed Texas boy. Something in his own nature complemented the role too. "I knew I had Doc the first time I heard Jim Boles read," Morse said.

I met Boles only once at an AFTRA gathering. I spotted him in the throng from publicity photos and started walking toward him, thinking how well this bony-faced man matched my mental image of Doc. But as I got closer, Boles seemed to shrink, down to only average height. He noticed my reaction. "I've never been tall enough for the roles I've played, like Lincoln. The stage audience can't really tell. And you can be tall as you like on radio."

Bole's wife, Athena Lord, played the part of Jerri Booker, the secretary to Packard and Long, in New York. (Gloria Blondel, sister of film actress Joan, played the role in Hollywood.)

Among the early supporting cast was Les Tremayne. He played the crippled gangster in "The Million Dollar Mystery" and appeared in the first New York serial, "The Fear that Creeps Like a Cat." Tremayne could have played the part of Jack Packard. He may have lacked the cantankerousness Thorson had naturally, but he could have played the part out of his skills as perhaps the most successful radio actor ever to ply the craft. He was the star of the *First Nighter* program (*not* Mr. First Nighter himself, who went to a play starring Tremayne with Barbara Luddy every week), the lead in *The Thin Man*, and the leading man and countless other characters in radio broadcasts from all three of the leading radio centers – Chicago, New York and Hollywood – at various times. For Morse he played the lead, the eldest son, in *Woman in My House*, which was originally a radio series reusing the early scripts of *One Man's Family* with the Barbour family name changed to Carter. In this series, he played the Michael Raffetto role. He did not get the Raffetto-type role on the New York-based *I Love a Mystery*, but he could have done well with it. His supporting roles lend a lot to the series on surviving recordings.

Another regular in the supporting New York cast was Robert Dryden. For the series, he took the part of a number of grungy Western characters, such as Jumpin' Dick in "Bury you Dead, Arizona," and a variety of thugs here and there. In the final few months, after Thorson left for the West Coast, he took over the role of Packard, sounding a great deal like the film actor, Lee Tracy, in his interpretation.

Morse's original concept for *I Love a Mystery* involved a trio of adventurers patterned after the most apparent of literary sources, Alexander Dumas' *Three Musketeers*. Originally, Jack, Doc and Reggie were known as the Three Comrades. Then after World War II and the obsession with the menace of Communism, the word "comrade" seemed to take on a negative connotation and the trio became known as Jack, Doc and Reggie. Actually, the untimely death of Walter Patterson broke up that particular combination rather soon. By 1942, the script said Reggie had returned to his native Britain to join the war effort and the combination became "Jack, Doc and Jerri Booker."

Other partners to join the roster included Michael, a rather ominous Frenchman who sounded like Peter Lorre; another secretary called Mary Kay Brown (later, when it was found that there was a movie actress by that name, changed to Mary Kay Jones), an Irishman named Terry Burke and a Swede named Swen.

Certainly the best remembered trio is Jack, Doc and Reggie – the name many people mistakenly call the series (such as television's *All in the Family* is often called *Archie Bunker*). Actually, more often it was a show with only a pair of heroes, Jack and Doc. Jack was always present, and in the New York series, Doc continued through to the end, with Reggie dropping out as Randall left for other work. In this repeat version, the alternate "comrades" were written out and their parts assigned to Doc. (In the original series, both Yarborough and Raffetto left the show due to a dispute with Morse over the Columbia movies of *I Love a Mystery*.)

On the Hollywood series, the character Doc was written out as recovering from a fall through a skyscraper in "I Am the Destroyer of Women." Jack continued, played first by Jay Novello and then by John McIntire. Jay Novello, whom the author met once in a line at the unemployment compensation window, never was quite right for the part of Jack. He was raised in Britain, of Italian parentage, and he never could quite shake that hint of Italian accent that served him well playing gangsters on radio and in movies in the then-accepted stereotype. He just could not quite bring off the tough-talking, all-American Jack Packard. John McIntire was much more satisfactory.

There had to be a first meeting of the three principal characters of *I Love a Mystery*, an "origin" in the terms of popular heroes of the pulps and comics. That origin occurred in China, whose nationalist forces the three have joined to fight the invading Japanese. The three soldiers of fortune find themselves together behind some debris, resisting an advance of Imperial forces. The odds are greatly against them, and it looks like the end. They make a vow that if they somehow survive this attack and get separated, they will meet at a certain restaurant in San Francisco's Chinatown the next New Year's Eve. Then the smoke and noise of battle obliterate the scene.

On New Year's Eve, Jack greets Reggie at the Chinatown hangout, and the two of them wait for Doc to appear. After some time, there seems to be nothing to do but drink a final toast to their missing comrade. But then Doc bursts through the door. He says the police are after him, and they want him for murder. The three decide they had better make tracks, and the chase is on. It wouldn't stop for years of thrilling, intoxicating high adventure. This was the first episode of *I Love a Mystery*.

The three men wind up borrowing a car "that wasn't exactly theirs," and near the town of Roxy they run into trouble. Witnesses to what they think is the attempted abduction of a young woman, they wind up being arrested by a posse of townsmen. Later in jail, as Reggie sleeps (being able to do it even on a jail bed), Doc complains that they should have taken the mob's guns away from them and made them eat them. Jack agrees that they could have done it easily (apparently there were only ten or twelve of these armed men, a mere irritant) but he wants to play along and see what is up. He finds out when he is taken to the office of the obviously corrupt mayor of Roxy and is told that the girl the boys saw was the mayor's daughter, being "protected" by the mayor's self-described "henchmen." The mayor wants Jack to take over the job of bodyguarding his beautiful but difficult young daughter. (Amusingly, the unsavory mayor was played by J. Anthony Smythe, the upstanding and virtuous Father Barbour on Morse's other show, *One Man's Family*.)

So began the first *I Love a Mystery* serial, which Morse identified on his scripts with a hasty scribble as "Roxy Gangsters."

Existing logs of the date and exact title of each serial differ, but the following list represents as accurately as possible the stories and the order in which they were written. After Jan. 16, 1939, exact dates are given where available. The show aired in fifteen-minute episodes, Monday through Friday, on the NBC regional network. The number of stations carrying it varied.

Episodes were as follows: "The Case of the Roxy Mob" (14 episodes), "Trouble at Sea" (12), "The Case of the Nevada Man Killer" (20), "The Turn of the Wheel" (20), "Whose Body Got Buried?" (15), "Escapade of the Desert Hag" (15), "Blood on the Border" (15), "Flight to Death" (15), "Murder Hollywood Style" (15), "Incident Concerning Death" (15), "Battle of the Century" (18), "The Blue Phantom Murders" (beginning Oct. 2, 1939; 15 episodes), "The Fear that Creeps like a Cat" (Oct. 23, 1939; 20), "The Thing that Cries in the Night" (Nov. 20, 1939; 15), "Bury your Dead, Arizona" (Dec. 11, 1939; 15), "The Million Dollar Mystery" (15), "Temple of Vampires" (20),

"The Brooks Kidnapping" (15), "Murder in Turquoise Pass" (15) and "The Snake with the Diamond Eyes" (20).

In 1940 the show became a thirty-minute nighttime program broadcast once a week on NBC coast to coast. Episodes were as follows: "The Tropics Don't Call it Murder" (Sept. 30, 1940; 14), "The Case of the Transplanted Castle" (Jan. 6, 1941; 9), "Murder on February Island" (Mar. 10, 1941; 9), "Eight Kinds of Murder" (May 12, 1941; 8), "The Monster in the Mansion" (Oct. 6, 1941; 7), "Secret Passage to Death" (Dec. 1, 1941; 13), Terror of Frozen Corpse Lodge" (Feb. 9, 1942; 9) and "The Secret Loot of the Island of Skulls" (Apr. 13 to July 6, 1942; 13 episodes and last of half-hour format).

The show went to a fifteen-minute format and was broadcast nationally by CBS beginning March 22, 1943. Episodes were as follows: "The Girl in the Gilded Cage" (Mar. 22, 1943; 15), "Blood of the Cat" (Apr. 12, 1943; 20), "The Killer of the Circle M" (May 10, 1943; 20), "Stairway to the Sun" (June 7, 1943; 30), "The Graves of Whamperjaw, Texas" (July 19, 1943; 15), "Murder is the Word for It" (Aug. 9, 1943; 15), "The Decapitation of Jefferson Monk" (Aug. 30, 1943; 20), "My Beloved is a Vampire" (Oct. 4, 1943; 25), "The Hermit of San Felipe Atapabo" (Nov. 8, 1943; 20), "The Deadly Sin of Sir Richard Coyle" (Dec. 6, 1943; 15), "The African Jungle Mystery" (Dec. 27, 1943; 10), "The Twenty Traitors of Timbuktu" (Jan. 10, 1944; 44), "I Am the Destroyer of Women" (Apr. 24, 1944; 15), "Corpse in Compartment C, Car 76" (June 5, 1944; 5), "The Thing Wouldn't Die" (June 12, 1944; 20), "The Case of the Terrified Comedian" (July 10, 1944; 21), "The Man Who Hated to Shave" (Aug. 8, 1944; 10), "Temple of Vampires" (Aug. 22, 1944; 20), "Bride of the Werewolf" (Oct. 16, 1944; 15), "The Monster in the Mansion" (Oct. 16, 1944; 23), "Portrait of a Murderer" (Nov. 17, 1944; 20), "Find Elas Holberg, Dead or Alive" (Dec. 14–31, 1944; planned for 16 episodes [scripts exist], last of original Hollywood series).

There seem to have been 46 serials (allowing for repeats, with a possibility for confusion due to retitled repeats) with the longest being "The Twenty Traitors of Timbuktu" at 44 quarter-hour episodes and the shortest "Corpse in Compartment C, Car 76" at 5 quarter-hour episodes (Morse said he wrote the latter in order to fill out a quota of episodes sold to a particular advertiser).

These programs were repeated with the New York cast from Oct. 3, 1949, to Dec. 26, 1952, on the Mutual Broadcasting System. Some stations delayed the show a week so that it could be run at an earlier hour in the day than its network origination (9:15 PM EST), so in some areas the show went into the following year and was heard for the last time on Jan. 2, 1953. The order was altered for rebroadcast, with "The Fear That Creeps Like a Cat" being the first of the repeat series but with "Find Elsa Holberg, Dead or Alive" again the final episode.

During the summer of 1948, Morse tried reviving the series with a variation on the format. As early as 1945 he had attempted to sell the adventures of Jack, Doc and Reggie as a complete story in half an hour, the standard format for such detective and mystery shows as *The Shadow, Ellery Queen* and *Sam Spade*. It was an attempt to adjust to the times. Morse did the series well, and it would have made a fine continuing series. It seems incredible that no sponsor picked it up. Morse sold the original format again late the next year, although the stories would be the repeated scripts in new productions.

The short-lived 1948 series marked the return of both Michael Raffetto and Barton Yarborough in their original roles of Jack and Doc, with Tom Collins playing Reggie for the first time. Morse thought the late Mr. Collins did a bad job of playing Reggie. Collins does sound as if he is forcing a youthful, carefree attitude on the character, but all in all his portrayal seems that of a competent professional. (Morse apparently had a great friendship with the original actor, Walter Patterson. Patterson's portrayal was incredibly underplayed, especially for radio, but very natural and convincing. Perhaps Tony Randall brought Reggie more assertiveness.) All in all, the cast for this trial series was excellent, with support from Morse regulars like Barbara Jean Wong, Jannette Nolan and Russell Thorson in noncontinuing character parts.

Here are all of the 13 episodes of *I Love Adventure* (actually the retitled *I Love a Mystery*) heard on ABC on Sunday afternoons during the summer of 1948: "The China Coast Incident" (Apr. 25), "The Great Air Mail Robbery" (May 2), "The Devil's Sanctuary" (May 9), "Pearl of Great Price" (May 16), "The Hundred Million Dollar Manhunt" (May 23), "The Girl's Finishing School Kidnapping" (May 30), "But Grandma, What Big Teeth You Have" (June 6), "Man with the Third Green Eye" (June 13), "The Girl in the Street" (June 20), "The Kwan-Moon Dagger" (June 27), "Assignment with a Displaced Person" (July 4), "Hearse on the Highway" (July 11) and "Ambassador Ricardo Santos Affair" (July 18).

The series began with Major Jack Packard being called to London to the richly appointed headquarters of a group called the Twenty-One Old Men of Gramercy Park, a secret order of influential men of all nations who attempted to guide the destiny of the world toward peace. Jack, Doc and Reggie were to become their chief agents if they could be found wherever the events of World War II had left them.

Jack alone handled the first case on the China Coast, a rather routine recovery of a missing secret formula, with the story now broken into the usual three- to six-minute scenes of most radio half-hour dramas. But at his next visit to the Twenty-One Men, Jack met Reggie York. It was the character's first appearance on a Morse program since 1941. Jack and Reggie worked together to prevent "The Great Air Mail Robbery," the midair piracy of a transatlantic plane by another aircraft. This was probably the best episode of the brief series, telling events that could have happened in thirty minutes of "real time."

Jack and Reggie handled a number of other cases for the Twenty-One, until the format of the series changed abruptly with the "Grandma, What Big Teeth" story. Jack Packard was back in Hollywood, running the A-1 Detective Agency again. Doc had been found and was with them – in spirit, at least, because he was out on another case. Reggie continued as chief sidekick. The story was a rewrite of an unsold 1945 audition with Reggie written to fill Doc's part. The story of a criminally corrupt grandmother and her innocent grandson was a good one, like all of Morse's scripts, but perhaps was not the ideal showcase for Jack and his partners.

The format change was probably due to small audience size and lack of response to stories of wartime-type espionage (the stories had been written a few years earlier) in a time when most people wanted to forget the war. There was also a character change: both Jack and Reggie now seemed as girl-crazy as Doc. Had somebody impuned their masculinity to writer Morse? Or had they developed the skirt-chasing proclivities attributed to servicemen?

Finally, Doc Long – the original Doc, Yarborough – returned in "The Girl in the Street" – but it wasn't much of a return. Jack and Doc hardly appeared in what was basically an anthology story about a military officer's wife and more intrigue. (The budget seemed to call for only one sidekick per episode, and Reggie never reappeared taking an apparent eternity to solve an arson case.)

Finally, Doc Long returned in all his glory in "The Kwan-Moon Dagger," a wild and woolly tale in the Morse tradition, even though it was credited to veteran radio scripter Sidney Marshal. One suspects Morse may have added some touches – like Doc calling up a movie studio to rent an alligator for him to wrestle to relieve his boredom.

But after another anthology entry and fair story about truck highjackings, there came the last episode of the series, in which Jack and Doc are hired to protect a South American ambassador and his feuding daughter and new wife. The boys find out the most dangerous part of the case is not crash-landing in the African jungle.

The series was a noble experiment – and in a perfect world, following the example of such programs as *Dick Tracy*, there would have been a serial featuring Jack, Doc and Reggie in *I Love a Mystery* on weekdays and a complete half-hour weekend case of *I Love Adventure*. In the real world, however, the title disappeared after these 13 weeks.

Each of the fifteen-minute chapters of the original *I Love a Mystery* series, whether presented singly each weekday or in pairs on one weeknight, was generally one long scene as in a stage play – no fades, cuts or music bridges. The first actor took the first line of dialogue and the action continued until the last actor delivered the last line of dialogue. This format gave a great feeling of reality, as if one were listening to fifteen minutes in the life of Packard and friends, perhaps eavesdropping from the other side of the door. Of course, the formula was not carved in stone; Morse occasionally did a scene-dividing fade, and often the chiming of a clock suggested a later hour. But for the most part there was only that single unit of time. The real time passage was generally realistic; the characters did no more than could actually be done in about a quarter hour. Of course, time was occasionally condensed for dramatic purposes. For instance, in the story "Million Dollar Mystery," Jack and the troubled heiress leave her house, walk across a park, enter a hospital and take an elevator up several floors in only about two minutes. Possible perhaps; a world record certainly.

A lonely train whistle began the program, suggesting travel, adventure, an eerie sound in the dark of night. Then came the announcer's billboard: "*I Love a Mystery,* featuring the adventures of Jack, Doc and Reggie – specialists in crime and adventure – in a new Carlton Morse adventure thriller...." (The wording differed a bit over the years, and of course the title of the current serial changed.) Then the magnificent *Valse Triste* theme, originally played on a great pipe organ, filled the room and the imagination.

A clock struck the hour, and the announcer, originally silky-voiced Dresser Dalstead, would name the hour and set the scene. "Four o'clock on a sultry afternoon on a tropical island somewhere in the Pacific. Jack is studying the map he managed to rescue from the sinking plane, while Reggie gets some much needed sleep. Doc is restless as usual, pacing up and down the deserted beach." (This is a composite opening of the present writer's invention.)

Carlton Morse's actual stories took place in many locales, although the tropics was one of his favorite locations. As in any writer's work, certain themes recurred.

There was often a sinister old mansion menaced by something unseen but definitely sinister. One or more beautiful young girls were in danger there, and like knights of old, the Three Comrades had to protect them – Reggie without thought of reward, Doc perhaps hoping for some reward from the lonely young thing and Jack grumpily but resigned to a destiny that put him at odds with the forces of evil and destruction. Stories of this type included "The Monster in the Mansion," in which an unseen killer played an organ rendition of Brahms' "Lullabye" to announce each death; "Bride of the Werewolf," in which mausoleum bells tolled each fatality; and perhaps the best of these old dark house thrillers, "The Thing that Cries in the Night," in which the murderer's sinister signature was the cry of a small baby. In a medium devoted to sound, it wasn't unusual for Morse to identify each menacing figure with its own distinctive note.

The baby-crying story is remembered by many people not by its true title but as "Faith, Hope and Charity," the names of three Martin family sisters who are stalked by the unseen Thing. Charity Martin is usually called "Cherry," rather than her biblical-sounding Christian name. Morse has the story identified in his files with the hastily penciled, "Hollywood Cherry."

The virginal Miss Martin is ripe for many things, but mostly psychoanalysis. She thinks she is being pursued by "Them" or "They" who did terrible things to her, like pushing her down stairs and slashing her arms with razor blades. But is it just paranoia when there are actual marks on her arms?

Her sister Faith, or Fay as she prefers to be called seems to go for every man she meets, even the family chauffeur. After Jack, Doc and Reggie are recruited by old Grandmother Randolph Martin to bring some order to the house of Martin, Fay shows up at the door of their guest room after one of her dates with Chauffeur Bob wearing only something she bought in France. Perhaps it is perfume – on radio you can use your imagination. Jack throws a blanket around her.

As for Hope, she is reported to talk in a vulgar way. On radio in the forties, you really had to use your imagination to believe that. She does make some suggestions about Fay coming to Jack's room, but Jack tells her, in a manner of speaking, to stuff it. He couldn't stand vulgarity.

The fourth woman in the house has the masculine name of Randolph Martin, no doubt that of some robber baron ancestor. She tries to run her family with the same iron hand with which she runs her several companies, but Grandmother Martin seems to fail miserably on the domestic scene.

The only male member of the Martin family is named Job, and if he is beset with troubles like his biblical namesake, he tries to drown them in a bottle.

The problems Jack, Doc and Reggie find in the Martin house began with the discovery of Chauffeur Bob murdered downstairs, clutching Fay's blood-splattered dress. The blood turns out to be that of a gangster who was murdered right in front of the table the loyal Martin employee was sharing with Fay at a nightclub. Fay changed out of the blood-splattered garment and left it up to Bob to get rid of. Somebody did not leave him enough time to take care of that.

Then when Cherry comes onto the scene and begins whispering about the mysterious "They" who are after her and all the Martins, and when she is pushed down the stairs, things begin to happen fast. The only warning the three investigators have is the cry of an infant somewhere nearby.

There was no real baby, only the cry of someone who had been trained as a radio actress, a certain Pauline West. Pauline West was the killer in the house. But who was Pauline West? Who were "They" who were out to get the Martins? It was left to Jack, Doc and Reggie to unravel these mysteries in further installments.

Following the events of the Martin case, the three adventurers leave town rather hurriedly because of trouble with both the law and the local Mob. They hop a box car on a departing freight train. The eerie whistle of the opening signature blends right into the sounds of the freight the three are riding for several episodes. This story belongs to Morse's picaresque tradition of stories told "on the go." Another story, "The Secret Passage to Death," begins on horseback and has the adventurous trio using nearly every other form of transportation as they attempt to carry an unconscious, hypnotized Chinese girl to San Francisco where an agency of the United States government is anxious to receive a secret she had. Rather similar events characterize "The Girl in the Gilded Cage," an alternate version where the secret-bearing Chinese girl is awake and a more talkative companion.

But in "Bury your Dead" the girl is from somewhere in Europe and the transportation moving Jack, Doc and Reggie is the freight train. What makes their ride interesting enough to cover a number of installments is the appearance in the same boxcar of a ponderous fat man and his beautiful young assistant. The man is known only as the Maestro and the girl, from somewhere near Russia, is named Natascha. The two do a magic act together, but are just now reduced to riding the rails. The Maestro is a self-proclaimed great man, whose "star is yet to rise" according to the girl. He is, he claims, a real magician with powers over the mystic forces. During the train trip, he seems to verify his claims by producing a corpse and making it vanish, and perhaps most impressively by turning Natascha into a tiger in the darkness and then bringing her human form back floating in a spectral radiance through the air.

Jack doesn't believe any of it, and he seems more in his own element when the train sidetracks at the virtual ghost town of Bury Your Dead, Arizona. The travelers take lodging at a relic of a boarding house run by a gun-wielding old gal who likes to listen at doors. She hears a lot, as the Maestro continues to work his ways, announcing that he is turning Natascha into a wolf and that later he will turn one of the wolves up on the ridge into a man. Seemingly he does it all.

After Jack, Doc and Reggie get in and out of any number of fights and traps, Jack exposes much of the Maestro's magic as illusion and trickery, but the man does seem to possess powers of mental suggestion, hypnosis and telepathy beyond the normal. Finally, Jack gets Natascha a job dancing in a nightclub – it isn't much, but better than riding freight trains with a fat maniac.

The hotel where the trio sign in after returning from Arizona to San Diego places them just down the hall from the room of Sunny Richards,

Les Tremayne, the "single greatest radio actor" in the opinion of many, in a recent photo. Tremayne, who played featured roles on the *I Love a Mystery* radio series as well as leads on *First Nighter* and *Thin Man*, would star again in the 1992 series of Harmon-directed productions of *I Love a Mystery*.

whose troubles, including the fact every man she gets near seems to die a horrible death, lead Packard, Long and York into the "The Million Dollar Mystery."

This story combined the touch of seeming supernatural menace from such stories as "My Beloved Is a Vampire" with the writer's brand of big-city gangster story. (Sometimes he would deal with rural thugs like those in the employ of prize-fight crazy Jim Ross who owned a ranch where Reggie would have to take on Big Swede in "The Battle of the Century.")

Usually Morse's gangsters were faceless thugs for the lads to knock over like tenpins. Some were given a humorous twist, and a poignant portrayal was given the chief gangster involved in Sunny Richards' troubles. A virile man now confined to a hospital bed by an accident, he vows that no man will have Sunny if he can't, and arranges for more "accidents" to strike her other suitors. Actor Les Tremayne gave an excellent interpretation of the role for the New York series in surviving recordings.

By the workings of fate, only a certain long run of New York episodes survives (random episodes of the Hollywood series also exist), but although many delicious stories are missing, this run does contain some of the best and most representative serials in the history of the show, including the most popular story ever. Sunny continues into this next adventure, begging to go along with the three adventurers on a Central American trip to clear her mind of her long ordeal. This journey eventually leads all of them into the most famous story of the series, "Temple of Vampires."

With Doc being the most lighthearted and Jack the most serious (and Reggie vacillating between their two influences), the trio was all in all, a rather carefree group, yet they were played against the most somber of happenings—frequently murder, and not infrequently seemingly supernatural evil. Events would often take them to some old deserted temple or ruin in some exotic place in the world. A number of Morse's most memorable tales belong to this tradition, including "The Snake with the Diamond Eyes."

Another memorable entry of the type, "The Stairway to the Sun," involved an ancient structure of stone steps leading up a mountain in Central America, the entryway to a lost plateau inhabited by life from every era of the world's history, from prehistoric pterodacty and cave men through mystic priests of recent centuries and perhaps to creatures of the Earth's future, beings evolved into supermen who subtly guide the destiny of governments and leaders. This story and its sequel, "The Hermit of San Felipe Atapabo," explored this fascinating land in Morse's deepest exploration into science fiction or science fantasy. "Hermit" was inspired by Hudson's *Green Mansions* and its tale of the bird girl, Rima. When that novel was made into a Technicolor film, Morse was stunned at how closely the opening shots of Rima's land matched the lost plateau he had imagined for the world of the "Stairway to the Sun." (It is too bad Hollywood never realized Morse's own creations so satisfactorily.)

The two serials set in this fantastic lost world are vividly remembered and highly regarded by the organized corps of fantasy fans. Yet they never quite received the fame of the story of Jack, Doc and Reggie, and Sunny on their plane trip to Central America.

"Temple of Vampires" seems to have become part of the popular consciousness. People still speak of something coming on like Gangbusters, and a real hard-working guy with no vices is a Jack Armstrong. These terms are used by people too young to have ever heard those radio programs. While the title of "Temple of Vampires" may not be recognized by all, many men and women seem to know the story from somewhere, perhaps from a parent or grandparent. Perhaps the story even has been repeated through a second generation, much like a folk tale.*

"Temple of Vampires" was another tale of perhaps the most enduring figure of the supernatural, the vampire. People in the urban twentieth century no longer dwell on the thought of ghouls devouring the flesh of corpses, or their neighbors changing into some beast of the surrounding forest like the wolf. But we are still fascinated by the thought of human-like creatures who come in the night to suck the life blood of the living, who live forever and who must sleep the day through in their coffins. Even today, there are people who believe vampires actually exist, and other people, men and women, who actually wish to be vampires.

There is discussion, argument and confusion over just what the attributes of a vampire are. Can vampires really change themselves into bats, or do they climb walls so swiftly with their flowing cloaks and depart equally fast, so that they *seem* like bats? Do they have to remain in their coffins, or is it merely a preference that can be abandoned in time of danger? Author Morse played on their variations brilliantly to create a totally realistic version of the vampire for a modern audience. If his vampires did not meet all the criteria of Bram Stoker's Dracula, they were myths for a developing America, not an ancient middle Europe.

The vampire has many psychological overtones. The creature who comes in the night and draws blood has sexual symbolism and fascination. As counterbalance to the menace in this story, Jack, Doc and Reggie also are symbolic of more than the forces of "Good" against "Evil." Sociologist Dawn Kovner has pointed out that the three heroes represent nicely the three elements of modern psychology: Jack is the ego – strong, forceful; Doc is the id – the child seeking pleasure; and Reggie might be regarded as the super-ego, the conscience trying to impose the standards of civilization on the others. The analogy is not perfect. Jack has elements of the super-ego in him, and to a lesser extent, so does Doc. Overall, the three are people, each of whom possesses elements of the entire human personality.

The story of "Temple of Vampires" begins with the three comrades flying off on a vacation adventure to Central America, accompanied by

---

Although scripts and recordings survive, they are not universally available. This story is worth delving into in depth. See Appendix for the author's interpretation of this classic episode.

Sunny Richards, the heroine of the previous story, "Million Dollar Mystery," who wants to forget all the violence surrounding the so-called Richards' Curse. On a flight over the Nicaraguan jungles, the group happily speculates on what to expect on landing at the next big town. Doc is looking forward to meeting some long-eyelashed senoritas. Jack wants to check out the speed of the plane. Reggie wants to find a native bar and get into a good fight, "sailor fashion." Although cautioned against it by her trio of protectors, Sunny is wondering if the local men are as good-looking as Doc reports the women to be. Then a stowaway introduces himself. He is Hermie, a seven-year-old boy, abandoned by his father on this plane.

It isn't a very safe plane for any of them. Jack's almost supernaturally attuned instincts soon detect something wrong with the craft's engine (later it is found to be caused by watered gasoline). Jack skillfully makes a forced landing – right next to a towering ancient temple. "A New York skyscraper rising right up out of the jungle!" Reggie exclaims.

The five people take what provisions they can and seek sanctuary in the stone structure. On the trail there they find a native, dead, drained of blood. Even with that omen, there is nowhere else to go. As they step inside the shelter of the temple, Doc sees something pass from one high-ceilinged wall to the other, something as big as a man, and without any clothes.

As the men have suspected, the seven-year-old boy turns out to be a problem. He wanders off and gets lost. Jack and Reggie go after him, and when Doc Long sees that man-like thing again – this time near his partners on a high stone staircase – he goes to their aid, leaving Sunny alone – but not for long. The black-robed priest of the temple, Manuel, appears before her and warns her that the Temple of Vampires is not a good place for little boys, or for beautiful girls.

In another encounter, they meet the misnamed priestess Angelina, who is certainly no angel. She kidnaps Hermie because she likes the little boy's red cheeks and white skin. The three men get the boy back, only to lose Sunny to Manuel. "It is the girl I want."

The priest and priestess have a disarming ability to seemingly fly from one wall of the old temple to the other in the dark. Their secret is finally found – ropes from the ceiling, on which they can swing, Tarzan-fashion, from one ledge to another. Willing to try anything, Jack and Doc swing on the ropes, leaving Reggie on guard. It works several times, but on one necessary move, Jack and Doc get their ropes twisted together, each clinging to a separate strand fifty feet above the stone floor lost in the darkness below. It is a bad spot to be in, and it gets worse when an earthquake strikes.

The old temple begins to fall apart. Huge jagged masses tumble past the two men in the dark to crash below. But the old structure does not collapse completely, not yet. The pair is left, in Doc's words, "Like two flies hanging from the ceiling."

The only way out, Jack concludes, is to climb the ropes, get on the stone arch to which the ropes are fastened and climb down to a ledge. Laboriously, wrapping the ropes around their legs to rest from time to time, they do it.

In the course of events, the adventurers discover the real vampires of the temple – huge, rapacious vampire bats, bred to gigantic size on human sacrifices. Today, we would call them mutants. Manuel and Angelina are only their priest and priestess, filling the bats' need for human blood.

The pair is reunited with Reggie York, who has guarded Hermie, and with Sunny, who has put up such a fight against Manuel he is almost glad when she is rescued. They all decide it is time to leave the temple, and just in time. A second earthquake strikes and the rest of the temple collapses on the "Sacred Vampires" and supposedly on the priesthood.

As they strain the watered gasoline through cloth into a rubberized air mattress (Sunny's suggestion) to be placed in the airplane's tank for a takeoff, Manuel shows up, the sole survivor of the priesthood. The natives are disillusioned with him now that their sacred temple has been destroyed. Then an arrow from the jungle strikes him – a wooden shaft through the heart of the vampire priest.

The takeoff is successful. Sunny decides to adopt Hermie. Jack, Doc and Reggie will soon be off on another adventure. And so ended, in the opinion of many, the greatest single adventure serial story in the annals of radio drama.

Films

Columbia Pictures began plans for a series of *I Love a Mystery* motion pictures in 1944. There were certainly wonderful ingredients for a memorable series of films from the Carlton E. Morse scripts, and a perfect cast was already assembled. But as usual, Hollywood had to change things.

One of the first changes the studio made was in the cast of the series. Michael Raffetto was not deemed suitable to play Jack Packard (even though he **was** Jack Packard, as nearly as any living person could be). For one thing, it was thought, he was too short. Though Raffetto was not a tall man, many other actors playing rugged detectives were not giants either (e.g., Alan Ladd). As a matter of fact, Raffetto did play quite successfully a police detective in a minor film of the same era, *Seven Doors to Death*. Though he was not the credited lead star of that film, it can be clearly seen that he would have made quite an acceptable Jack on screen, and of course the voice would have carried him. The part was given to tall, handsome Jim Bannon for the film series. He certainly looked the part, but his acting range was much more limited than Raffetto's. It would be easy to dismiss Bannon as wooden, but he did learn to play heroes with some acceptability only a few years later, notably cowboy Red Ryder. Curiously, Bannon had been on the *I Love a Mystery* radio show, but only as an announcer reading the Oxydol soap commercials. It isn't clear whether this had anything to do with his getting the film contract; perhaps it was mere coincidence.

At a convention of Western actors in the 1970s, Bannon recalled that making the series was quite enjoyable, mainly for all the good times he had playing cards off the set with Bart Yarborough. He confirmed the consensus that Yarborough was one of the most charming men anyone could ever meet. Radio actor Forrest Lewis said he looked on Bart as a brother. It became Forry's bittersweet job of taking over many of Bart's roles in various radio series after Bart's fatal heart attack. A master of voices, Forry could sound as much like Barton Yarborough as any other person could. (Yarborough was not on radio playing Doc Long immediately before he died—Jim Boles was.)

Thankfully, Barton Yarborough did get to play Doc Long on screen, but the radio cast was slighted. Yarborough was given fourth billing, when he certainly should have been given at least second. His part was downplayed in number of lines and time on screen, as well. Yarborough was an experienced screen actor, playing many supporting roles. He can be seen, for example, as the second Dr. Frankenstein's well-meaning, apparently British assistant in *Ghost of Frankenstein*.

Apparently both Raffetto and Yarborough felt that they had been treated unfairly by Morse, holding that he should not have sold the film rights unless the two were guaranteed star billing. "It was out of my hands," Morse said. Almost no one has the ability to dictate such cast demands on an adaptation to another medium. The two radio actors went on strike against the *Mystery* program (although they continued on Morse's *Family* show). The radio show continued for nearly a year without them, showing that despite the great contributions of these radio performers, it was Morse's writing that kept the wheels turning. Raffetto and Yarborough had buried the hatchet deep enough to return as Jack and Doc in the brief revival as *I Love Adventure*.

With Barton Yarborough as Doc Long being the most interesting thing in the films to radio fans, the movie series rolled. The first film, under the series title *I Love a Mystery*, was based rather faithfully on Morse's radio serial "The Decapitation of Jefferson Monk." It just misses being a classic film on the basis of Jim Bannon's one-dimensional Jack Packard. Though Raffetto would have been ideal, one can imagine how good it would have been with one of the established stars then doing "B" mysteries playing Jack—Lloyd Nolan, Ralph Bellamy, even Randolph Scott (before he turned exclusively Western). And of course more of Barton Yarborough's Doc Long would have helped.

The storyline followed Morse's script and retained some of his dialogue.

Doc (Yarborough) and Jack (Bannon) try to find signs of life inside a tomb in the second *I Love a Mystery* movie, *The Unknown* (1945), remotely based on the Morse radio story "The Thing that Cries in the Night."

Jefferson Monk (actor George MacCready, always seeming a bit weird) is a man who has the mixed fortune to exactly resemble a centuries-dead religious leader of an Eastern sect. The Great One's body has been mummified and perserved over the countless decades for worshipers to visit. But finally, the head is beginning to deteriorate and has to be replaced – with Jefferson Monk's. The High Priest is perfectly willing to purchase Monk's head. Of course, Monk would only be given a limited time to enjoy the wealth before the head is claimed and taken to its sacred resting place. To get away from the supposed madman, Monk accepts the deal. But as his time is running out, he begins to regret the arrangement and seeks the help of Jack and Doc in averting the loss. As calmly as in his radio guise, Packard (Bannon) tells Monk to take it easy and not to lose his head.

Director Wallace MacDonald and producer Henry Levin produced an acceptable film of Charles O'Neal's screenplay from Morse's work. The radio creator was given a rather curious credit, a title that read, "Based on the popular radio program, *I Love a Mystery*, written and directed by Carlton E. Morse." Some reviewers and film historians made the forgivable mistake of thinking Carlton Morse directed the film. He did not; in fact, he has said he "never cared for those pictures." The true director, MacDonald, is credited later with an only slightly larger title card.

The Devil's Mask (1945) was the third and last *I Love a Mystery* feature, with Jack (Bannon) and Doc (Yarborough) and a featured player holding an unbilled shrunken head. There was a hint of the wonderful jungle-based thrillers by Morse, but no single story source can be identified.

As the O'Neal screenplay develops it becomes uncertain whether there is an actual curse or merely a mundane plot against Monk by his wife (Nina Foch)—or if some even deeper deception is involved. Yet there is a head to be taken and an appropriate atmosphere of the supernatural.

Probably the best sequence in the film comes early on with Jack and Doc sitting in a bistro and spotting Jefferson Monk for the first time. After engaging him in conversation, the two save Monk from a dangerous burn from the flaming specialty of the house. The manager offers to replace Doc's damaged coat. "It's not the whole coat, just a sleeve," Doc says, dismissing the matter.

Leaving the restaurant and going on to a foggy San Francisco street, Jack and Doc are again face to face with danger as a car nearly runs them down.

For these moments, the spirit of the radio series comes most nearly to life.

There is less success in the other two films of the short series, *The Unknown* and *The Devil's Mask*, also released in 1945. While *The Unknown* can be seen as being remotely based on the Morse story "The Thing that Cries in the Night" (with Faith, Hope, and Charity), it is hard to see what specific Morse story might have inspired *The Devil's Mask*. A shrunken head from South America and a prowling leopard are involved.

These Columbia films did not quite come off, but they were not deliberately wrong-headed. In fact, the Public Broadcasting System liked the first entry well enough to run it in a series of film classics.

Television

The attitude of the next attempt to film *I Love a Mystery* was just plain wrong. In 1966 Universal made a television movie of the show, again under the series title. At that time the *Batman* "camp" craze was at its height. The stories of Batman and Robin, translated directly from the comic books, seemed so ridiculous to an adult audience that they were funny – in fact hilarious. Someone decided that the same could be done with some famous old radio show. *I Love a Mystery* was chosen.

One of the reasons for the success of the Morse program was that no matter how fantastic the situation in which Jack, Doc and Reggie became involved, the heroes themselves and the other characters remained totally human and believable. But the television movie's comic-book style meant that no one could believe in the characters or the situations.

Morse thought David Hartman (later *Good Morning, America* host) was well cast as Doc, and he even rather liked young Hegan Beggs, who played Reggie (although he played the role not as an upper-class Englishman like Morse's Reggie, but as a working class "Beatle" type). But talk show host Les Crane as Jack was impossible. He smiled ingratiatingly, posed, sometimes even simpered and generally hammed it up. Crane was awful, but in all fairness Laurence Olivier could not have saved the script.

In a unique conception of adaptation that could have been effective and interesting, one story of *I Love a Mystery* was simply laid on top of another. "The Fear that Creeps like a Cat" was put on top of "The Thing that Cries in the Night." Ida Lupino was cast as Randolph Martin, now the mother (not the grandmother) of the three beauties, Faith, Hope and Charity (and striking beauties they were too). She gave it a nice comic turn, with a hint of kinky sex. Miss Lupino also became the maniac from "Fear that Creeps" who keeps lions for bizarre experiments. Other characters and incidents were similarly combined.

The movie, which was a pilot for an unsold series, can be credited, if it be credit, to producer Frank Price and director-teleplay writer Leslie Stevens. They certainly chose a wonderful subject. Perhaps they executed it the way they did because of demands from network executives for Batman-like camp material. As it was, it was decided that even the camp-crazy sixties were not ready for this, and the film was not actually released to television until the seventies.

Anything with any elements of *I Love a Mystery* can't be entirely bad. It has its moments, and indeed some people like the television film a lot. But it has to be appreciated on the level of a *Mad* magazine parody, not a reasonable adaptation of the real thing.

Comics

Carlton E. Morse agreed to let syndicated cartoonist Don Sherwood adapt *I Love a Mystery* to comic strip format for newspaper publication in the eighties, some thirty years after the radio series had left the air. Sherwood was a very realistic artist, and he made the faces of his Jack and Doc resemble old photos of actors Raffetto and Yarborough, with Reggie a creation of his own. Since the original radio scripts depended on cliffhangers, the plotline worked well in a continuing daily strip (although, of course, much of the original dialogue was missing). The strip began with "The Fear that Crept like a Cat," which had begun the New York radio series and had been the partial basis for the television movie.

There was a limited success in getting the strip into certain European publications, but it could not be successfully sold to American newspapers. The continued story strip was on the way out in the eighties, with many old favorites already gone and those left on shaky ground. It was not the time to launch a new story strip.

Books

After the death of his first wife, Patricia, Carlton E. Morse decided to publish some of his work in book form. Impatient with book publishers and knowing they might take long years to publish the series of books he had in mind, Morse decided to publish his own books. First offering his "straight," non-genre novels, *Killer at the Wheel* and *A Lavish of Sin* to good critical response, Morse at last offered what most of his fans had been yearning for, the first of his novels of *I Love a Mystery*, featuring Jack and Doc: *Stuff the Lady's Hatbox*.

The story contains contemporary references and is set in the present, yet the characters and situations might seem more at home in Dashiell Hammett's thirties. How many ladies today have hats, much less hatboxes?

After Jack and Doc at least temporarily recover a hatbox stuffed with a quarter million dollars from crooked gamblers in Las Vegas, Doc is roused out of his well-earned sleep by the beautiful heiress Linda Holliday – sister of Hillie Holliday, who originally "borrowed" the cash. The girl knocks relentlessly on Doc's hotel room door.

> "This better be an emergency like fire and floods and the earth a breakin' apart, or the management's a gonna find a corpse in the hallway." He yanked open the door. "Why, hello, honey." His voice became soft and seductive, a sort of masculine cooing. Actually, all he saw through sleep-bleared eyes was a beautiful girl. "I hope you brought your nighty on account this is a bedroom and I ain't half through sleepin'—" Suddenly his eyes and brains cleared and he exclaimed, "Linda Holliday! What **you** doin' in Las Vegas?"

The wealthy girl is interested to hear that Jack and Doc have recovered the hatbox full of money, and that Jack has it in his room at that moment. Of course, she doesn't know that this is just the beginning of the trouble Jack and Doc will find themselves in. The novel recaptures the spirit of the radio series delightfully while adjusting for an adult audience.

This entirely new adventure of the Triple-A-1 detectives was to be followed by an adaptation of one of the best of the radio serials (Morse's personal favorite), *The Widow with the Amputation*, and later by another more serious novel, *The Book of Monetti*.

Dedicated fans had to wait over thirty years to get collectible "premiums" for *I Love a Mystery* (see next section), but when they arrived, they could not have been better—except possibly for more radio episodes from this truly wondrous example of American popular culture.

Premiums

There was only one *I Love a Mystery* premium or giveaway, a photo of Jack, Doc and Reggie, circa 1940, for a letter of request. The listeners did not seem to think the actors matched up to their mental images of the heroes (a frequent complaint received by most radio drama series) and no more giveaways were made. The same actors could be seen in the pages of many family album type premiums from Morse's *One Man's Family* show. Some photo stories of the group's spectacular travels appeared in newspapers and in *Radio Guide* and *Radio Mirror* magazines.

There were commercials on the show offering such things as packets of flower seeds, but since these had no connection in word or picture to *I Love a Mystery* or Jack, Doc and Reggie, they have no interest to fans or collectors.

Jack Armstrong, the All American Boy

Juvenile adventure serial, weekdays (exceptions), beginning July 31, 1933, CBS; later NBC Red; NBC Blue; syndicated transcription; to last, June 28, 1951, ABC (retitled *Armstrong of the S.B.I*).

Creator-original writer: Robert Hardy Andrews **Later writers:** Talbot Munday, Col. Pascal Strong, Kermit Slobb **Directors:** James Jewell (most notable), Pat Murphy, David Owen, others **Jack:** Jim Ameche (1933-38), St. John ("Sinjin") Terrel (1938), Stanley (Stacy) Harris (1938), Frank Behrens (1939), Charles Flynn (1939-43, 1944-51), Michael Rye (aka Rye Billsbury) (1943) **Billy Fairfield:** Murray McLean, John Gannon, Roland Butterfield, Milt Guiou, Dick York **Betty Fairfield:** Scheindel Kalish, Sarajane Wells, Loretta Pynton, Patricia Dunlop **Uncle Jim Fairfield:** James Goss **Coach Hardy:** Arthur Van Slyke, Olan Soule, Les Tremayne **Captain Hughes:** Don Ameche, Jack Doty, Franke Dane **Blackbeard Flint:** Robert Barron **Weissoul, the Spy with a Thousand Faces:** Herb Butterfield **Announcers:** Franklyn MacCormack (most notable), David Owen, Tom Shirley, Truman Bradley, Bob McKee, Jack Lester **Others:** Naomi May, Marvin Miller.

Jack Armstrong was the *perfect* American Boy. In the thirties, the popular conception was that young America wanted a flawless ideal to try to emulate. The concept had to be right for those times. In the midst of a Great Depression bringing widespread unemployment and poverty, no one, young or old, seemed to be interested in hearing how flawed the human condition was. As a boy during that era, the present writer needed no one to tell him of his trouble getting along with the other kids – especially *girls*. I wanted an example to lead my way out of Christmases with a wind-up train instead of a Lionel Electric, to free me of the grey winter small town boredom of Mount Carmel, Illinois. I certainly wanted to be like Jack Armstrong – at least until I could grow up and be like my greater idols, Tom Mix and the Lone Ranger. Yes, I wanted to be like Jack – although there was always the wraith of wimpy, gosh-wowing Billy Fairfield looking suspiciously like a mirror image of myself.

Jack Armstrong was born in the mind of Robert Hardy Andrews, a writing phenomenon who could produce other radio prototypes like *Ma Perkins* and *Just Plain Bill* on command at the press of a button in his better-than-computer brain. According to his own letters (supplied by Dr. Fred King), Andrews, hardly conjuring a frown when requested by General Mills to produce a classic adventure serial, was inspired by a box of Arm and Hammer baking soda to come up with the name "Jack Armstrong." In recent years, it has been claimed (probably erroneously) that a real-life person named Jack Armstrong, who had many of the qualities of the fictional Jack and who was a friend of a General Mills executive, inspired the use of the name. This namesake, never an actor on the show or otherwise connected with it, save as inspriation, died in the mid–1980s after a career in the military.

The first storyline in 1933 put Jack and his friends from Hudson High School, Billy and Betty Fairfield, at the then ongoing Chicago World's Fair. From the first Jack was a master of all sports, and this sequence concentrated on the aquatic ones. This skill at athletic activities and a similarity in names that bespoke personal qualities, he owed to the early dime novel Frank Merriwell.

So it was that the show opened re-echoing another image-inspiring name: *Jack Armstrong* . . . JACK ARMSTRONG . . . *Jack Armstrong, the All-American Boy*!

This billboard was followed by the equally celebrated theme, sung by a quartet called the Norsemen:

Wave the flag for Hudson High, boys,
Show them how we stand!
Ever shall our team be champions,
Known throughout the land.

Human memory is faulty, and radio reception was sometimes imperfect, so that some people seem to remember other lyrics like "Every fellow should be a champion" or "ever challenging we champions" for that elusive third line, but the first version above is strongly believed to be the one and only accurate rendition.

In the early days the theme went on the "Boola Boola Boola" and a second chorus which for most of the later run of the show became the *closing* theme and a purely commercial one:

Have you tried Wheaties?
They're whole wheat with all of the bran
Won't you try Wheaties?
For wheat is the best food of man!
They're crispy and crunch the whole year through
Jack Armstrong never tires of them
and neither will you.
So just buy Wheaties
The best breakfast food in the Land!

The tune came from the 1920s song, "I'm a Jazz Baby."

The show would then open with a commercial – during some periods an incredibly *long* commercial, up to three minutes of a solid pitch for Wheaties, Breakfast of Champions. By the late thirties, Jack Armstrong's Training Rules would be incorporated – Get plenty of sleep, fresh air and exercise; use plenty of soap and water; and eat healthy foods like Wheaties. Endorsements by leading sports figures such as Bob Feller and Joe DiMaggio would also be offered, usually re-enacted but occasionally with the ball player in the studio giving an incredible bad reading.

Of course, when there was a giveway offer for a premium, like the Pedometer, the commercial was about that, and those were actually interesting, really firing our imagination to produce a fearful longing for the object of our induced desire. We sent in our dimes and Wheaties box-tops and could only wait out the days until it came, checking the mail twice a day (not unrealistically; there were two mail deliveries a day back then).

The first storyline about the Chicago World's Fair had Jack crash his motorboat during a race and seemingly be swept away forever on the dark waters of Lake Michigan. But the timely arrival in a "crash-proof" airplane of Captain Hughes, the first "adult authority" figure, prefiguring Uncle Jim Fairfield, saved Jack.

Just after the turn of the new year, 1934, Jack and his friends went to Canada and gave aid to the Mounted Police (who seemed to get along fine without Jack's help before this). During this Northwest adventure, Jack picked up the inevitable husky dog. This produced the first contest and first premium offer. The listeners were invited to "Name the Dog." Winning name: Arrow Champ (submitted by Betty Fisher of Toledo, Ohio). Photographs of Jack, Betty Fairfield, and Arrow Champ were offered.

From Canada's frontier, Jack and company went to the American West, the Castle Ranch in Arizona. Jack defeated the usual cattle rustlers with the help of an unnamed black horse. Another contest produced the horse's name – Blackster – and another photo, of Jack and his new mount.

In September 1934, all of Jack's listeners were preparing to go back to school, so to give some greater identification of the audience with Jack, the

Jack Armstrong, the All-American Boy, played by Charles Flynn, circa 1940. (Courtesy Rev. Robert E. Neily)

All-Amercian Boy and his friends prepared to return to their hometown of Hudson and its high school. In all the years the show was on the air, Jack would occasionally touch base with Hudson High for a day or two, or sometimes even a few weeks, but he never really spent enough time there to graduate. (And he did *not* graduate – not for seventeen years.) Of course, in the modern provision for "Life Achievement" he learned enough of the world and its ways to earn a *college* degree.

Even while at Hudson High, Jack Armstrong did not lead an ordinary student's life. As would happen again and again over the years, sinister forces were at work in 1934 at Hudson. In this case, it was a gang of counterfeiters. To further complicate Jack's life, his friend (but never his girlfriend) Betty became seriously ill. A doctor relayed life-saving instructions over a Magic Dial brand radio. Another contest produced winners of fifty radios.

During these early couple of years, the *Armstrong* program had been broadcast six days a week for fifteen minutes – not just Monday through Friday, but Monday through Saturday. Probably deciding most kids spent all of Saturday outside playing and away from the radio, General Mills dropped the sixth day. The last Saturday show was November 3, 1934.

These shows interrupted the regular storyline and dramatized some kind of ballgame with Jack – baseball, football, etc. He played them all, won them all.

But the sponsor also added to the audience coverage made by *Jack Armstrong*. In October of the same year, they added to their live network broadcasts a chain of stations playing prerecorded transcription discs of the show. The transcriptions had to be made up three weeks in advance to be shipped to the stations.

The sponsor wanted the transcribed episode to be the same as the live show, so that all over the country Jack would be in the Far North or the American West at the same time. So the scripts had to be written far in advance and the actors did the script for an individual episode first for the transcribed services before the live performance three weeks later.

During this period, Jim Ameche became established as the voice of Jack Armstrong. His richly vibrant voice hardly sounded "boyish." His brother, Don Ameche, played Coach Hardy on the series for a time, but their voices were so similar, Don stepped out of the picture, leaving Jim as the lead, unchallenged by another commanding voice like his own. Don went on starring in movies, right up to the present writing, and Jim was very successful in broadcasting until his death in the mid-1980s. Jim was positive that he was the original "Jack," and the sometimes credited St. John Terrell followed him, and only briefly.

Though several others played Jack briefly, the best remembered All-American Boy is Charles Flynn, living in happy retirement today. It is fair to say that the symbol of eternal youth does not look elderly even today, but seems a man of vigorous middle years.

In 1986, Charlie Flynn and the author, among others, appeared at a convention of the Society to Preserve and Encourage Radio Drama, Variety and Comedy in Los Angeles. We appeared in a short sketch I wrote of a Jack Armstrong parody, where Charlie was again Jack and I played Billy, along with Fred Foy, announcer of *The Lone Ranger*, and other cast members. In our discussion afterwards, Flynn told of a story evocative of doing *Jack Armstrong* and early radio in general.

Jack Armstrong's friends: "Uncle" Jim Fairfield, played by Jim Goss; Betty Fairfield, played by Sarajane Wells; and Billy Fairfield, played by John Gannon, circa 1940.

The show was a water show, with all kinds of ship sound effects. The sound effects man had an immense tub of water for it ... Between shows [for different time zones] John Gannon [Billy] and I came in with a bottle of bubble bath and dumped it into the water. The show started at 6:30 and he started churning the water, and the bubbles started to rise and the sound of the water went down and down until it was just *sssss* [a hiss] .... The two of us fell down laughing and Jim Goss and Sarajane Welles who were playing Uncle Jim and Betty had to carry on for a minute. When the show was over, [director] Ed Morse came over and said "You're fired!" ... He relented the next day.

After all, Flynn and Gannon really were nearly as young as the parts they played. Only the fictional Jack could be grimly dedicated all the time.

The next serial adventure of Jack Armstrong near the start of 1935 concerned the strange disappearance of a $20,000 postage stamp. The theme of stamp collecting got into the next premium offer too. The line between the drama section of the show and the commercial for the premium was always blurred on *Armstrong* and other similar serials. So the offer stated Jack wanted his listeners to send him a nickel for his beginning stamp collector's kit so that he could use the money for an operation for his ailing mother. The Federal Trade Commission did not like the idea of children being solicited to help finance surgery on a fictional person. They laid out some dos and don'ts. (One of the things advertisers were not to do was to suggest that if the little buddies out there wanted to keep the show on the air, they had better shell out those nickels and dimes and box-tops. Despite this, all the shows often implied this in their spiel, and not inaccurately.)

In March 1935, Jack Armstrong set off for South America, a continent he would spend much time on during his radio career. The All-American Boy with his friends, the young Fairfields, searched for a lost city of gold deep in the Amazonian jungles. Finding it, after a series of traps and escapes, they started home, only to crash land on a remote island and become involved in a buried treasure adventure.

Jack and his friends spent the summer at a resort hotel where fur smuggling was going on and where the hotel got burned down during this illicit activity. In need of a summer job, Jack could not apply at McDonald's in those years before the restaurant chain came on the scene. So he thought he would try to get on at a laboratory where they were trying to develop atomic energy. The lab must have been hoping for somebody with at least a few years of physics, but finally decided a high school boy who was certainly well-traveled would be just the ticket.

While atomic energy was just a theroy in those days, it was often referred to in science fiction magazines and the *Buck Rogers* comic strip and radio series. Jack Armstrong would have a number of brushes with nuclear power, some of which ended better than this first encounter, which had Jack diving out of a window to escape perhaps the first atomic explosion. Fortunately, the atoms did not know how to do it right at this time, and there was only a tiny blast, and almost no radiation—sort of like a water heater blowing up.

Around Christmas 1935, the Armstrong crew was enjoying a really White Christmas in the City of White Eskimoes up around the Arctic Circle. The storyline was concerned with the search for pitchblende, an atomic ore that was a source of radium. During a fierce storm, Jack helped a rival ship's crew by carrying a rescue line across the frozen ice on foot. (This show, and episodes following, with Jim Ameche as Jack, are the earliest known transcriptions to survive and have been put on L.P. recordings.)

After his Arctic adventure, Jack returned to Hudson to work on a newspaper and to hold some contests for its fictional readers and his real listeners.

Following the program's first summer vacation, *Jack Armstrong* returned in 1936, now written by Talbot Mundy, a genuine adventurer himself, a prolific and respected fantasy and historical novelist. Mundy sent Jack off on the *China Clipper* to Shanghai where he and Billy and Betty Fairfield met up with Uncle Jim Fairfield, the commanding but warm father figure who would be featured in most of the coming years of the program.

Jack was carrying a jade talisman from a friend of Uncle Jim's, and a Chinese tried to take it away from him, only to lose a dragon talisman he was carrying. The dragon piece was the clue to an ancient city buried beneath the sands of the Gobi Desert. The story was reflected by a Dragon Talisman Chart Game premium for listeners.

At the start of 1937, Uncle Jim took Jack, Billy and Betty off to Africa for still another retelling (from many movies and fiction pieces) of the search for the Elephants' Graveyard, a mythic place where dying elephants lumbered to die and where, naturally, reposed a fabulous treasure in ivory tusks. This serial became the subject of *Jack Armstrong and the Ivory Treasure*, a Big Little Book (half pictures, half text), a tangible treasure itself, capturing moments out of the ephemeral air of the radio series. A Moviescope viewer offering 3-D scenes of the African trip was a premium offer.

The radio serials were becoming year long affairs, with one storyline blending into another, with old villains seemingly left behind, only to return again, in a leisurely mosaic of adventure. The pacing was similar to the soap operas heard earlier in the day. Other afternoon thrillers like *Tom Mix* generally wound up the story in about three weeks. *The Lone Ranger* with a later and more adult audience usually wrapped up everything in one half-hour show (although there were some continued serials).

After summer vacation in 1937, the program was back with a storyline about a search for Jack's old friend Captain Hughes. One might suppose that the good captain was off looking for another job, since he had been clearly replaced by Uncle Jim. It was the elder Fairfield who took his niece and nephew and their friend, Jack, to Egypt at around the start of the new year to outwit a gang of tomb robbers around the Great Pyramid.

To help the folks from Hudson High communicate with each other, there was an Egyptian Whistling Ring. Signals could be sent by use of the spinning siren of the ring. Naturally, it was another premium offer. The spell of Osirus' image and the ankh symbol for good luck caught many imaginations.

As the pre–World War II years continued, Jack fought modern pirates after sunken treasure in the Indian Ocean, then had to solve "The Mystery of the Iron Key," and then after a brief return to Hudson, he was off to South America again to take part in an air race. Returning from Rio de Janeiro, one plane was forced down by the villains and Betty and another girl were held captive in an underground city. Jack, Billy and Uncle Jim tried to find the girls, traveling through a maze of winding tunnels and passages. They used a pedometer, called a Hike-O-Meter, to check how far they had gone down each passage. With such a wonderful device, they succeeded. Many wonderful things could be accomplished with this glorious gadget. On February 9, 1939, it became a premium offer, and over one million were mailed out. Child movie star Shirley Temple sent in a hand-lettered order. The pedometer became one of the most successful Jack Armstrong promotions and one of the most famous radio premiums ever offered by any program. The sight of its round, blue enamel rimmed dial evokes a whole lost world to those of a certain age.

No wonder that over the years the pedometer was offered several times, at least once as a Ped-O-Meter, on the *Armstrong* series, and on other shows sponsored by General Mills such as *The Lone Ranger* and even on Quaker Cereal's *Sergeant Preston of the Yukon*. As late as the 1970s, the back of the Wheaties cereal box offered a Jog-O-Meter to keep up with that fad. It may have worked as well as Jack Armstrong's model, but they forgot to put in the pinch of magic.

But a radio hero never rested. With his Torpedo Flashlight premium to light his way (they moved 6,600,000 of these because you didn't have to go to the trouble of writing in for it—it came over the counter with two boxes of Wheaties), Jack was on the trail of the Grand Lama of Tibet to deliver to him a sacred scroll.

When Jack finally reached the Grand Lama, the venerated person gave Jack some advice, a philosophy of life. Only ... he was only echoing back Jack's own philosophy, the one he always lived by.

Grand Lama: Tell the boys and girls of the United States this world is theirs, and they may use it as they will. As they are, so shall their world become. If they have hearts of gold, a glorious new golden age awaits us all. If they are brave, they shall find a world of chivalry.

If they are honest, all riches shall be theirs. If they are kind to one another, they shall save the whole world from the malice and the meanness and the war that is tearing its heart. Will you take that message to the boys and girls of the United States, Jack Armstrong? Jack: Yes, sir, I'll be proud to do it. I'm going to spend the rest of my life trying to live that message!

And Jack Armstrong did live that message. Of course, kindness could not turn aside a Hitler, but millions of young men who grew up with Jack Armstrong fought a war not for personal gain but with a sincere belief that they were fighting and dying to bring sanity and hope to a whole world. There was little doubt or hesitation during World War II. Those who fought tell me, and I know those of us at home felt, it was a war of Good against Evil. For a time at least, the philosophy of the Grand Lama and of Jack Armstrong lived.

There were a few other globe-girdling adventures ahead for Jack, before World War II sent him after spies and saboteurs at home. Charles Flynn became Jack in the fall of 1939, and Jack went after another buried treasure in the West Indies. Jack enjoyed the search for such lost loot, but since he never kept any of the valuables for himself, he never retired before hitting twenty-one and could still enjoy the thrill of the hunt. The Cuban government did reward Jack and his party for locating this treasure by giving Uncle Jim a great diamond. While Uncle Jim pondered what charitable prupose to put this great gem to, all returned to Hudson High. Two villains, Professor Lorenzo and Lal Singh, an East Indian, determined to steal the diamond. They followed the party from Hudson around the world, as Jack and his friends tested a new airplane on a 10,000-mile trip – and also tested a new premium, the Magic Answer box, sort of a portable Ouija board. It told who was telling the truth – a valuable tool around the likes of Lorenzo and Lal Singh.

Another adventure took Jack and his party to mysterious Easter Island, returning a set of 13 statues of ancient kings in the image of the long-faced Easter Island monuments. These were clues to lead to even greater treasure. A certain Captain Anthony Badger tried to take the treasure from them, but a badger proved no match for a sly old fox like Uncle Jim.

On September 30, 1940, Jack Armstrong began one of his best and most representative adventures, concerning a search for the missing Professor Loring and a source for Uranium 235 which was thought in 1940 (correctly, of course) to be a source of atomic energy. Fortunately for every fan, every historian, much of this long serial has survived on transcription disc, transferred to tape, and is available from many collectors and radio clubs. This is no doubt the best example of *Jack Armstrong* to survive, and probably the best and most representative example of any of the classic afternoon adventure serials of radio. It was written by Col. Pascal Strong, a career Army officer who spent much time in the Philippines.

A recurring character, Blackbeard, a modern pirate, got involved in the search for Loring – on the wrong side, of course. Like Long John Silver in the novel *Treasure Island*, Blackbeard often assured Jack and his friends that he was really on their side and had their best interests at heart, a prototype of the lovable – or at least likeable – villain.

Aiding Jack was another premium, the Dragon's Eye ring with a green stone held in the mouths of two crocodiles on either side of the band. The ring glowed in the dark, a quality much overdone in premiums, but when it was fairly new as here, it fascinated young minds with its eerie glow. With the aid of the ring (and a renewed pedometer offer) Jack Armstrong and crew trekked through the Philippine jungles in search of the lost professor and his prophetic knowledge of atomic energy. On the way, they did learn something of the nature and customs of the Philippine people. While not really intended as educational, the program could not help but impart some knowledge to youthful listeners. The unbelabored moral tone was one of friendliness, cooperation, helping others.

At the end of the 1940 season, Jack and his friends found the professor and defeated (but did not destroy) the villains with the aid of an autogyro. In some areas of the country, the program went on through the summer, and Blackbeard and his cohorts were around to make it hot for a few months more.

In the fall of 1941 the program offered what should have been a classic radio premium – a Sound Effects Kit, which included cellophane paper to crumple to simulate fire, metal plates to drop for a crash and other items. It was not a popular offer. Perhaps it reminded the listeners that Jack's adventures were just a radio program put on in a studio with actors at mikes and a sound effects man in the corner. Listeners wanted to believe it was real. Offering a sound effects kit was like sticking a finger in the eye of imagination.

The war was on in 1942 – just weeks after the attack on Pearl Harbor, December 7, 1941 – and Jack Armstrong was involved. Too young to join the armed forces by the storyline (in real life, actor Charles Flynn would soon be in the United States Navy), Jack nevertheless did his part. He tracked fifth columnists all around the world and helped protect a Secret Bombsight which became another premium, a toy that dropped tiny bombs on paper ships. Even this early in the war, the device was made of wood, not rationed metal. In an attempt to make it authentic in some degree, General Mills executives searched through libraries for diagrams of bombsights, drawing the attention of the F.B.I. The Bombsight today is for some reason exceptionally rare, and examples have sold for over $250.

Wartime propaganda took over the program and Jack's adventure in a prophetic atomic submarine was opened by a new theme, "Spread Your Wings, You Eagles and Fly," and a Wheaties commercial that urged listeners to write a letter to a Fighter Corps flyer.

In 1943, Jack and his friends managed to get passage to North Africa where they routed out Nazi spies in Morocco.

Another adventure at home had the band from Hudson High fighting black marketeers in the United States. As the war drew to a close in 1945, Jack was up against plain old gangsters in a war between the Silencer and the Black Avenger. When both were brought to justice, the Silencer was revealed to be a famous missing scientist, Victor Hardy, who developed amnesia ten years before and had lived a life of crime under his sinister alias. In a really incredible turnabout, much more illogical than most of the carefully developed plots on the show, the one-time gangster the Silencer, now restored to mental health as Vic Hardy (and duly pardoned) started up the Scientific Bureau of Investigation – the S.B.I. – to fight crime (a subject Hardy was intimately acquainted with) and to repay society for his misdeeds. A noble motive, but even kids must have wondered how well a big time gangster, even a reformed one, would be accepted as the head of a major law enforcement agency. Hardy and the S.B.I. were clearly euphemisms for Hoover and the F.B.I. It was easy to picture J. Edgar Hoover as the F.B.I. chief, but then he had never previously been John Dillinger! (Even so, Hoover's permission was sought and granted for use of the similar-sounding S.B.I. name.)

The show began to take on an authoritarian tone, as family member Uncle Jim was replaced by the authority figure, S.B.I. Chief Vic Hardy. By this time, the radio director was Jim Jewell, who had moved over from the Detroit *Lone Ranger* series to Chicago. In the words of one of the later *Jack Armstrong* announcers, Jack Lester, the late Mr. Jewell "acted like a little Hitler – he even looked like Hitler, with his little mustache."

Jewell was not an entirely unlikeable person, but he was an autocratic director. At times, he would level all his criticisms on one actor, practically reducing the man or woman to tears. During one such demonstration against another actor, talented performer Art Hern did something rarely done in radio or elsewhere – he laid his job on the line for a fellow worker. "Mr. Jewell," he said, "I don't care to be associated with a production that treats its actors in that manner." Jewell backed off.

Jewell was a hard taskmaster, but certainly a major talent in developing several of radio's greatest adventure series.

Jack Armstrong continued on into the post-war world, with Jack now working as an agent for Hardy's S.B.I. Some of the story titles suggest the scope of his adventures – "Jack Armstrong in South America," "The Lake of Mystery," "City of the Sun God," "On the High Seas," "The Night Riders," "The Secret Base," and "The Devil's Castle."

Finally, during the summer of 1947, there was a story about mysterious attacks on a circus, "The Phantom of the Sawdust Trail," and this became the last continued serial of *Jack Armstrong*. The series would continue, but after August 22, 1947, would be heard as a complete story told in a single half-hour installment. Director Jewell was familiar with this format from his work on the *Lone Ranger*, and he successfully translated the old serial format to this. The new format seemed to fit the late forties and early fifties, helping radio compete with television a little longer. It might be called "instant gratification," but the serials had come to seem too long and drawn out for a fast-moving age.

At first, *Armstrong* alternated with another series, *Sky King*, sponsored by Peter Pan peanut butter on weekdays. So on the first week *Armstrong* would be heard Monday, Wednesday and Friday, and *King* on Tuesday and Thursday. But the second week, *King* was on Monday, Wednesday and Friday, and *Armstrong* was heard the other two days. It split the advertising costs exactly in half, so it cost the sponsor no more than a quarter-hour show five days a week, figured over a two-week period. But it was somewhat confusing. Some newspapers inaccurately listed *Jack Armstrong* as being on the air for a half-hour five days a week. Eventually General Mills agreed to buy the Monday-Wednesday-Friday slot permanently for *Jack Armstrong*, and *Sky King* was heard only on Tuesday and Thursday.

The sixteenth episode in the new half-hour format, which aired on October 7, 1947, was a memorable episode called "Hurricane Destroyer." In it, Jack and his friends fly through a hurricane to test a device which they hope can destroy a hurricane before it reaches shore with its destructive force. Artificial lightning is fired from the wings to break up the storm. On the show it works, and in real life somewhat similar attempts have been made using cloud seeding.

Of course, in the old days when Jack was searching the South Seas for a missing inventor with the secret of atomic energy, such a single plane flight would have been only one incident, not a whole story. But like a well-crafted short story, the hurricane flight tale did have a beginning, middle and end.

Another later story, "Clear and Tracks," concerns a trip on a train that becomes a runaway down a steep mountain slope. Jack saves the train from derailing by firing a rocket motor bolted to the floor of a freight car, using the thrust as a brake. Again, a single incident but developed into an interesting story.

For the next three years hundreds of exciting episodes with fascinating titles were broadcast. Examples: "Great Lunar Rocket," "Jungle Shadows," "Danger Under the Sea," "Devil and the Pumpkin," "Medicine Men of the Everglades," "Mystery of the Trans-Coast Limited," "Blue Water and Black Gold," "Fog Island," "Danger–North of Singapore," "The Five Hundred Hitter," "The Spook Train," "Billy Throws a Bommerang," "Atomic Footprints," "Cobweb Castle," "Ghost Riders of Cripple Creek" and finally, on June 1, 1950, the last broadcast of *Jack Armstrong, the All-American* ("Boy" dropped out somewhere along the way). It was called "Mystery of Holiday Lodge," and it was the last show with the famous echoing call of "Jack Armstrong . . . JACK ARMSTRONG . . ." and the closing Wheaties theme.

It was not quite the end for the character Jack Armstrong, however.

To face the challenges of the television a new series was devised to alternate with *The Lone Ranger* in a later time period. The new show was heard on Tuesdays and Thursdays, and he was called *Armstrong of the S.B.I.* Jack was on hand, with Betty to help him (although Billy had departed for other climes), and of course Vic Hardy was in command. The first show, September 5, 1950, was called "Wise Guy." Grimmer, less imaginative titles followed: "Death and the Dollar Sign," "A Wife for Judas," "Voice of Treason," "The Undertaker's Funeral," "Commuter to the Grave."

The new series featuring Jack Armstrong seemed to be modeled after *David Harding, Counterspy* – another fictional radio version of Hoover and the F.B.I. The good-natured campus hero of Hudson High just did not make it as a deadly earnest government agent. On June 28, 1951, there came an episode called "The Deadliest of the Species," about a female drug smuggler closed in on by Armstrong and Hardy. When her male accomplice will not surrender, Jack Armstrong, the one-time All-American Boy, guns down the crook. It was the end, the last broadcast with Jack Armstrong, even as *Armstrong of the S.B.I.*

There was no mention that this was the final show, no recognition of Jack Armstrong's record of eighteen years on the air, inspiring several generations of kids, only a notice to tune in for a new show next week (the short-lived *Mr. Mercury*, about a circus detective).

Jack Armstrong was a classic and his name has gone into the language meaning a straight-arrow, do-gooder. But he was not too good to be believed, not by millions of kids.

Motion Pictures

There was only one Jack Armstrong movie, a 1947 serial of fifteen chapters from Columbia Pictures, appropriately called *Jack Armstrong, the All-American Boy*. The film was produced by Sam Katzman and directed by Spencer Bennet, who died in 1987 at age 94 after a wonderful career that lasted through many of the great years of Hollywood and through the entire span of the motion picture serial. Bennet worked as an assistant on the silent *Perils of Pauline* and, after directing many silent and sound serials, piloted the very last ever made, *Blazing the Overland Trail* (1956). The *Jack Armstrong* serial was one of his best, featuring John Hart as Jack.

John Hart said around 1975, "There wasn't much you could do with Jack as an actor interpreting a character ... I just played him as a younger version of myself, and hoped I seemed enough like the Big Man on the Campus."

Hart was believable, and his clean-cut good looks seemed a perfect realization of the image created on radio by Charles Flynn's voice. (Flynn would have made a good visual Jack, too, suggesting a more raw-boned, "folksier" Jack.)

The other casting was acceptable too, with a somewhat beefy Joe Brown as Billy, pretty Rosemary La Planche as Betty and Pierre Watkin as a more austere Uncle Jim. (Watkin also played the banker who gave a "warm handshake" to W. C. Fields in *The Bank Dick*.) Like the new comic books coming out at that time, the movie serial returned to the glory years of the radio series, reflecting themes of the thirties and early forties more than the series' then present preoccupation with the Scientifiic Bureau of Investigation. The serial did not forget Vic Hardy entirely, however. Vic was portrayed by Hugh Prosser as a scientist working in Uncle Jim's factory who was kidnapped, and his rescue was one of Jack's goals.

Vic Hardy was held captive in a spaceship which became an artificial satellite of the Earth. This movie serial was one of the first visualizations on screen of the man-made satellite theory and deserves a footnote in history for that.

The escapes in the *Armstrong* serial were often more plausible than in some serials. The first chapter ends with Jack and Billy caught in a laboratory explosion. Chapter Two opens with the door to the place collapsing outward and letting the two heroes fall away from the full force of the explosion. It may have been a minor point, but it had a touch more realism than the hero going through some terrific explosion as in many other films, then merely getting up and dusting himself off.

There were no other films of Jack after this. There was talk in the 1980s of translating him into a Saturday morning cartoon like Superman and the Lone Ranger, but a Jack Armstrong in a modern setting, no doubt given a taste for rock and roll, just wouldn't fit.

Jack Armstrong belongs in a more idealistic past. His voice echoes out of Radioland even now, rowing with Billy toward Uncle Jim's yacht, the *Spindrift*, riding gently in the warm waters of the Sulu Sea. There is a creaking of the oars, the splashing of the water. And Jack looks ahead dreamily, thinking of what can be done if his friends and he can discover the secret of atomic energy they are seeking.

JACK: Billy, when I think of this country of ours, with millions of homes stretching from sea to sea, and with everybody working and pulling together to have a nation where people can be free and do big, fine things – why it makes me realize what a terribly important job we've got ahead!

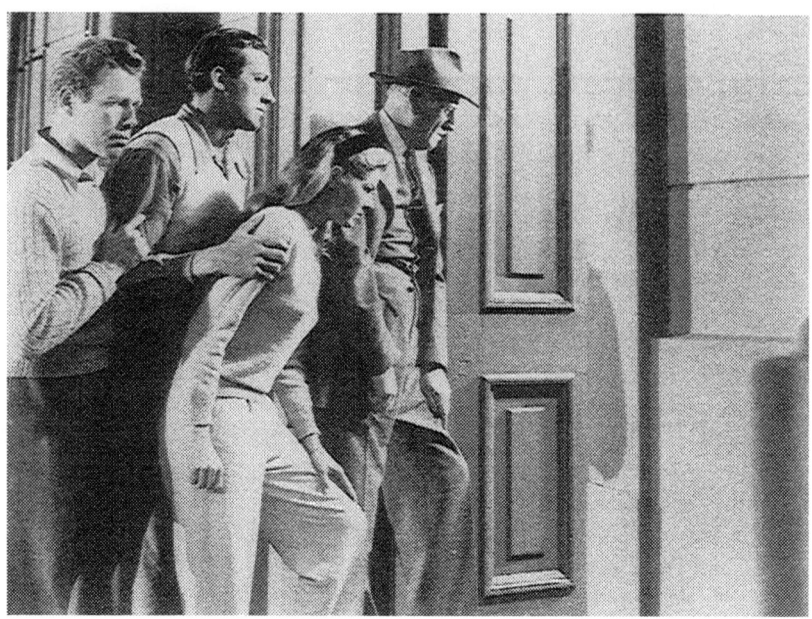

In the 1947 movie serial version of *Jack Armstrong*, Billy (Joe Brown), Jack (John Hart), Betty (Rosemary La Plance) and Uncle Jim (Pierre Watkin) open the door to danger. (Courtesy Dr. Fred King)

BILLY: I'll say!
JACK: If we can ... discover where those pitchblende desposits are located, why we'll learn how to use all that energy in the atom. And we'll use it for the good of the whole world!

Somewhere it is always 1939, and somewhere Uncle Jim leads Jack, Billy, and Betty on to high adventure and high ideals.

Comics

In November 1947 the first issue of the *Jack Armstrong* comics magazine appeared.

The comic book reflected more of the program's past than its then current series of half-hour S.B.I. crime cases. Uncle Jim was back, taking Jack, Billy and Betty off on splendid adventures all around the world.

The magazine was a bit livelier than most of the publications that came from the Parents Group, also publishers of the "educational" *True Comics*. The first issue started off with a routine "Arctic Mystery," but the second story introduced "The Man with a Million Faces"— Doctor Proteus, who looked like a withered mummy when not in one of his many disguises. He was a recurring villian probably based on the more modestly billed "Man of a Thousand Faces" from radio. Defeated by Jack, Proteus is dragged away yelling, "No jail can keep me from getting even with you, Jack Armstrong!"

The book was a fair series, but artwork from the likes of the routine Jack Sparling and stories that soft-pedalled action, horror and sex could not long compete successfully with super-heroes like *Superman* or *Captain Marvel* or the oncoming books of E. C. with a more sophisticated approach to art and story, but a much more violent and sexual one. The *Jack Armstrong* comics ended with No. 13, September 1949. There was also a brief syndicated strip of *Jack Armstrong* with the same attitude as the comic magazine.

Books

There was little merchandising of the famous *Jack Armstrong* name outside of General Mills' own premium offers. Two exceptions during the 1930s were two "Big Little Books" from the Whitman Publishing Co. These little volumes still appear in a new batch every decade or so, keeping the name alive, so most people know that they were about 4½ by 3-5/8 inches and about an inch and a half thick with 432 pages (as in the case of the first volume discussed). One page was of text with dialogue and description as in a novel, and the other page was a drawing, with caption beneath. Books adapted from comic strips merely had the comics panels doctored, with dialogue balloons removed.

Jack Armstrong and the Ivory Treasure was an original Big Little Book, not adapted from a comic strip, so original illustrations were done by Henry E. Vallely. Vallely was arguably the finest artist ever to do original work for the B.L.B. series, a really unique craftsman who should have had a famous syndicated comic strip to make him rich and famous as *Flash Gordon* did Alex Raymond or *Terry and the Pirates* did Milton Canniff–but who did not. His clear, clean drawings for this *Jack Armstrong* book and others are marvels of economy of line and function by suggestion. He was at least touched on the shoulder by genius.

Ivory Treasure was a Big Little Book No. 1435 in 1937, credited to author Leslie N. Daniels, Jr., but based on radio scripts by Talbot Mundy. In the story, Jack and his usual companions were racing the villainous Lopes to find the horde of tusks where the elephants went to die. Opposing either competitor in finding the treasure was the mystical figure of Boo-loo-la, the Elephant Man whose sacred trust was protecting the elephants. Finally after Jack defeated a native chief in a trial by combat (using something that sounds a bit like judo or karate) and won his way through to the Graveyard, Jack explained to Boo-loo-la that the fortune in ivory would be used to protect the living species of elephant, and won his support. One hopes that there is an old bank account somewhere still drawing interest for that purpose—the African wildlife needs help today even more badly.

The second Whitman publication, now called a "Better Little Book," was No. 1432 (a non-sequential code number), *Jack Armstrong and the Mystery of the Iron Key* (1939), also illustrated by Vallely with no author credit and based on radio scripts by Mundy about British India, maharajahs, villainous Hindus, and the mysterious "key," symbol of power.

There were no known large "store" items with the famous *Jack Armstrong* identification, like a bicycle or even a football, but apparently in the late 1940s General Mills decided to let some outside sources use the famous name for comics, films and a few toys.

Premiums

The usual requirement for a premium was a Wheaties box-top or some other part of the box. Sometimes coins were required; a dime was usual, but early offers were as low as a nickel and some were as high as a quarter—a stiff price for the 1930s. The premiums were as follows, listed alphabetically with year and approximate value in 1992 (assuming average condition).

Airplane, Sky Ranger (1940; over the counter with two Wheaties boxes, six million distributed; $50), American Boy magazine subscription (1938; $20), Answer Box, Magic (1940; regular offer, over 600,000 sent; $65), Banner, WAFC (1942; 940 sent to school rooms; $200), Baseball Pencil, Bakelite, (1939; test, under 1,000 sent; $50), Baseball Pencil, Luminous (1940; test, about 1000 sent; $75), Baseball Pencil, 100th Anniversary* (1939; $35), Baseball Pencil, Wooden (1943; $35), Bat, Wheaties Baseball (1937; low distribution; $150), Bon-Bon Dish (1934; $15), Bombsight, Secret

In the Baseball Pencil package and other premiums there was a "bounce-back" offer—a coupon for still another premium. These are always the rarest premiums. Without the constant drive of the commercial and in the program itself to get kids to respond, these bounce-backs got little response, but proved a valuable negative reenforcement, establishing that the program did do an effective job of selling. Thanks to Dr. Fred L. King's privately photocopied Jack Armstrong Encyclopedia, we have a much more complete list of bounce-backs and test offers than on most series of this type. During 1939 Jack Armstrong offered these very rare bounce-backs, with only dozens of responses. The items often were not highly desired, since they were not closely identified with the storyline of the show or personal childhood memories. Nevertheless, any of these items if authenticated by accompanying Armstrong papers is now worth up to $100. Such items included: Golf Ball Offer, Baseball Folio, Champion Belt, Baseball Cap, Baseball Scrapbook, Sports Compass, Weathercaster, (footnote cont.)

(1942; on the air, about 450,000 sent; known sale at $250), Bowl, Breakfast of Champions (1937; $35), Bracelet, Gardenia, Luminous (1940; a Betty Fairfield premium offered on only a few broadcasts, nearly 200,000 sent; known sale at $250), Cap, Baseball (1934; test, fewer than 50 sent; $35), Charm Booklet (1937; low distribution; $15), Christmas Spoon (1933; $20), Comic Books, Miniature four (only slightly miniaturized to about 6 x 8 in.; 32pp.; paper covers with banner "FREE w/Two Boxes of Wheaties"; rare as premiums or comics; almost never found mint due to Scotch-type taping to boxes) including WHIZ COMICS Miniature (1948; $50), CAPTAIN MARVEL Miniature (1948; $50), FLASH COMICS Miniature (1948; Kubert art; $60), FUNNY STUFF Miniature (1948; low demand content; $15), Compass, Wrist (1937; test, about 3,000 sent; $75), *Cub Pilot* Newspaper & Dog Tag (1945; $50), Dish, Shirley Temple (1935; $35), First Aid Kit, Junior Ace (1939; test, about 500 sent; $100), Flashlight, Torpedo (1939; commonly found, six million, over the counter, red, black, other colors; $15), Football Game (1937; brief regular offer; $30), Football Game, Big Ten (1937; $30), Game, Talisman Chart (1936; $75), Goggles, Army (1947; Army surplus; $20), Grid-O-Scope (1939; football premium; $35), Hand Grip Developers (1933; $35), Heliograph Distance Finder (1937; low distribution, about 1,200 sent; $50), Hike-O-Meter (1939; name change for Pedometer; $50), Indian Arrowhead Offer (1935; test, 2,500 sent; $60), Library of Sports (1943; 18 booklets; $3 ea.), Light Kit, Safety Signal (1939; $60), Listening Squad Kit (1940; test, under 500 sent; $75), Model Planes, Tru-Flite, No. 1 (P40 & Zero), nos. 2–7 (1943; light pasteboard to be assembled in deference to wartime rationing, over 3 million sent; $40 ea.), Model Ship, Sloop (1934; test, fewer than 50 sent; $35), Moviescope Viewer, 3-D (1937; test & regular offer; $65), Mug, Shirley Temple (1935; $30), Parachute Ball (1947; $20), Pedometer (1939; over the air offer; $50), Pencil Offer (1939; $15), Photo, Betty (1934; $20), Photo, Hockey Players (1935; $15), Photo, Jack (1934; $35), Photo, Jack Armstrong on his horse (1934; $30), Photo, Weissmuller (1933; $10), Photos, 1934 World Series (Cardinals and Tigers), autographed (1934; $20), Photos, Set of three (1934; over the air, over 110,000 sent; $60), Picture Book, Jack Armstrong (1941; test, about 750 sent; $35), Pitcher, Shirley Temple (1936; $45), Postage stamps, 200 (1948; $30), Propeller Plane Gun, Shooting (1933; over the air, over 400,000 sent; $75), Ring, Baseball (1938; $30), Ring, Dragon's Eye (1940; test and over the air, about 390,000 sent; $190), Rock Crystal (1935; $20), Rocket Chute (1939; test, about 100 sent; $100), Safety Belt, Blackout (1941; offered briefly on *Armstrong* as test with about 2,000 sent, mainly offered on another General Mills show, *The Lone Ranger*, with over 500,000 sent; $95), Signal Mirror, Navy (1947; Navy surplus; $20), Six Man Football Book (1938; $15), Sound Effects Kit (1941; on the air, over 100,000 sent; $45), Stamp Collecting Offers ("A" through "E," also "Oriental," minor misc.) with Jack Armstrong packaging (1935; $30), Sugar & Creamer Set (1934; $25), Sun Watch, Frank Buck Explorer (1948; offered on *Armstrong* show with appearances of the real Frank Buck; $65), Telescope, Explorer (1937; $35), Training Kit, Cub Pilot Corps, with manueverable "wind tunnel" type model trainer (1945; $200), Water Pistol (1933; test item, 555 sent; $150), Wee Gyro

Sports Neckerchief, Pedometer (limited offer), Sun Glasses, Mystery Baseball Game, Lie Detector, Strongheart (the movie dog) Wrist Band, Whistling Pencil, Fingerprinting Kit, Distance Finder.

(1934; test, about 31,000 sent; $30), Whistle, Crocodile, Luminous (1941; test, under 1000 sent; known sale at $350), Whistling Ring, Egyptian (1937; $65), Write a Fighter Corps Kit (1942; on the air, about 150,000 sent; $75).

Premiums apparently disappeared after 1948, although the series remained as *Jack Armstrong* until 1950 and as *Armstrong of the S.B.I.* until 1951. There may have been some later premium offers shared with other General Mills shows like *The Lone Ranger*, but no such records have been found. As a half-hour show, the program may have appealed to a more mature audience of teens and adults, less responsive to premiums.

Little Orphan Annie (aka Radio Orphan Annie)

Juvenile serial, 15 min., five times weekly. Began April 6, 1931, and ended spring 1943. Aired on NBC, sponsored by Ovaltine, 1931–40 and on Mutual, sponsored by Quaker, 1940–43.

Director: Alan Wallace **Writers:** Roland Martini, Ferrin N. Fraser, Day Keene, Wally Norman **Little Orphan Annie:** Shirley Bell, Janice Gilbert, Floy Margaret Hughes (West Coast) **Joe Corntassle:** Allan Baruck **Mr. Silo:** Jerry O'Mera **Mrs. Silo:** Henrietta Tedro **Daddy Warbucks:** Henry Saxe, Stanley Andrews, Boris Aplon **Clay Collier:** Hoyt Allen **Aha, Chinese cook:** Olan Soule **Sandy:** Brad Barker **Announcer:** Pierre André **Others:** Harry Cansdale, St. John Terrell, James Monks.

"Who's that little chatterbox – the one with the pretty auburn locks?" Half the world might recognize the description, but most would know the little orphan waif named Annie only from the stage musical and the movie, or from the current comic strip by Leonard Starr. None of this has much to do with the original comic strip created by Harold Gray called *Little Orphan Annie*, or with the radio program of the same name that in 1931 became one of the most popular children's shows on the networks.

The comic strip began in 1924, and by the 1930s was one of the top five strips nationwide, but in those days more kids knew Annie from her radio appearances than from her comic strip adventures. As Richard Marschall points out in his book *America's Great Comic-Strip Artists*, the newspaper feature *Little Orphan Annie* depicted the adventures of a small girl but wasn't really intended for children. In fact, Annie herself seemed ill at ease in the presence of other kids. On the radio, though, she was really a kid, maybe eight or ten years old, that young listeners could identify with. Most other children's shows – aside from such marginal things as *"Coast-to-Coast on a Bus"* and *"Let's Pretend,"* which you had to be kindergarten age to appreciate – were about grownups or at least teenagers such as Jack Armstrong. Annie and her little friend Joe Corntassel really seemed to be children who were trying to cope with a strange and complex adult world.

The show originated in Chicago and was written and produced by the advertising staff of Ovaltine, the instant-coca mix that you added to milk to make a chocolate-flavored concoction. Like Coco-Malt, a similar mix that sponsored *Buck Rogers*, it was favored by kids who hated the taste of milk but were compelled to drink it for reasons of good health and vitality. Most kids had never heard of Ovaltine before *Little Orphan Annie* came along on the family radio. That was before the days of supermarkets, and most of the goods at the corner grocery were displayed out of reach, and not in easy view, behind the counter. Despite the Great Depression, sales of Ovaltine must really have skyrocketed after *Little Orphan Annie* began. "Leapin' lizards!" someone at the manufacturer's Chicago headquarters must have cried in amazement – emulating Annie herself – upon looking at the latest sales figures.

In its earliest days the show had to be done twice each day, for the nationwide radio network had not yet been established. In the East and Midwest a cast headed by Shirley Bell as Annie did the show from Chicago, and in the West another cast, this one with Floy Margaret Hughes, broadcast from San Francisco. In 1933, when NBC went nationwide the Chicago cast became the permanent one. Other cast members were Allan Baruck as Joe Corntassel and Stanley Andrews as Daddy Warbucks. Andrews later achieved a certain measure of fame as the original host of television's *Death Valley Days*.

Five forty-five in the afternoon was "Little Orphan Annie Time" to kids in the 1930s, who all became familiar with the opening theme song, which was rendered by an unidentified group:

Who's that little chatterbox,
The one with the pretty auburn locks?
Who can it be?
It's Little Orphan Annie!
Always wears a sunny smile,
Now wouldn't it be worth the while
If you could be
Like Little Orphan Annie?

That song – which, by the way, was given away as sheet music in one of the show's first radio premiums – was followed by the dulcet voice of announcer Pierre André, the erstwhile Uncle Andy, actually provided an occasional

"Arf!" in the person of Sandy, as did Shirley Bell, though the role ostensibly was played by Brad Barker, certainly an appropriate name. No other kids' show had a more reassuring voice than André's to introduce the show, not even *Jack Armstrong*, which at various times had Truman Bradley, Franklyn MacCormack and Paul Douglas as the announcer. After he had sold the daily requirement of Ovaltine, Pierre André set the scene and Annie was off on another adventure.

The earliest sequences of the show were derived from the comic strip storyline originated by Harold Gray himself. On the farm of Mr. and Mrs. Silo, near the town of Simmons Corners, Annie met Joe Corntassel, a boy of her own age who lived just down the road and who remained her companion, as faithful as Sandy himself, on subsequent adventures, long after he disappeared from the comic strip. Presumably this was to give boys who listened to the show someone to identify with besides a mere girl, however spunky and enterprising she might be. Actually Harold Gray originally intended a boy hero, Little Orphan Otto, but comic strip impresario Joseph Medill Patterson, to whom he submitted the strip, growled that Otto "looks like a pansy" and ordered, "Put skirts on the kid." Thus Annie was born, created to look a little like a popular movie heroine of the day, Mary Pickford.

In their radio adventures Annie and Joe didn't stay long on the farm. Falsely accused of stealing money to buy candy they hopped a freight train to the city where they tracked down the real culprit and cleared their names.

As in the comic strip, Annie on the air had a Daddy Warbucks who appeared on the scene from time to time, more frequently on the radio show than in newspapers. A millionaire who had made a fortune in World War I – that is, "war bucks" – he fell to the depths, mentally and financially, in the Great Depression. Only through the inspiration and encouragement of Annie – "We may be down, but we ain't out, Daddy!" – did he manage to regain control of his business empire. This development was handy for the creators of the radio storyline, for it enabled them to put Annie and Joe aboard Daddy Warbucks' yacht and sail them off to the South Seas.

Their further adventures were a lot more thrilling, too. In Simmons Corners about the most exciting thing that happened to them was getting lost in the woods. In the South Pacific, on one occasion, there was a mutiny, and Annie, Joe and Daddy Warbucks were compelled to walk the plank. Fortunately there was a desert island nearby, which the mutineers, being typical bad guys, had somehow overlooked. Taking refuge there, Annie and her friends found that it wasn't deserted after all; it was the home of cannibals who besieged them in an abandoned stockade, a scene more or less copied from *Treasure Island*. Annie rescued them from this peril by fashioning masks of her own face which she stuck in the gun-ports of the stockade, causing the ignorant savages to suppose that the fort was manned by a whole army of small redheaded girls, a terrifying prospect indeed.

Masks like those that scared away the cannibals were offered to listeners of *Little Orphan Annie* who sent in a dime and the inner seal from a jar of Ovaltine, allowing them to scare their friends and family members in a similar fashion. This was only one in a series of radio premiums offered by the program which had pioneered in such an enterprise. The most famous *Annie* premium, and one of the most famous ever offered on a children's show, was the Shake-Up Mug. As Pierre André announced at the end of each episode, "It's Little Orphan Annie's very own Shake-Up Mug... with a beautiful, new and different picture of Annie and Sandy right on it. You put the special orange shake top on it when you shake up your ice-cold Ovaltine, then lift the top off, and presto! You have a special Little Orphan Annie mug to drink right out of. Here's the way to get it. Take out all of the thin aluminum seal you find under the lid of a can of Ovaltine and mail it, together with ten cents – one dime – to cover the cost of mailing and handling, to the Wander Company, 180 North Michigan Avenue, Chicago, Illinois. Then in a few days the postman will bring you this brand new Little Orphan Annie Shake-Up Mug to have and keep for your very own."

Even earlier, in the 1920s, before radio became a nationwide phenomenon, the Wander Company had offered a mug with Uncle Wiggily pictured on it, but this earlier premium is unlikely to have sold as widely as the Orphan Annie version plugged so assiduously on the air. It's uncertain which was the first radio premium, the Shake-Up Mug or another mug, a small chinaware one with still another picture of Annie and Sandy on the side, but it is the Shake-Up Mug that everybody remembers. It was said to be made of "genuine Beetleware" and to hold "8 full ounces."

Ovaltine offered numerous other premiums over the years, some of which could be purchased in dime stories: badges, secret manuals, code devices, a silent dog whistle, a periscope, a model circus with animated animals and clowns, and even Orphan Annie Talking Stationery (when the notepaper was unfolded, a likeness of Annie seemed to be moving its lips as if reading the message on the paper). Aside from the Shake-Up Mug, the most popular premium was the decoder pin or badge. A new one was offered every year, though many of them differed only superficially from one another. Such a device enabled listeners to decode secret messages provided at the end of each broadcast, usually giving advance information on upcoming developments in the current sequence involving Annie and Joe. The decoder was offered after a failed earlier attempt at secret messages, supposedly accessible only to Annie's secret club members. The messages were given in a simple substitution code that even the least intelligent kids in school were able to crack after hearing it once.

In 1940 disaster struck Annie, something that even the resourceful Daddy Warbucks couldn't prevent: She lost her sponsor. She was down, but she wasn't out, for Quaker Puffed Wheat Sparkies (a brand name that was later dropped) picked up the option for another two years. Annie's former sponsor, Ovaltine, had taken up with an aviator,Captain Midnight, and in the new series Annie soon found herself playing second fiddle to another aviator, Captain Sparks. Once the central character, she was now only a little girl sidekick like Joyce, her counterpart on *Captain Midnight*, or Jane on *Tom Mix*. Even Annie's club, the Safety Guard, was turned into Captain Sparks' Secret Guard, the counterpart of Captain Midnight's more famous Secret Squadron. At the last she had little to do but gasp "Leapin' lizards!" when Captain Sparks pulled his plane out of a power dive or turned the tables on the villain.

Like Annie of the radio show, Annie of the newspaper strip suffered a change, although she continued until 1968, when creator Harold Gray died. The strip, rechristened "Annie" after the stage and film musical, continues under the hand of Leonard Starr but has little connection with the past. On the radio, sometime in the war-torn year of 1943, Captain Sparks disappeared from the skies, and even radar has not been able to locate him. With him, wraith-like at the end and lamented only by fans of her earlier incarnation, was Little Orphan Annie, once the heroine of the radio series, leaving behind only the ghost of her "sunny smile" and a fading memory of her "pretty auburn locks."

Films

There was a "B" picture of *Little Orphan Annie* in the thirties, and a lavish "A" production filmed in the seventies from the hit stage musical, but they were so far from any connection with the radio show or even the comic strip that they do not seem to be proper subjects for consideration here.

Premiums

The premiums offered were as follows, listed alphabetically with sponsor, date and approximate value in 1992 (assuming average condition).

Adventure Books (6) (Ovaltine, 1934; $25 ea.), Airplane, Folding Wing "Wright Pursuit" (Quaker, 1941; $100), Badge, Membership, Mysto-Snapper (Clicker) (Quaker, 1941; $30), Badge, Mysto-Snapper (Quaker, 1941; $25), Badge, Signaller (Quaker, 1941; $35), Bandana (Ovaltine, 1934; $40), Belt and Buckle, Code Captain (Ovaltine, 1940; $150), Book About Dogs (Ovaltine, 1936; $40), Book, Recipe (Quaker, 1941; $30), Book, Snow White Cutouts (Whitman) (Ovaltine, 1938; $135), Bracelet,

Identification (Ovaltine, 1934; $35), Bracelet, Identification Tag (Ovaltine, 1939; $30), Button Card (Ovaltine, 1930; $70), Button, Annie (Ovaltine, 1930; $70), Button, Joe (Ovaltine, 1930; $300), Cap, Secret Guard Insignia (Quaker, 1941; $45), Card, Membership (Quaker, 1941; $15), Christmas Card Set (Ovaltine, 1937; $35), Circus Action Show (Ovaltine, 1936; $120), Cockpit, Aviation Training, Captain's Sparks (Quaker 1941; $150), Comic Book, "Sparkies," Book 1 (Quaker, 1941; $55), Comic Book, "Sparkies," Book 2 (Quaker, 1941; $50), Comic Book, "Sparkies," Book 3 (Quaker, 1941; $45), Commission, Captain's (Quaker, 1941; $45), Commission, Captain's (Quaker, 1941; $35), Decoder, Mysto-Matic (Ovaltine, 1939; $45), Decoder, Slideomatic, Paper (Quaker, 1941; $105), Decoder, Whirl-O-Matic, Paper Board (Quaker, 1941; $100), Dog Whistle, Three-Way, with Sandy's Head (Ovaltine, 1940; $50), Election Mailer (Ovaltine, 1930; $35), Emblem, Captain's, Glow Wings (Quaker, 1941; $150), Foreign Coin Folder (Ovaltine, 1937; $35), Game, Treasure Hunt (Ovaltine, 1933; $70), Glassips (Ovaltine, 1936; $45), Goofy Circus (Ovaltine, 1939; $125), Goofy Gazzetts (3) (Ovaltine, 1939; $25 ea.), Handbook, Safety Guard (Quaker, 1941; $150), Handbook, Secret Guard (Quaker, 1941; $150), Kit, Detecto, Secret Guard (Quaker, 1941; $30), Lucky Piece (Ovaltine, 1934; $25), Manual (Ovaltine, 1934; $55), Manual (Ovaltine, 1935; $55), Manual (Ovaltine, 1936; $45), Manual (Ovaltine, 1937; $50), Manual (Ovaltine, 1938; $75), Manual (Ovaltine, 1939; $70), Manual (Ovaltine, 1940; $90), Manual, Captain's Secret (Quaker, 1941; $100), Manual, Captain's Secret (Quaker, 1941; $80), Manual, Code Captain (Ovaltine, 1940; $45), Manual, Flight (Quaker, 1941; $35), Manual, Silver Star (Ovaltine, 1934; $25), Manual, Silver Star (Ovaltine, 1935; $25), Manual, Silver Star (Ovaltine, 1937; $30), Manual, Silver Star (Ovaltine, 1938; $45), Map of Simons Corners (Ovaltine, 1936; $55), Mask, Orphan Annie (Ovaltine, 1933; $60), Mug, 50th Annie-Versary (1982; $25), Mug, Annie, Ceramic (Ovaltine, 1932; $55), Mug, Beetleware (Ovaltine, 1933; $50), Mug, Beetleware (Ovaltine, 1935; $50), Mug, Shake-Up (Ovaltine, 1935; $55), Mug, Shake-Up (Ovaltine, 1938; $105), Mug, Shake-Up (Ovaltine, 1939; $60), Mug, Shake-Up (Ovaltine, 1940; $60), Mug, Shake-Up, Film (1982; $20), Mug, Shake-Up, Radio and Film (1982; $20), Mug, Shake-Up (Ovaltine, 1930; $50), Mug, Uncle Wiggily (Ovaltine, 1930; $35), Outfit, Nurse, Secret Guard (Quaker, 1941; $80), Penlight, Secret Guard (Quaker, 1941; $35), Photo, Annie, Face (Shirley Bell) (Ovaltine, 1932; $50), Photo, Annie, Waist Up (Shirley Bell) (Ovaltine, 1932; $50), Photo, Joe (Allan Baruck) (Ovaltine, 1932; $35), Photo Frame (Ovaltine, 1938; $35), Photo Stamps (Ovaltine, 1938; $20), Pictures, Magic Transfer (Ovaltine, 1935; $60), Pin, Captain's Safety Guard Magic Glowbird (Quaker, 1941; $190), Pin, Code Captain Secret Compartment (Ovaltine, 1939; $65), Pin, Decoder (Ovaltine, 1935; $25), Pin, Decoder, Sunburst (Ovaltine, 1937; $35), Pin, Decoder, Telematic (Ovaltine, 1938; $45), Pin, School (Ovaltine, 1938; $30), Pin, Secret Society, Bronze (Ovaltine, 1934; $15), Pin, Speedomatic Decoder (Ovaltine, 1940; $50), Puzzle, Tucker County Race (Ovaltine, 1933; $40), Ring, Altascope (Quaker, 1941; $150), Ring, Annie, Face (Ovaltine, 1934; $55), Ring, Birthstone (Ovaltine, 1936; $140), Ring, Mystic Eye (Look Around) (Ovaltine, 1939; $70), Ring, Secret Compartment, Triple Myst., Silver Star (Ovaltine, 1938; $500), Ring, Secret Guard Initial (Quaker, 1941; $500), Ring, Secret Guard Magnifying (Quaker, 1941; $850), Ring, Secret Message, Silver Star (Ovaltine, 1937; $110), Ring, Signet, Two Initial (Ovaltine, 1937; $95), Ring, Silver Star (Ovaltine,

1936; $30), Scribblers (Tablets), Secret Guard (Quaker, 1941; $35), Shadowetts, 6 (Ovaltine, 1938; $35), Sheet Music (Ovaltine, 1930; $10), Stamp, Rubber, Secret Guard (Quaker, 1941; $30), Sun Watch (Ovaltine, 1938; $35), Talking Stationery Set (Ovaltine, 1937; $60), Whistle, Three-Way, Annie's Head (Quaker, 1941; $70).

The Lone Ranger

Half-hour Western drama. Began Thursday, Feb. 2, 1933 (better research replaces often-published Jan. 30 date), WXYZ Detroit. First irregularly scheduled, then Tuesday, Thursday, Saturday through Nov. 25, 1933. Later (with Silvercup bread beginning as first sponsor) moved to Monday, Wednesday, Friday. The series went to be the founding cornerstone of the new Mutual Broadcasting System in 1936, then also joined NBC Blue (which later became ABC) in 1937, remaining there (under sponsorship of General Mills' Cheerios, Kix and Wheaties beginning in 1941) until the last original broadcast, on Sept. 3, 1954. Reruns remained on ABC until 1956, when the rerun series moved to NBC for five half-hour episodes a week until 1958.

Producer-Creator: George W. Trendle **Chief writer and editor:** Fran Striker **Other writers:** Felix Holt, Bob Green, Sheldon Stark, Bob Shaw, Dan Beatty, Tom Dougall, Gibson Scott Fox **Director:** Jim Jewell, Al Hodge, Charles Livingstone, Fred Flowerday **The Lone Ranger:** George Seaton (first, 1933-35), "Jack Deeds" (once), Jim Jewell (once), Earl Graser (1935-41), Brace Beemer (1941-54), (Emergency substitutes: Jay Michael, Fred Foy, perhaps others) **Tonto:** John Todd **Dan Reid** (nephew): Ernie Stanley (questioned), James Lipton, Dick Beals **Butch Cavendish:** Jay Michael **Thunder Martin:** Paul Hughes **Clarabell Hornblow:** Elaine Albert **Announcers:** Harold True, Brace Beemer, Harry Golder, Charles Woods, Bob Hite, Fred Foy **Others:** Rollon Parker, Jack Petruzzi, Herschel Mayal, Ted Johnstone, Amos Jacobs (Danny Thomas), Bob Maxwell, John Hodiak, Frank Russell.

"From out of the past come the thundering hoofbeats of the great horse, Silver... the Lone Ranger rides again!"

So concludes the introduction to the classic radio series, almost as if written in some premonition that this great character would be remembered from the past and resurrected in various forms for the grown-up children who once listened to his radio adventures–and for their children, and even their grandchildren.

Of course, those men around George W. Trendle during the creation of the series were not planning on creating an immortal figure. They wanted a commercial presentation to make some money and keep the radio station, WXYZ in Detroit, in business.

But even then, business executive Trendle professed idealism, bearing the standard for the American dream. Most of his contemporaries doubted his sincerity, as the statements they left behind reveal. The present writer had a fairly lengthy correspondence with Trendle in his waning years. It was difficult to find anything warm or other than businesslike in the man. He had a humorless fixation on the goal at hand. Yet he professed patriotism and service to the youth of his country.

As with all the great popular heroes, the Lone Ranger seemed to be distilled from generations of storytelling. There was more than one mysterious masked rider in the days of the real Old West, perhaps the best known being the poetry-mangling outlaw Deadwood Dick. Fiction and movies offered the double-identity caballero Zorro. The books of Zane Grey gave us *The Mysterious Rider* and *The Lone Star Ranger*. There were even minor pulp magazine stories here and there which made specific reference to their hero as "The Lone Ranger." (At least two real-life Texas Rangers were called "the Lone Ranger" at one time or another.) But these were the usual forshadowings of legend. It all came together in Detroit in the 1930s.

There are many versions of how the famous series about the Masked Man was created. One version was given in a 1939 *Saturday Evening Post* article, taken largely from the statements of Trendle. It bore some relationship to reality, but seen from today's viewpoint, it was not the final word.

In his fine, long (444 pages) book *From out of the Past: A Pictorial History of the Lone Ranger* (Holland House, 1988), Dave Holland gives the story of the creation in more detail than ever before. Only a few new items and interpretations can be added to this fine account.

Some people have told the present writer they heard the Lone Ranger in the Buffalo, N.Y., area years before hearing it start in the Detroit area on WXYZ in 1933. The statements of these men and one woman are similar. It is known that during 1932 and perhaps a bit before, Fran Striker wrote and helped produce occasional episodes of a western series called *Covered Wagon Days* on WEBR, Buffalo. In those pioneering, unstructured days of radio an episode of the *Covered Wagon* series was put on "whenever Striker could put one together," Buffalo area broadcaster Paul Harris observed. The stories were nominally anthology entries, tales where the hero changed each time. Could one of these heroes have been a masked avenger of justice? It wouldn't have been that unusual – it was a fairly common theme. That he was actually called "the Lone Ranger," a name created at a conference at WXYZ years later, seems unlikely.

Such speculations are fun, but Dave Holland has taken away most of the mystery surrounding the most famous of the West's mysterious riders. His research reveals that the Striker family still has copies of the *Covered Wagon Days* scripts and they state there is no character that appears in more than one of the stories. One wonders if these scripts have been thoroughly read to see if even one contains the appearance of a masked mystery man hero. One wishes for a guide to the plotlines of all these shows.

It is known that Striker selected *Covered Wagon Days* script No. 10, about gold miner Ezra Holten trying to protect himself from claim jumpers, and interjected the Masked Man into it to make script No. 1 for *The Lone Ranger*. Such rewrites and reuse of material are common among overworked writers. Yet would the reappearance of a plot from another show on the *Lone Ranger* series make a strong enough impression on a number of people for them to recall it after nearly half a century? Coupled with Striker's distinctive style of plot and dialogue, it would appear so.

Another explanation is that these people from the Buffalo area have that age-old craving to be "on the inside", to have secret information not known to the masses, and have simultaneously come up with the same story. It is possible. There was a common folk tale told by many people over the years that the soap opera matriarch of *Ma Perkins* was played by a man. There simply is no truth to that legend. From first episode to last, some twenty-seven years later, Ma Perkins was always played by the same lovely lady, Virginia Payne.

The existence of *Covered Wagon Days* is an established fact; its degree of resemblance to *The Lone Ranger* program has been questioned. Fran Striker wrote not only this series but a number of others for early radio, including such science fiction/fantasy thrillers as *Ultra Violet* and *Dr. Dragonette*. His plan was to syndicate these scripts to individual stations for a fee (four dollars for a 1,000-watt station) to be performed by a group of local actors and production people. Radio drama was (and is) so vastly less expensive than a visual performance for television or movies that it was common for local radio stations to put on their own dramas without network affiliation. On any given night in the thirties, a radio listener could sample not three different programs, or eight or ten, but dozens. Given a magic radio that could tune in every station in the country, this hypothetical listener could have tuned in hundreds of different dramas. Since stations could only reach a limited area before fading out or being blocked by a competing signal from another station, Fran Striker could sell the same wares to many different market areas.

At one of Striker's potential markets, WXYZ Detroit, one of Trendle's staff, dynamic writer-producer Jim Jewell, phoned Striker about gaining his services. At first it was for cops and robbers thrillers for a series called *Manhunters* featuring, among others, Warner Lester, criminologist. Now Jewell needed help on a new series station owner Trendle wanted, a Western.

Trendle told the WXYZ head of dramatic production to come up with a Western program idea. Jewell had written a number of episodes of a series called *Curley Edwards*, about a cowboy who, Jewell would later claim, masked himself with a bandana at times to act in secret for justice. Trendle considered this format, but was not enthusiastic about it.

An executive conference was called. This meeting has been written about many times. Unfortunately, no verbatim transcript was made, either by written notes or a sound recording. Only the memories of those there were left, tapped by many researchers over the years.

When the author suggested to Trendle in 1968 that the Lone Ranger was the result of a compromise between the ideas of those present, Trendle responded, "There was no compromise. I was the boss. What I said went."

Yet those talented men (no women were present) were there to do more than listen to Trendle talk to himself. They speculated, they suggested. As boss, Trendle had the final word as to what suggestions to accept.

One of the earliest recorded recollections of that meeting came from Jewell to a free-lance writer Tom Eldredge, Dave Holland revealed.

In late 1932, Jewell met in WXYZ offices in the Macabees Building in Detroit with Trendle and acting station manager Harold True. (Others would hold the station manager title around this time, including Howard Pierce and Brace Beemer, but Jewell said True was the man who was meant when it was stated that the station manager was there.)

Trendle recalled that the group met for a generalized discussion of a Western series. Jewell made it more specific: they were there to listen to a performance of his series, *Curley Edwards and his Cowboys*, and evaluate it. In a separate interview, True concurred.

After listening to Jewell's show, Jewell recalled Trendle as saying, "It's a great idea; go ahead and develop it." True recalls Trendle as saying, in effect, "It needs development." The agreed concept was development. It was not finished, not ready to go ahead. No one liked the title, or by inference the lead character. A new character was needed.

Most people agree that Trendle went through a refrain that has been replayed, expanded upon and edited many times in the retelling over fifty years. The station owner had always liked Westerns, with their little morality plays. In the silent movies of his youth, he had liked Douglas Fairbanks as the masked Robin Hood, Zorro, and another favorite was daredevil horseman Tom Mix. There wasn't any prominent Western series on the air that Trendle noticed (apparently missing the afternoon serial *Bobby Benson and his H-Bar-O Rangers*). This new character should be a combination of all these elements, and he needed a name more distinctive than Slim or Curley.

It was the moment of fate. A name came into Jewell's head from somewhere. "A name like... 'The Lone Star Ranger'."

True nodded thoughtfully. "Not bad. But Zane Grey had a book by that title. There was a movie too. How about... *The Lone Ranger!*"

The three men looked at each other. Could they hear, faintly in the background, a trumpet playing the first few notes of the "William Tell Overture"? Not quite yet.

The boss spoke. "That's it – the Lone Ranger. Jim, I want you to write up some scripts about this Lone Ranger."

The meeting broke up. Each went away with different memories of what had happened, a veritable *Rashomon* in Motor City. George W. Trendle recalled he had created a new program format by talking the matter over with his employees. Jim Jewell remembered he had been told to make a few changes in his program, *Curley Edwards*, and convert it into *The Lone Ranger*. Station manager Harold True remembered that he had given a great new character his name.

A more objective analysis might conclude Trendle had made a business decision to create a new Western program, and had used excellent judgment as to what would be successful.

Producer Jewell had been told to make a silk purse out of a sow's ear, and although a very creative individual, he would prove ultimately unequal to the task.

Manager True had made one excellent suggestion. He could hardly take credit for the entire concept, but in a perfect world he would have gotten some reward for his service. It isn't a perfect world, though, as the lawyer he later consulted told him. He was working for Trendle, and was only doing his job in coming up with useful ideas, which then became the property of Trendle. He was "bitter" over his dealings with Trendle. (He was not the only one.)

In the long run, it took more than the idea of doing a Western radio show, or expanding on an existing one called *Curley Edwards*, or even coining a colorful name like the Lone Ranger.

The series certainly could have gotten along without ever knowing *Curley Edwards*. It might have survived even without the Lone Ranger name, as *The Mystery Rider* or *The Masked Avenger*. (Those names and others were used for countless "inspired" follow-ups in movies and printed fiction. Radio seemed to steer clear of any exact imitation.) The one thing needed to make *The Lone Ranger* an everlasting classic was the genius of Fran Striker.

Striker would be called a workaholic today. In the thirties, he worked literally night and day not out of any morbid compulsion to make ever more money, but to ensure the very survival of his family. Not only his wife and children, but his parents, grandparents, aunts and uncles were dependent on him for food and shelter. Then, as now, many people were homeless. Many people without money, even if they still had a place to live, were too proud to beg and starved to death in their own homes. One working relative often meant the survival of a whole family. In the Striker clan, it was Fran who was inventive enough to create his own job.

There were other people who wrote for radio, but the pay was so low — two, maybe four, dollars a script – it was hard enough for one person to eat. But Striker hit on the idea of syndicating his scripts, of getting more than one use out of each one. Most stations covered only a one-city area, so they had no objection to other stations, perhaps halfway across the nation, using the same story. A script submission to Striker in one of his many radio jobs, this time at WEBR, from Phillips H. Lord, later to be a power in radio as creator of *Gangbusters*, gave Striker the idea of creating "Fran Striker Continuities, A Broadcast Ideastudio and Radio Word Shop."

It was as the operator of this company that Jewell contacted Striker, reportedly on the recommendation of Harold True. First he wrote *Manhunters*, about an active Scotland Yard inspector, a retired Scotland Yard inspector and Warner Lester, criminologist – the latter part played on the air by director Jim Jewell with his own Scandinavian accent.

Then came the famous conference, and Jewell sent Striker a letter to make the requirements absolutely clear. An existing carbon reads: "Will you write up three or four Wild West thrillers using the central figure the Lone Ranger...?"

Jewell had tried to fix up his old *Curley Edwards* to suit Trendle, but he couldn't seem to come up with the version of *The Lone Ranger* the station owner wanted. The dramatic director instructed the writer to include "all the hokum of the masked rider, rustler, Killer Pete, heroine on the train tracks, fighting on the top of box cars, Indian badman, two gun bank robber, etc." Obviously, Jewell had a superior, cynical attitude that Striker never did. Striker's characters were real to him, even one as noble as the masked man who sacrificed everything, even his identity, in the cause of justice.

At this point, Striker selected that tenth script of his old series, *Covered Wagon Days*, and added the mysterious figure of the Lone Ranger to aid prospector Ezra Holten in his fight against claim jumpers.

The story followed a basic format that was used for many years. The problem was clearly set out before the masked man arrived on the scene. There was already a nominal hero or protagonist – in later years, often a young rancher or lawman or military officer; here, a determined prospector. Then the Lone Ranger would appear, as a sort of guardian angel, and help the central character win out.

In the closing years of the series, this old format was not always used. Many of the later stories were tales of the Lone Ranger himself. They would begin with the Lone Ranger finding a clue to a robbery – a tobacco pouch, for instance – and tracking down the owner, the leader of the gang. One reason for the more straightforward story was that the show was shorter –

five minutes had been lopped off the program for a local newscast or other programming. Commercial time had been increased, too, so that the actual story time on a program, which in 1938 was about twenty-six minutes, had decreased by nearly a third by 1954 to about eighteen minutes. Yet even in these more abridged episodes, the traditional format of the masked man coming on the scene to help somebody solve a problem reoccurred.

In this first story, the Lone Ranger only appears to deliver two messages: one in a note wrapped around a rock, tossed through a window; the second in a whisper from the shadows. In the finale, the Lone Ranger rides up to deal out justice to claim jumpers, then rides away.

The unrefined original opening suggested the polished, distilled one of later years. It went like this:

> Throughout the entire West, in those turbulent days, were circulated stories of a masked rider, a picturesque figure that performed deeds of the greatest daring. A modern Robin Hood ... seen by few, known by none. Whence he came and where he went, no one ever knew. Few men had dared to defy this *Lone Ranger*, and those that had were found dead. The daring adventure of the Lone Ranger, the mystery rider, will be presented in this new series of programs.

When the character became fully formed, no one was found dead on his account. He only shot to wound, or more often to smash a weapon with a silver bullet. The precious metal was a constant reminder of the high cost of human life. That silver came from the masked man's secret mine, operated by a retired Ranger named Jim who took out just enough for his own needs, the Lone Ranger's silver bullets and other expenses.

The announcer introduced those first characters to be aided by the mysterious masked man. "Old Ezra Holten was a prospector and with his wife had given the best years of his life in the endless search for gold in the West." The old couple came on stage, to the microphones:

> Millie: Yew got back sooner'n I thought you would this time, Ezra.
> Ezra: Yep, I ... I was too broke, Millie, tuh stay around the town.
> Millie: It's jest as well yew was broke.... I can't understand why yew always have tew buy drinks for all the men that hangs on...

Ezra's fortunes changed after the Lone Ranger brought to justice those men trying to steal his gold claim.

In the closing, the announcer told us:

> You have met the most picturesque figure in the entire West, the Lone Ranger. From out of nowhere, he rides his fiery horse, taking the lawless country by storm, taking the law into his own hands, defying the crooks and the guardians of the law.... Remember, when you hear a hearty laugh, and fast hoofbeats coming from a distance, watch out for the Lone Ranger. He is riding like the wind, to bring help to someone who needs help, and retribution to one who needs punishment.

Then there would be the sound of approaching hoofbeats, a hearty laugh from the Lone Ranger and again the hoofbeats, fading out. The laugh would be replaced by an equally hearty cry that would become much more famous.

In the cast list, the Lone Ranger is described as having a "very even, *mild* voice, but clear and pleasing as well as a voice of authority" (emphasis added). Mild? All the surviving recordings and memories reveal that the Lone Ranger as produced by WXYZ always had a very forceful, commanding voice. Striker may have envisioned his being somewhat more underplayed, but such was not to be (and probably would not have worked, in a medium as barren of subtleties as early radio).

The only person to get name credit in the first script was Jim Jewell. The Jewell Players and the station WXYZ were also mentioned. For years, only the station itself, which George W. Trendle must have considered an extension of himself, was credited in the closing. "You have just heard another of the famous Lone Ranger dramas, originating in the studios of WXYZ Detroit."

In the first script, Striker has the Lone Ranger using silver bullets – like the silver-tipped arrows he remembered Robin Hood using in an old story – and silver horseshoes for his horse or "hosses" (plural). Some accounts have these items coming from Detroit conferences. Perhaps they were relayed to Striker (though correspondence doesn't show it) or perhaps it is a case of an executive staff taking credit for ideas of creative personnel.

In the second script, Striker gives the horse a name, Silver. Researcher Dave Holland states that the horse was not described as white until Script No. 14. But who ever heard of a horse named Silver being anything else but white? "Silver" refers to his color as surely as "Blackie" would. (Perhaps a horse could be a sorrel and called Blackie for a black-hearted, mean disposition, but it would be unusual.)

The first script written was not the first script performed. Trendle liked the second script written better – it had more of the flavor he wanted. In this one, the masked man had his famous horse Silver and at least the beginning of his famous cry.

This first broadcast of Striker's follow-up to his initial script concerns clearing Jeb Longworth of false murder charges brought against him by the real killer, Cal Steward. The masked man tries to clear his friend in a confrontation with Cal.

Cal: Folks around here aren't going to be troubled by you any longer. I'm going to kill you right now, Lone Ranger!
Sheriff: *(Distant)* Oh no you ain't, Cal Steward. Put up your hands... I heard all that was said, and I guess it's you that'll be tried for the murder of Higgins, not Jeb!
Ranger: You see, Cal, it takes brains sometimes to out guess guns! I was so sure that you'd take advantage of me when I was unarmed, and so sure of your boasting nature, that I left a little note for the Sheriff to be by that window tonight, if he wanted to hear the confession of the real murderer! I think I'll be leaving...
Man: Sheriff... He's grabbed his guns... (Door open and slam... ad lib shots... running feet... shouts of men, etc... horse's hooves..)
Ranger: Come Along, Silver... That's the boy... Hi yi... (Hearty laugh) Now cut loose... and away...

Note that even in the first show's script, Striker has written "Hi Yi..." as a call to Silver. It was his attempt to suggest cowboy yells like "Yi... Yi... Yippee" but to make it a bit different, more distinctive. He experimented with "Hi Yi Ho... Silver" and "Hi Yi Yo Silver," but Dave Holland finds that in Script No. 12, Striker typed out "Hi Yo Silver... Away..."

There are various stories of the actor, Stennius, and the director, Jewell, experimenting with various cries to the horse. The cry may have been a variation on the old English call "Heigh Ho." In an interview with writer David Rothel, Jewell confirmed this version. Striker listened to the shows, and he may merely have been trying to phonetically reproduce the cry he was hearing. But he may have been trying to lead it in the direction he thought was the final version. It was he who set it in type for all time.

For copyright and trademark purposes the official name of the Lone Ranger's horse is "Hi Yo Silver." There have been other Silvers – cowboy star Buck Jones had one – but only one Hi Yo Silver.

Another piece of the Lone Ranger vocabulary which has become a part of the American language is the friendly greeting the masked man and his Indian friend have for each other, "Kemo Sabay." Director Jim Jewell wrote the phrase into the scripts, getting it from the name of an Indian-style boys' camp his father-in-law ran as far back as 1915, Kamp Kee-Mo Sah-Bee.

According to Jewell it meant "trusty scout." Through usage (the change that takes place in all language) it has also come to mean "faithful friend." Of course, popular culture never created two trustier scouts or more faithful friends than the Lone Ranger and Tonto.

It was Jim Jewell who first suggested the idea of a partner for the masked man. On February 15, 1933, he wrote Striker: "It might be a good idea also to [give the Lone Ranger a sidekick], and Indian half-breed who always stands ready at his command to help him . . . ." Of course, after Striker named him Tonto (having consulted a map of Tonto National Park, not being sure if that was the best possible name), he eventually became a full-blooded Indian. Only the villains were "half-breeds," apparently so as not to offend either camp.

Some have charged that Tonto was treated as a second class citizen, a servant. Perhaps in the earliest episodes he was, but later the masked man only made suggestions as to the division of labor: "You make the fire, Tonto, while I unsaddle the horses." And "tonto" does not really mean "stupid" in Spanish, as sometimes claimed – it means wild and fired-up. A real-life Indian known to Jim Jewell was sometimes accused of being "tonto" when he took on a bit too much firewater. The name might be no more insulting than calling James Butler Hickok "Wild Bill." The tone was set in a show from the last years of the series. The Lone Ranger and the local sheriff are waiting for Tonto to show up.

> Sheriff: I'm looking forward to meeting Tonto.
> Ranger: He's one of the finest men I've ever met, Sheriff. I owe my life to him many times.
> Sheriff: Any man would be proud to have a friend like Tonto.

So say we all.

Tonto spoke in broken English, a not entirely inaccurate representation of the way some Indians who had English as a second language spoke. This was radio, and dialect helped listeners keep in mind what the character was supposed to look like – in this case, and Indian. Other dialects were big in early radio for similar reasons: Irish, Swedish, Jewish, Italian, French, Hillbilly, "Rube." etc. One publicity handout explained Tonto spoke many languages – several Indian dialects, Spanish, and so on – but had trouble with proper pronouns in English.

On several occasions, Tonto had to carry on without his masked friend and did fine. He was certainly accepted as co-hero by young listeners. In the 1950s, one of the writers under Striker, Sheldon Stark, in effect made Tonto the hero of his own series, under the name *Straight Arrow*. The man who often had written about Tonto now chronicled the adventures of a full-blooded Comanche warrior who posed as rancher Steve Adams but rode out on his palomino, Fury, with his old-timer sidekick, Packy, on the trail of justice, dressed in Comanche garb from head to foot.

The part of Tonto was played from first to last by John Todd, a lifelong actor on the stage, on radio, wherever the work was. He began the part in his sixties and concluded it in his eighties. Some say he fell asleep during shows in the last years, others that he read *Reader's Digest* during scenes in which he did not appear. At any rate, when nudged Todd would sometimes blurt out, "Gettum up, Scout!" when the scene took place in a hotel room or on a Mississippi riverboat.

There was one other important "character" in the show, even before the introduction of the Lone Ranger's nephew, and that was the narrator.

It was Striker's and the show's style to use a narrator throughout the dramatic portion of the show. By the late forties, most radio shows used a narrator very sparingly, letting the actors explain what was happening in their dialogue. The narrator generally only set the scene. In some shows, only a muscial bridge separated the scenes and the announcer only read the opening and the commercials. But on *The Lone Ranger*, the narrator could be expected to interject himself anytime: "The wily crook pulled a gun from under his coat on the unsuspecting Tonto, and smiled in satisfaction" or "The Lone Ranger urged Silver up the slope, only to see in alarm a great boulder rolling down towards them."

Harold True was the first of several narrators. Brace Beemer handled the job on many occasions; Dave Holland accuses him of sounding "bored." Well, it wasn't the job he wanted. From the first, he had made it clear he wanted to be the Lone Ranger. Harry Golder was a fine narrator for many years, with a kindly uncle quality, but with a certain tension in his voice suggesting excitement.

But then, in 1948, there came Fred Foy, and he literally made many people forget that there had been any others before him. He was *the* announcer, perhaps the greatest announcer-narrator in the history of radio drama. He pronounced words like no one else ever had – "SIL-ver," "hiss-TOR-ee." But hearing him, you realized everybody else had been wrong.

Trendle made him Brace Beemer's understudy. In the rehearsals, and once on the air when Beemer couldn't make the show, he did the part of the Lone Ranger. If the show had gone on another decade and Beemer had retired (or, alas, died, as he did in 1965), Fred Foy would have taken over and done a fine job. He might not have done so well at public appearances, though. Trendle told him to take riding lessons, but he only tried it once.

But Foy narrated better than anyone. He continued doing voice work, mainly in television, for many years, serving as Dick Cavett's talk show announcer for some time. He is still heard selling products, often various record collections, on television.

In his first script, Striker suggested *The Lone Ranger* might use the theme song of his old show, *Covered Wagon Days*, or even "Beyond the Blue Horizon." That was not to be, of course.

As head of production, Jewell selected the theme music, Rossinni's "William Tell Overture" – or more specifically, the section of it known as "The Ride." (Another segment, "The Storm," was used for two different early radio series, *Flash Gordon* and *Jungle Jim*.) It came from a 1927 RCA Black Seal recording by maestro Rosario Bourdon and the Victor Symphony. The trumpet call comes out of the final pastoral notes of "The Storm" in a live performance or modern recording, but since there had to be breaks in old 78 rpm sets, each record of which could go only for a maxium of four minutes or so, the trumpet call begins cleanly. It became a call to adventure for decades. It's been said only a true intellectual can hear the "William Tell Overture" and not think of the Lone Ranger. It would also take a person almost totally alienated from popular American culture. Phyllis Diller said with a leer that when she heard the famous music, she thought of Tonto. Certainly no other music so suggests a man riding, riding on through obstacles on a mission of destiny.

The other music was good, too. Not all of it was classical. Much of it was used from the *Lone Ranger* movie serial after its 1938 appearance. Many people thought for years the music had to be from some obscure classical pieces and tried to trace it down. Finally, a book by Reginal Jones, *The Mystery of the Masked Man's Music*, revealed these themes to be by Alberto Columbo, William Lava, and other Republic staff composers.

After the theme was chosen, the show was ready to go on the air, at least for a tryout.

Most printed sources say *The Lone Ranger* premiered January 30, 1933, the night the Michigan Radio Network came on the air. But extensive descriptions of the offerings of that new network (down to a three-minute song by a duo) reveal no airing of the masked man's adventures. There may have been a "tryout" broadcast on January 20, largely based on the memory of director Jewell. A printed notice in the *Detroit Evening Times* for February 2, 1933, definitely states, " 'The Lone Ranger'... makes his bow in a new dramatization series to be heard three times weekly on WXYZ starting at 9:00 p.m. today...." This must have been at least the first regularly scheduled broadcast.

Who played the Lone Ranger on that first broadcast?

From memory, George W. Trendle has said it was "a man named Deeds." But Trendle's memory was faulty on a number of points.

Fran Striker's original script for that first show exists, and in a notation in his handwriting he states that the Lone Ranger was played by "Stenius" – George Stenius, later to be known as George Seaton, a prominent Hollywood writer-producer-director on such films as *The Bridges at Toko-Ri*. John Todd, later Tonto, played a sheriff.

The early Lone Ranger, believed to be a rare picture of radio actor Earle Graser in costume on horseback (he was not an experienced rider).

Jim Jewell also remembered hiring Stenius for the part after auditioning him while he was doing *Elizabeth the Queen* on stage in Detroit. The actor's widow recalled her husband stating he was the first Lone Ranger "and I never knew him to tell a lie." (Perfect casting!)

If Jewell was responsible for hiring Stenius/Seaton, he was also responsible for his leaving the show after two and a half months. The radio director went to see some one-act plays Stenius had written and afterwards exclaimed "How can you waste your time acting when you write so well!"

Stenius took the praise to heart and left his acting role of the Lone Ranger to pursue his literary endeavors.

Then came Jack Deeds, although people may not have been remembering his name just right after half a century. He was a dapper man with a fine voice, but he couldn't seem to stand up under the ferocious directing technique of Jewell. He got through at least one show during the third month of the series but did not show up for the next performance. Jewell himself, with a natural Scandinavian accent, went on for Deeds, trying unsuccessfully to adopt a Texas drawl. It was the only time Jewell played the part.

In a desperate rush, Jewell auditioned all the men in the drama club at Wayne State University. From this group he selected Earle W. Graser (pronounced "grah-zer," not "grass-er"). Graser won the audition on Sunday, April 16, 1933, and played the Lone Ranger on the air for the first time on Tuesday, April 18.

Graser had a fine voice and a naturalness and ease of delivery his successor Brace Beemer would not have. But if Graser made the Lone Ranger a real person (and many think he was the best man ever in the part), it was Beemer who made the Lone Ranger larger than life, a seemingly superhuman champion of justice.

Trendle seemed to like to play a game of denial with his employees. If there was something they wanted, he saw to it that they didn't get it. Foremost was money. Everybody was underpaid, even by the miserly standards of the day. In the early days, actors were paid $5 for doing three shows a week—that's about $1.66 a show for a *total* of $5.

But beyond adequate salaries, Trendle denied them other side benefits they sought. Fran Striker sought security for himself and his rather large family. The station owner tantalized Striker with hints of giving him a percentage of the character for which he had made the greatest creative contribution. It never happened. Striker was a wage slave till the day he died.

Brace Beemer, the towering, barrel-voiced figure who could command grown men when he was still a boy, a thirteen-year-old sergeant in World War I, wanted to play the part of the Lone Ranger from the day he heard about the show. But for years, Trendle denied him that privilege, while having him pose for the photos they sent out of the Masked Man—he looked the part as well as sounded it. He also played the Lone Ranger, riding a white horse, at the Ranger's first public appearance, when a crowd of ten thousand youngsters went mad at the sight of their hero and rushed out onto a football field, threatening to crush man, horse and each other. They were stopped in their tracks by Beemer's ringing command—"Steady, Rangers!" But Trendle did not think this man was ready to play the popular hero. He kept him as the narrator and bread salesman until fate decreed otherwise.

After Graser's death there was another WXYZ staff conference. A talented actor was dead, but the Lone Ranger lived. As was said of another immortal fictional character, Sherlock Holmes: "Those who have never lived, can never die." Trendle expressed formula regrets but declared "the show goes on." Different memories have different people being suggested to replace Graser. Could Al Hodge be moved over from his role of the Green Hornet? How about announcer Mike Wallace? Now the famous news commentator, Wallace was once active in radio as a newsman, and as an announcer and actor in radio drama. He announced *Sky King* and played the lead criminologist on *Crime Files of Flammond*. Another announcer, Jay Michael? He was too strongly identified with villain roles. Finally, Charles Livingstone, the director after Jewell left for Chicago to do *Jack Armstrong* and other shows, suggested Brace Beemer.

It is difficult to believe that it would take so long to think of Beemer. He and Graser sounded very much alike, particularly when Beemer first assumed the role (Beemer's voice got deeper and more authoritative as he got older). Moreover, Beemer looked the part—he had had the dubious distinction of posing in costume for all the early photos of the Lone Ranger, and making personal appearances in the role, while someone else played the part on the air and collected the paychecks. Graser was slight of build and was no horseman in real life, whereas Beemer grew up on a horse farm.

Beemer had been narrating *The Lone Ranger* off and on for years. Records reveal he had been the narrator in June and October 1934, December 1938 and again in July 1940. He may have been doing it on other dates, too; the records are incomplete. He was not the narrator on the show for Graser's last performance, April 7, 1941 ("Sixty Days for Life," in which the masked man tricks crooks into exchanging a sixty-day stay in jail for life sentences). Beemer was also playing the part of Sgt. Preston of the Northwest Mounted Police on *Challenge of the Yukon*, then only a weekly show with a limited audience. Years later, Beemer would return to the role of Preston after *The Lone Ranger* became recorded reruns. He did live, complete broadcasts as the Mountie with the great dog, Yukon King, in 1954–55.

The Boss, Trendle, told Striker to break Beemer into the role easily; the audience would have to get used to him and not be introduced to a new voice suddenly. It is possible that such care was not really needed. Some radio collectors who are experts at identifying voices argue over whether certain recordings featured Beemer or Graser. They sounded *very* similar. Most listeners probably could not tell the difference.

While Striker came up with an excellent transitional series, "easing Beemer in," his work was not without argument, according to the late actor Curley Bradley, Golden Age radio's last Tom Mix. Bradley knew all the Detroit radio people well, and he said Striker was such a close friend of

Graser and so devastated by his death that he wanted the Lone Ranger to actually die in the drama, perhaps prompting Tonto to take his mask and search for a time for a new Lone Ranger. Trendle reportedly axed that idea. "There is one Lone Ranger and he lives forever!" According to Curley Bradley's account, Striker then came up with a wounded Ranger who would slowly recover and speak more as time went by.

In the first of five transitional episodes, Tonto found the Lone Ranger badly wounded at the ranch of his old friend, Mustang Mag. She spoke to Tonto – and to all the worried listeners. "I want you to know that I'm sure of one thimg... *The Lone Ranger is goin' to ride again!*"

The Lone Ranger's agile mind was still working. His strength was gone, but not the "resourcefulness" that had made him known the length and breadth of seven states. With a few whispered words, and painfully scribbled notes, the masked man gave Tonto instructions how to stave off a range war. "Ride for us both" were among Beemer's first words as the Lone Ranger.

There were other missions for Tonto during the next few shows. But the Lone Ranger did not seem to be getting better – he seemed to be getting worse. The Indian knelt beside the masked man's bed. "An Injun prayin' to his Creator," Mag whispered. "First time... Tonto... shed tear," the Indian told her later.

Criminals intercepted a telegram the Lone Ranger had sent to Washington, explaining his delay in getting certain important papers delivered. The crooks decided to seize those papers for blackmail and to kill the Lone Ranger in the bargain.

As in all good Westerns, the Calvary arrived in time to prevent that and to bring an Army surgeon to aid the masked man.

In the final show of this important sequence, other outlaws had a wagon train loaded with gold trapped in a canyon. It was another mission, another call to duty. The Lone Ranger struggled from his bed, rose to his feet. Was he taller now? His voice was deeper and gone was the natural, easy-going quality of Earle Graser.

His footsteps still testing the path cautiously, he made his way to the side of his great horse. "We'll be riding again, Silver." And ride he does at the head of a posse to save a gold train from outlaws. He encounters the first of the crooks, who is foolhardy enough to attempt gunplay. "I just shot your gun away, Lance! The next shot might come from one of the men who'd shoot to kill!"

Mustang Mag's old timer sidekick, Missouri, speaks for us all. "Jumpin' Juniper, it's great to hear your voice like that!"

But the best was yet to come. For the first time in two weeks, seemingly a lifetime on radio, the Lone Ranger raised his voice (now in the matchless timber of Brace Beemer) and cried out to a waiting nation: *"Hi Yo Silver, Away!"*

Beemer would be the Lone Ranger until the final live broadcast on Friday, Sept. 3, 1954, and would continue to do commercials and public service announcements to aid certain charities until the end of the network reruns, first on ABC, then NBC, until 1958. Beemer did some promotional announcements for syndicated reruns from Fred Flowerday's Special Recordings, then Charles Michaelson, Inc. (these are still used) shortly before his death from a heart attack while playing cards with friends at his Oxford, Michigan, horse ranch in 1965.

The fame of the Lone Ranger grew as he added more stations: the Michigan Radio Network, then Mutual, Don Lee and NBC Blue (later just the Blue Network and finally ABC). There were sponsors coming on board. Broadcast Corned Beef Hash toyed with sponsorship and may have gotten a few trial broadcasts in the can; records aren't complete. Then came more of a natural, Gordon Bakery's Silvercup Bread; then Gingham Bread, Merita Bread in Southern states; and finally General Mills, introducing its new product Cheeri-Oats in 1942 (called Cheerios after 1945).

Doing the radio series was a lot of work for production people and the actors. There were many more rehearsals in busier radio cities than Detroit, where *The Lone Ranger* was usually the only network broadcast going out of the city on a particular day. In New York, Hollywood and even Chicago, the busy actors would be hurrying to and from other shows, hiring stand-ins to take their places in rehearsals until they could get there.

According to the various directors, there were no casual read-throughs as were common on other shows. All rehearsals were on microphone, actors standing in place, learning to move in and out to suggest movement.

After a first read-through, there was a rehearsal for timing. An experienced radio writer such as Striker or any other of his staff knew to make the script about the right length; usually a double-spaced page equaled one minute. But different scenes are played in different ways. A heated argument runs faster than lovers exchanging words as they look at the moon. An explanation of a mystery has to be done more slowly and meticulously than a description of a gunfight. So scripts had to be cut for time, and occasionally small additions had to be made. Somehow it was more often a cut— the process was usually called "making your cuts."

Then came a "production rehearsal" where the recorded music and a combination of live and recorded sound effects were added to the mix.

One of the best sound effects departments in the business was at WXYZ, whose technicians included Fred Flowerday (later a program director), Ernie Winstanley (later an actor) and Gibson Fox (later a writer for both the radio

Opposite: **Brace Beemer, the longest-running radio Lone Ranger, in costume with his Silver (the Lone Ranger is a copyrighted trademark of Lone Ranger Television/Palladium).**

and television *Lone Ranger*). They had not just a "gravel box" to strike toilet plungers into, but a box with gravel, clay, rock and other surfaces as called for. Real harness with bits of buckles and trim was shaken for effect.

Gunshots were made by various devices – striking a cardboard box with a ruler, then a leather cushion with a cane, then by releasing a rat trap fastened to a metal drum. Near the end of the series a recording of a real gunshot was used, and by the 1950s the show was relying too much on these recordings. Even on static-filled old AM a listener could hear the disc recording being cued up. The sound man would let the effect begin to play – without going over the air – then give the turntable half a turn or so backwards and physically hold the turntable with his hand until the director gave him the cue. The sound effect would come on instantly, at least in theory. In these days before digital perfection the sound effect might not be quite instantaneous. One heard, "Tonto, I'm going to shoot the gun out of his hand!" Hisss... BANG! The surface noise from the recording was heard too many times to be funny. It indicated a certain slackening of standards in the closing days, as did the scripts which told often a very simple tale of things that happened directly to the Lone Ranger, instead of his intervention in somebody else's problem.

After the sound effects and music from commercial recordings and those supplied by Republic Pictures were set, the cast and crew were allowed fifteen minutes to go to the bathroom or get a drink of water. (Actually, many claim that the drink very often was not water.)

Now came the first of three live broadcasts, to different time zones. All the people began arriving at about three in the afternoon for the first show. Various production people – Jewell, Livingstone, etc. – have varying memories about exactly when those shows were.

It is a matter of record in many newspapers and magazines (such as *Radio Mirror*) that the *Lone Ranger* was on the air live over the Blue Network, later ABC, at 6:30 PM Central Standard Time. That had to be the first live show. The program would be heard in New York and other Eastern zone cities at the same time, but at 7:30 Eastern Time.

Then, after only a thirty-second gap, the next live performance would begin for the Mountain time zone, and finally, after another hour, another live show for the West Coast.

In the closing years, the second live broadcast, which was recorded for later rerun syndication, was probably played for either the mountain or Pacific zone. (Memories and records are inexact on the point.)

The earliest broadcasts of the series came from a Detroit skyscraper, the Macabees Building, which also housed the offices of Trendle and all of WXYZ. (It became the home of WDET later.)

After 1943, and until the final live broadcast, the program along with all the WXYZ dramas and the offices of Trendle and his executives and

Striker and his staff of writers were moved to the Mendelssohn mansion at Iroquois and Jefferson. The huge old home from another era became the "Jefferson studios."

The dramas were done in Studio D (the old living room), the sound effects were done on the reconditioned sunporch. Fran Striker had his office just above that room and could be seen and heard working late into the night on scripts.

The living room was not turned into a chrome and steel antiseptic cell. It still retained a fireplace and a flowered rug, with the old 44 microphones set up in the center. Apparently, the acoustics were fine. For over a decade the "masked man" (unmasked, in an open-necked sport shirt) and all the others performed in the millionaire's living room.

This Jefferson building was now, in essence, WXYZ. But WXYZ was no longer the property of Trendle and his largely silent partner, John King, with whom he had formerly run a string of silent movie theatres (when King was known as Kunsky). They had sold the station for $3,650,000 to the new American Broadcasting Company network. Trendle retained ownership of the dramas, eventually buying out King.

In the early years of *The Lone Ranger* many tales were written and performed but not recorded. Some of the scripts have survived but not all. Only human memories still conjure up many exciting adventures of those early days. Noted collector Bill Thailing recalls a story of the early thirties where the Lone Ranger was trapped in an explosion on a bridge, and only his black mask was found floating on the water.

Writer and critic Redd Boggs remembered the days before the story of the Lone Ranger's origin in an ambush of a group of Texas Rangers had been established. Until the story was given in the movie serial in 1938 and revised for its first radio broadcast in 1941, no one knew from whence came the Lone Ranger. Characters on the show and listeners at home would both speculate on his origin.

The show seemed to indicate that the Lone Ranger wore a mask not just to hide any face, but to conceal a famous face, one that would be recognized if not for the mask. Could the Lone Ranger be some other famous personality of the West – Buffalo Bill or Wild Bill Hickok disguising himself as the Lone Ranger for some of his adventures? But these men seemed to have as full a career as the masked man. The Lone Ranger was too busy to be leading a double life. Could he be somebody leading a new life after his life was thought to be over? Could he be Billy the Kid, not really dead from Sheriff Pat Garrett's bullets, but living a new life to redeem himself for his past mistakes? Not likely, since there came a series of stories in which the masked man met all these characters. Could he have been one of those great heroes thought killed at the Alamo, but secretly surviving to carry on his great work – somebody like Davy Crockett or Jim Bowie?

Such were the speculation of the listeners in those early days. But the scripts of Fran Striker and his fellow writers at WXYZ suggested that people would be surprised if they could see the face beneath the mask, they would find that face "hard to believe." Would the face of one young Texas Ranger, a trooper serving under a captain, be enough to prove so startling? Apparently, not even Trendle or Striker had yet decided just who the man was behind the mask.

Then came the 1938 Republic serial *The Lone Ranger*. It told an origin for the masked rider. But it was not just the concoction of the movie studio. In his book, *His Typewriter Wore Spurs*, Fran Striker, Jr. told that the senior Striker was in correspondence with the studio and passed on a number of suggestions about the plot. It seems that the ambush of the Texas Rangers, all of whom were left for dead, must have been his idea since he embraced it so fully in the radio shows thereafter. He was under no obligation to do so. Other elements, such as the masked man's true name turning out to be Allan King, were rejected. Some radio fans have criticized the plotline about the "five Ranger suspects" as not being true to the radio version. But there was *no* established radio origin for the Lone Ranger at this time, so there was nothing from which to deviate. It was a good plot device to keep the audience guessing who was the real Ranger as one by one the suspects got killed off.

Correspondence reveals that Trendle did not like the five suspects plotline, but he may not have been aware of just who contributed it. He could have disapproved it even after his chief writer had submitted it, though it seems unlikely that Striker would even have submitted such a concept without discussing it with Trendle. Three years passed after the 1938 serial, and in 1941 in a story called "A Girl to Aid" the origin of the Lone Ranger was presented in dramatic form, with the future Ranger, his brother and Tonto having speaking parts. Before, characters had spoken of these events only in description, in past tense. And here, Trendle and Striker agreed with the filmmakers that the Lone Ranger had been one of a group of Texas Rangers ambushed and left for dead. One survived.

Striker added a new note. Even before Tonto arrived on the scene, a pretty young girl found the wounded ranger and helped him to a cave where the Indian later discovered him. This mysterious girl who aided the Lone Ranger at the beginning of his career was only a part of the longest-running plot line on *The Lone Ranger*. It concerned his efforts to destroy the notorious Legion of the Black Arrow, a group headed by men in high places who planned to subvert the U. S. government and seize power for themselves. The story was no doubt inspired by a number of real-life subversive groups such as the Klu Klux Klan and considering the year in which the programs were produced, perhaps the German-American bund. Trendle, as producer, may have seen the Black Arrow as more resembling the Soviet Union with

The five "Ranger suspects" from the first movie serial of *The Lone Ranger*, 1938: Lee Powell, George Letz (George Montgomery), Hal Tafiaferro, Lane Chandler (not identified in original caption), and Herman Brix. The notation "M.B.S." identifies the radio show's network, the Mutual Broadcasting System.

its communist agents "everywhere." In the storyline of the series, members had a black arrow tattooed on their arms, although some agents must have had to forego the mark to ensure the secrecy of their membership. With an actual mark or only a psychic one, these agents of the Black Arrow were spread across the West to do their work in destroying the American nation.

Though brave men and women tried to resist, their cause might have been lost had they not had a leader, a mysterious rider who appeared out of the night, aided by a stalwart Indian, to strike back at these other night riders. This masked man rode a great white horse, and his ringing command to that magnificent mount seemed to lift the hearts of those who felt fear and oppression. Many a heart beat faster at the cry *"Hi-Yo, Silver–Away!"*

The masked man and Tonto began to discover criminals with the tattoo of the Black Arrow on their forearms. At first, there were only the usual mail robbers and rustlers. But as the masked man fought on, he discovered the Black Arrow in higher and higher places.

At first, the mysterious girl who had helped the Lone Ranger appeared in each story and left a clue to aid him against this dark legion. But finally she seemed to have done all she could in the great struggle, and the masked man and Tonto fought on alone.

In an early encounter with the band, then working the rather modest racket of cattle rustling, the masked man talks about the Black Arrow with the local sheriff.

> Sheriff: All I know about the Legion of the Black Arrow is this: It ain't healthy to talk about it.
> Ranger: The Legion of the Black Arrow must be smashed, Sheriff. If it isn't, the United States will fall! It's a huge secret organization whose purpose is to overthrow the government. Especially here in the West. . . .

In the same story (at least in the comic strip adaptation of it), the masked man and Tonto fight six killers *with their hands tied behind their backs*. Through fast footwork and forceful shoulder thrusts that would put an NFL linebacker to shame they send the half dozen crashing into stone walls and unconsciousness, allowing the finest team in the West to escape and bring help to round up a veritable army of Black Arrow henchmen.

At one point the Lone Ranger thought that he had found the leader of the Black Arrow, but he was wrong. The man he suspected was murdered by higher ups and the fight had to go on.

There were four great leaders of the nefarious group, and one by one, the Ranger and Tonto brought each of the leaders to justice.

But even after the Black Arrow had been broken up, the Lone Ranger could still tell a crooked rancher, "There's something in your past that you will never be able to live down—you were a member of the Black Arrow."

Even when it was not mentioned, one could suppose many of the crooks and killers the Lone Ranger would bring in after 1942 had worn that brand of dishonor.

There were many other criminals who would feel the impact of a silver bullet against their gun hand. The masked man seemed totally democratic in handing out justice; he would expose a confidence man trying to fleece a young girl of her inheritance, or help a young man falsely accused of bank robbery. Some of these crimes seemed too "small potatoes" for this heroic figure. The story seemed to fit him better when it was of grander scale, when the Lone Ranger was on a special mission for the president on which "the future of the West depends."

According to WXYZ, it was the Lone Ranger who was instrumental in getting the Western Union telegraph lines through to join the nation together, at the special assignment of President Lincoln. He gave similar aid to the building of the Union Pacific railroad.

He fought shoulder to shoulder with Buffalo Bill against renegade Indians to protect the wagon trains of homesteaders, opening up the West to civilization.

There was General Custer and his foolhardy attacks on Indian forces that were both larger and more wisely commanded than his own. The masked man tried to turn him from his ways, but even the Lone Ranger could not always win.

But when gallant old Sitting Bull had to surrender, it was the masked man who saw to it that he was given fair and honorable treatment. This sequence formed the last "connected series" of stories during the last year of live broadcasts.

The Lone Ranger helped Wild Bill Hickok tame the town of Deadwood by disguising himself as Hickok, letting the lawman be in two places at once and giving him twice the odds to defeat the badmen.

Knowing that no man is all bad, the Lone Ranger tried to get Billy the Kid to turn from his criminal wildness, but it was Sheriff Pat Garrett's guns that spoke the last word.

The Lone Ranger was everywhere, helping, protecting, striking for justice. In the words of one early version of the ever-changing introduction to the program, "More than any other man, it was the Lone Ranger who finally succeeded in bringing law and order to the West."

One of the masked man's greatest exploits came in 1945 (listener's time) when it came to him to save the secret of "the power of the Sun" from foreign spies against the United States.

A partially destroyed secret paper from a high government official told the Lone Ranger to be on the lookout for a man "wearing a silver bullet." The rest of the message was missing. The masked man and Tonto speculated on what was meant by "wearing" the bullet. Was it stuck in his gunbelt among other more usual lead bullets? Could he have it on a string around his neck? When they finally found the secret agent, they saw he was wearing a silver bullet on a ring on his finger. The ring would become one of the premium offers of the program. The listeners' ring would contain a tiny device that slowed flashes of light supposedly from atoms being destroyed. The flashes could be seen in a dark room when a red plastic finned cap was removed. The fins were added to make the design both a silver bullet and an atomic bomb replica. The Lone Ranger Atomic Bomb Ring, despite obvious anachronisms, became perhaps the most successful of all such premium offers, with over three million distributed. There is hardly a collection of such premiums that doesn't inculde one of these. It is "common" as a collectible, but still more valuable than many others no one is interested in.

There are four episodes in the tale of how the Lone Ranger captured the spies and saved a meteorite to allow American scientist to begin their studies which would eventually liberate the power of the Sun. The "miniseries" (not that the term was in use then) extended just over a week in listening time. Remembering it before recordings were unearthed, the author had thought it lasted many weeks. It made quite an impression on listeners.

There were other sequences of connected stories or outright serial episodes in the history of *The Lone Ranger* program, which was normally a story complete in half an hour. Many of us who actually heard the show on its first run can remember these best.

Besides the lengthy series about the Black Arrow, there was a three-parter about the Son of Silver. Another story "arc" (another term not in use then) took the masked man to the Barbary Coast and had him fighting those who shanghaied innocent men as sailors against their will, and others who smuggled opium.

The most significant sequence of stories came in 1942 when the Lone Ranger found his long lost nephew, Dan Reid (see *The Green Hornet*). As Dave Holland observed, no one knew he had a nephew or that he was long lost until now. But it was a great story and introduced a teenage boy as a regular on the series. Other shows specifically for kids had had juvenile characters for a decade or so (such as Tom Mix's young wards, Jimmy and Jane). But because the show was not exclusively for children, Dan Reid would appear only in about every third show, or about once a week.

Of course, Dan was in every episode of the series that introduced him. The masked man and Tonto found him being raised by a kindly old pioneer, Grandma Frizby. The Lone Ranger was struck by what a fine boy Dan was, as he helped Grandma Frizby and him fight against the criminals who were trying to take over the entire territory. But the struggle was too much for the elderly frontierswoman. As she neared her final sleep, she told of saving Dan from a wagon train attacked by Indians, where his mother had died. She had raised him as her own, but the photo she had saved of Dan's parents revealed to the Ranger that Dan's father was his brother, Dan, Sr., and his sister-in-law, Linda. The masked man promised to raise Dan as his own son. And he answered Grandma Frizby's last request, to see his unmasked face. "It's a good face," she said.

Dan was away at a boarding school much of the time, but he visited his "friends" regularly. Dan could not call the masked man "uncle" openly or otherwise compromise his secret identity as Ranger Reid. No first name was ever given for him on the show to add to the air of mystery. A book, *Radio's Golden Age* (aka *The Big Broadcast*) by Buxton and Owens, supplied the first name of John, copied by the film *The Legend of the Lone Ranger*. Dan Reid referred to his uncle as "Sir," not unheard of in educated families before the turn of the century.

A decade of listener time passed, and Dan aged almost as much as the real time which passed. He grew from a boy of perhaps fourteen to a young man in his twenties. He had a number of romances that did not get very serious, with young women ranging from a charming Indian princess to a double-identity female outlaw. In more than one story he wore the Lone Ranger's mask to mislead bandits. It was suggested that "one day Dan may wear a mask and ride for justice," implying that Dan Reid might become the Lone Ranger when the one we knew was killed in action or could no longer carry on due to the weight of years. That never happened.

Any career of Dan Reid as a masked crimefighter is lost to radio history, but his son Britt Reid became the Green Hornet.

For a twentieth anniversary show near the end of the live broadcast series *The Lone Ranger*, the masked man and Tonto took Dan back to the place where it all began, Bryant's Gap, where Butch Cavendish and his gang ambushed a group of Texas Rangers led by Captain Dan Reid and including his younger brother. We heard a recap of the origin where the captain asked his brother to take care of his wife and son, if the brother survived and the captain did not. Of course, with the help of Tonto, the younger brother did survive to become the Lone Ranger and to capture all the Cavendish gang.

But as fate would have it, Cavendish escaped and followed his nemesis to Bryant's Gap for a final confrontation. Despite a gunshot wound, the Lone Ranger engaged Cavendish in hand-to-hand combat. But weakened, about to be strangled by the other man, the Lone Ranger lifted his feet and sent the murdering outlaw over the edge of the cliff. While the Lone Ranger made it part of his creed not to take human life, this seemed to be an exception. One could say that the masked man was only freeing himself of a death grip, and it was incidental Cavendish went over the cliff edge. But it seems Striker was saying some villainy is too great not to be rewarded with death. In listener time, the world had gone through a great war that included Nazi atrocities nearly beyond human comprehension. Some villains had to be met with more than a flesh wound or the destruction of their weapon.

As Cavendish lay at the foot of the cliff, the Lone Ranger unmasked for a dying person, even as he had earlier for Grandma Frizby. He wanted Cavendish to see the face of the one Ranger who had ended his reign of evil. "Wished I could have died without... knowing," Cavendish gasped out with his final breath.

Later, as Dan knelt beside the grave of his father, the Lone Ranger and Tonto renewed a vow they had made at this same place so long before. Tonto spoke for them both. "As long as me live, as long as you live... me ride with you."

Films and Television

The first Lone Ranger serial was made by Republic in 1938. Because the right reverted to Trendle, who did not preserve the film's negatives, the

Lone Ranger serial and its sequel were lost for many years and have only surfaced in recent years in faulty condition – scratchy, splicey, with printed Spanish subtitles at the bottom of each frame. Two chapters were not found in this print, which allegedly came from a print shown over and over for years by a missionary near the Central American jungles to bring in a crowd of locals whom he could then hit with a sermon. The missing chapters, including the last, were found in France and have French dubbed onto them; a second version has a very recent English dubbing by a well-meaning fan, but alas an amateur.

If a better print could be found for more accurate viewing, *The Lone Ranger* might be recognized as the finest Republic serial of all, even surpassing *The Adventures of Captain Marvel*. As the best from Republic, many would regard it as the best of all serials. William Witney and John English directed both.

In the opening of Chapter One, "Heigh-Yo Silver," a renegade military man, Captain Smith, assumes the identity of a government official, Marcus Jeffries, who he has summarily murdered. The man now known as Jeffries (distinguished-looking character actor Stanley Andrews) summons his henchmen, Kester (John Merton), Felton (Tom London) and another played by Jack Ingram. He tells them to string along with him and wealth will be theirs. With his fake identity of a presidential representative, Jeffries is sure "Pretty soon all of Texas will be seeing things my way."

Atrocities followed – mostly stock footage from old John Wayne films – and a band of Texas Rangers who fought in the Civil War hear of the group as they are riding home. They determine to do something about them. Only the captain (Edmund Cobb) is seen closely enough for identification as a Jeffries henchman leads them into ambush. (Later radio versions would have this captain the brother of the Lone Ranger, but in the film he is not so identified.) The Rangers fight bravely against their hidden attackers, but eventually all are cut down.

Onto this scene of silent death comes the Indian Tonto (Chief Thundercloud). Tonto finds one ranger with a spark of life. Lifting his eyes in a silent prayer, he smiles. (As an actor, Thundercloud always made it a practice to smile a lot, perhaps in an effort to erase the image of the Indian as stone-faced and emotionless, and to make his Indian characters more friendly and human.)

After a long bout with fever, the single survivor awakes, his head wound covered with a bandage that hides his face. Tonto tells him that he is the only one left from the band of ambushed rangers. "The Lone Ranger," the wounded man says. His fingers clutch the Texas Ranger star he wore. "I'll never rest until those deaths are avenged!"

The voice belonged to Billy Bletcher, onetime silent movie comic and character actor in the talking era, who dubbed in all the dialogue for the Lone Ranger. A short man at only five feet two inches, with a large mustache, he sounded a thundering *basso profundo* voice, perhaps even deeper than then current radio Ranger Earl Graser. Strangely, he seemed to anticipate the more booming voice of Brace Beemer, who would not become the Ranger on radio for three more years. Over a decade later, in 1950, radio producer Trendle hired Bletcher to come to Detroit, home base of the radio series, to be on call as Beemer's understudy. No transcription of any performance of Bletcher as the Lone Ranger has ever been uncovered, but Bletcher claimed in interviews a decade later to have appeared "many times." Actors often want to make their parts seem more important than it really is, but Bletcher may have confused full dress rehearsals with shows that actually went out over the air. It is possible that Beemer took things a bit easier in later years and used a stand-in (Bletcher) for the run-throughs, a common practice for stars on many radio shows. Bletcher reportedly returned to Hollywood because he couldn't stand the Detroit winters.

Soon the Lone Ranger is riding his great horse, Silver (origin unexplained here) and causing a great deal of trouble for Jeffries' private army.

A spy believes he has evidence that one of five men is the Lone Ranger. The suspects are Allen King (Lee Powell), Bert Rogers (Herman Brix, later known as Bruce Bennett), Dick Forrest (Lane Chandler), Bob Stuart (Hal Taliaferro), and Jim Clark (George Letz, who later used his middle name for his last name, Montgomery). They have differing occupations and abilities, as will be brought out over the course of the chapterplay. Primarily, each of the five seems to the audience to be a potential Western hero. In earlier years, Chandler and Taliaferro (the latter under the name Wally Wales) had starred in minor Western films, as would Lee Powell later. Brix and George Montgomery would go on to make important "A" films. Each man was a reasonable candidate for the mask. Many in the audience thought the elegant, distinguished Herman Brix would be the "winner," and the script even went that way for a time. But it was eventually decided the unknown Lee Powell would receive the honor. Perhaps it was thought he would be cheaper to hire for a sequel or series. As it happened, Powell made only a few more films before joining the Marines in World War II and dying in service to his country.

Many think the real star of the serial was stuntman Yakima Cannutt, who did the riding and fighting for the masked man in every chapter. He was not the only man to wear the mask in the film. Careful analysis of the frames can detect Powell, Montgomery and others wearing the black visor. Once source claims all the suspects were seen in the mask at one time or another to confuse the audience. But it was Cannutt who more often wore the mask and did all the dangerous work as the Lone Ranger. Since the Lone Ranger has the body of one man, unknown to the moviegoer, and the voice of another, he seems no single one of the suspects but only the Lone Ranger himself.

Stuntman George DeNormand doubled Chief Thundercloud as Tonto. DeNormand heard what paint horse he was to ride, a pinto rather incorrectly referred to as "White Feller" in the film, after an earlier white horse Tonto had ridden on the show, later replaced with Scout who matched the color scheme of the movie horse. The stuntman know what he had to do with this mount, famous for his mean and balky disposition. The day before shooting began, he took the horse out and rode him over the roughest territory around, up and down ravines, through underbrush, riding the surly but unfortunate horse until it was so tired at the end of the day it could hardly stand up. Thereafter, George had no trouble with the horse on the picture. Animal lovers may not approve of George's solution, but the life of the stuntman can be at stake. Many have been killed by unruly horses.

Several stuntmen and wranglers were reportedly killed by the famous Rex, King of the Wild Horses. It is said famous stuntman, Yakima Cannutt, took an even sterner hand with Rex than George DeNormand did with Tonto's horse. Cannutt is said to have beaten the murderous Rex to the point of unconsciousness with a two by four to show him who was the boss. In the real world of movie making, everything can't be as nice as the virtuous conduct in the storyline of a "B" Western.

Jeffries' militia quickly rounds up the five suspects and prepares to execute them. Fortunately, Tonto is still free and sends the men a message in sign. Tonto can clearly be seen telling the captured men to prepare to leap onto their horses and ride like the wind, a reasonable sentiment. (Unfortunately, at another point in the serial, stock footage of this identical message in sign is used to mean something entirely different.)

Tonto drives a captured stagecoach between the prisoners and their would-be firing squad, and the five leap aboard the coach. As the chase goes on, each man transfers to a harnessed team horse and cuts free. A large group of stuntmen worked that day – Cannutt doubling Powell, Joe Yrigoyen probably for Brix, Cliff Lyons for Montgomery, and George DeNormand for Chief Thundercloud, among others. The coach, cut loose from its team, turns over and blocks the path of the pursuers.

At a safe place, the Lone Ranger assumes his true identity (and the voice of Bletcher). He will ride Silver, who emerges from somewhere, and go to the Old Fort to warn the settlers of an attack they have learned of while imprisoned. The identity of the speaking Lone Ranger and the listening "suspects" is hidden.

At the fort, the masked man dispatches a Jeffries spy in an explosion that might have been a cliffhanger in itself. (In fact, one of the earliest releases of the battered Spanish-subtitled print used the explosion as the end of Chapter One.) But the real climax comes as the Lone Ranger stands in the shattered doorway of the fort and single-handedly tries to drive off a troop of Jeffries' raiders with a pair of blazing six-guns. But there are too many. The horsemen seem to ride over the vastly outnumbered Lone Ranger.

But Chapter Two reveals that the Lone Ranger has only fallen back to a safer position and summoned the settlers to turn back the riders. It was a bit of a cheat, not too common in Republic serials.

As the serial continues, the Lone Ranger tries to help another federal representative, Blanchard (George Cleveland) and his daughter Joan (Lynn Roberts), whom the crooked Jeffries has captured, as well as the settlers suffering at the hands of the impostor.

There is plenty of action – gunfights, fistfights, explosions, horse falls, coach wrecks. And one by one the Lone Ranger "suspects" die. Jim Clark, the youngest, is the first to go. But perhaps the moving death is that of Bob Stuart. Jeffries' raiders find out that Stuart's uncle (unbilled silent screen "Tarzan" Elmo Lincoln) is making the silver bullets for the Lone Ranger's six-guns. They murder the strong old blacksmith and steal the silver for the bullets. Bob Stuart vows revenge and traces the killers to a cantina, where he enters a card game with them. Stuart antes up with silver bullets for chips. A gunfight against impossible odds begins. Stuart obviously knows his is going to his death. The other Ranger suspects ride to his aid. One crook sees the disarmed Stuart on the floor and aims a shotgun at him. "This is your finish, Lone Ranger!"

But in the next chapter, the real Lone Ranger says, "No, it isn't!" and shoots the man with the shotgun before he can fire. The other men get the already wounded Stuart back to their cave hideout but he doesn't last long.

The last chapter brings a final confrontation at the secret cave. Gunfire brings down the rock roof on much of Jeffries' henchmen – and on Dick Forrest. Only King and Rogers are left among the suspects. The two ride for help from the federal cavalry. One is shot from his horse; the other transfers to Silver and puts on his mask. The Lone Ranger is truly alone again (at least among the suspect five) and is riding for justice.

The calvary and the settlers round up the last of Jeffries' army, and there is a final hand-to-hand contest between the Lone Ranger and Jeffries. The two men, in a deathlock, roll over the edge of a cliff, even as Sherlock Holmes and Moriarty were supposed to have done.

Later at the cave, Blanchard, his daughter, Tonto and other friends conduct a memorial service for the Lone Ranger who has brought law and order to the state of Texas. But even as they consign him to immortality, the ringing cry of "Hi-Yo Silver!" echoes through the vault. No, the Lone Ranger cannot die, no more than mankind's hope for justice.

The masked man tells the group that his work here is done, and he must ride on. Joan Blanchard asks if he can't show them his face. For the first time, the Lone Ranger does what always before he would seemingly rather

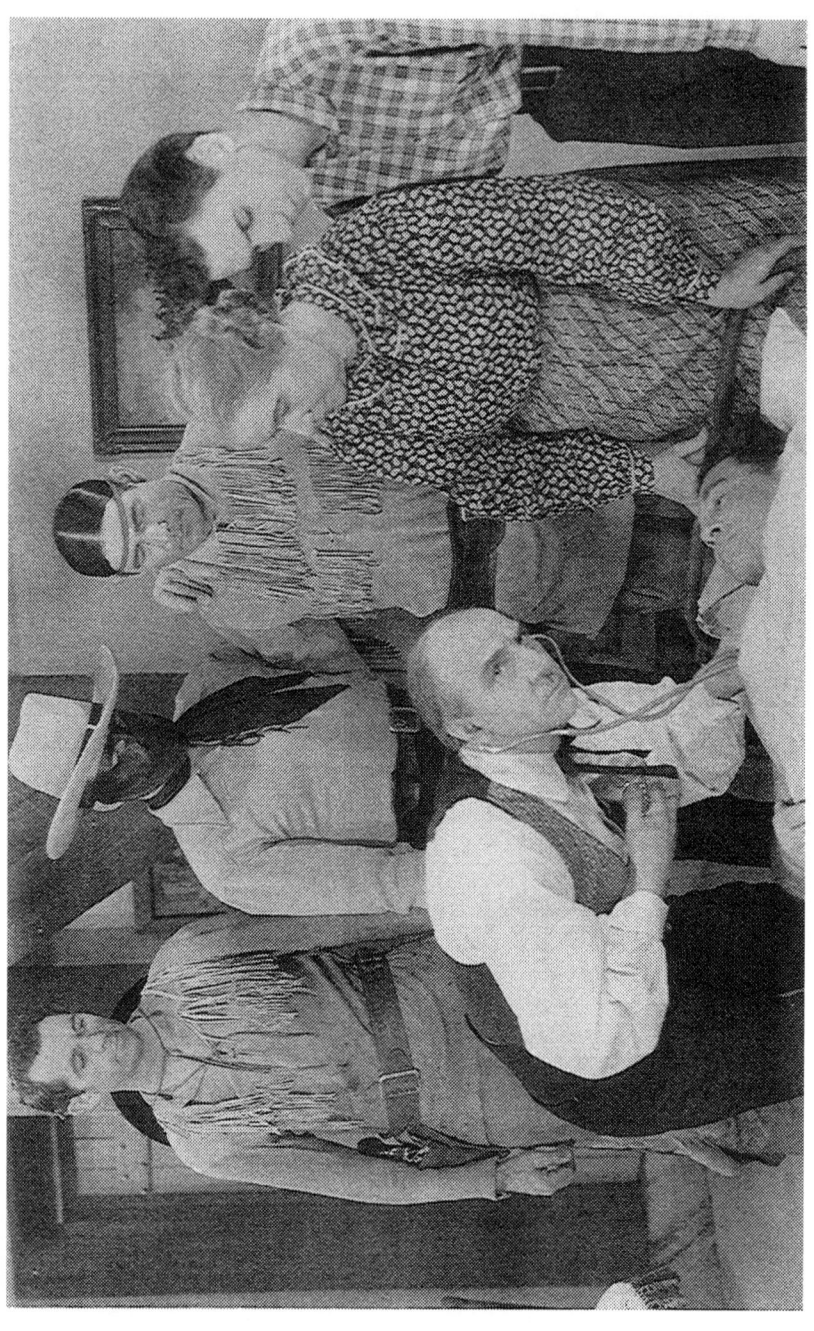

die than do – he takes off his mask. It is the face of Allen King (Powell). Then he and Tonto ride away with a final "Hi-Yo Silver."

Scriptwriter George Plympton, who contributed to countless serials including this one – though his work on *The Lone Ranger* was uncredited – later groused that the Ranger would have been better off with no mask. True, many honest ranchers mistook the masked stranger for a cattle rustler or a stage robber, but unmasked he would have lost his legendary identity as the embodiment of the unknown.

There was a new face under the mask in the sequel serial, *The Lone Ranger Rides Again* (Republic, 1939). In fact, the face was evident much of the time, unmasked. For the second Lone Ranger screen vehicle, Lee Powell was passed over and an established star, Robert Livingston, was introduced in the lead role. The well-known player had been (or would be) the leader of the Three Mesquiteers 20 times, compared to only 8 times for John Wayne, 13 for Tom Tyler, once for Harry Carey and in a classic case of miscasting, once for whiskered comic Al ("Fuzzy") St. John. Livingston had also starred in the first sound Zorro film, *The Bold Caballero* (an early color film) and had played another masked Zorro type, the Eagle, in a previous Republic serial, *The Vigilantes Are Coming*.

The audience knew Livingston and Livingston knew the audience, not that he liked them or Westerns very much. Late in life, he openly stated that he had had the potential to be a great actor, and had been unfairly put in horse operas. He often attended Western nostalgia conventions, but only for the money paid him, he was quick to explain. Months before his death, in a wheelchair, he accepted an award from Gene Autry at a Golden Boot ceremony. Although he had been speaking animatedly with friends before accepting the award, he made no comment whatsoever on stage.

Livingston had a deep, commanding voice that was quite suitable for the Lone Ranger. In fact, he sounded quite similar to then-current Ranger Earl Graser. But following the lead of the first serial, whenever Livingston put on the mask, he spoke with the even more barreling tone of voice artist Bletcher.

Livingston was doubled as the Lone Ranger by Yakima Cannutt, once again behind the mask. Cannutt had doubled Livingston before (as in the previously mentioned *Vigilantes* serial) but he was not as perfect a match for Livingston as he had been for Powell. Moreover, Livingston had certain distinctive mannerisms that Cannutt could not duplicate. Audiences were less demanding and more unsophisticated about such things then, and probably few in the 1939 audience noticed or cared.

Opposite: *The Lone Ranger Rides Again*, the 1939 movie serial, offered Robert Livingston as the Masked Man, Chief Thundercloud as Tonto, second and third from the right, with other featured players.

In this serial, the civilian name of the Lone Ranger is Bill Andrews, not Allen King as the first serial had established. No one seems to know why. Republic Studios and Hollywood in general always seemed to play fast and loose with famous characters from other mediums. One explanation (that probably gives filmmakers too much credit) was that neither Allen King nor Bill Andrews was the true name of the Lone Ranger; each was merely a name he temporarily assumed for the present assignment. The film could not have used the name Reid for the masked man, because that had yet to be established, in the story of finding his nephew Dan Reid in 1942 on radio.

In this second serial, Chief Thundercloud returned as Tonto and Duncan Renaldo was added as a new partner, Juan Vasquez. Westerns were tremendously popular in Mexico and all through Central and South America. Mexican heroes and heroines were often introduced at the side of some Yankee star like Gene Autry. Contrary to some accounts, Mexican villains were very seldom seen. Even if the villain might *seem* a Mexican, there was a line of dialogue to prove otherwise. "Remember—you are Portuguese in Mexico" would dispel the idea in a Buck Jones serial, and in early John Wayne feature, the sheriff says of a badman, "He looks like a Mexican ... he talks like a Mexican ... but remember, he's *not* a Mexican!"

Actually, the heroic Duncan Renaldo was not Mexican, either. He always maintained the Latino image on screen, but he grew up in Europe and was born, he thought, in Spain. Other sources say he was born in Yugoslavia. Renaldo had an almost incredible life and career. He began as a director, helming the first silent film óf Bela Lugosi, then went on to become a leading "Latin lover" on the screen, "second in popularity only to Valentino" in his own estimation. He was the romantic lead in the early talkie *Trader Horn*, with Harry Carey as the Trader and Edwina Booth. There was talk of wild parties on the African location shoot, and Renaldo fell into disfavor. He was literally reduced to sweeping out the studio at Republic when producer Herbert J. Yates discovered him, raising him to at least featured roles in many serials and features. During World War II, Renaldo became an advisor to Franklin D. Roosevelt on Latin American affairs. Political enemies reported he was in the country without a legal passport and he served a year in prison—shortened only one day by a presidential pardon (not too much favoritism was to be shown). But with his civil rights restored, Renaldo was asked by the government to replace Gilbert Roland as the Cisco Kid in a series of pictures. Roland portrayed Cisco as a murdering, womanizing dog, causing riots in South America. It was Renaldo who created the popular if whitewashed version of Cisco as a true Robin Hood friend of the people, protector of women. It was this portrayal that he brought to television in the fifties with great success.

Renaldo's character was one more of a long line of co-heroes or people helped by the Lone Ranger in all his various incarnations. The ending suggested Juan Vasquez might be more than a person in trouble rescued by the masked man, that he was to become a permanent sidekick along with Tonto, but Republic offered no more sequels and this never happened.

The second serial, offered the usual well-executed fights and chases, Republic style, but without the device of the five Lone Ranger suspects and with an unmasked Lone Ranger clearly in sight much of the time. The second serial lacked the suspense and special appeal of the first. The direction by William Witney and John English was as good as in the first, and Jinx Falken (sometimes styled Falkenberg) was a lovely leading lady, but Ralph Dunn was an unimpressive lead heavy, exercising typical villainy in leading the cattlemen to take over the homesteaders' property. He was no match for the Lone Ranger. It was almost no contest.

Barry Shipman, Franklyn Adreon and Ronald Davidson worked on the screenplays of both serials. Lois Eby and George Worthington Yates contributed to the first and were replaced by Sol Shor on the second. Perhaps the script needed the woman's touch of Ms. Eby or the input of Mr. Yates, who did go on to write some major "A" films. Probably most lacking was the first serial's uncredited input of the great Fran Striker, who deserves to be recognized as a significant American author.

Republic issued an edited feature version of the first serial under the title *Hi-Yo Silver*, with a new introduction by character actor Raymond Hatton as an old-timer telling the story to his grandson. This was the last film appearance of the Lone Ranger for a decade.

In 1949, George Trendle decided to bring his successful radio series to the new medium of television. This time he vowed to have complete control. He went to Hollywood and auditioned several movie actors to play the part, including Clayton Moore, who had just played another famous masked character in the Republic serial *Ghost of Zorro*. Trendle was pretty sure Moore would do. He asked, "Do you think you could play the Lone Ranger, Mr. Moore?" To this, Moore frequently recounts saying, "Mr. Trendle, I *am* the Lone Ranger!"

And Clayton Moore did become the Lone Ranger to several generations. He has been identified with the character for over forty years. The radio generation can still remember other voices of the famous masked rider of the plains, and perhaps there is a faint buzz in Moore's ears from the reruns of the radio series, still on the air, starring Brace Beemer and extending Beemer's identification with the role to some sixty years. When the Gene Autry Western Heritage Museum offered a tribute to the Lone Ranger in 1991, the gunbelts, saddles and photos of Brace Beemer were given equal billing to those of Moore.

In the pilot episodes of the new television series, and for several episodes following, Moore did an imitation of the inflections of Brace Beemer in his dialogue. Actors always want to establish their own style, so one might assume that he was directed by Trendle or one of his staff to "do" Beemer. Beemer actually wanted to do the part of the Lone Ranger himself on television as well as radio, but it did not happen. For one thing, he was needed in Detroit to do the radio show for another five years after the television version started.

The first television episode was faithful to the 1942 radio "origin" story and bore some similarity to the version used in the 1938 serial. A band of Texas Rangers is led into ambush by a treacherous guide, and one man survives to be found by Tonto and nursed back to health. That last survivor, that lone ranger, takes a vow to bring the killers of his comrades to justice.

Chief Thundercloud was still alive when the series began, looking much as he had looked a decade earlier. (He appeared in some Gene Autry TV episodes made during the same period.) But a new Tonto was sought and found in handsome, dignified Jay Silverheels. There couldn't have been a better choice. Silverheels was stuck with the broken English from the radio show (necessary to identify Tonto as being an Indian on a medium whose audience could not see him) and did not like it. Some episodes had him speaking to Indians in Indian dialect translated for the viewer, and he was allowed to be much more eloquent. Silverheels was not always kind in recalling his role of Tonto, saying in one interview that Tonto was little more than an idiot, but Moore and Silverheels, the actors, always remained friends. It was just their horses, Silver and Scout, who did not like each other, according to Moore, and would begin biting at each other if a scene required them to stand side by side for long.

It took three episodes for the new masked man to find his great horse Silver and to bring to justice the instigator of the ambush, Butch Cavendish, played by Glenn Strange. These first three episodes, "Enter the Lone Ranger," "The Lone Ranger Fights On" and "The Lone Ranger's Triumph" were all filmed on location and looked like some of the better "B" movies to come out of Hollywood. The on-location look continued through later episodes like "Legion of Old Timers," in which the Masked Man and Tonto secretly help some aged cowboys defeat a band of crooks and regain their jobs, and "Pete and Pedro," about two feuding pals who call armistice long enough to help a girl save her ranch.

By the time of the tenth episode, "High Heels" (about a vain little man who wears high heels to appear taller and is stopped by the Lone Ranger from entering a deadly duel to prove himself), something had happened to the production values on the series. There were almost no exteriors now, and everything was photographed on a sound stage, even supposedly exterior shots of rocks and trees. A very few short scenes of the Lone Ranger and Tonto riding separately and together were filmed and inserted. There were a few other standard action scenes such as the Lone Ranger bulldogging a man in a black vest off his horse. This shot was used as the climax of several episodes. Often the villain would take off the coat he had worn throughout the episode and put on a dark vest. The viewers with the best memory then knew what shot was coming up.

Still, even on the crowded sound stage, Clayton Moore, Jay Silverheels and their opponents performed some exciting fights, vigorous but short. Violence was to be downplayed by Trendle's order.

While Harry H. Poppe was given credit for directing most of the early episodes, old-time action film director Breesy Eason was on hand and gave invaluable consultation about staging the series.

The scripts were under the supervision of story editor Fran Striker and sometimes were written by him, so the series stayed close to the spirit of the original radio show. But no longer were there vast armies of Indians being attacked by equally large troops of cavalry, or huge cattle drives invaded by hordes of rustlers. Usually there was one crook with one sidekick who was causing trouble for one man, or maybe one married couple, and one Lone Ranger and one Tonto to put everything right. Add a very few townspeople and perhaps one perplexed local lawman, and that was the cast.

For a time there was a second Lone Ranger. For the 1952-53 season, John Hart replaced Clayton Moore, after having played a bad guy with graying hair in earlier episodes. There was a contract dispute—Moore wanted more money, and from George W. Trendle it was not a likely prospect. Hart was handsome and easy to like, but he seemed very young. He told the author he interpreted the part as being like a military officer, stressing duty, honor, loyalty, discipline.

Trendle wanted this replacement Ranger to be made up to look exactly like a painting the producer had made. Each day of shooting, Hart would sit in the chair and have makeup elaborately applied. He used the time, he said, to study his script. Afterwards, he would wash his face down to his natural tan and go on the set.

Hart may have been somewhat better than Moore in assuming the disguises of other characters within the story. Moore usually did a comic exaggeration of his old prospector or a Mexican bandit. Hart more seriously acted the parts of those disguises. In one story, as the Lone Ranger is in the makeup of an older man, Hart is asked his name. He says a memorable line: "Folks sometimes call me Mr. Justice."

After one season, Moore returned. The John Hart episodes were not rerun for years to solidify the image of Clayton Moore as the Lone Ranger, but in more recent times, those Hart programs have been put back in the package distributed to television stations. Hart has even done more recent guest appearances as the Lone Ranger, including one on *Happy Days*. Both Hart and Moore are warmly accepted by the new copyright owners for a big 60th anniversary celebration.

After 182 black and white episodes there came a change to full color for 39 episodes. There was more than an addition of color, though. Trendle now had sold all rights to film producer Jack Wrather. While Wrather did not ruin the show he did change it. His own writers took over from Striker, and the show had less of the feel of the radio show. The new writers misunderstood the Lone Ranger's character at times and had him seem like a Sunday school teacher. The real masked man was just, but he was firm. At times in the radio series, the Lone Ranger would ominously tell even sympathetic characters to come along with him "if you want to save yourself a lot of discomfort." He would not kill a man, but he told many a hard case, "Drop that gun or my bullet will break your arm." In one of the Wrather episodes, in beautiful color, the Lone Ranger declines to escape from jail to save his own life when given a clear opportunity because jail breaking is against the law. Of course, the Lone Ranger and Tonto had escaped jail hundreds of times before on radio and television. He was an armed vigilante trying to bring law and order out of the chaos of the West, not a prissy teacher giving a civics lesson to a small boy.

There were two feature length movies from Wrather that were essentially expanded television episodes with Moore and Silverheels: *The Lone Ranger* and *The Lone Ranger and the Lost City of Gold*. They were both well made pictures, and the first one sometimes shows up on lists of the best Western movies. This film brought back all those missing people from the radio series—large groups of Indians, settlers and cavalry. The second one was lower budgeted but gave the Lone Ranger a chance to romance a lady—but she was a crook, and he was only in one of his many disguises as a goateed Southern gentleman. The first film allowed Moore to be his own comic relief, as a bowlegged old prospector.

Then in 1981 came *The Legend of the Lone Ranger*. Many fans were offended by the copyright owners' treatment of Clayton Moore, who was told he could not appear in his mask and devalue the new film with his aging image. To many, Moore *was* the Lone Ranger. His own idea, that he find a new younger man to take over in the story and pass the mask to him, was not a bad one. Or he could have appeared in cameo at the opening and set the scene for a time when he was younger and bring in the younger actor as himself at an earlier age. But it is just as well Moore had nothing to do with this terrible film. It should have been aimed at the same audience as a Disney film or *Star Wars*, but its constant profanity and excessive violence made it unsuitable for that audience. The idealistic Lone Ranger would hardly appeal to those seeking Clint Eastwood or Serge Leone. The film could satisfy no one.

Michael Horse as Tonto was fine, a fit successor to Chief Thundercloud and Jay Silverheels, but Klinton Spillsbury as the Lone Ranger was unacceptable. His ineffectual voice was dubbed by Jim Keach. Spillsbury was credible in a jacket as lawyer John Reid, but when he put on the tight-fitting shirt of the Lone Ranger (with a modern styled rodeo hat and machine-made mask) he looked too limp and wasp-waisted to get the job done.

When Buffalo Bill and General Custer were brought on, with less substance than wax dummies, it was too much. Two animated television series of *The Lone Ranger* were better than *Legend*, even with the introduction of science fiction elements like giant talking frogs. (The vocalizations, first by Michael Rye and then by William Conrad as the masked man, were fine.)

At one *Legend* showing, when at the end of the movie President Grant (Jason Robards) wonders "Who was that masked man?" one theater-goer yelled out, "Well, it sure as hell wasn't the Lone Ranger!"

Comics

The comic strip adventures of *The Lone Ranger* first in the syndicated King Features strip in newspapers and then in its reprints in giveaway and newsstands comic books, were always well done, but never quite at the forefront of the best comics ever created.

The writing was always good and perfectly in character with the radio series since the early scripts were by Fran Striker, who usually adapted earlier radio plays. The writers who followed him in later years faithfully mimicked his style.

The art was usually interesting, but it didn't have the freedom it might have had if the artist were creating the scenes instead of depicting what was given him, and often scenes were too dependent on dialogue (not surprisingly, considering the comics were based on radio plays).

But children, the author included, loved the Lone Ranger comics. I still remember the time when I was six or seven, home from school with a miserable cold, when my mother came in and asked how I would like to see some new Sunday comics of the Lone Ranger. How could that be? I asked. This was only Wednesday, and so far as I knew there was no Sunday comic strip of the Lone Ranger. But she surprised me. The St. Louis *Post-Dispatch* had put out a special four-page supplement introducing two new Sunday features with four installments, alternating top and bottom. (The first Sunday *Lone Ranger* strip had appeared earlier, on Sept. 11, 1938.) The second new strip was about a dog (possibly *Napoleon*), but the attraction was the handsome, red-shirted masked man. I read the section over and over, forgetting about my cold, and kept these special comics for months, perhaps years, before they got lost.

The strip had a charm and vigor, as drawn by Ed Kressy, but also a sort of crudeness and inappropriate comedic look – too "bigfoot" cartoonish, as artists say.

The strip was written by the artist's wife, Maryland Kressy, from Striker radio scripts supplied by WXZY. Mrs. Kressy recalled to Dave Holland how Trendle and company made an avalanche of requests for changes in his art: draw the masked man taller, draw Silver more supple, draw Tonto wiser-looking. Despite the hard work Kressy put into his atmospheric effort, probably what was wanted was a better artist. Jon Blummer, who created *Hop Harrigan* for DC comic magazines, tried out but made the error of imitating Kressy's style and character models.

A new look came into the strip on Sunday, March 12, 1939, when Charles Flanders took over the art after leaving *Secret Agent X-9*, a strip originated by writer Dashiel Hammett and artist Alex Raymond, a stunning combination of talents who nevertheless did not produce a masterpiece in *X-9*. Flanders followed them creditably, and excelled on *The Lone Ranger*, now fully scripted by Striker.

In the masked man's world as depicted by Flanders, the characters looked more serious, more realistic, more credibly violent. The Lone Ranger himself looked older, slightly heavier and coincidentally rather like Brace Beemer, who would assume the role on radio in a few years. At first, Flanders continued Kressy's style of putting in pupils in the eye-holes of the mask, at least in closeups, but this gave the Ranger a startled or even fearful expression. Soon it was decided just to leave the eye-holes blank. Little Orphan Annie had gotten along without pupils in her eyes for a long time.

On March 13, 1939, Flanders began his first daily serial about crooks attempting to ruin an oil well driller for their own purposes. The artist got more deeply into his subject even in the few weeks the story took, so that by the end of the story, as the masked man faces a crook, one can practically hear that booming voice.

Most of the story is told in panels of the Lone Ranger facing a crook or talking with Tonto, with a heavy emphasis on dialogue exchanges from the radio scripts. The best panel in Flander's first effort is an evocative rendering of a desert supply wagon being pulled by a team of mules. The *Lone Ranger* strip had found its artist, and he stayed with it for the next thirty-three years.

Toward the last, Flanders' hand became less sure and, perhaps by an unconscious effort of the artist to reflect himself in his character (as often happens with cartoonists), the masked man began to look fat, his face round and shapeless. There came a warning from the front office, King Features or the WXYZ organization, one supposes, and the masked man's jaw line became firmer and squarer, and the drawings had more detail. The strip hung on until December 1971.

Dell publications was bringing out a series of comic magazines of *The Lone Ranger*, the first 37 issues being reprints of the Flanders strip. But George Trendle did not like the way they hacked and cut the strip to fit the magazine format, and he decreed new stories beginning in No. 38. Artist Tom Gill and writer Paul S. Newman took over and did a creditable job. (These two also were involved with the newspaper strip at various times.) The stories looked and read clean and quick, but somehow lacked the substance of the older material. Comic strips may not be considered "deep" subjects, but everything has a certain depth, and the comic books had less depth than the old strips. The change from the red shirt and dark pants of old to the television image of the masked man in a powder blue uniform did not appeal to the old fans, but the public came to accept the "uniform" look, a far cry from the earliest radio-inspired depictions of the Lone Ranger in a checked shirt and dark vest.

A final try at a newspaper strip for the masked rider of the plains was attempted in 1981, thanks to a movie about which enough has been said. Writer Cary Bates and artist Russ Heath produced an admirable creation, vastly superior to its film inspiration, but the market for continued adventure strips in newspapers was slipping to hover at zero. Fewer than sixty papers carried the new version. The masked man rode into the sunset of newspaper adventure strips on April 1, 1984.

Thanks to collectors, the comics of the Lone Ranger have never really disappeared. Strip collectors are fairly rare, but many save the comic books from Dell and other sources.

The very first Lone Ranger comic book was a 1938 giveaway from an ice cream company (or a group of them, perhaps with different names in different areas of the country—no company name is evident). It featured artwork that has been credited by some to Henry Vallely. If it is Vallely, he is certainly not at his very best in this tale retold from a 1935 exploit (with the Lone Ranger and Tonto riding double on Silver, before the Indian was given his own mount).

Vallely was also associated with the Lone Ranger by illustrating the Big Little Books of alternating text and picture pages from the thirties. Those little volumes presented some of his best art, and he was a very fine "commercial" artist. His line was so light and clean and airy, it was not perfectly suited to the dusty, sweaty world of the Old West, although his Lone Ranger illustrations are outstanding. If Vallely had ever been given a newspaper strip, his name would be as recognized as that of Alex Raymond or Hal Foster.

To a kind of throw-away kids' book series, often scratched out by hacks whose drawings one could not even understand, Vallely brought real art. Why a man of his transcendent ability choose to work in these circles, one can but wonder.

Vallely's work can be seen in *The Lone Ranger Follows Through, The Lone Ranger on the Barbary Coast* and *The Lone Ranger and the Secret Weapon*. Various illustrators worked on other Big Little Books titles such as *The Lone Ranger and his Horse, Silver,* . . . *and the Vanishing Herd,* . . . *and the Secret Killer,* . . . *and the Menace of Murder Valley,* . . . *and the Red Renegades* all the way through to . . . *Outwits Crazy Cougar,* a 1968 revival of the format.

Books

There were full-size novels, too, from Grosset and Dunlap. The first one, *The Lone Ranger*, was written by reliable professional scribe Gaylord DuBois. His byline appeared on the first edition, but Trendle decreed that "Fran Striker" would replace his name for reasons of conformity. Striker did write all the rest of the total eighteen, based on his radio scripts, including *The Lone Ranger and the Mystery Ranch,* . . . *Rides Again* and . . . *Rides North.* The last is the story of the Lone Ranger's finding his lost nephew, Dan Reid.

The incredibly prolific Striker also managed to turn out eight novels for a pulp paper magazine of *The Lone Ranger* in 1937, juggling his material in dazzling fashion, reusing radio scripts and prefiguring the comic strips and hardcover novels that would follow.

The story of the comics and all the juvenile books is a part of the whole story of the Lone Ranger – the story of a man with money, George W. Trendle, and a man with talent, Fran Striker.

Striker's talent was to look into the hearts of children and grownups alike and to know what their ideals were – to know that if they were only strong and brave enough, they would love nothing better than to spend their lives like the Lone Ranger and Tonto in helping their fellow man.

Premiums

The premiums offered on the radio show were as follows, listed alphabetically with sponsor (when known), date and approximate value in 1992 (assuming average condition).

Airbase (Kix, 1943; $85), Airbase Cereal Box, Complete (Kix, 1943; $100), Album, Victory Battles of 1942-45 (1945; $15), Badge, Chief Scout (1934; $75), Badge, Deputy, Secret Compartment (1949; $25), Badge, Miami Maid Safety Club (1937; $30), Badge, Safety Scout Membership (Silvercup Bread, 1937; $15), Bandana (1949; $30), Belt, Safety, Glo-In-Dark (1941; $40), Belt, Texas Cattleman's Lone Ranger Scenes, Leather (1941; $45), Belt, Tonto, Beaded Leather (1952; $25), Billfold (1942; $50), Blackout Kit (1942; $45), Blotter (1938; $10), Book, Christmas (May Co; $25), Book, Coloring (Merita, 1951; $15), Book, *Lone Ranger Ranch Fun* (1951; $15), Book, *Lone Ranger*

The Lone Ranger

and Tonto Health and Safety (Merita, 1955; $25), Booklet, "How Lone Ranger Captured Silver," 7 Ch (1934; $25), Booklet, "Legend" (Good Food Guys, (1969; $15), Boxes, Cereal, Complete (Wheaties, 1951; $125 ea.), Boxes, Cereal, Back Only (Wheaties, 1951; $35 ea.), Branding Iron Initial Stamper, Unmarked (1956; $20), Bullet, Silver, w/Compass and Secret Compartment (1947; $45), Bullet, Silver, 45-Caliber Secret Compartment (1941; $30), Bullet, Solid Silver (1938; $15), Certificate, Safety Club (1938; $10), Charter, Deputy Club (1951; $25), Coin, 17th Anniversary, Lucky Piece (1949; $15), Coloring Contest Drawing, From Pkg. Back, Ea. (1951; $15), Combat Insignia Album and Stamps (1942; $30), Commission, Chief Scout (1934; $15), Cut-Outs, Lone Ranger (Merita, 1951; $65), Decoder, Paper (Weber's Bread, 1943; $65), Figures, Movie Ranch Wild West Town, Plastic (1951; $50), Flashlight Gun w/Secret Compartment Handle (1949; $75), Flyer, Introduction (Kix, 1941; $10), Folder, Deputy Secret (1949; $25), Frontier Town, Uncut, Four Sections (Cheerios, 1947; $150 ea.), Frontier Town Complete Cereal Boxes (Cheerios, 1947; $250 ea.), Frontier Town Package Backs (Cheerios, 1947; $35 ea.), Gun (Victory Corp., 1942; $30), Hike-O-Meter (Wheaties, 1951; $15), Indian Head Dress and Bead Set, Tonto (1964; $25), Kit, Jr. Deputy: Card, Tin Badge, Plastic Mask (1951; $30), Kit, Movie Membership (1951; $15), Kit, Safety Club, w/Letter, Photo and Card (Merita, 1950; $70), Letters, Safety Club (Various, 1938; $10 ea.), Manual (Victory Corp., 1942; $45), Manual, Secret Writing (1938; $25), Map, Hunt (1938; $75), Map, Old West (1951; $25), Mask (Merita, 1934; $15), Mask (1943; $35), Masks (2), Lone Ranger, Tonto (Wheaties, 1951; $25), Masks (6), Other than Lone Ranger or Tonto (Wheaties, 1951; $20), Membership Badge, Safety Club, Star (Bond Bread, 1938; $30), Membership Badge, Safety Club, Star (Butter-Nut Bread, 1938; $30), Membership Badge, Safety Club, Star (QBC Bread, 1938; $30), Membership Badge, Safety Club, Star (Eddy's 1938; $30), Membership Card, War Bonds (1943; $15), Michigan Network Photo (1933; $25), Neckerchief, Shirt and Mask (1949; $55), News, Safety Club, Vol. 1, No. 1 (8/39) (1938; $20), News, Safety Club, Vol. 1, Nos. 2–6 (1939; $15 ea.), Pedometer, Aluminum Rim (1947; $20), Photo (Kix, 1941; $15), Photo (Sepia) 1938; $15), Photo, Black and White (Silvercup, 1938; $20), Photo, Campfire (1938; $20), Photo, Four-Color (1938; $15), Photo, Lone Ranger (1934; $10), Photo, Silvercup Color (1938; $15), Photo, Tonto (1934; $10), Photo, WGN (Station) (Horlick, 1938; $20), Pin, Military, Unmarked (1942; $85), Pinback, Merita Safety Club (Merita, 1934; $20), Pinback, Safety Club (1934; $20), Pinback, War Bonds (1943; $15), Pistol and Targets (1951, $35), Portfolio, National Defenders Secret (1941; $60), Postcard (Bond Bread, 1938; $15), Postcard, Chief Scout, First Degree (1934; $10), Postcard, Chief Scout, Fourth Degree (1934; $25), Postcard, Chief Scout, Second Degree (1934; $15), Postcard, Chief Scout, Third Degree (1934; $20), Postcard, Contest, Color, Giveaway Comics (1954; ?), Poster (1938; $15), Poster, Lone Ranger, Life Size (1951, $150), Poster, Tonto, Life Size (1951, $150), Poster, Win Silver's Colt (1941; $200), Recipes, Ho Ling's (1938, $25), Revolver, Rapid Fire (1951; $25), Ring, Atom Bomb (1947; $50), Ring, Filmstrip Saddle, w/16mm Lone Ranger Scenes (1951; $100), Ring, Flashlight (1947; $50), Ring, Look-Around, National Defenders (1941; $55), Ring, Movie Film, w/8mm Marine Corps Film (1949; $60), Ring, Movie Film, w/o Film (1949; $30), Ring, Photo (1941; $500), Ring, Secret Compartment, 4 Versions (1942; $325), Ring, Six Shooter (1947; $50), Ring, Weather (1943; $45), Safety Club Pledge Letter (1934; $12), Shirt, Polo, w/Hi-Yo Silver Design (1941; $40), Siren, Warning,

National Defenders (1941; $100), Stationery Sets (8 Different), Test Premiums (Victory Corp., 1942; $100), "Story of His Mask and How He Met Tonto" (1951; $10), "Story of Silver" (1951; $10), Story, "How to be a Lone Ranger" (Merita, 1951; $25), Tab (Good Food Guys, 1969; $20), Tab (Victory Corp., 1942; $30), Tatoo Decals (1944; $25), Token, Good Luck (used to expose images in glow-in-dark surfaces) (1938; $10).

The Shadow

Began as an unnamed character of *Street and Smith's Detective Story Hour*, CBS, July 31, 1930; was named in first season. Appeared on *Street & Smith's Love Story Hour, Blue Coal Radio Revue*. First broadcast under series title, *The Shadow*, January 1932. Ran twice weekly on CBS, Oct. 1933-spring 1935, with all appearances as host-narrator of half-hour drama occurring between these dates. Began as central character of half-hour mystery-adventure story on Mutual in the double identity of Lamont Cranston and the Shadow, Sept. 26, 1937, to Dec. 21, 1954. Revived as syndicated rerun feature, 1963, intermittently to present.

Directors: Clark Andrews, Bourne Ruthrauff, Jerry Devine, others **Writers:** Harry Engman Charlot (1930), Edward Hale Beirstadt (1937), Alfred Bester, Max Erhlich, Jerry Devine, others **Consultant:** Walter Gibson **Music:** Rosa Rio, organist, others **The Shadow:** James LaCurto (1930), Frank Readick (1931-35), (Others, including Robert Hardy Andrews reported, but documentation not established) **The Shadow/Lamont Cranston:** Orson Welles (1937-38), Bill Johnstone (1938-44), Bret Morrison (1943-spring 1944, fall 1945-54), John Archer (fall 1944-spring 1945), Steve Courtley (fall, 1945, six episodes) **Margo Lane:** Agnes Moorehead (1937-38), Margot Stevenson (1937 summer series, second to play part though she inspired the role), Marjorie Anderson (began 1938), Judith Allen (1944-45), Laura Mae Carpenter (1945), Lesley Woods (1945), Grace Mathews (1946-49), Gertrude Warner (1949-1954), others as substitutes **Police Commissioner Weston:** Ray Collins, Santos Ortega, Dwight Weist, others **Moe "Shrevie" Shrevnitz:** Alan Reed, James LaCurto (the original Shadow), others **Others:** Everett Sloan, Richard Widmark, Alice Frost, Arthur Vinton, Kenny Delmar, Carl Frank.

The Shadow is one of the great figures of fiction, and one of the most enduring characters of the once popular world of radio drama. The Shadow is still a part of the language, and a new series of comic magazines of his adventures has appeared. There is talk of a movie about the eerie master of men's minds. His radio adventures are hardly buried, having been rerun in major markets for nearly three decades (they were withdrawn from radio play for a few years but are at this writing once again available). Recordings of the radio shows are available in many record stores.

Cloaked by night itself, the slouch-hatted figure distilled into one identity a century of phantom figures, both heroes and villains, from popular melodrama. Many of these characters who hid in the dark and appeared to terrorize both the guilty and the innocent were even named the Shadow. English novelist Charles Dickens was one of the earliest to use the name of the Shadow in the mid-nineteenth century. He speculated upon a "a certain shadow which may go into any place... and be supposed to be cognizant of everything... I want to get up a general notion of 'What will the shadow say about this, I wonder?... Is the Shadow here?'" He was in countless dime novels as a figure of mystery, and in a dozen turn-of-the-century plays. In the early part of the twentieth century, Mary Roberts Rhinehart presented a character of mystery who worked his ways in the dark, one who eventually appeared in novel, stage plays and several film versions. The character was called the Bat, but bore similarities to the Shadow. (Cartoonist Bob Kane has given credit for his creation of *Batman* to inspiration from both the Bat and the pulp magazine of the Shadow.)

"If ever a mystery character created himself in his own image, that character was the Shadow," observed Walter Gibson, who wrote the Shadow novels under the name Maxwell Grant. "To say that the Shadow sprang spontaneously into being would be putting it not only mildly, but exactly."

Even after the appearance of the radio series and novels of *The Shadow*, that mysterious name was given to other characters in other examples of popular entertainment. A "B" Western of the '30s *Riders of Durango Valley*, featured a masked character known as the Shadow. (Since both the chief heavy and cowboy star Bob Steele wore the costume at various times for various purposes, the Shadow might be considered both the hero and the villain of the piece.) The Shadow first appeared on the air as only the narrator/host of anthology stories about other people. His position was similar to that of Rod Serling on *Twilight Zone* or Nancy, the old witch of *Witch's Tale* or the later Raymond, the host of *Inner Sanctum*.

The year was 1930 and the program was *Street & Smith's Detective Story Hour*. On Thursday, July 30, the Shadow first sent his mocking laugh out over the airwaves. At this time, the figure was so mysterious he did not even have a name. The author of the radio scripts, Harry Engman Charlot, gave him the name of the Shadow. Some five years later, Sept. 28, 1935, Charlot was found dead at thirty-five in a cheap hotel on the Bowery—poisoned. Not even the Shadow seemed to get to the bottom of that mystery.

The radio program was meant to promote the sales of the *Detective Story Magazine*, but news dealers complained that customers kept coming to them asking for the magazine about the Shadow, or "that Shadow magazine." Since there was no such publication, Harry Ralston, general manager of

Street & Smith, decided to create one. He contacted prolific magic and mystery writer Walter Gibson to write the first of the Shadow's adventures in print. Many more followed.

There has been a lot of confusion as to the exact details of the Shadow's long radio career, and perhaps all the fine points are not nailed down even at this point. One chance for error came from the title of the first program on which he appeared. The *The Detective Story Hour* was actually only thirty minutes long; the term "hour" was ubiquitous and euphemistic in early radio. A children's "story hour" on a local station might only be fifteen minutes long. There are no known surviving recordings of the Shadow from his "narrator only" period.

A recording of the first broadcast featuring the Shadow as a full-fledged central character on his own show does exist. Walter Gibson found the script to the first episode, or at least a number of pages for the script by Edward Hale Bierstadt, another prolific author who had written the *Warden Lawes of Sing Sing* radio series, in publishing company files. Gibson had visited Bierstadt at his Maine cottage and been technical advisor on this script and a number of later ones, to set the radio series on the right path. The author of the novels filled in the missing scenes from the first script from his phenomenal memory for publication. However, the program's recording proved a number of changes had been made even from the script pages that survived. The master crimefighter's right-hand man from the novels, Harry Vincent, was present in the script. But according to authority Anthony Tollin, producer Clark Andrews thought a female interest would work better, so he interjected a "friend and companion" for the Shadow. The lovely Margo Lane was based on Andrews' own girlfriend, actress Margot Stevenson.

The two most significant changes in the radio series from the novels of the Shadow were the introduction of the feminine interest, Margo, and the character's ability to employ literal invisibility, not merely being very difficult to see as he glided about the shadows in his black cape.

The radio show, particularly in its later years, did not live up to the great potential in the unforgettable character of the Shadow. Mostly written by writers who churned out scripts about gangsters and hoodlums for such mundane series as *Big Town* and *Mr. District Attorney*, the radio series of *The Shadow* often had the Master of Darkness up against commonplace criminals, such as the smugglers of illegal aliens in "Death Rides High" (Frank Kane, author, May 11, 1947).

Yet somehow, the potential of the Shadow could not be ignored and many of the episodes dealt with dark, seemingly supernatural events and the Shadow's own wonderful powers.

During Orson Welles' original tenure, most of the stories dealt with the fantastic. (The authors of most of these episodes are unknown.) The Shadow debuted with "The Death House Rescue" (Edward Hale Bierstadt, author, Sept. 26, 1937), a fairly mundane tale of a last-minute reprieve for a wrongly convicted man, but by "The Temple Bells of Neban" (Oct. 24, 1937) the Shadow was explaining the Far Eastern origin of his near-supernatural hypnotic powers and battling a woman who shared many of his abilities.

For a summer season of recorded shows played at varying times and dates in 1938, Welles as the master of men's minds displayed other telephatic talents in "Power of the Mind" and in a tale of a European man setting himself up as lord of an island of the South Seas, "The White God." Other titles evoke their subject matter: "The Hypnotized Audience," "Death from the Deep," "Murders in Wax," "Tenor with the Broken Voice" and "Caverns of Death."

When a less famous actor, Bill Johnstone, took over the starring roll in the fall of 1938, the style and quality of the scripts did not change. "Night Without End" (Oct. 16, 1938) concerned the efforts of a scientist to block out the sun and produce perpetual night. Another mad scheme involved causing the death of anyone who made an E flat sound in the busy city, an early anti–noise pollution campaign. Newsboys eagerly whispered the headlines about "Murder in E Flat" (Nov. 4, 1938).

Horror continued to make its presence felt in "The Night Marauders" (Peter Wright, Oct. 1, 1939) concerning a murdering gorilla and its mad keeper, and in the story of a man who seemingly returns after being executed for murder to kill again in "The Return of Carnation Charlie" (George Lowther, Feb. 4, 1940), a story repeated on the series with changes and variations over the years.

Margo Lane was at the side of Lamont Cranston through all of these adventures, a friend and companion to the wealthy young man about town with a secret side. For all her fidelity, she was usually awarded only some peril from which the Shadow would rescue her. One of the best of these "Margo menaced" tales was "Death Prowls at Night" (Jerry Devine, March 23, 1941) in which Margo is won away from Lamont by a suave doctor who also happens to be a werewolf and wishes to initiate Margo into the joys of running through the night as a four-legged beast. In the end, the doctor's willpower is no match for that of the Shadow, of course.

A number of actors played the Shadow over the years. The original in the role (as a full-fledged central character) was Orson Welles. Another was Bret Morrison. His voice was beautiful, but Morrison was the opposite of the Shadow in appearance. Not tall and lean and black-haired, Morrison was of only average height, rather plump and bald.

The many re-runs of Morrison's long run in *The Shadow* radio show earned him only a one-time check for $100.

One of the actors who replaced Bret Morrison for part of a season of *The Shadow* was John Archer. Also a well-known movie actor, Archer was

Bret Morrison in costume as his famous character, the Shadow, circa 1945.

visually more like Lamont Cranston than Morrison, and his vocal performance was excellent too. He projected a sincerity and very masculine kindness that many stars of the forties had.

The original *Shadow* radio series had also been performed before a live audience in the thirties and forties. "When I became the Shadow," Morrison said, "I would slip behind a screen [some sources say an enclosed announcer's booth] so I would be invisible to the studio audience too. That part went over, but even though I was slender in those days and had my hair, I often got the impression the audience was disappointed in my appearance." Of course, no one could live up to certain mental images, and disappointment in the actual looks of radio performers was a frequent happening. But Bret Morrsion may have been a bit less like his projected image than most. Nevertheless, his vocal performance as the Shadow was outstand-ing; he could project culture and breeding as Lamont Cranston and the menace of an avenging angel of justice as the Shadow.

Bret Morrison always gave a very special reading to those famous lines, "Who knows what evil lurks in the hearts of men? The Shadow knows!"

It is his voice that rings out when one reads a printed script such as "The Final Hour" (Jerry McGill, Oct. 31, 1954), a show that aired only nine weeks from the end of the series. This story so near the end has the same theme as the very first broadcast adventure of the Shadow – saving an innocent man from execution. As the hours tick off to the midnight hour of execution, the Shadow goes to Walker, the witness whose perjury is sending young Jim Martin to the chair. The real killer, Marty Barton, is with Walker in a bar, alternating threats with reassurances to keep the perjurer in line. As these two part for a moment, the Shadow makes his entrance.

Walker: (Gasps) ... The chair moved!
Shadow: Wait, Sam Walker! Don't call to Barton. He wouldn't believe a chair could be moved by unseen hands.
Walker: Unseen hands?
Shadow: And an unseen presence speaks to you.
Walker: (Dazed and frightened) Speaks! Yes. I am hearing it or I'm going crazy!!
Shadow: The voice is as real as the fear and remorse that are slowly destroying your mind, Sam Walker.
Walker: What ... where are you?
Shadow: Not behind you. Not in dark corners of this bar. I am right here, in front of you, close enough to touch you.
Walker: (Verge of panic) No! It can't be. It's my mind!
Shadow: Of course! For I have the power to remain unseen, invisible to the eyes of men with tormented minds such as yours. But I am real.
Walker: No, not real.
Shadow: (Slow and measured) So real, I could reach out and touch your trembling hand that clutches the empty glass you have drained of the last bitter dregs of the false courage of the coward!

Walker: Who ... Who are you?
Shadow: Many men and women, such as you, have known me as the Shadow.
Walker: The ... Shadow!

After more pressure, Walker breaks and agrees to tell the truth. The Shadow prevents Barton from killing Walker, and the terrified man admits his lies to the governor before midnight, "The Fatal Hour."

The story had some of the Shadow's best "terrify the suspect" business, but was a pretty simple one. It had to be. The script only ran some twenty pages, compared to nearly forty pages a decade earlier when the program ran a full half hour with only three brief commercials for a single sponsor, the Blue Coal company.

By 1954, the program only ran 25 minutes and some eight of those were taken with spot commercials and public service announcements. The actual story content was only about that of a fifteen-minute program during a more prosperous era of radio.

Very few of these later, multi-sponsored episodes of *The Shadow* are known to survive. They were recorded on magnetic tape, and after running once on the Mutual network, the program was erased and the tape reused. The older programs from the thirties and forties had been put on sixteen-inch disc recordings, and even if these transcriptions were tossed into the garbage can, they could be and often were salvaged by cast, crew or other interested persons.

It was the survival of these old discs that allowed longtime radio syndicator Charles Michaelson to revive *The Shadow* on radio beginning in 1962, with WGN Chicago being the first station to air the nostalgic old favorite. Michaelson found great success with *The Shadow* and eventually added many other favorites including *The Lone Ranger, The Green Hornet, Sherlock Holmes, Sergeant Preston of the Yukon, Gangbusters*, and others. Unfortunately, not enough recordings of many old favorites survived to make a rerun package, but there were enough episodes to make the Shadow live again.

Since that 1962 revival, the master of men's minds has not been away, appearing not only on radio again but on albums (even with two newly recorded episodes for MGM Leo Records), new novels and classic reprints, comics, coloring books, etc.

The Shadow has entered modern American folklore. Symbolic of the frightening power of conscience, he also represents the world of radio drama more than any other single character. He is an icon of justice, yes, but not a simple or comforting one. He is a frightening representation of mystery itself, the unknown. He leaves us wondering – *What really lurks in the heart of the Shadow?*

Films

The Shadow first appeared on the motion picture screen less than a year after he first came to prominence on the radio and in his own magazine.

In 1931, Universal released a series of two-reel subjects, "The Shadow Detective Series." These were part of the "Selected Short Subjects" that accompanied a major feature film in the thirties and forties and even into the fifties. About thirty minutes in length, they told short stories that added variety to the main feature. Most two-reelers were comedies (the Three Stooges, Edgar Kennedy, etc.) but often in the silent era and occasionally into sound, they were drama, Western or mystery. Probably the most successful of these dramatic two-reelers in the sound era was MGM's *Crime Does Not Pay*. Universal's Shadow series did not prove so enduring. Prints are not even known to survive.

From the titles and writing credits, we do know these two-reelers were adapted from the mystery stories in Street & Smith's *Detective Story* magazine, like those the Shadow hosted on radio. The series consisted of *Burglar to the Rescue*, *Trapped*, *Sealed Lips*, *House of Mystery*, *The Red Scare* and *The Circus Show-up*.

The casts were good for that era. Silent movie hero (and later Western heavy) Walter Miller appeared in the third and fifth titles, probably still as a leading man. The last title featured Sally Blane and Polly Ann Young, both minor stars, not merely featured players.

While it isn't known for certain, quite possibly the radio Shadow (probably Frank Readick at this time) recorded the film Shadow's narration at Universal's New York studio. Presumably it did have the Shadow as narrator to justify the title. At this time movie studios frequently featured radio singers, announcers and comedians in shorts and features to satisfy the audience's curiosity about their appearance. Again, it isn't known if the Shadow made any kind of onscreen appearance. It was already a standard cinema technique for mysterious characters to be seen merely as a shadow on a wall, and the Shadow's image in these shorts may well have taken such a form.

Six years would pass before the Shadow appeared on the movie screen again. Rod LaRocque had been a leading man in the silents, and although obviously aging in 1937, he took the title role in *The Shadow Stikes* (Grand National). It has been said that Larocque played Lamont Granston (sic), but this may be merely a typographical error in the credits. In the body of the picture, he seems to be called "Cranston" by other actors. He spends most of the film impersonating a character named Randall, a lawyer the criminologist is pretending to be.

Opposite: The earliest film version: Rod LaRocque wears the cloak in *The Shadow Strikes*.

Only twice does La Rocque appear as the cloaked Shadow. He does not seem menacing, his tone natural and conversational. When the Shadow has the drop on him, one crook asks, "What kind of game are you playing, Shadow?" The cloaked avenger replies lackadaisically, "You might call it a kind of solitare."

Grand National tried again, and La Rocque returned as Lamont Cranston in *International Crime* (1938). A number of the Shadow's agents and associates appeared, including reporter Clyde Burke (William Moore), cab driver Moe "Shrevy" Shrevnitz (Lou Hearn), and Police Commissioner Weston (Thomas Jackson). One Shadow regular who didn't make it was the Shadow – Cranston never donned mask and cloak in the picture, the last of the brief series.

Although based on a *Shadow* magazine novel, a rare one written not by Gibson but by Ted Tinsley, the film was more inspired by the radio show, giving Cranston his radio sidekick, Miss Lane (but with a first name of Phoebe, not Margo) and even giving him a profession in radio, that of a crusading radio reporter out to smash subversive fifth columnist agents.

Finally, in 1940, Columbia Pictures gave the screen the first acceptable image of the Shadow in a fifteen-chapter serial called *The Shadow*. Talented actor Victor Jory looked and sounded like the Shadow, with his angular, striking looks and a laugh as scary as that of any radio Shadow. Jory played in many radio dramas over his career and could have easily done the part on the air, though he never did.

Much of the physical action of the Shadow was performed by Jory's stuntman, George DeNormand. DeNormand was shorter and stockier than Jory (he was a better match for Spencer Tracy, whom he doubled all of Tracy's career) but the action went so fast, the audience wasn't supposed to notice.

"The damned cape got in the way every time," DeNormand said. "If these guys really were going out doing these things for real, they would get rid of the cape after the first time. You don't get in a fistfight in a cape."

Jory and DeNormand got along well, but the actor wanted to do anything he really could do himself. One scene called for him to jump down six feet onto a pair of hoods.

"Hell, George, I can jump six feet. You don't have to do that for me," Jory reportedly said.

But when he got up six feet, Jory hesitated. "He was up six feet, but he was looking down the height of his body, so he was looking down twelve feet," DeNormand said.

"You do it, George," Jory finally said.

Veda Ann Borg played Margo Lane in the serial. Some sources say she played "Martha Lane" but that was merely a slip of Jory's tongue in one scene. Borg was not ideal for the society girl, Margo. She went on to play

Victor Jory puts the arm on Jack Ingram to save Margo (Veda Ann Borg) in the 1949 movie serial of *The Shadow*.

earthier types, gun molls and dance hall hostesses, and even here her accent was too coarse.

The chief agent of the Shadow, Harry Vincent, finally made it to the screen in the person of minor actor Roger Moore (not the star of the same name from a later era). This actor, too, was ill suited to his part, seeming more like a minor hood. He also combined the role of Shrevy and drove a cab for Cranston.

It was the central portrayal by Victor Jory of the Shadow that made the serial, however. He was the pulp version – the slouch-hatted, cloaked avenger, with two guns and two ready fists. But the appeal of the radio show made itself felt in the opening of the later chapters: Jory with a voice-over, "I am the Shadow!" and the mocking laugh. (The radio opening was too long to fit over the fast roll of the credits).

Another bit borrowed from the radio series was the inclusion of an invisible man. It was not the Shadow here but his nemesis, the Black Tiger. He made himself invisible only long enough to walk to a desk and pound a gavel for order among his ring of crooks, and occasionally brandish a gun. The movie producers must have felt that radio fans would expect somebody to become invisible, so at least the villain would. A better solution might have been to have the Shadow cloaked and creeping most of the time, but let him assume his invisibility for a few special tasks.

The storyline of the serial had Cranston fighting the Black Tiger's attempts first to wreck and then to take over the U. S. transportation system. There were a lot of good action scenes, but the cliffhangers unfortunately lacked imagination. Many chapters ended with an explosion from which the Shadow miraculously emerged the next chapter, brushing off his cloak. Most serial heroes were given only one such miraculous escape per serial. (The other escapes had to be logically explained.)

Probably the repetition of the cliffhangers was not so obvious when the chapters were viewed a week apart over a period of months, and memory failed about some chapter ending of weeks before. The serial was a legitimate attempt to bring the Shadow to the screen, and given the low budget alloted serials, it succeeded on its own level.

A few years earlier, an imitation of the Shadow from the pulps, the Spider appeared in a Columbia serial, *The Spider's Web*. For some reason, this turned out to be an even more faithful and lively adaptation than Columbia's version of *The Shadow*. Both serials about the cloaked crimefighters were directed by James W. Horne, who also directed Laurel and Hardy and who liked to interject bits of humor in his serials. Unlike the Spider, there was no second serial featuring the Shadow.

The master of darkness next appeared in series of features starring the hero of many serials, Kane Richmond. The good-looking Richmond had already appeared in Republic's *Spy Smasher* (1940) as a costumed avenger who owed something to the Shadow, as do nearly all such characters. Now he was in the Monogram feature, *The Shadow Returns* (1946). Like the serial, this feature presented the Shadow as his pulp incarnation, getting into gun battles with crooks in warehouses, swinging down on them on a rope and pulley.

Barbara Reed was cute and believably wealthy as Margo Lane—perhaps a bit more scatterbrained than her radio incarnation, but some of the radio plays were also making her seem a bit fey by this time. Shrevy was also on hand as portrayed by Frank Sully, who supplied more comic relief than required. In fact, *Behind the Mask* (the same year) was almost a complete farce with Richmond attempting to retain some dignity for himself and his character but being portrayed as a bumbling idiot in his investigation. Margo even puts on the Shadow disguise and is laughably inept. (In his writings, Gibson had women pose as the Shadow several times, but in earnest.)

The best of the features is *The Missing Lady*, an early directorial assignment of Phil Kaufman, who went on to direct *The Right Stuff*. Kaufman took the material seriously and presented a Shadow much more like the radio character than either of the other two Kane Richmond films.

There is a certain ambiguity about his presentation of the Shadow. Is he really invisible except for the shadow on the wall, or is it merely the point of view of the audience that makes it seem that way? Yet the actors seem to be looking at nothing in particular, rather like the blind, so one feels that the master of darkness is truly unseen. In his search for the Lady—a valuable statue involved in a murder case—the Shadow uses the radio technique of terrifying the suspects into revealing more than they wish to do. If *The Shadow* serial is the best presentation of the pulp version of the dark avenger, *The Missing Lady* is the best film version of the radio Shadow.

There was one more Shadow feature, released more than a decade later by Republic and called *Invisible Avenger* (also known as *Bourbon Street Shadows*). The film was intended to be the pilot for a Shadow television series, but it didn't sell. As with a number of pilots during this era, it was released to theaters as a feature. Richard Derr played Lamont Cranston, who had the hypnotic power to cloud men's minds. In this version, not only Cranston brought the secret from the Orient, but one of his teachers as well, the mystically gifted Jogendra (Mark Daniels). Together, they fought crime in New Orleans. The premise was probably more interesting than many during the early days of televison, but it was neither the radio or pulp version of the Shadow; more than a distant cousin, but perhaps only a half-brother to the master of men's minds fans knew from Walter Gibson's novels and the eerie thrills generated by the radio voices of Orson Welles, Bill Johnstone, Bret Morrison, John Archer and the rest.

It is rumored that a half-hour pilot film for a Shadow television show was made, starring Clayton Moore (television's Lone Ranger) as Cranston. There was also a short demonstration pilot (perhaps ten minutes) made and largely written by producer Stanley Ralph Ross just after Wonder Woman appeared on the home screen. These films have not been publicly seen.

Near constant talk goes on of a major film about the Shadow, but as yet, this big budget feature remains as invisible as the cloaked master of darkness himself.

Comics

Gibson-Grant, a seemingly inexhaustible writing machine, wrote the first six years of Shadow stories of *Shadow Comics*, beginnning in March 1940.

Issue No. 1 was virtually an anthology of all the Street & Smith fiction magazines past and then present. It featured not only the master of darkness but dime novel heroes from the early part of the century, Frank Merriwell (the original "All-American Boy") and Nick Carter, Master Detective (who would continue to appear in almost all issues of this comics magazine). The Shadow's pulp companion, Doc Savage, also made an entrance here and returned to these pages after his own comic died.

Early issues featured the art of Vernon Greene, who also collaborated with Gibson on a short-lived Shadow daily newspaper strip. Greene was good, atmospheric and technically accurate. He did adaptations of such Gibson novels as *Lingo*, which was used in the first issue.

Unfortunately, Greene was not around long, and most of the art was by the Jack Binder shop. It ranged from just plain bad to adequate.

After the first few issues, Gibson began using the radio version of the Shadow, a man who could become completely invisible by hypnotic power. The change was presumably made by editorial order; it must have been thought the "completely invisible" version was better known to young buyers just learning to read. One inspiration was rendering the Shadow when invisible in dark blue outline with light blue shading. It had a different look from any other comic on the stands.

In later years, a really outstanding comics artist did *The Shadow* – Bob Powell. Everything he did was good, and *The Shadow* was nearly his best.

During his comics writing, Gibson created such recurring villains as Monsterdamus, an evil man who had lived for centuries, and also introduced as a supporting character Shadow, Jr. The cloaked boy seemed a bit silly and was never developed for a strip of his own. A young boy really doesn't know much about the evil in the human heart and can't muster up a suitably sinister laugh.

The senior Shadow knew of those things, and has returned in recent revivals from several different companies. Archie Comics in the sixties introduced a hatless, blond Shadow in a version that at first had a few flaws, then became disastrous when the Shadow donned a "long underwear" superhero uniform. In the Seventies DC had a faithful version drawn by Mike Kaluta that didn't sell well enough. While they had rights to the Shadow, DC had him meet up with Batman who humbly admitted the Shadow was his idol and inspiration. An eighties revival of the Shadow at DC presented "adult" sexual situations and lots of bloody violence, which may have helped the sales some but not enough. Rival Marvel Comics simultaneously presented a Shadow "graphic novel" (a long, hardbound comic book) through some rights loophole.

In 1989, DC presented still another version under the revised title *The Shadow Strikes*. It took the Shadow back to his best era, the thirties, with talented writing by Gerard Jones and art by Rich Magyar. The atmosphere worked much better, and after a dozen issues, the publication was continuing.

Comic book series come and go, but in some form the Shadow will be around forever.

Magazines and Books

Walter Gibson, writing as Maxwell Grant, created the Shadow for the series of novels appearing in the pulp magazine carrying the famous character's name, beginning with *The Living Shadow* in April 1931 and concluding after 325 issues and eighteen years with *The Whispering Eyes* in the summer of 1949. Gibson wrote 282 of those novels himself.

The connection between the *Shadow* magazine and the radio series was so great that neither can be considered an adaptation of the other. They grew together, constantly cross-influencing one another.

The *Shadow* magazine was an attractive and haunting thing on the newsstands. The covers were beautiful and frightening, like medieval paintings of scenes of the Black Death. The black-cloaked figure was at once scary and appealing as depicted by such cover artists as George Rozen and Graves Gladney. Equally effective were those like Orban and Cartier who drew the black and white interiors. It was apparent where the Knight of Darkness' anger was directed, toward crooks and gunmen threatening the innocent. He would never hurt someone on his side, against criminals and bad men. But as to those others, those who had turned their faces from the light, he seemed little inclined towards mercy. The two big black guns in his fists blazed out sudden justice to the guilty.

In reality the Shadow seldom killed. He used his bullets to frighten and scatter hordes of criminals with near misses, slugs fanning their coattails or screaming by their ears. Another pulp magazine competitor and something of an imitator, the Spider, did shoot to kill. And he ran up a ghastly total, killing a hundred in a single novel, many thousands in the whole series. It became bloodily gruesome.

Always a magician, whether working on stage with Houdini and Blackstone at the moment or not, Gibson conjured up a tale of a cloaked figure rescuing a young man just before a suicide leap and swearing him to this Shadow's crusade against evil. As he wrote the story on assignment, Gibson consulted another Street & Smith pubication, a Horatio Alger book, to form some idea of structure and chapter lengths and combined the names of two Alger characters to create "Harry Vincent," the Shadow's new recruit and chief assistant. Gibson's story, *The Living Shadow*, was accepted and Gibson went on to write most of the 325 magazine novels that followed. Most of the others were by Theodore Tinsley and Bruce Elliot; one was written by Lester Dent, creator of that other great pulp character, Doc Savage. All the stories appeared under the house pseudonym of Maxwell Grant. A complete professional, Gibson did not mind, preferring to keep his own name for nonfiction works on magic, such as his *Houdini Escapes*.

Another important name was involved – one for the Shadow's chief alter ego. Gibson decided he should be a man of wealth, with a sprawling

New Jersey estate. He wanted something strong and memorable with two syllables fore and aft. In going through some notes on a Houdini theater tour, he came across the name "Baillie Cranston," a theatre manager in Scotland. The first name was not quite right, but in consulting a list of names Gibson found "Lamont," which sounded like a family, one of wealth and position. So the Shadow's other identity would be Lamont Cranston.

With *The Shadow Unmasks* (Aug. 1, 1937), Gibson revealed an even deeper secret of the Shadow. He was not even really Lamont Cranston. He only *posed* as the real Cranston (who was still alive, traveling abroad and being overwhelmingly cooperative). In his deepest identity, the Shadow was Kent Allard, a famous aviator long thought dead. This identity was never explored in the radio series, comics or other appearances of the Shadow. Even in most of the later novels, the Shadow is Lamont Cranston, an identity so familiar that he even thinks of himself as Cranston.

Gibson was an incredibly prolific writer, and a good one for all his tremendous output. He generally wrote a Shadow novel in eight days, turning out four pages an hour or thirty pages a day in eight or nine hours. But he could get on a roll and sometimes produce two sixty-five thousand word novels in a single week.

Gibson was perhaps not as great a writer as Victor Hugo or Robert Louis Stevenson, but he shared some of their abilities at storytelling and moving characters from one peril to another without overwhelming the audience with repetition and improbability.

Gibson seems to have used his love and knowledge of stage magic to power his tales. The Shadow was a master magician, always dealing in illusion (his seeming invisibility and omnipresence) and misdirection. One of his more obvious talents at misdirection was the ability to steer the gunfire of his enemies away from him.

Like the great radio writer Carlton E. Morse, Gibson was also a master at stalling. For many a chapter in the long saga of Shadow novels, the master of men's minds sat alone in his secret sanctum, writing notes to himself.

He was still at it as late as 1976 when Walter Gibson wrote a new novelette for *The Shadow Scrapbook* (Harcourt Brace Jovanovich, 1979).

A bluish light shone down upon the surface of a polished table, amid surrounding blackness. Two long-fingered hands moved into the glow like living things. One hand drew a pad and pen from the darkness; the other stretched into the gloom and pressed an unseen switch that gave an audible click. A tiny yellow light glimmered in the dark beyond the bluish ray. A quiet voice came an amplifier: "Burbank speaking."

The response was whispered: "Report."

"Final report on Rangoon Ruby. Revised list of probable or potential purchasers..."
As Burbank recited the names, the long-fingered hand wrote them deftly, swiftly on the pad. This black-walled room was the secret sanctum of The Shadow, master of darkness, who used reports that came through Burbank to plan campaigns against coming crimes....

The secret sanctum was only one more card in Gibson's hand of tricks. Gibson has freely discussed in interviews and his own writings his work in doing the Shadow novels. It appears that he preferred doing those novels that were based on factual research. He singles out *Mox* (Nov. 15, 1933), a tale of an actual small town detective in a setting Gibson knew from his early days reporting for the press. A further entry was *Crime Circus*, (April 15, 1934) another story based on solid research. In his story conferences with *Shadow* magazine editor John Nanovic, he pushed such types of stories and often got approval to proceed with a two- or three-day lead to go to a certain local and research a business or community history. It was incredibly short time for almost any writer, but with Gibson meeting a semimonthly schedule, it was all that could be allowed.

Yet Gibson reveals that the letters from the readers voted for more master villains, super-criminals that would really test the mettle of the master of darkness. By implication these were not his own personal favorites, but Gibson a consummate professional, turned out what was required.

The Shadow novels were often too bland and mundane for a small boy. Many of the scenes took place at the Cobalt Club with Cranston smoking cigars with Commission Ralph Weston and pumping him for police information, or at dinner parties at country estates. But like the movies of the era, the magazine was attempting to appeal to a broad spectrum of the audience, not merely to thrill-seeking youngsters. Still, the letter-writing readers seemed to prefer to read of the Shadow swinging into action, both big .45s blazing as he fought a madman out to rule the world. As Maxwell Grant, Gibson provided such menaces in *The Grey Fist, The Black Falcon, The Crime Master* and *The Cobra*, all in 1934.

The greatest single villain of the novel series was undoubtedly Shiwan Khan, an Oriental menace who claimed to be descended from Genghis Khan. While it was never explicitly claimed, he might also have shared the bloodline of Dr. Fu Manchu. This villain curiously had many of the hypnotic and mental powers attributed to the Shadow himself in the radio series. Although Gibson claimed to have given the Shadow hypnotic powers in the novels before the radio program did so, they were certainly underplayed. In one of the Khan stories, the Shadow specifically thinks to himself that he does *not* have the mental powers of Shiwan Khan because he devoted himself to a broader development of skills needed in his work, presumably the martial arts skills of hand-to-hand fighting and marksmanship needed for dealing with the criminal element.

The Oriental mastermind first appeared in *The Golden Master* (Sept. 15, 1939) to challenge the Shadow – unsuccessfully, but it was a hard fight. *Shiwan Khan Return* (Dec. 1, 1939) had the Asian genius attempting to steal the products of other brilliant men, great scinetific inventions, to help him in his world conquest. But it took more than machines to conquer the steel nerves and iron will of the Shadow.

For an unprecedented third time the villain returned, claiming to be *The Invincible Shiwan Khan* (Mar. 1, 1940). Now he took over the entire underworld in his plans for global subjugation. This had gone on long enough. As with Sherlock Holmes and Professor Moriarty, there had to be a final settlement of "those matters between" Shiwan Khan and the Shadow.

In *Master of Death* (May 15, 1940), the Shadow cried "To the death!" as he prepared to engage Shiwan Khan in combat. The outcome? The next issue of the magazine was not called *Shiwan Khan*. The Oriental mastermind, though presumably dead, did return in comic book stories in the sixties and the eighties, but he remained dead in the novels.

Although a semimonthly magazine is a transitory thing, the readers and the publisher realized that the Shadow was making for himself a lasting place in popular culture. As early as the thirties, the first novel, *The Living Shadow*, and two others were reprinted in book form.

After the end of the *Shadow* magazine in 1949, fans and collectors sought those few hardcovers and back issues of the magazine. While many were lost to wartime paper drives, other survived and many people still own representative collections of the magazine. A few boast complete runs.

It was not until 1963 and the successful revival of the radio series in syndicated reruns that a new book of the Shadow appeared – a really new, original novel by the series creator, Walter B. Gibson, now under his own name. The book, a Belmont paperback, was *Return of the Shadow*. Neither Gibson nor the man who posed as Lamont Cranston had lost any of his abilities. Classic reprints had been planned to follow, but instead Belmont opted for more originals by the prolific paperback scribe Denis Lynds under the time-honored Maxwell Grant byline. While not distinguished, these eight books were acceptable pastiche, much like the many imitations of Conan Doyle's Sherlock Holmes stories.

Soon there came reprints of Gibson's original stories in several different forms: a hardbound Grosset & Dunlap book reprinting three Shadow novels (1966); seven paperback novels from Bantam (1969–70); a single paperback from Tempo (1969), and twenty-three titles from Pyramid/Jove paperbacks (1974-78). There was a large omnibus of two titles from Dover in 1975, and a series of Doubleday Crime Club reprints beginning in 1975.

When Otto Penzler edited a collection of essays on *The Great Detectives* (Little, Brown, 1978) written by the detectives' creators, he included along with Lew Archer by Ross MacDonald, Michael Shayne by Brett Halliday and Mr. and Mrs. North by Richard Lockridge, the Shadow by Maxwell Grant (Gibson). Once only a "lurid pulp," the Shadow at last was recognized as one of the greatest characters of mystery fiction of all time, and Gibson as one of the greatest then living mystery writers.

There is an old saying to creative people: "Your greatness will be recognized after you are dead." Walter Gibson lived a long life, a long enough time for cynicism to pass and acceptance to begin. The creator of the Shadow lived to see himself venerated for his masterful abilities and to see his creation become one of the immortals of the world of fiction. The Shadow had the last laugh.

Premiums

There were two sources of premiums for the Shadow: the magazine and the radio show. Neither one issued a vast array of items. Both the publication and the radio series were aimed at a general audience, including probably more grownups than kids. Too many premiums might have tended to make the character seem juvenile.

Magazine premiums began in 1933 and included a Shadow Club metal badge (worth an average of $65 in 1992), a Shadow Club tie-pin stud ($95), a Shadow Club Rubber Stamp ($60) and a Shadow Club Paper Sticker Seals (set of 10 or more; $30).

Radio Premiums offered included the following, listed alphabetically with date and approximate value in 1992 (assuming average condition).

Ink Blotter, Blue Coal/Shadow (1941; several designs; $25), Match Book, Blue Coal/Shadow (1941; $30), Photo, Shadow (masked actor Frank Readick), "compliments of Blue Coal" (1937; $95), Ring, Shadow Blue Coal Glow-in-the-Dark* (1941; $700), Ring, Shadow Glow-in-the-Dark (1947; from Carey Salt, black stone, crocodile design; $95).

A number of other items were offered for sale in the pages of the *Shadow* magazine and sold in stores. But these items do not qualify as "premiums," items that were giveaways or sold at cost. These commercial items included an Official Shadow Hat and Cloak (price $1; worth several

*The "stone" is a lump of Blue Coal; sidebands have a cloaked likeness of the Shadow, all plastic. This is arguably the most sought after single radio premium, only exceeded in value by the multi-unit (some 60 items) Lone Ranger Frontier Town.

hundred dollars today), a Shadow Game, Shadow Holster Set with gun, mask, handcuffs, whistle and flashlight (some $400 today; none are known to exist), Shadow pencil light and other items. There were also posters for the magazine, the radio show, the movies. Any letter from the magazine or radio show bearing a Shadow letterhead or likeness is worth at least $15.

Sherlock Holmes

Half-hour mystery drama occasionally serialized. Began Oct. 20, 1930, on NBC and continued intermittently on NBC, ABC, Mutual and again NBC until 1955 with an ever-changing cast (see cast list) dominated by Richard Gordon in the early years. The show reached the height of its popularity with Basil Rathbone and Nigel Bruce as Holmes and Watson, 1939–46.

Directors: Basil Loughrane, Joseph Bell, Tom McKnight, Glenhall Taylor **Writers:** Edith Meiser, Bruce Taylor (Leslie Charteris), Dennis Green, Anthony Boucher, Howard Merrill, Max Ehrlich **Sound Effects:** Bill Hoffman **Musical Director:** Graham Harris **Sherlock Holmes:** William Gillette (1930, first show), Richard Gordon (1930–31, 1932–35), Clive Brook (1930, part season), Louis Hector (1931–32), Basil Rathbone (1939–46), Tom Conway (1947), John Stanley (1949), Ben Wright (1950), John Gielgud (1955) **Dr. Watson:** Leigh Lovel (1930–35), Harold West (1935–36), Nigel Bruce (1939–47), Alfred Shirley (1949), Wendel Holmes (George Seldon) (1949), Ian Martin (1949), Eric Snowden (1950), Ralph Richardson (1955) **Moriarty:** Louis Hector, Orson Welles **Interviewer for George Washington Coffee:** Joseph Bell **Mrs. Hudson:** (housekeeper) Mary Gordon, Jeanette Nolan, others **Irene Adler:** Jeanette Nolan, others **Mycroft Holmes:** J. Scott Smart, others **Announcer:** (Bromo Quinne) Knox Manning **Announcer:** (Petrie Wine) Harry Bartel **Others:** Agnes Moorehead, Harry Neville, Lucille Wall, Bill Shelley.

Few figures loom larger in the realm of radio mystery than Sherlock Holmes. He was not the first mystery figure on radio; the evil Dr. Fu Manchu and his detective nemesis, Nayland Smith, started in 1929. Holmes may not have even been the detective creation most identified with radio; the Shadow could have a stronger claim. But for class and staying power and universal appeal, as has been observed, there was no police like Holmes.

The short stories and books about Holmes and Watson by Sir Arthur Conan Doyle were recognized as classics even in the lifetime of the author. The hawk-nosed sleuth was based on Dr. Conan Doyle's teacher at medical school, Joseph Bell, for his insightful diagnosis of what ailed patients. The author decided it was time for a detective who applied the scientific method and "built up" his case, observation by observation. And there was Dr. John Watson, about whom there has been as much speculation as Holmes. Was Watson a man of normal intellect who only seemed dense in comparison to the near superhuman Holmes? In his only filmed interview in 1930, Conan Doyle spoke of Watson as Holmes' "rather stupid" friend. But he was loyal and courageous and loved by generations of readers, moviegoers and radio listeners.

If Conan Doyle was within Sherlock Holmes, Holmes was within Conan Doyle. The writer-physician tried his hand at several real-life cases, in one instance clearing a minor civil servant of charges of animal mutilation. If his cases and his results were not as spectacular as those of Holmes, it might be because reality was not plotted and controlled by Conan Doyle. In short, Doyle was not given the puzzles and the opponents that he himself gave Holmes.

By 1930, the year of Conan Doyle's death, Holmes and his Watson were known to all the world, already probably the most famous fictional characters of all time. Many did not even believe they were fictional; Conan Doyle stated he had received requests for Holmes' autograph and even thinly veiled offers of marriage for the detective. The myth of Holmes' being a living man is still nurtured by the organization of Holmephiles under the blanket name of the Baker Street Irregulars, even as the detective approaches the age of a century and a quarter. Holmes was anything but an ordinary man.

It seems hard to understand how selling such a massively popular creation to radio would be a problem, but it was. Edith Meiser, new to the profession of radio writing after a turn at acting, had tried to sell a Holmes radio series as early as 1929, but it took her until 1930 to get NBC to put the show on the air with one of her scripts adapted from a Conan Doyle original.

Eventually she went through the complete canon (even repeating one of the classics from time to time) and went into creating new tales of Holmes based on incidents in the originals. Today, producing Sherlock Holmes pastiches seems almost a cottage industry, but Meiser was one of the first and one of the best to do it. Her final association with Holmes came in scripting a daily comic strip about him in the fifties.

Over the years, other outstanding writers such as the creator of the Saint, Leslie Charteris (writing as Bruce Taylor), distinguished actor-turned-author Denis Green and critic and mystery writer Anthony Boucher sometimes spelled Miss Meiser for a season or two, but she always returned. In recent years, actor-producer-writer Ken Greenwald has released on commercial cassettes with new introductions by original cast members some of the Green-Boucher radio stories, which he later wrote into book form. The

Meiser-scripted comics have also been reprinted in magazines and softcover books.

The first actor to portray the great detective in a Meiser script was stage actor William Gillett. A recording of a single scene he did as Holmes reveals that by the time of recordings and radio, Gillette had grown quite elderly and sounded not the least British. He sounded rather like an old American farmer. No doubt he was dashing in his youth, and the public is always loathe to let its heroes go.

Gillette agreed to do only the initial broadcast of the series, and thereafter he was replaced by Broadway's Richard Gordon. Fellow radio actor and coincidentally writer of some Holmes pastiche novels Frank Thomas recalls Gordon as something of a John Barrymore type. Once walking down a street at an hour far too early in the day for the actor, Gordon urgently asked Thomas, "What is that woman's name coming this way?" Thomas looked. "I don't believe I know her. Why?" Gordon shuddered. "I believe she was my third wife and I need to know how to address her if she speaks."

Gordon was clearer headed as Holmes, but his voice was not clearer. The few surviving recordings show he used a strange, high-pitched tone that made him completely distinctive in the sea of voices of early radio, but not comfortable to listen to.

Gordon's Watson, Leigh Lovell, opened the show by greeting G. Washington Coffee announcer Joseph Bell (what a strange coincidence that Holmes' first radio announcer had the same name as the man who inspired his fictional creation in Conan Doyle's mind). The old doctor led Bell into his study to sit beside the crackling fire and have a steaming cup not of tea, but of G. Washington coffee – "the best cup of coffee that can be found!"

While they sipped their favorite beverage, Watson recalled the days of his youth in 1880, when he was around twenty-eight. The time factor worked in 1930, but of course by the 1950s Watson would have been a very hale centenarian still spinning his tales of an age long ago.

Screen actor Clive Brook also appeared as Holmes for a time during that first season of 1930-31, but Gordon returned until 1935. He was replaced by Louis Hector for one season, then returned for the 1936 series, along with a new Watson (Harold West) first heard with Hector. The absences of Gordon are probably explained by his going on the road with a play, his stagecraft taking precedence over the radio show for reasons of personal commitment and probably larger salary.

For three years, the great detective was off the airwaves, but finally he returned in 1939 with the actor many believe to be his greatest portrayer of all, Basil Rathbone, along with Nigel Bruce as Watson from the hit movie of the same year, *The Hound of the Baskervilles*.

The new sponsor was Bromo Quinine Cold Tablets, and announcer Knox

Manning did not solicit an open endorsement from Doctor Watson. But he still visited the study and listened to Watson spin his tale. One obvious device that was never used was that of having the actor protraying Watson sound older as the tale-spinner and younger in the story set before the turn of the century. Nigel Bruce was probably not capable of such vocal dexterity, but other radio actors in the part were voice specialists who could have done it. As it was, Bruce as Watson sounded elderly even in the scenes of his youth. Apparently it never bothered listeners.

In a typical episode, "The Disappearance of Lady Frances Carfax," Dr. Watson's introduction takes the listeners back to the rooms he shared with Sherlock Holmes on Baker Street. Watson has just returned from an outing, and Holmes immediately deduces that Watson has not been playing billiards or taking in a play but rather having a Turkish steamed bath. Even the omniscient Holmes has to ask why.

Watson: Because for the last few days I've been feeling rheumatic and old. A Turkish bath is what we call an alternative in medicine – a fresh starting point – a cleaner of the system.
Holmes: You say that you have had it because you need a change. Let me suggest that you take one. How would Switzerland do?
Watson: Switzerland?
Holmes: Yes, old chap. First-class tickets to Lausanne, and all expenses paid on a princely scale.
Watson: ... But why?
Holmes: I'm afraid some evil has befallen the Lady Francis Carfax.

And so it has. The pair from Baker Street is called upon to rescue the still-living Lady Carfax from her own coffin.

Bruce and Rathbone were just intrinsically "right" in the parts, but when one reviews the old recordings objectively, their performances were far from perfect. At times it seemed that Rathbone had not even bothered to read the script, much less rehearse it. At times he would start addressing a character in a hostile tone, and halfway through, realize that he was supposed to be sympathetic and change his reading. Perhaps over-examining the show from a later perspective, one can even seem to detect that Rathbone was bored with the show on occasion.

As for Bruce, the "bumbling" of his beloved character, Watson, was also a part of his natural personality. At times he would garble a line beyond all recognition.

Of course, neither Rathbone nor Bruce was primarily a radio actor. In movies, an actor can do retakes. On stage, he can rehearse many times and if he flubs a line in one perfromance, there is always one coming up. In the days of live radio, or even in the early days of transcriptions, one had to get it right on the initial try. Even transcriptions had to go fifteen minutes without an error. Only years later did Bing Crosby introduce tape where mistakes could be edited out. The old crooner was no longer a boy tenor, and he occasionally hit a clinker that he did not want to go out over the air. Still, even by the fifties, many dramatic shows were put on transcription disc, requiring an error-free quarter hour or so. (*I Love a Mystery* was one such dramatic show. Surviving recordings do reveal that if a bad enough error was made early in the episode, the show could be started over, as when Doc Long says of a trouble-maker not "We'll tan his thick hide" but rather something like "We'll twine his slick side.") So, during virtually the entire existence of radio drama, a radio actor was supposed to be one who could get it right the first time.

Many screen actors other than Rathbone and Bruce often did not get it right the first time on the air. Gloria Swanson may have been the worst screen performer on radio. In several appearances on *Lux* and *Suspense* it seemed she did not deliver a single line without problems. James Stewart was a superb radio actor in various anthology appearances and in his own series, *The Six Shooter*. Rathbone and Bruce were somewhere in the middle. Yet the mistakes they made on the air did not matter. To listeners at home, they simply *were* Holmes and Watson, and they could do no wrong.

The Baker Street duo led fans through familiar adventures such as *"The Sussex Vampire,"* in which a child seems to be threatened by an occult menace; *"The Bruce-Partington Plans,"* in which Holmes saves a secret weapon from foreign agents with the help of his brother, Mycroft (appropriately played by radio's *Fat Man*, J. Scott Smart on the Bromo-Quinine series); and "A Scandal in Bohemia," in which Holmes meets "the women," Irene Adler, who outsmarts Holmes in keeping him from retrieving evidence of her romance with the King of Bohemia, although she renounces the king, saying she is now loved by a far better man. (Can it be she means Holmes? Her recently acquired husband seems only a strategic gambit.)

Besides such familiar tales, writers Meiser, Charteris, Green and Boucher also wrote versions of other stories, some only alluded to in Conan Doyle's works. These included the hideous tale of the red leech, "the shocking affair of the Dutch steamship *Friesland*, which so nearly cost both our lives," the singular affair of the aluminum crutch and the remarkable account of the man who stepped back into his house to fetch his umbrella and was never more seen in this world.

One of the most effective new tales was written from such a passing reference in Conan Doyle's stories. The "Giant Rat of Sumatra" turns out to have been injected with bubonic plague, and it is about to be unleashed on a helpless London by the evil Professor Moriarty. The mad scheme is halted when Holmes and Watson set afire the creaking old ship in whose hold the giant rat resides. The detective lights his pipe and declares it a satisfactory smoke.

Moriarty appeared many more times on the air than in the books. Holmes put down his plots week after week.

The Rathbone-Bruce series returned to one of the original books, *The Hound of the Baskervilles*, and serialized it over a number of weeks. In one surviving recording, Watson and Sir Henry Baskerville speculate on the nature of the enemy who struck against Sir Henry not only on the fog-shrouded Moors but in the heart of London. They speculate that the ghostly hound of legend may be able to transform itself into a man to commit more evil. It is mere speculation, of course, but for a time the feeling of the supernatural inherent in this tale may turn it (on radio, at least) into a werewolf story, or at least a werehound story. In the end, of course, Holmes proves the Hound is a real dog, but one trained for insidious ends by a human master.

In 1946, Rathbone moved to New York to perform on the stage, leaving Nigel Bruce and *Sherlock Holmes* behind in Hollywood. While in New York, no doubt to augment his income, Rathbone took on a radio series sponsored by the new Fatima cigarettes and called *Tales of Fatima*, involving the queen (or was it goddess?) Fatima. In the program, Rathbone played himself, actor Basil Rathbone. While appearing in some play he would become involved in a murder mystery. In his dreams Fatima, whose small statue he always carried, would come to him and give him some cryptic clue to the solution of the mystery. At first the dream sequences were elaborate, involving long exchanges between Rathbone and Fatima. Later, Rathbone (and the audience) would only hear Fatima in an echo chamber speaking one enigmatic line. It was obviously a far cry from *Sherlock Holmes* and lasted only one season.

The Holmes program continued in Hollywood with Bruce still as Watson and a new Sherlock, movie star Tom Conway. The brother of George Sanders, Conway had been good as "The Falcon" in films, and he was okay as Holmes. The trouble was, he just was not Basil Rathbone.

The series might have continued, except that as director Glenhall Taylor said, the Conan Doyle estate kept asking for greater and greater fees. Finally, the producers could not afford to pay the estate. They tried changing the show, turning it into *The Casebook of Gregory Hood*. The new show, about a modern day detective who ran an importing business, featured regular radio actors. It was not a terrible show, but it was not *Sherlock Holmes*, any more than *Tales of Fatima* was. The perfect combination required Holmes and Watson, Rathbone and Bruce, but that ended on May 27, 1946. Bruce continued with Tom Conway until 1947.

Next, perhaps after a more equitable agreement with the estate, the character of Sherlock Holmes moved to a series produced in New York with little known John Stanley as the detective and Watson credited to George Seldon (an old stage name for someone doubling a part, but here just covering the name of actor Wendell Holmes, since it was thought Holmes playing Watson would be confusing to the public). These episodes were fairly enjoyable, but they lacked something – Rathbone and Bruce.

The situation wasn't much improved when the series went back to Hollywood with Ben Wright as Holmes, and Eric Snowden as his medical companion. The old sponsor, Petri Wine, was back, along with many of the supporting actors from the Rathbone-Bruce program. This series ran until March 8, 1950.

There was one final U.S. radio network appearance for *Sherlock Holmes*, even though it was an imported production made by the British Broadcasting Corporation in London. In the last days of American radio drama, several series of this sort were imported, including *The Scarlet Pimpernell, The Third Man, The Black Museum* – the last two featuring American Orson Welles working in England. The British series was fine, starring John Gielgud and Ralph Richardson as the detective and the doctor. It ran January 2 until June 5, 1955, and was repeated on other stations, right up until the present. It was put out on phonograph records and cassettes and was for years the most accessible Holmes radio series.

The high point of the Gielgud-Richardson program is the telling of "The Final Problem" with Holmes apparently falling to his death into a Swiss waterfall, dragging with him the embodiment of all evil, Professor Moriarty. And what a Moriarty here – the great Orson Welles in a one-time guest appearance. (Years before, Welles had played Sherlock Holmes himself on his *Campbell Playhouse* anthology.)

Fortunately, the following week came "The Adventure of the Empty House," in which Holmes returns and appears before a fainting Watson. Holmes' death was a hoax to confound his enemies. After the capture of the last of Moriarty's lieutenants, Col. Sebastian Moran, Holmes is free to return to Baker Street. The elder Watson, telling of those earlier days, savors the moment. "Sherlock Holmes back in Baker Street, and a thousand cases still before us. Yes, yes."

What happier moment could there be?

Films

Many complete books, as well as shorter essays, have been written on the Holmes stories by Sir Arthur Conan Doyle, and on the films made from them. The purpose of the present volume is to include scarcely available information on often neglected radio characters. Still, in the interest of a certain standardization of format, a brief survey of the cinema of the master sleuth will follow. Consult such books as *Deerstalker* by Ron Haydock and *The Detective in Film* by William K. Everson for a more detailed picture.

Sherlock Holmes in 1903 was the first detective to appear on film. The film, *Sherlock Holmes Baffled*, lasts less than a minute and depicts Holmes not noticing a burglar entering his apartment. A copy exists, and the film is sometimes included in film anthologies.

Many other early silent films of Holmes have been lost. Those that survive reveal that the silent cinema was not really a showcase for Holmes, who could not easily display his ability at making deductions or learn clues from the answers of suspects. Holmes came home when talkies came in, and he could talk and listen to the other characters.

Eille Norwood flooded the market playing Holmes in both two-reel and feature length British silents in the early 1920s. One feature, one of several silent versions of *The Hound of the Baskervilles*, was shot in such modest surroundings that Henry Baskerville seemed less a knight of the Realm than a successful butcher. As a group, the films were of low budget and low inspiration, and so numerous they forced out other possible makers of Holmes pictures.

Still, the character was too famous to be ignored altogether. Stage star John Barrymore appeared in the first important American film of Conan Doyle's detective, *Sherlock Holmes* (1922), with the Satanic-looking Gustav von Seyfferitz as Moriarty. Rolland Young was Watson. This Samuel Goldwyn production was heavy on melodrama and lurid action, but popular with the audiences. At last report master film preservationist Kevin Brownlow was literally trying to put the pieces of the negative back together to make a watchable version for public consumption.

Clive Brook became the first Sherlock Holmes to talk on screen in 1929's *The Return of Sherlock Holmes*. He made a handsome and distingusihed, if rather humorless, Holmes. As in most Holmes films up to this point, the detective was automatically moved up to modern times out of his gaslight era. Here Holmes was experimenting in his impressive if unrealistic laboratory with death rays–at least rays that could kill a car engine and trap a bank robber for Scotland Yard. A minor director, Basil Dean, helmed the production, probably because he had directed stage plays and was believed to know how to direct the new element of dialogue.

Brook returned as Holmes in a comedy sketch for *Paramount on Parade* the same year, and in 1932's *Sherlock Holmes*, a Fox film. Reginald Owen was on hand briefly as Brook's Watson, replacing H. Reeves-Smith from the earlier film. Watson might have been around less because this time Holmes had a romantic interest carried over from the Gillette stage play, Miriam Jordan in the role of Alice Faulkner. Director William K. Howard knew how to make a thriller, and the film became a good one, if not an ideal vehicle to show off the deductive reasoning of Holmes.

The two Brook features can sometimes be seen on television at four in the morning on commercial stations, and a bit earlier on PBS.

Brook's Watson, Reginald Owen, graduated to the role of the great detective himself in *A Study in Scarlet* (1933) but looked too pudgy and old to possibly be the hawk-faced Holmes. Still, Owen became the only film actor to play both Holmes and Watson.

Britain produced an admirable Sherlock Holmes in Arthur Wontner. He was intelligent, yet warm and charming. His angular face and body looked the part. The only problem, alas, was that by the time talking pictures came in, he was really too old for the role. His pictures often began with the detective being called out of retirement for "one last case." His Watson was played several times by a youngish though graying actor named Ian Fleming (not the author of the James Bond novels of a later generation). Fleming appeared too young to have been this Holmes' companion at Baker Street during an earlier period.

The first Wontner entry was *Sherlock Holmes' Fatal Hour* (1930). This followed Conan Doyle with some faithfulness, featuring Norman McKinnell as a rather low-key Moriarty robbing banks and trying to hide from the master detective behind a high society facade. Critic William Everson found the direction reminiscent of the German silent cinema.

Wontner strolled back onto the film stage in *The Sign of Four* (1932), with Ian Hunter stepping in as Watson. Director Graham Cutts followed the Conan Doyle story accurately. With Ian Fleming back as Watson, Wontner next appeared in *The Missing Rembrandt* and *The Triumph of Sherlock Holmes* (1935), a retelling of Conan Doyle's "Valley of Fear." Moriarty was played by Lyn Harding as a big, boisterous man, something of an Irish tavern keeper turned very, very nasty. Too much of this film is spent away from Holmes and England in a long flashback, supposedly taking place in the old American West with a total lack of conviction.

Wontner, Fleming and Harding returned for the last of the series, *Silver Blaze*, released years later in 1940 in the United States as *Murder at the Baskervilles*, to cash in on the success of the U. S. hit *Hound*. In the British film, Henry Baskerville has Holmes and Watson visit him at Baskerville Hall, many years after the events of the ghostly Hound, and plans to show them his prize race horse, Silver Blaze (combining elements of two Conan Doyle stories) – except the horse is missing, kidnapped by Moriarty in one of his less spectacular crimes. It seemd a minor case both for the criminal mastermind and the great detective, but Arthur Wontner went through the motions with class.

In two other British entries, Raymond Massey gave Holmes almost the dignity of President Lincoln, his later role, in *The Speckled Band* (1931), and

Robert Rendell, usually a man of action, seemed too eager and insufficiently deductive as Holmes in still another remake of *Hound* (1932).

Then Hollywood batted one out of the park with the 1939 hit version of *The Hound of the Baskervilles* with near perfect casting of Basil Rathbone as Sherlock Holmes and Nigel Bruce as Dr. Watson. Actually top-lining was romantic star Richard Greene as Sir Henry.

Also in the cast was a bearded Lionel Atwill as a country doctor so suspicious he could not be the surprise villain in the film, although Atwill returned in a later film as the greatest of all Holmes foes, Moriarty. Another player who would wind up at Unversial later with Rathbone, Bruce and Atwill was John Carradine playing the butler, Barryman (changed from "Barrymore" of the book, so as not to remind audiences of John Barrymore, who Carradine resembled enough in manner to impersonate on radio in a bit of outright audience deception on the Rudy Vallee program.)

Sidney Lanfield has been called an inappropriate director for the subject matter, but since he showed up a number of other directors before and after who attempted the *Hound*, it can probably be said he did well. The story was shot on American sound stages dressed to resemble exteriors of the British countryside (then unavailable because of the ongoing war in Europe, even if studios had wanted to go on location, as they seldom chose to). But the audience had the "willing suspension of disbelief." Even to a child of six, it was obvious that the background in some scenes (process shots) was "just a picture," but who wanted to dwell on it? A more serious problem was the almost complete lack of a musical score to highlight the mood and the action.

The *Hound* and its sequel, *The Adventures of Sherlock Holmes* (1939), were set in the gaslight period, unlike most of the earlier sound films. In the sequel Rathbone and Bruce, now with top billing, were joined by another player who would soon follow the team to Universal: after this second Twentieth Century-Fox offering: George Zucco as Moriarty. This time, Holmes' old foe was out to steal the Crown Jewels, and was diverting Sherlock with an elaborate murder scheme against a young woman (Ida Lupino). One of Holmes' disguises is so good during a party scene that the audience is actually fooled for a moment.

Just over two years later, Universal released the first of its Sherlock Holmes films. Rathbone, who had played Holmes for Fox, was actually under contract to MGM and was "on loan" to Universal for all the Sherlock Holmes pictures he made there. (The radio show stated Rathbone appeared through the courtesy of MGM, and Bruce through Universal, where they

Opposite: **Basil Rathbone as Holmes, actress Ida Lupino, and Nigel Bruce as Watson in the 1939 Fox film,** *The Adventures of Sherlock Holmes,* **where the two men continued their radio roles.**

were making the Holmes series.) But rights to Basil Rathbone's services and to the Conan Doyle character were obtained, and the series went ahead.

Many people were displeased that Holmes and Watson were moved up to modern times in the Universal series. No doubt it was cheaper to shoot in a contemporary setting than in period, and the current issues of World War II—spies and traitors—could be explored. And Holmes was still Holmes—or perhaps it should be said Basil Rathbone was still Sherlock Holmes to the audience. If Nigel Bruce was not quite the image projected by Conan Doyle's works, it was the image most people began to attribute to Watson.

Critics have said Rathbone overacted as Holmes, but it is difficult (though not impossible) to overact as Sherlock Holmes. The character is himself an actor who wishes to dramatize events and dazzle audiences with his deductions and solutions.

The Voice of Terror (1942) ushered Holmes into the modern world of Nazi spies, with Thomas Gomez playing his menacing opponent. He may have been seen by the world at large as merely an overweight villain, but Gomez considered himself a leading man. "The whole picture usually revolves around me," Gomez said. And he was right; the great Holmes was only reacting to his sinister plans. John Rawlings offered adequate direction.

With the second film, Roy William Neill took over direction of the rest of the Universal series. He and the Universial technicians managed to achieve a delicate atmosphere of shadowy intrigue that multimillion dollar productions now try for, often unsuccessfully. It is no wonder that these modest "B" pictures have been shown constantly on television for the last thirty years. One Los Angeles station, KTTV, ran these dozen films over and over in a regular weekly slot in prime time for nearly twenty years.

In *Sherlock Holmes and the Secret Weapon*, Holmes vies against Moriarty (Lionel Atwill, not as innocent as he was in *Hound*) to decipher the code of the Dancing Men (from the Conan Doyle story). Holmes solves the problem, and Moriarty discovers it by accident. A secret bombsight is at stake. Moriarty traps Holmes and begins draining the blood from his body drop by drop (at Holmes' own suggestion, a stall for time).

But in the next episode, *Sherlock Holmes in Washington* (1942), Holmes faces a former Moriarty (George Zucco, from *Adventures of Sherlock Holmes*), now just a Nazi spy out to get another coded message. *Sherlock Holmes Faces Death*, from the same year, had Holmes trying to solve still another code, the Musgrave Ritual (from a Conan Doyle story). The life-size chess game will lead to a Regal Charter Land Grant worth millions.

Gale Sondergaard appears as the Spider Woman, a darker and more sinister screen version of Irene Adler who uses one of the tricks Holmes used against Irene—she uses a fake fire to get Watson to rush to the hiding place of a valuable object and reveal its location. This character appeared in a spinoff film of her own, not surprisingly called *The Spider Woman Strikes Back* (not a Sherlock Holmes film).

The next entry is the favorite of many. *The Scarlet Claw* (1944) is the mark left by a phantom killer in the wilds of wartime Canada. Holmes faces his eeriest menace since the hound itself. The series swung toward the horror pictures Universal was famous for in the next title, *Pearl of Death*. Rhondo Hatton, an actor who had become a distorted giant though a glandular condition, was featured as "the Creeper," sometimes also called "the Spine Breaker." The Creeper, like the Spider Woman, got his own non-Holmes film. This character was somewhat artificially grafted onto Conan Doyle's old plot about something being hidden in one of six small busts of Napoleon – the hidden object this time being the fabulous pearl of the title.

The horror was more atmospheric in *House of Fear* (1945) as Holmes and Watson found the reason for murder lying behind Conan Doyle's own Five Orange Pips. *The Woman in Green* (1945) offered the detective another female opponent somewhat reminiscent of Irene Adler, plus the master villain behind her, a returned Professor Moriarty (now played by Henry Daniel). Their plot was to make wealthy men believe they had committed crimes known as "the Finger Murders," that resembled those of Jack the Ripper, thus forcing them to pay blackmail. Of course, Holmes put an end to the villainy.

Among those onboard the passenger ship in *Pursuit to Algiers* (1946) was John Abbott as a mysterious, eccentric traveler. Abbott's distinctive, half-lidded eyes made him look like the description of Moriarty in the Conan Doyle books, and he would have made an excellent chief menace to Holmes. The real menaces in this picture, including Martin Kosleck, were not strong enough to raise any doubt that Holmes and Watson would get the young king of a friendly nation through to his homeland safely.

The next film also involved travel (and the low expenses of shooting on cramped sets suggesting ships or trains). *Terror by Night* (1946) followed a train through the night as Holmes and Watson attempted to guard a precious jewel. This entry is perhaps the one that pictures Watson at his most dense.

For the final Universal entry, Holmes faced another beautiful but deadly foe, Patricia Morison, in *Dressed to Kill* (1946), the plot of which involved a search for counterfeit Bank of England pound note plates.

Kindly, white-haired Mary Gordon was on hand in many of the films as the landlady at Baker Street, Mrs. Hudson. She can be heard on some of the radio broadcasts, although radio performers such as Jeanette Nolan also did the part some of the time. Dennis Hoey was often on hand as a rather dense Lestrade on screen.

Since the Universal series, there have been a number of individual attempts at a Holmes movie, but not a theatrical series again. Notable was Hammer Films' 1959 version of *The Hound of the Baskervilles* with Peter Cushing making a striking and effective Holmes though he was criticized for being too short. Cushing seemed short only when mechanically compared to other actors—otherwise, his warmth and intelligence dominated. Andre Morell as a dashing Watson and Christopher Lee as a rather dour Sir Henry were also fine. The hound itself was up to muster, as well.

Television

An early television series of Holmes featured a too-handsome Ronald Howard as the detective and H. Marion Crawford as a conventional Watson. The stories tended not to take the world of Baker Street seriously, virtually lampooning it. Other attempts at television productions of Holmes followed, down to the currently shown series from the BBC starring Jeremy Britt, an actor of stunning ability. Unfortunately Britt plays Holmes as such a frenetic, half-mad eccentric that he hardly seems a human being.

Premiums

In 1933 G. Washington Coffee offered two different volumes of *Sherlock Holmes Stories*, one with a photo frontispiece of Richard Gordon as Holmes, the other with one of Leigh Lovell as Watson. These two small hardbound volumes are valued at an average of $25 each in 1992. A 1936 wall map of "Sherlock Holmes' London" from Household Finance, a better display item for collectors, brings an average of $68.

Sky King

Juvenile serial, began on ABC October 28, 1946, as a quarter-hour show Monday through Friday. In 1947 became a half-hour complete story airing twice first week, three times next week, alternating with *Jack Armstrong* weekdays. Became established on Tuesday and Thursdays in 1948; moved to Mutual 1950–54. Sponsor: Peter Pan peanut butter.

Series Creators: Robert M. Burtt, Willfred G. Moore **Producer-Director-Chief Writer:** Roy Windsor **Writers:** Abe Burrows, others **Sky King:** Roy Engel (1946-47), Jack Lester (1947-49), Earl Nightingale (1950-53), Carlton KaDell (1954) **Clipper:** Johnny Coons, Jack Bivens **Penny:** Beryl Vaughn, Beverly Younger **Jim Bell:** Cliff Soubier **Martha Bell:** Viola Berwick **Sheriff:** Stanley Gordon **"Peter Pan"** (girl commercial spokesperson): Jean Mowry **Announcers:** Mike Wallace, Pierre André **Others:** Clarence Hartzel, Norman Gottchak, Richard Thorne, Art Hern, Ken Nordine.

Sky King was one of the last of the classic juvenile serials to appear on radio, and it came close to combining the elements of all the earlier prototypes. It might be considered a combination of *Captain Midnight* and *Tom Mix*, but it is also owed something to several others.

The aviation theme was apparent from the title. The show was created by Robert M. Burtt and Willfred G. Moore, both pilots in real life, who indeed created most of the series on radio built around aviation. They started with the fairly realistic *Air Adventures of Jimmie Allen*, a young boy who wanted to be a flier like his idol Speed Robertson, then developed the larger than life, pulp magazine/comic book–inspired *Captain Midnight*, marked time with World War II Air Corps pilot *Hop Harrigan* and finally put it all together with *Sky King*.

Schyler "Sky" King had been a military flier like Hop Harrigan, only Sky had been in Naval Air. He didn't have a colorful secret identity like Captain Midnight, but his own name had a "superhero" sound to it. Surely a King would outrank a mere captain.

There was a home and a family for Sky King. His Flying Crown ranch in the modern West (with a specific location near Grover, Arizona) seemed much like Tom Mix's TM-Bar. But unlike such heroes as Tom and Captain Midnight, he was not just a guardian to young wards, he was a genuine uncle. (So were the Lone Ranger and Uncle Jim Fairfield on *Jack Armstrong*.) His niece and nephew were Penny and Clipper King, and while there was an attempt to give the youngsters equal time, Penny seemed to become the more important in the story. Jane had eclipsed Jimmy on *Tom Mix* too. Part of a long tradition, Penny was a heroine whose inspiration could be traced back to Jack Armstrong's friend Betty, or even to *Little Orphan Annie* who sat in the copilot's seat next to Daddy Warbucks and later Captain Sparks.

As a genuine uncle, Sky King was rare. Young listeners seemed to want a family group, but they didn't want a real parent to put the pressure of reality on their escape. One of the few examples of a real father in escapist fare is Charlie Chan, who in books, films and radio had his Number One Son and some later additions since he was fruitful and multiplied.

Part of the family unit of the juvenile radio serial generally included an "old-timer," sort of a grandfather figure. Tom Mix had the Old Wrangler and later Sheriff Mike Shaw. (Jack Armstrong's "Uncle" Jim Fairfield was similar but contained elements of the more vigorous older "idol.") On *Sky King*, the old-timer was Jim Bell, the ranch foreman. He had both moments of comedy and the wisdom of age. (The actor, Cliff Soubier, was still going strong as a lay minister at age ninety.)

More unusual for such series was a grandmother figure, Jim's wife Martha. The Lone Ranger had several rough and tough older women with hearts of gold, such as Clarabell Hornblow. A later series, *Straight Arrow*, would feature Mesquite Molly to lend motherly support to radio's great full-blooded Comanche hero. But such female supporting characters were rare.

The writers, Burtt and Moore, seemed to think a strong hero needed an equally strong adversary. On *Captain Midnight*, the Secret Squadron leader's nemesis was the evil spy, Ivan Shark. Sky King got perhaps an even more threatening menace, Dr. Shade. Sort of a combination of the Shadow and the Hunchback of Notre Dame, this creature prowled his castle on the plains of Arizona and brooded ill for Sky and friends. But times were changing and kids were no longer prepared to listen to a hero fight a single menace, day after day, week after week, and seemingly get nowhere. Dr. Shade began the series, and reappeared from time to time, but was never the regular villain that Ivan Shark was on the other aviation show.

The beginning of the King family saga took the group around the world to Europe and Asia in quarter-hour installments. But these serials often took Sky away from his home base, and the Western elements of horses and rangeland that were part of the show's appeal.

Jack Bivens as Clipper and Beryl Vaughn as Penny in a 1950s publicity photo for Mutual Radio's *Sky King*.

With pressure from the newly born television medium and from other radio shows still going strong, the *Sky King* program and *Jack Armstrong* made a unique pact. They would adopt the half-hour complete story format used for many years by *The Lone Ranger* with very little imitation. Moreover, the two shows would share the half-hour of radio time exactly equally. One week Sky would be on three times, and the following week only twice, then three times again. So sometimes *Sky King* would be on Mondays, Wednesdays and Fridays and other weeks on Tuesdays and Thursdays. The same was true for *Jack Armstrong*. It was an interesting experiment, but it caused confusion in newspaper and magazine listings, and in listeners' minds. Eventually, in only a year or so, one sponsor had to bite the bullet and buy an extra fifteen minutes a week. General Mills and Wheaties bought the extra time for Jack, and Sky began being regularly heard only on Tuesdays and Thursdays for Derby Foods' Peter Pan peanut butter. Later, Derby shaved its time a bit more by cutting the program to only 25 minutes. The 25-minute program had become a fairly frequent radio staple because of the need for a 5-minute newscast at various points. To a listener, the dramatic effect of a 25-minute show was no different from that of a 30-minute one, but the shorter length must have required tighter writing, devoid of padding. In later years, the five-minute spot after Sky's was filled by *Bobby Benson*, the Kid Cowboy leader of the B-Bar-B Riders, introducing a couple of songs by Tex Fletcher.

Both shows took a while to settle into the approximately half-hour format, and many of the early episodes were really just "incidents," not real stories with a beginning, middle and end. One half-hour *Sky King* episode, for example, concerned the rescue of a prisoner from a band of renegade Arabs, a story that would have been a mere fragment of one of the old serials. A lot of loose ends were left unresolved. But as time went on, very complicated plots were unfolded in the half-hour format. Eventually, the story would always begin around the Flying Crown ranch and would involve a Western element such as a cattle stampede or the robbery of a Frontier Days stagecoach. From there, the plot might take Sky, Penny and Clipper anywhere in the world – to the fog-shrouded streets of London or the Amazon jungle of Brazil. As Westerns grew even more popular due to early television the stories tended to be placed more and more in the West, always involving one of Sky's aircraft – the prop-driven *Songbird* most often, but occasionally his jet, the *Black Arrow*. Although a civilian, Sky had an aerial cannon mounted in the *Black Arrow* and occasionally engaged in dogfights with menacing planes. (The radio show was less concerned with reality than its television counterpart.)

The series made creative use of format, as has been pointed out. Another innovation the program employed was a semi-serial, composed of connected complete stories. One example was a stolen necklace of nine gems that had been divided among nine thieves. When put back together, the nine gems would reveal a coded secret message of great importance. In each of nine episodes, Sky King would defeat and capture one thief, scattered somewhere in the world, until he found the ninth gem and the completed secret message. Adding to the continuity was the employment of new individual planes for Penny and Clipper, and a contest for the listeners to name the planes. Whatever the winning names, the two teenagers rarely if ever seemed to use those new planes again. Perhaps the King family found it just could not afford so many planes; it did make them seem just a bit too stinking rich. The format, however, was clever. It encouraged regular listening like a serial but delivered more content than the average serial installment, and a listener could miss a broadcast and still enjoy the shows that followed. It was a refinement of the sequence in which the Lone Ranger on his own series captured one member or more of the notorious Black Arrow organization (no connection to Sky's jet) each show, as he worked his way toward the top man.

Rather late in the series, it was decided that Sky should have a great horse to ride on the ground, equal to the *Songbird*. He captured and tamed a great Palomino that was traveling with a wild horse band. His new horse, Yellow Fury, continued to appear a bit more frequently than those small planes for the two kids. The name might have been conceived more carefully since the show just before Sky's every Tuesday and Thursday was *Straight Arrow* and the horse, also a Palomino, was simply Fury. So the two heroes, back to back, each had a horse called "Fury." (Sky did not always call his trusty steed by his full name.) Since the two men were separated in story time by a century or so, it can be assumed they were not sharing a horse.

Roy Windsor took over the writing from the series creators and was also the producer-director. He continued an active career in broadcasting for decades. His radio scripts were adapted to the television series of *Sky King*, and he contributed to the revival of radio drama in *CBS Mystery Theatre* in the 1970s. He died in 1987 at age 75.

He first cast Roy Engel as the rancher-aviator. Engel would work up real emotion by the end of the half-hour shows and snarl that the villains were going to spend the next thirty years in prison. Whatever the crime—game-pouching, treason, bank-robbery—they were always headed for thirty years in the slammer. He must have known a really tough judge.

Off camera, Engel could work up a pretty good rage. Reportedly, during one dispute with the production staff, the late actor whipped out a real gun and fired a warning shot into the control room wall, shouting, "You can't talk to Sky King like that!" Eventually Engel went to Hollywood and played character parts in a number of Westerns—some owlhoots but also some honest sheriffs not unlike his radio image.

Succeeding Engel was Jack Lester, the perfect Sky King. Jack had been born in cattle country in Enid, Oklahoma, and he learned to ride military style at the University of Oklahoma. All the great screen cowboys—Tom Mix, Buck Jones, Ken Maynard, Tim McCoy—rode cavalry fashion, upright and steady, and Jack followed in a great tradition. (Old-time range cowboys actually rode with their elbows pumping like wings, bouncing up and down.) Later, Jack Lester became a skilled pilot.

Jack Lester, who played the role of Sky King, in a recent photo.

Jack's voice always carried sincerity and conviction. He was much in demand as a versatile actor, appearing in supporting roles on *Tom Mix*, soap operas such as *Romance of Helen Trent*, and in such early television shows as *Hawkins Falls*. Today he can be seen on television as a commercial spokesperson, Neil the Mechanic, for a brand of automotive belts.

During the radio era, besides acting, Jack Lester was active as an announcer, doing the last season of the serialized version of *Jack Armstrong* among many other assignments. His announcing skills would come in handy even on the new show in which he starred.

The announcer on *Sky King* was Myron "Mike" Wallace – the same Mike Wallace of television's *Sixty Minutes*. Then as now, Wallace was a man of many interests, one of which was the stock market. Before each afternoon show, Wallace was on the phone with his broker. He kept cutting it closer and closer, getting to the studio just before the show went on live like most radio shows of the period. "Mike," Lester said, "you're not going to make it one of these times."

There came a particularly active market day and Wallace indeed did not make it before the program went on. The cast looked at one another. "Penny" couldn't double the announcer. Jack Lester hitched up his belt and did his own introduction, leading up to his own first line of dialogue. "And we find Sky in the Flying Crown ranch-house with Penny and Clipper, as he says..." (now as Sky) "Kids, there's something funny about those cattle disappearing from the north range...."

Lester recently said, "I pitched it high for the announcer, and dropped it low for Sky. The sponsor was so tight with money, I was afraid they would ask me to do both parts as a regular thing – for the same money, of course. Maybe Mike thought of the same thing. He was on time after that."

Earl Nightingale was the new "Sky King" after Jack Lester left due to the usual contractual differences. Nightingale played Sky for several years, but his real love was in the financial world. For years, he had a program offering inspiration and investment tips which, together with sales of tape recordings on the same subject, made him very wealthy. His business activities took him away from the show nearly half the time, and he was substituted for by radio veteran Carlton KaDell, who eventually became the regular in the leading role.

The other members of the cast all had active careers in Chicago radio and television. The boyish sounding "Clipper" became "Uncle" Johnny Coons in early Chicago television, bringing afternoon fun to another generation of kids.

Coons and Beryl Vaughn left their roles eventually, and another pair of juvenile actors moved over from the discontinued *Captain Midnight* series. Jack Bivens and Beverly Younger became Clipper and Penny, just as they had played Chuck and Joyce on the other flying show. The show sounded a bit like *Captain Midnight* then – so much so that one actor from those days said the Midnight series had changed its name to *Sky King* and gone on. In actuality, the two shows had coexisted for some four years.

Though he did not play a regular role, Norman Gottchak was in almost every episode, playing everything from a Grover, Arizona, storekeeper to a foreign spy. He was one of radio's talented "voice" men, fulfilling the same function on *Sky King* as Forrest Lewis did on *Tom Mix*.

Among the many other semiregulars was Clarence Hartzell, whom Jack Lester describes as being "perhaps the only true genius I ever worked with." His vocal range was not as wide as Gottchak's, and he was limited to playing a certain elderly eccentric type. He is best remembered as Uncle Fletcher on *Vic and Sade*, but he also appeared on *Scattergood Baines*, *Lum and Abner* and *One Man's Family*. The two later series he did from Hollywood, before returning to the more sincere, supportive world of Chicago radio. He also wrote many scripts and musical compositions there, playing a number of instruments himself.

When all these talented people put their skills together, *Sky King* became a whirlwind half-hour of adventure. One story, "The Mark of El Diablo," had a lot of pounding hooves and gunshots, mysterious riders in the night and a black stallion who seemingly brought death of the enemies of one who called himself El Diablo ("the devil" in Spanish), a sinister masked figure who was opposed by Sky King and his friends.

At one point, El Diablo captures Penny and crusty old Jim Bell, but they know Sky King will not be far behind. The crook needs to know the whereabouts of a certain individual Sky had flown to a secluded spot.

El Diablo: If you try stalling –
Penny: Wait – I'll tell you where Zack Morely is.
El Diablo: Talk fast.
Penny: At a waterhole. It's near a strange-looking rock, pointing up like a finger. I'll take you there in the *Songbird*.
El Diablo: A waterhole. Now I'll find it without you.
Jim: It's Sky – he's coming! (*Sound effects: Hoofbeats of several horses, hold under*)
Penny: And he's bringing all the ranchers with him.
El Diablo: He couldn't be!
Penny: Sky – Sky, it's El Diablo!
Jim: On that black stallion, Sky!
Sky: I see him, and I'm going to see what's under that black mask!
El Diablo: No, you don't!
Clipper: (coming on) Sky's bull-dogging him like a wild-eyed steer!
Sky: I've waited a long time for the pleasure of meeting you...
El Diablo: You won't get me!
Sky: And this is a really big pleasure! (*Sound effects: terrific punch, body falls*)
Clipper: You knocked him loose from his mask.
Sky: Just as I thought – Link Higgins.

Link Higgins, alias El Diablo, has been striking his victims with a horseshoe mounted on a club, throwing the blame on the innocent black stallion, as part of a scheme to drive the ranchers off their mineral-rich land. There is no doubt that for his devilry, El Diablo will earn the inevitable "thirty years in prison." Even more certain: "Once again, Sky King has won out in his constant fight for justice!"

Television

The *Sky King* television show was a lot calmer and more realistic than the radio show. On television, Sky seldom wore a gun in the days of the modern west. Even horseback riding was at a minimum. He stuck to his aircraft, the prop-driven *Songbird*, most of the time. The plane was a Cessna P-50 in the first season but later became a Cessna 310-B, which was good for a thousand miles of cruising at an average of 210 mph. The typical young viewer might have guessed a speed for it about three times that, but only when Sky King was at the controls.

Although many of the early television episodes were based on radio plays by Roy Windsor, they set a more deliberate pace and were as logical and well thought-out as most adult shows of the era.

Through his own convictions, or perhaps a fear of looming censorship, producer Jack Chertok was presenting a deliberately more criticism-immune, family oriented show than the radio version. The radio series contained so much action and so many fistfights, gunfights, dogfights in airplanes, chases on horseback and dizzying changes of exotic locale that it sometimes seemed shrill and hysterical. The radio show was fighting to stay alive, and it did, coexisting with the television version for several years and outlasting such radio giants as *Jack Armstrong* and *Tom Mix*.

But television was a new medium and the calculations had been correct—parents would observe with more care what programs their kids enjoyed. Not that such "toning down" was a bad thing. To translate the average radio story of Sky King to the television screen then or now would have taken the budget of an Indiana Jones film.

Early television episodes were, according to collector John McCarthy, limited to such things as a stagecoach stolen from a Frontier Days celebration—a good excuse for Sky and the rest to wear their guns and fanciest Western outfits in contemporary times. The stagecoach contained hidden money from a real robbery Sky discovered.

Another story concerned enemy agents who were dropping bombs on the buildings of a U. S. Air Force base from fake weather balloons. Sky managed to shoot one down from a borrowed fighter plane, and it was up to old Jim Bell to nail the spy on the ground in a somewhat comic fistfight.

The *Songbird* took Sky, Penny and Clipper to many places in the West. They took over a mine and ran it for the owner to trap one employee who was stealing valuable shipments from the air freight. Another time, Penny decided boys had a better lot in life than girls and posed as a boy, succeeding long enough to get involved with crooks trying to steal an important secret from an old man. She couldn't be a boy, but she acquitted herself well as a girl, helping Sky make his capture.

The television Sky King was Kirby Grant. He was a good-looking man with a good voice that wouldn't disappoint Sky's many radio fans. He grew up on a Helena, Montana, ranch and had done a World War II tour of duty as an Air Force flight instructor – credentials enough to make him the famous "flying cowboy." As a boy, he had dreamed of a career as a concert violinist like his idol, Fritz Kreisler. But the six hours a day of practicing left no time for anything else – such as a developing an interest in girls – and he turned to less demanding music, playing and singing with a five-piece band. While on tour, the group played for Chicago crime czar Al Capone. They expected only five dollars apiece, but the gangster believed in conspicuous consumption and peeled off a hundred dollar bill for each. The band members had a sumptuous meal at the best restaurant in Chicago – at a $1.75 a plate.

A stint as a radio singer in Chicago took him to Hollywood in 1937. After only dubbing vocals for actors who looked better than they sang, his slim good looks soon got him before the camera.

Kirby Grant got an impressive start in movies filling John Wayne's boots. *Red River Range* (1938) had a complicated plot and was one of Wayne's last "B" Westerns before *Stagecoach* made him a major star. The story had Wayne as Stony Brooke, leader of the Three Mesquiteers, on an undercover assignment. His old friend, Tex Riley (Kirby Grant) pretends to be Brooke so the trio will be complete (with Crash Corrigan and Max Terhune as fellow Mesquiteers), fooling the crooks. With so large a cast and so busy a script, Grant did not have a lot of screen time, but he was established as a Western hero from the first.

Other Western starring roles followed, starting with *Bad Man of the Border* for Universal in 1945 (musical parts having filled the interim). He made a solid series and an attractive cowboy star, but Universal saw "B" picture profits dropping. When their standing Western town burned down, they quit.

Later, Grant would do another outdoor series for Monogram, about a Canadian Mountie and his dog, rather similar to *Sergeant Preston of the Yukon*. Grant's dog was Chinook, and the series was based on James Oliver Curwood novels, from *Trail of the Yukon* (1949) to *Northern Patrol* (1953).

Grant got the part of Sky King by auditioning for it. He did a scene as Sky with "Penny" – played not by Gloria Winters, who got the role but with

Kirby Grant as television's Sky King.

Barbara Whiting, who had played teenagers on radio. Young Ron Haggerty completed the King family as Clipper.

They worked hard in those early days, six days a week from sunup to late at night. The exteriors were done in Apple Valley near Victorville (now site of Roy Rogers' museum) where the high desert is similar to the named locale of Arizona, where some scenes were actually shot. The cast and crew returned to the Hollywood studios for interiors two and a half days of the long week.

Though each episode was being brought in for around $9,000, the peanut butter sponsor was dissatisfied and dropped out. Eventually a new sponsor, Nabisco cookies, would come along, but Grant did not know that and found another job as a writer-director for Wilding Pictures in Chicago, a company that made such industrial films as a fifteen-minute tour of a steel plant.

It was there two Sky Kings met. Radio's Jack Lester worked as an actor on some of Wilding's films, and the two men exchanged stories about playing the famous flying cowboy, Lester recalled.

Grant was called back to Hollywood to make new episodes of *Sky King*. He took the role seriously, realizing he was a role model for young viewers. He stated that he was not naïve enough to think he could stamp out juvenile delinquency, but he believed that a character with ideals and principles could not help but have some positive influence on young people, if only a slight one.

Grant would not club or gun-whip a criminal, no matter how bad. Television's *Wyatt Earp* introduced gun-whipping of opponents as an acceptable act, a more "adult" attitude. Grant did many of his own fights and much riding himself, although like all action stars he did use stuntman doubles.

Some of the trickier flying was doubled for him too, even though he was an experienced pilot. Curiously Grant would at times copilot the man doing the stunt. On one occasion, he flew with a strange man in a twin Beechcraft. The other pilot had been asleep in the car, but roused instantly and went to the plane. With Grant at his side, he lifted the plane off and started flying straight for two poles thirty feet apart.

An immediate crash looked certain. Grant took a deep breath and thought how interesting life can be. Then the pilot turned the airplane on its side and flew between the two poles. The man had known what he was doing; he just hadn't told Grant.

Over a number of seasons, Kirby Grant and Gloria Winters made 130 television episodes. Gloria met her future husband while the rest of the cast had lunch, leaving "Penny" tied to her seat, a "prisoner." Ron Haggerty left after the first season to join the Air Force in real life. Explanation for his absence: Clipper had joined the Air Force.

The original negatives of many of those 130 episodes were lost in a warehouse fire. Only 77 are thought to have been saved, though some of the others may exist as positive prints in the hands of private collectors. Still, 77 episodes is a respectable number for a rerun series. For years they lay in vaults, perhaps because of some legal dispute between producers and old sponsors. An occasional episode of *Sky King* would be seen in a "Festival of Early TV." But in 1988, the CBN cable network began running the *Sky King* series again nationwide. The shows look in great shape, although a few have mismatched end credits with the wrong supporting cast. It remains to be seen how many episodes will appear.

Kirby Grant is not here to see it happen. After surviving open-heart surgery and other illnesses, he died in a one-car accident in 1985 while en route to Cape Canaveral to see a space shuttle launch. He had been invited by one of the astronauts, a boyhood Sky King fan. In the years following the television show, Grant had continued to make public appearances and had represented such institutions as Sea World in Flordia. He and his wife ran a Sky King Youth Ranch for homeless teenagers in the 1970s. At one time, he had a plan to film new episodes of *Sky King* at the ranch and to let the general public in, making the ranch a tourist attraction. He even promised fans he would try to bring back a new radio series in which he would play Sky King (for the first time on radio). He could never quite get this plan off the ground as easily as he did the *Songbird* in all those episodes.

Shortly before his death, Kirby Grant, Gloria Winters and Ron Haggerty appeared together on television in a reunion of old television show casts. All looked in fine shape, ready to go back before the cameras and make another series about a slightly more mature family, perhaps with Penny and Clipper married to spouses and parenting young "Pennys" and "Clippers" of their own.

Comics

Sky King appeared in only one known comic, a giveaway called *Sky King and the Runaway Train*, a sixteen-page regular size comic book offered in 1964 by television sponsor Nabisco. Though not high in collector value – a perfect copy is worth only about eight dollars – it is rare.

There was also a short-lived attempt at a newspaper strip of *Sky King*. Collector Richard Gulla remembered seeing it as a Sunday page in the Chicago *Sun-Times* in the early 1950s, artist and writer unknown. The character of Sky was drawn after the likeness of radio actor Earl Nightingale, Gulla recalled.

More familiar to many people were the Sunday comics and comics magazine ads for many of Sky's premiums. They were drawn in comics style and occasionally had dialogue balloons. Even though they did not feature a miniature adventure as similar Tom Mix advertisements did, the *Sky King* ads were a colorful and nostalgic part of the world of radio and early television.

Premiums

Many Sky King premiums were offered simultaneously on radio and television. On radio, the premium was incorporated into the storyline. This was never done on television, due to the rerunning of the episodes long after the offer was over. The premiums were as follows, listed alphabetically with date and approximate value in 1992 (assuming average condition).

Address Stamping Kit (1950; personal name & address stamper with ink pad, size of aspirin box; $45), Ring, Aztec Indian (1947; $95), Ring, Electronic Television (1949; behind plastic screen, small photos of Sky and others; $80), Ring, Magi-Glo Writing (1949; glows in dark and has miniature ballpoint pen; $65), Ring, Mystery Picture (1947; turning top changes from Sky to him in sinister disquise via polarization – almost never found in working order due to fading polarization; $150), Ring, Navajo Treasure (1950; $80), Ring, Radar Signal (1948; $80), Ring, Teleblinker (huge ring with telescope and miniature Naval-style signal blinker; $80), Signal Scope (1947; tube with mirror, whistle, luminous band, magnifying glass, code chart; $45), Writer, Spy-Detecto (1949; metal, oblong with code dial, magnifier, raised alphabet strip and built-in ink pad; $65).

There were a few later television only premiums such as a Nabisco postcard with a color photo of Sky (worth only about six dollars). All actual radio premiums were offered by Peter Pan peanut butter, the only radio sponsor.

Superman

Juvenile serial. Began as a syndicated 15-minute serial three times a week in 1938, running until 1940. Then as follows: 2/12/40–1942, Sustaining, Mutual 3x/wk; 8/31/42–1943, Sustaining, Mutual, 5x/wk, 15 min.; 1943–46, Pep, Mutual, 5x/wk, 5:15 PM, 15 min.; 1946–49, Sustaining, Mutual, 5x/wk, 5:15 PM, 15 min.; 1949 (Winter-Spring), Sustaining, Mutual, 3x/wk, 30 min.; 1949 (Fall)–1950, Sustaining, ABC, Sat., 30 min.; 1950–1951, Sustaining, ABC, 2x/wk, 30 min.

Producers: Robert and Jessica Maxwell **Chief Writer-Director:** Jack Johnstone **Other Writers:** Mitchell Grayson, George Lowther, others **Directors:** George Lowther, Allen Ducovy, others **Sound Effects:** Jack Keane **Superman, (alter ego for Clark Kent, reporter):** Clayton (Bud) Collier (1940–50), Michael Fitzmaurice (last season only) **Lois Lane, reporter:** Joan Alexander **Jimmy Olson, copy boy, later cub reporter:** Mitch Evans (substitute) **Perry White, managing editor:** Julian Noa **Beanie, office boy:** Jackson Beck **Batman:** Stacy Harris, Matt Crowley, Gary Merrill, Bret Morrsion, Don McLaughlin, others **Robin:** Ron Liss **Narrator:** Jackson Beck, George Lowther, Frank Knight **Others:** Ned Wever (the Wolf, and other roles), Mandel Kramer, Robert Dryden, George Petrie, Guy Sorel.

The Superman radio series began in syndication in 1940, only two years after the first publication of the genre-creating comic strip. The broadcast series was as innovative as the print version. In fact, the comics borrowed a number of the elements of the radio series, primarily the introduction of copy boy (later cub reporter) Jimmy Olsen as an important character, and the invention of the radioactive element Kryptonite from Superman's home planet as his greatest menace.

The casting of Clayton "Bud" Collier was inspired. His ability to speak as Clark Kent in a high voice, then change his tone to monumental depth and power when it became "A job for . . . *Superman!*" was impressive and unique. The difference between Kent and the man of steel was unmistakable, yet there was no doubt both voices came from one man. None of the many other people who have portrayed Superman in various media could duplicate this vocal duality.

In the opening weeks of the series, Kent's voice was perhaps too high, almost comical. But as the months wore on, Kent spoke in a rather commanding masculine tone himself, just never as forceful as the superhuman man of steel.

Reportedly, Collier made a few personal appearances as Superman in full costume, but with the addition of a football helmet. The new gear was in response to an incident of one kid sneaking up on him to swing a baseball bat at his head to see how "super" he really was. In interviews Collier said the cast really sent the script up in rehearsals to get the improbabilities out of their system, so they could do the broadcast dead serious. One anecdote tells of the cast undressing Collier during a live broadcast while he had to keep the grave tone of the man of steel. A visiting sponsor's representative put a stop to that.

In the sixties Collier, who admitted that he had not wanted to do the *Superman* series and was even "ashamed" of it (probably "embarrassed" would have been a better word), grew nostalgic and asked people to send him recordings of the show if they had them. He even returned to voicing Superman in a series of Saturday morning cartoons, along with other cast members such as Joan Alexander ("Lois"). He was better known as a television game host by this time, on such programs as *Beat the Clock* in the fifties and *To Tell the Truth* in the sixties. A circulation problem brought on his final illness in the seventies.

The opening of the very first broadcast nearly had the classic introduction down: "Faster than an airplane... More powerful than a locomotive... Impervious to bullets..."

There was no sound effect but the rushing wind of Superman's flight. But soon the opening was in final form:

Announcer:	"Faster than a speeding bullet... [Sound effects: Passing bullet] More powerful than a locomotive... [SFX: Locomotive] Able to leap tall buildings in a single bound... [SFX: Rushing wind, hold under]
Man:	Look–up in the sky!
Woman:	It's a bird!
2nd Man:	It's a plane!
Man:	It's Superman!

On the initial episode only, Superman was thought by the woman to be a "giant" bird.

Bud Collier, circa 1950, who played Superman on radio.

The sound of Superman in flight was reportedly accomplished by combining a recording of shrieking wind with that of an artillery shell screaming through the air. The sound effects men became adept as slowing the "flying" recording by hand to suggest the man of steel swooping down, stopping the turntable to suggest him dropping down to the ground. It was different from a mere wind effect, and one of the most identifiable sound effects in all of radio.

The introduction, explaining Superman's origin and powers, changed over the years, but it was generally agreed he "came to Earth with powers and abilities far beyond those of mortal men" and that he worked in secret as Clark Kent, "mild-mannered reporter for a great metropolitan newspaper." It wasn't until 1942 that he was said to fight for "Truth, Justice, and the American Way."

In the first program of its long run, the *Superman* series opened with a reasonable depiction of the last days of the planet Krypton when scientist Jor-El and his wife Lara send their infant son, Kal-El, in an experimental rocketship toward Earth, just before the moment of Doomsday. Episode Two was pretty silly, one of the worst of the entire series. Superman grows up on the long flight, educating himself in the process. Immediately on landing on Earth, he rescues an old man and a boy from an out-of-control vehicle and they suggest their strange new friend get a job on a newspaper and call himself – just out of the blue – Clark Kent. Longtime chief writer and director of the show Jack Johnstone denied in 1987 that he had written that particular script. If he did, he apparently could not remember it.

Early sequences of the program often had the young reporter going off on expeditions in the jungles, the Arctic or the South Seas, doing more of this than reporting the crime beat in Metropolis for the *Daily Planet*. These were adventures perhaps more appropriate for Jack Armstrong, the All-American Boy, but experimentation was needed to find out exactly what to do with Superman. Moreover, the show was just starting out in low-budgeted syndication. These stories of vast and uncivilized territory often left Clark with only one or two people to talk to during a whole episode. Small cast, small expense.

Fortunately, unlike almost every similar radio adventure serial, almost the entire run of the show has survived on transcriptions (although often rather battered and poor sounding ones) and the various stages of the series can be clearly heard on the episodes that have been released.

As the program became more established and successful as a transcription feature, the cast was expanded.

Around the fiftieth episode of the program, when Clark Kent goes searching for the lost explorer Alonzo Craig in the Arctic, he is accompanied by only two characters, an old sea captain and a bewhiskered guide. The whole story is told with only Kent/Superman and these two companions, with a little doubling of grunts and shouts from hostile natives. Kent eventually discovers Craig, who has lost his mind and become a tribal witch doctor, and brings him back to civilization and sanity.

Later, the series featured more of the regulars such as *Daily Planet* editor Perry White, reporter Lois Lane (the only young, adult woman regularly a co-star in this type of afternoon thriller) and most often teenage Jimmy Olson, copy boy and later cub reporter.

Many of the early radio serials feature Jimmy Olsen as virtually a full partner to Kent/Superman. He is as important in the series as Jack Armstrong was to Uncle Jim Fairfield or Jimmie Allen was to Speed Robertson. Of course, unlike Jack Armstrong or Jimmie Allen, Jimmy Olsen did not have the program titled after him. (Many years later, he did achieve his own comic book title.) In the story, Jimmy traveled everywhere with Kent, with the usual father/son relationship clearly established. Though as close as family members, Jimmy always politely referred to his mentor as "Mr. Kent."

In one adventure out West with Tumbleweed Jones, a cowboy who uses a bow and arrow instead of a six gun, Jimmy Olsen refers to his pal back home, Jackie Kelk. That was the real name of the actor playing Jimmy; he was giving himself a plug. Most radio shows did not give actor credits in those days.

Bud Collier never mentioned his own name, but for several shows in which he was working with Naval intelligence in 1941 he had to explain why Clark Kent, alias Superman, sounded as if he had a bad cold: He had been dictating war news all day long and was hoarse.

These globe-trotting adventures have very much the feel of the thirties, a time between wars. One excellent example of this type of story concerned the experiences of Kent and Jimmy aboard the *Clara M.*, "last of the clipper ships." It was an old style sea story with a peg-legged villain, Pete Barnaby, as well as a ghostly presence on board known as "the Whistler" for obvious reason. There were storms and waves, winds and sails, men overboard and men mutinying. There was a stowaway, young Pug Flanagan, a rougher-edged companion for Jimmy, and a medical operation performed at sea by Kent with radio instruction from another vessel. Of course, the mysterious Superman appeared from time to time to rescue people from the sea, or to quell an unruly crew with his superhuman powers. But the story of the ship and the sea remained paramount. Finally, the last villain was put in irons and the Whistler was revealed to be only the wind passing through a set of pipes mounted in the classic wooden figurehead adorning the bow of the craft.

During these stories, Clark Kent was really only "mild-mannered" in the standard introduction to the show. He displayed courage and initiative, and on several occasions knocked cold some threatening foe with a "lucky punch." Jimmy complimented Mr. Kent on one occasion by telling him he was "a lot like Superman." Certainly on radio, Kent was more like Superman than he ever was in the comic strip or in the movies. It must have been decided that on radio, Kent could not be portrayed as a complete coward or fool and become heroic only after a switch to Superman. Such a contrast may have been deemed too great for young listeners to understand. So on radio, Kent was a very capable young man, but he became a miracle worker when he switched to the man of steel. In the radio stories, Superman's appearances had to be kept to a minimum. Superman could resolve any problem too quickly for a daily radio serial to last several weeks if he stayed on stage all the time. Usually Kent was prevented from becoming Superman so as not to give away his secret identity to others such as Jimmy or Lois.

There was even a treasure map found on the old sailing ship, but no one ever went searching for that treasure. The real world seemed to be intruding on these old-fashioned stories from the thirties (with the influence of an even earlier tradition going back to Stevenson's *Treasure Island*). As Kent and Jimmy returned to Metropolis on a more modern freighter, World War II brought the series into the world of the forties. The ship on which our friends from the *Daily Planet* was traveling was mined by agents with clearly German accents to blow up its shipment of nitrate for explosives, destined for an allied port. Though Clark Kent professed neutrality, Superman displayed distinct hostility to these Nazi agents.

The next story might as well have been set during the middle of World War II, although it was 1941 before America entered the combat. Enemy agents with German names and accents are out to seize an experimental submarine developed for the U. S. Navy, one that can dive to greater depths than heretofore known, past 250 feet. The wartime characterizations of Nazis were in full force, even in this early story. They are portrayed as total monsters with contempt for all human decency. A captured Editor White gives an impassioned speech to the effect that he has fought against the scourge of war all his life, but if that is what it will take to rid the world of such depraved subhuman creatures, he will carry a gun himself. Superman returns a torpedo aimed at an American ship to the submarine of the German-accented agents, blowing it up and striking the first American blow of the war (albeit fictional).

Next, there was an attempt to return to the stories of the thirties, with Kent and Jimmy going to the Far North to solve the mystery of the "White Plague," a curse upon a lumber camp supplying paper to the *Daily Planet*. Revealing the man behind the seemingly supernatural events seemed "too small potatoes" for the mighty Superman in those eventful times.

Just before Pearl Harbor, Dec. 1, 1941, Superman was in South America looking for a group of American engineers who had been captured by the Lost Tribe of the Incas, an intelligent, sophisticated group who preferred to steer clear of the white man. Nevertheless, Superman wins the Incas over by creating a new river to bring them water for crops, power for their mills. The engineers will be allowed to build a new highway through their homeland to help join North and Sough America together for interhemispheric defense (suggested by the real-life Pan American Highway). On their return to the States, Jimmy Olsen, though "only fourteen," tries unsuccessfully to enlist in the Navy and Clark Kent receives a commission as an undercover Secret Service officer. (In the comics, he never officially served in the armed forces. He failed the physical by accidentally looking through the wall with his X-ray vision and reading the wrong eye chart.)

One of Kent's first tasks as a Secret Service officer was to track down a spy ring led by the dread Leopard Woman. For most of the war, Superman would fight these enemy agents at home and abroad. One of his greatest foes was Der Teufel ("the devil" in German), a Nazi scientist who developed an atomic gun whose rays must have been similar to those of Kryptonite. The rays from the atomic gun were harmful to Superman, but thankfully not fatal.

To escape the constant pressure of wartime events, Superman would sometimes return to searches for lost explorers and the solving of seemingly supernatural mysteries such as a ghost car causing highway accidents near a dude ranch.

It was during the "Ghost Car" story that Jackson Beck first appeared on the *Superman* radio series. The man who would become that program's most famous announcer – one of the great announcer-narrators in the medium – Jackson Beck was first heard on *Superman* in an acting role, in Program No. 317, February 18, 1942, as a South American goucho named Alfredo. Some fifty years later, Beck is still voicing television commercials for Superman's old sponsor, Kellogg's cereals, and is still one of the announcers most in demand in broadcasting, at past eighty years of age. His voice and skill haven't changed. Though he lives quietly and alone since becoming a widower, he is reported to make more than a million dollars a year.

It was Beck who told the story of Superman's adventures, then turned listeners over to announcer Dan McCullough who would tell the benefits of eating Kellogg's Pep – the main benefit being the prize inside the box. Each box contained a model warplane that could be constructed from wood, or later cardboard. Finally, with metal rationing ending with the close of World War II, listeners were offered the classic Pep comic buttons, dime-sized pinbacks with a different comic strip character on each: Superman, of course, and Little Orphan Annie, Moon Mullins and many more. "They are metal and will last a long time." Many onetime listeners still have theirs after forty years.

Sometimes Superman would return to the same story twice. "The Dragon's Teeth" was one such serial, a story of a set of jade pieces that gave the secret of eternal health and life. The earliest version in 1940 contained a good many racial insensitivities about the Chinese. When repeated after the War, they were removed – a good thing for Superman, self-proclaimed champion of tolerance and good will.

Another repeated story was that of the "Voice Machine." It was presented just before and after World War II, and it was even condensed as one broadcast during the single season of complete half-hour stories on *Superman*. This series of half-hour scripts was repeated virtually in full when the show moved from Mutual to ABC, with Michael Fitzmaurice replacing Bud Collier in the title role. Fitzmaurice had a beautiful deep voice, but he was never able to change it from Kent to Superman the way Collier had so brilliantly and convincingly.)

The miraculous power of Dr. Roebling's Voice Machine was that it could be adjusted to pick up any sound from the past, anywhere on Earth. The demonstration used was tuning in on Abraham Lincoln delivering the Gettysburg Address. Kent, Lois and editor Perry White felt that such a device could bring about world peace – no nation could keep its war plans secret. (Of course, it has often been evident when some nation has been plotting war – in reality prior knowledge is not sufficient protection.) Beyond question, it was a valuable invention and Roebling's greedy nephew tried to steal it for himself.

As the guilty nephew and his wife fled in their car, the red-caped Superman dropped into the road in front of them and stopped them with his more than human strength.

Unfortunately, the man of steel could not stop the revenge-seeking nephew from smashing the Voice Machine on a return visit. But as Clark Kent, his prodding and suggestions helped the old inventor repair the fabulous device. Then, halfway through the usual length of a serial, the scriptwriter seemed to run out of ideas and the story became one of ordinary crime and gangsters discovered by a chance tuning of the Voice Machine.

In 1945, near the end of World War II, Superman performed one of his many rescues, this time of an unconscious boy from a drifting rowboat. The man of steel notices the boy is wearing a red vest with the letter "R" on it, under his more ordinary clothes. "Great Scot," Superman intones "if this is who I think it is, this is serious business!"

The listeners were invited to think it over until the next show to see if they knew who the boy was. He was Robin, the boy sidekick of the famous Batman – as the show put it – "the most fabulous and glamorous figure in the whole world, save only Superman himself."

Later Robin, in his civilian identity of Dick Grayson, tells Clark Kent of the disappearance of Batman. After an attack by armed men at their home, Dick heard one of the men mention the name of Zoltan. Using that clue, the two crimefighters go to Zoltan's Wax Museum, where through a window the boy thinks he see Batman – but he is a wax figure.

As the story develops, it turns out that Zoltan has a process of keeping people in suspended animation in his wax statues, not only Batman but a group of Allied scientists he is planning to ship to Germany to be used against the forces of democracy. Superman discovers the scheme and first frees Batman, tearing off the covering of "wax," which is actually a compound harder than steel. Then for the first time on radio (and after only in a few comic book panels and symbolic covers) the two most famous costumed characters in popular entertainment meet. Batman's first concern is for Robin and the imprisoned scientists, but after learning of their safety, he expresses his thanks to the man of steel.

This would hardly by their last meeting. Batman became a regular on the *Superman* radio series, appearing in about every second story from then on. Robin did not appear quite so often; Batman showed up alone about half the time.

Stacy Harris was apparently the first actor to play Batman on the show. He had been one of the early Jack Armstrongs. Midway through the second story in which Batman appeared—a rather routine mystery involving an amusement park—the part of the cowled crusader was taken over by Matt Crowley, who earlier had been Buck Rogers and who would be Mark Trail, the outdoorsman whose series would replace that of *Superman* five years later. Ron Liss was the regular Robin.

A number of other actors are recalled to have played Batman at one time or another—Bret Morrsion (radio's Shadow), Don McLaughlin (David Harding, Counterspy), Richard Kolmar (Boston Blackie), etc. Memories may have been faulty; transcriptions of shows with these actors have not yet turned up.

Naturally, the plan must have been for Batman to "spin off" (as they would say years later in television) to a series of his own, but it never happened. There are reports of an "audition" or pilot show in which Batman spoke in usual American tones as his civilian identity, Bruce Wayne, but in a British accent as Batman. Some sort of voice change to help the radio listener separate Bruce Wayne and Batman was the obvious intention, and not everyone could do Bud Collier's two-tone trick. It might have been better for "millionaire playboy" Bruce Wayne to have used the British accent or a cultured, affected upper class tone, and for the rugged Batman to have remained All-American. In the thirties, Al Hodge playing the Green Hornet had anticipated all these radio voice changes by playing publisher Britt Reid as an educated gentleman and the Green Hornet as a growling tough guy since the Hornet was generally suspected of being a crook and was not recognized as a crimefighter.

On the *Superman* radio series, however, Batman and his alter ego, Bruce Wayne, were portrayed in exactly the same tone of voice by the various actors.

Shortly after the amusement park mystery, the greatest serial story in the more than twelve-year run of *Superman* radio series began. It was a story of Superman's greatest menace, Kryptonite, and how it became embodied in a human menace, the Atom Man. The story involved Batman and Robin and a league of the most dangerous villains the man of steel had faced. It went on for months, and at times it looked as if Superman was facing death – even as if he were dead. At one point the demonic Nazi, the Atom Man, drove Superman to his knees with bolts of green Kryptonite lightning, and announcer Jackson Beck asked, "Is this the end of Superman? The end of truth, justice and the American way?" This serial was the greatest blockbuster of all Superman radio serials.

Kryptonite, the radioactive element from Superman's destroyed home planet, Krypton, had come to Earth as a meteorite, and had been found and used against the man of steel by a racketeer in an earlier story. But it was all thought to have been destroyed except for a small piece kept for research in the Metropolis Museum.

A villainess, the Scarlet Widow, has one of her henchmen steal the Kryptonite from the museum. She then proceeds to extort a million dollars from some of the man of steel's old enemies, including Der Tenfel and the Laugher, a sinister chuckling gangster. They could pay her and eliminate their greatest menace forever.

Der Teufel obtains a portion of the Kryptonite for his own purposes and returns to his native Germany with it. In 1945 the nation had been conquered, but according to the story, a group of dedicated Nazis was plotting "the next war." The Nazis were such complete villains, writers of popular entertainment could not seem to let them go – or perhaps stories involving the Nazis had already been planned or written before the war ended.

In a secret cave inside occupied Germany, Der Teufel begins his plan to create an Atom Man, a living human being in whose veins will flow the deadly radioactive Kryponite, greatest menace to Superman and therefore the greatest menace to the forces of right and justice. To create this creature of pure evil, Der Teufel selects a simple soldier, Heinreik Milch, who will assume the power of the Atom Man, but who (like Superman himself) will pose as an ordinary American – an employee of the *Daily Planet*, known connection to the man of steel. He will use the American name of Henry Miller (no connection with the writer of erotic literature, one presumes, or else he would be after Lois to read his writings and give him her reaction).

Mason Adams played the part of Henry Miller, the Atom Man. In fifty years as a voice actor, he played many roles, but a *TV Guide* article suggested that the Atom Man might have made the greatest impression on him.

Stark confrontations between good and evil are always memorable: Sherlock Holmes and Professor Moriarty, Van Helsing and Dracula. This match-up of Superman and Atom Man was of similar intensity.

As the Atom Man tests his powers, there are several encounters between him and Superman. Miller needs to use a converter device to activate the

Kryptonite in his blood. With the converter on, he can shoot Kryptonite bolts of green lightning to subdue the man of steel. Although these Kryptonite bolts can drive Superman back, send him to his knees, even make him unconscious, they do not seem to have the power to actually *kill* him.

Miller is irked that he does not have sufficient power to destroy Superman. The radioactive poison in his blood seems to affect his mind. He rants and raves that he *could* kill the man of steel, but he fails to prove it.

Superman is so hard pressed by these events that he has to take a desperate action. He goes to Batman as Clark Kent and reveals his secret identity to the cowled crusader. He will need his help as he has never needed help before. Batman does help him, running down vital clues as to the whereabouts of the various conspirators involved in the elaborate scheme to use Kryptonite to destroy Superman, the worst of all featuring the Atom Man.

Then at last, after times when Superman seems near death, or even dead, there comes the final confrontation between the two most powerful men on the face of the earth. With a merciless plan to drive Superman into the open, the Atom Man threatens to blow up the dam above the city and drown every man, woman and child in Metropolis. The man of steel meets his foe face to face in a stand of woods near the dam, for a terrible battle.

Atom Man: Come closer, I dare you. You're afraid of me. Superman is afraid of me.
Announcer: Gasping for breath, his mighty muscles weakened by bombardment of atomic power, Superman clings to the top of a tall tree, regaining his lost strength. But the Atom Man whirls about, his strange meshed hands outstretched, forked green lightning hurtling from them, to shrivel the trees in his path, to rend and uproot them, to send them crashing to earth with a roar like Jovian thunder...
Atom Man: Now for you, Superman...
Announcer: His eyes gleaming like a madman's, the Nazi monster points his hands at the tree where Superman clings, laughing triumphantly as green lightning strikes the giant trunk and coils around it like a pair of twined snakes, uproots it and hurls it, scorched, to the earth. As Superman falls to the ground, wrapped in the crashing branches, the Atom Man rushes toward him...
Atom Man: Now I've got you! This time you are through!
Superman: No, keep away!
Announcer: His atomic power raking and exploding the earth and branches about his fallen foe, the Atom Man races forward, but suddenly there is a violent burst of wind,

a blur of red and blue, and Superman bounds from the ground, slashing upward into the heavens, like a comet...

Through force of will more than physical strength, Superman has saved himself for another moment. But the merciless Atom Man hurls bolt after bolt of otherworldly energy after the man of steel, causing him to drop like a stone into the waters of Metropolis Lake.

The Atom Man rants deliriously over his triumph, his reason gone. But then after long minutes, a flying form streaks upward from the waters and grabs the creature that was once a human being and carries him far aloft.

Five thousand feet up, Superman warns the Atom Man to hold still while he rips away the converter device that frees the Kryptonite racing in Miller's bloodstream. Superman has won – or would have if he were dealing with a sane man. Miller continues to send Kryptonite radiation through the man of steel from the grip he has on his shoulders. Supermans warns Miller he is getting weak, near unconsciousness, and he cannot help but drop the Atom Man. Though privy to great power, the Atom Man's body is mortal.

Finally Superman's grip weakens. The Atom Man falls, screaming, his sanity returning long enough that he knows he is about to die. A moment later, Superman loses consciousness, and he plunges a second behind his mightiest foe.

Two bodies strike the earth near the shore of the lake. But only one figure stirs and revives. It is Superman.

His old friend Inspector Henderson of the Metropolis police and an Army general rush to help him and to extend their thanks to Superman for saving the city from the disaster of an exploded dam and for ridding the world of the menace of the Atom Man. "You don't owe me anything, I'm fighting for the same things you are – the end of tyranny and intolerance."

The long story – perhaps the longest serial in the history of the *Superman* radio series – was not yet over. Some of the other villains in the plot, like the Scarlet Widow, had to be accounted for.

A scientist in league with the fat gangster, the Laugher, recovers a small piece of Kryptonite and manages to use it first to render Superman unconscious and then to place him in a cyclotron, an "atom smasher" in which the man of steel may be finally destroyed. But Superman's allies, Batman and Robin, save him from that trap. Superman quickly snatches up the professor and the gangster and sees to it that the "last known" piece of Kryptonite is destroyed "forever."

There would be other fragments of the dread element located by enemies in the future years, other cases in which Superman needed the help of Batman and Robin, other menaces hovering over Superman's friends, Lois Lane, Jimmy Olsen, editor Perry White, office boy Beanie, Inspector

Henderson, private detective Candy Myers. But the moment of his greatest triumph was surely the destruction of the essence of evil, the Atom Man.

Films and Television

The first film appearance of Superman came in the wonderful animated short subjects of Max and Dave Fleisher. If not too distracted by alluring visuals, one could recognize the voices of Bud Collier and other radio cast members giving a familiar sound to these cartoons. Later, other voice actors would be used. Collier reportedly got tired of leaving New York City and traveling to a place in New Jersey just to dub the four or five lines needed for Superman in these shorts. Apparently, the producers were not prepared to offer him enough money to make it sufficiently interesting.

Most critics think the realistic animation of these shorts has never been surpassed or even equaled. They cannot be compared to the simple, often crude adventure cartoons of Saturday morning television; indeed, this 1942 Fleisher series may well be the finest example ever produced of cartoons not involving funny animals. In them one can see Superman taking on Einsteinian physics by bending a ray of light from the destructive ray machine of the "Mad Scientist" (the first entry), or battling flying robots in "Mechanical Monsters" or rescuing Lois from a King Kong-like ape in "Terror on the Midway."

In 1948, Superman first became a live action figure on screen in the Columbia serial *Superman*.

The first live action Superman was Kirk Alyn. Producer Sam Katzman phoned Alyn to drop around to his office to try out for the role of Superman. Alyn said he would be glad to. He had worked for the "king of 'B' pictures" before in a corny musical, *Pistol Packin' Mama*, and did not mind doing so again. Of course, he had seen *Superman* in the newspaper comics and knew roughly who the character was, but his conversations with the author suggested that he did not really know yet how "super" Superman was and thought he was more like Batman—a real stong guy who could beat up crooks.

When he arrived at Katzman's office, the secretary, who he knew, was pleased and relieved to see him. "Oh, Kirk, I'm glad you are here. We've had a parade of weightlifters, circus strongmen, and wrestlers trying out for Superman. They were impossible. At last, a real actor."

Katzman's effusive greeting died in his throat. He was shocked to see Kirk wearing a beard and goatee for a costume picture he had just made. "It shaves off, you know," Kirk told him.

There was a representative of DC Comics, probably Whitney Ellsworth, in the office. He and Alyn became friends later on, but Alyn did not know him at the time. Katzman said, "Let's show this gentleman your build. Take off your shirt."

Alyn took off the shirt. For some reason, Kirk Alyn looked much more muscular in person than on film, with well-defined weightlifter biceps. He was taller and broader chested than George Reeves, television Superman, but on film he did not look it. Alyn always appeared slender and graceful on film – usually an asset, but not when portraying the strongest man on Earth. Some have said he looked so young, a mere stripling, that he appeared to be more Superboy than Superman. Actually (although he did not admit it at the time) Alyn was forty when he first played the man of steel.

Katzman and the man from the publishing company seemed satisfied with a shirtless Kirk. "Now, Kirkie, would you mind taking off your pants?" the producer asked.

"Wait a minute," Kirk said. "I don't take off my pants that easily."

They laughed, and Kirk let them see if his legs would measure up for Superman.

Eventually, he was fitted for the Superman costume. Unfortunately, in 1948 double-knit fabrics had not yet been invented, and the best they could do was a sweater material, which could not be as form-fitting as the costume Adam West would wear as Batman in the sixties television version of *Batman*, or the outfit worn by a later screen Superman, Christopher Reeve. The Kirk Alyn costume was colored to look best on black and white film – gray (for blue) and brown (for red).

The costume was so revealing that it soon proved impossible to use a double for Kirk Alyn in the more dangerous scenes. The audience could see the way he was built and the way he moved. He was a trained dancer, and they could see his face. There was no shielding of the face with a hat brim as typically used with serial stuntmen. Kirk practically had to *be* Superman in this low budgeted film without a stuntman or elaborate special effects.

It was his ballet training, Kirk believed, that allowed him to move gracefully as the man of steel. It was not the first time he had performed in tights. As a dancer, he had taken some great leaps, but the longest one came when he had to jump down twelve or fourteen feet from a large packing box in the film. He was also frequently required to rescue Lois Lane (Noel Neil) or Jimmy Olsen (Tommy Bond). Dummies were used sometimes, but other times the real people had to be used for close or medium shots. In one scene, Superman carried the woman and young man from a smoke-filled fire scene, one under each arm.

"Kirk, you're Superman," director Spencer Bennet complained. "Everything you do should be effortless. But I could see the muscles in you neck straining."

"Spence," Alyn said, "I'm not really Superman. Those were two real people, not dummies, I was carrying. I do have to strain a bit."

Kirk Alyn was the first on-screen Man of Steel in the 1948 serial, *Superman*. Alyn was also a radio actor in such 1940s shows as *Portia Faces Life*, and in Jim Harmon's 1975 series, *Curley Bradley's Trail of Mystery*. ("Superman" is a copyrighted trademark of DC Comics Inc.)

Bennet, who made many silent and sound movie serials including the two Superman serials and the very last serial made, *Blazing the Overland Trail*, prided himself on bringing a picture in under budget. When he did that for Katzman, the producer figured he was being given too much money, and his budget was cut back each time. Bennet reported he was actually embarrassed at how cheap some of the last serials looked. On *Superman*, he was given a reasonable budget. Although in his fifties, Spencer Bennet persisted in a long practice of showing stuntmen and actors how he wanted a stunt done by doing it himself.

Because there would only be one chance at it, Bennet did not preview one stunt for Kirk. For the Chapter One cliffhanger, Superman was to hold a broken train rail in place for the locomotive to pass safely over. The crew of a real train was altered to the appearance of a cloaked figure on the tracks. The camera crew "cheated" the angle so Kirk Alyn would be over on a parallel track, but very close to the one the train passed over. The production crew pulled well back, and Kirk was left alone. The train approached. It roared by, wheels clanking furiously. The wind tugged at Kirk's cloak, threatening to drag him under the wheels. He held on to the rail with all his non-superhuman strength to keep from being dragged under the speeding train.

Afterwards, the crew came back and someone told him, "You really looked great, Kirk." He later said he thought to himself, "An actor will do anything, so long as they tell him he looks good doing it."

In the first serial, Superman fights the villainous Spider Lady (Carol Forman), who uses Kryptonite against him to seize a powerful secret weapon, the Reducer Ray. But she is defeated in the end by the man of steel, who wears a protective lead lining under his uniform to make himself immune to the deadly rays from the unearthly element. (One might question why he did not always wear such protective gear. Perhaps it itched.)

In the second serial, *Atom Man Vs. Superman* (1950), the man of steel fights both his old nemisis Luthor (Lyle Talbot) and the booming-voiced Atom Man, in black robes and a huge idol-like head. (Only the name for this character had been taken from the radio series.) Even the smallest child in the audience soon discerned than Luthor and the Atom Man were one and the same. There was far more gadgetry in the second serial, and more action with Superman.

George Plympton was chief writer on both, although his screen credit varied. He was sensitive about the plausibility of his scripts – which were supposed to be entertaining, not necessarily believable. He once showed the author a newspaper clipping about a man falling out of one plane and landing astride another one. "I put that in a serial, and they said it was not believable. But it really happened," Plympton said.

For the second serial, there were some scenes of Kirk Alyn flying in costume. He was painfully suspended on wires for a long time. Only a few medium shots were used, and the wires showed. In both serials, the flying scenes of Superman were accomplished by turning the man of steel into a cartoon, a line drawing. A more realistic animation with a wash drawing, similar to a painting, could have been done for a few thousand dollars more, but producer Katzman declined.

Excellent scenes of a man flying had been done by Republic in *The Adventures of Captain Marvel* (1941) and *King of the Rocket Men* (1945). But this was Columbia, not Republic, who had lost the bid to make the first *Superman* serial in 1941 when the screen rights went to Paramount for the cartoon series. Republic instead made a serial of Superman's greatest newsstand rival, Captain Marvel.

Columbia's Superman serials belong to an era past the Golden Age of the serial, but they have a charm and dedicated following of their own.

In 1951, *Superman and the Mole Man*, a theatrical feature, appeared with a new Superman, George Reeves, and a new Lois, Phyllis Coates. The picture was produced by the radio show's producer, Robert Maxwell, and was obviously a pilot for a television series. Reeves was acceptable in the role, but the film suffered from a lack of flying scenes (there was only one brief swoop to save someone falling off a dam) or indeed of any action scenes at all, to speak of. The story of treating mysterious little visitors from beneath the earth with respect and tolerance seemed consistent with the theme of racial and religious tolerance hammered home by the radio series for years. (Both the theatrical feature and the first television show were written by Maxwell, the latter in collaboration with comics editor Whitney Ellsworth.)

It was not a surprise to see George Reeves return as the man of steel in a half-hour television series later that same year. Many of the early episodes seemed much like stories from the radio series. Some – for example "The Haunted Lighthouse" with its ghostly goings-on and "The Stolen Costume," where in his only television appearance, the radio series' private detective character, Candy Meyers, helps Clark Kent recover "something valuable" from the hands of criminals – can be documented as originating on radio.

These radio type stories served the *Superman* series well. Because there was more Clark Kent than Superman, they were cheap to produce and helped the fledgling series survive. They were also more realistic in an age that demanded realism. As the series became more firmly entrenched, Superman himself came on the scene more and more, and the stories featured him performing more and more spectacular feats.

Eventually the DC Comics representative, Whitney Ellsworth, took over as producer, and often as writer, in collaboration with onetime prolific pulp magazine scribe Robert Leslie Bellem. "Jimmy Olsen, Boy Editor" (1953), with a self-explanatory plot; "Superman Week" (1954) "The Wedding of Superman" (1955); "Superman's Wife" (1957); and "The Perils of Superman" (1957) all were stories from the comics magazine. Now the television shows were even in color, like the comics, for those lucky few who could afford the expensive new sets. Unfortunately, this Superman empire, so closely controlled, did not represent the most creative use of the character. Those who were the correct age at the time loved both the television show and the comics, but from the distance of adulthood, one must objectively say that the stories, both broadcast and printed, were often silly and trivial. According to them, Superman's greatest problems came from being a celebrity in demand. He was famous for being famous.

It was not until *Superman: The Movie* (1978) that the man of steel was given serious attention as one of the great folk heroes of all time. With the direction of Richard Donner, and the production of Ilya and Alexander Salkind, the film became a brilliant vehicle for the character, albeit a somewhat schizophrenic one. The movie could be seen as three films.

It was a high-tech science fiction film with metaphysical symbolism (like the spaceship carrying the infant Superman resembling a plant spore or a sperm). It told the end of the world Krypton with a great star, Marlon Brando, playing Superman's father, Jor-El, looking both handsome and dignified despite his weight.

It could also be seen as a pastoral, idyllic version of the baby Superman arriving on Earth, being adopted and growing up in a farm community. Serial star Kirk Alyn had been suggested to play Superman's father on Earth, Pa Kent, but that role went to a major star Glenn Ford. Alyn did play Lois Lane's father with film and television Lois, Noel Neil, in a cameo. Little of the scene survived in the theatrical release, but the full scene was shown when ABC aired the movie.

Finally, Superman had his first adventure against villain Lex Luthor and his stooge (Ned Beatty) who were portrayed as comedic threats rather like those in the 1966 *Batman* television show. This conflict of themes shouldn't be surprising, since dozens of writers and perhaps hundreds of advisors contributed ideas. What was used mostly came from Robert Benton and David and Leslie Newman. Prominent credit was given best-selling *Godfather* author Mario Puzo.

The casting of Christopher Reeve as Clark Kent and Superman (an incredible coincidence of names in the similarity to television's George Reeves) was a masterstroke. He was young and new, but powerful in physique, character and charisma. He changed impressively from the bumbling reporter to the superhuman man of steel in a way that George Reeves had never done on television, or even Bud Collier on radio. Kirk Alyn had changed into two distinct characters in the movie serials, and in a commendable gesture of appreciation, Christopher Reeve acknowledged Alyn's inspiration.

Three more Christopher Reeve movies have been made, with varying box-office success, and there is talk of a *Superman V*. The movies had added a whole new chapter to the saga of the man of steel, but with their hugely expensive special effects and casts loaded with international stars they owe a little to the simpler films and easygoing radio adventures of another era.

Comics

Superman was the most influential comics character to appear in magazine format. Superman's first appearance in a single story in the June 1938 *Action Comics* (an anthology of strips, also including *Zatara the Magician* and others) sparked not only the success of that magazine, not only the success of the publishing company (DC, from *Detective Comics*, a slightly earlier companion magazine), but the success of the whole fledging comic book industry. *Famous Funnies* had appeared as early as 1933, making it the first regularly and continuously published comics magazine, but it offered only reprinted Sunday newspaper comic strips such as *Buck Rogers*. Other comic books followed in this vein, and some began publishing some or all new material. Notable from DC were *New Fun Comics* in 1935 and *Detective Comics*. The latter was the first comic book devoted to a single theme (mystery), save a short-lived competitor a few months before. But it was the appearance of Superman that caused *Action Comics* to sell out on the stands, to be reprinted four times, to create dozens of competitors, to inspire hundreds of new publishers to try for the jackpot and to give comic books enough impetus to survive even to the present day. Many other beloved staples of the thirties and forties have disappeared into the shadows of time – pulp fiction magazine thrillers, Big Little Books, Saturday matinee movie serials, radio drama – but comic books survive in a nationwide network of specialty shops and limited newsstand display. Without Superman, it is doubtful that the genre would still exist, except for an occasional paperback special.

A number of complete books have been written on the Superman comic books, so the present work will not attempt to cover them in equal detail. Instead it will touch on a few points that influenced the radio series.

It might be noted that I am the first person to ever write about comic books in an amateur fan magazine, a "fanzine." I wrote a piece called "I Remember Comic Books" for Charles Lee Riddle's science fiction fanzine, *Peon*, in which I acknowledged the inspiration of my now late friend, Rick Sneary, and his article elsewhere, "I Remember Flash Gordon," devoted to the Sunday newspaper strips (but not about comic books). After my article in the fifties, there would appear other fanzines, Richard Lupoff's *XERO* (also written in part by myself, and admittedly inspired by my work) in 1960, and Jerry Bailes' and Roy Thomas' *Alter-Ego* in 1961. Neither Rick Sneary or myself have ever been credited in the official histories of comics fandom.

The youthful creators of Superman were Jerry Siegel and Joe Shuster. They created a single character who has earned over a billion dollars, and an industry that has earned more billions, but they lived in poverty for many years. As did virtually all writers and artists for comic books (as distinguished from syndicated newspaper strips), Siegel and Shuster signed away all their rights with the very first story, earning $150. Siegel said they received *six dollars* for the original drawing for the first cover.

In 1976, Jerry Siegel sent out a form letter to many people in comics and popular arts fields detailing the story of how he and partner Joe Shuster had been deprived of all income from *Superman* while Shuster had been going blind and Siegel had been in the Army in World War II. Artist Shuster was reduced to living on welfare, and writer Siegel went to work for the post office. Mainly through the efforts of contemporary comic artist Neil Adams to expose the truth to the public through appearances on national television, the new owners of DC, Warner Communications, finally provided a pension to each of the creators, reportedly $30,000 a year each at first. Later improvement were made.

On the six-dollar first cover, Superman is seen lifting an automobile over his head as a bunch of hoodlums flee in terror. He is wearing a red cape, blue tights and shirt with the letter "S," red shorts over the tights and red boots. The costume looks rather rough hewn, almost homemade. An early comics panel showed the man of steel fastening his cape on with a safety pin. As time went on, both the visuals and the concepts became much slicker, but they lost some of the charm and vitality of this early work.

Inside, there was a single-page synoptic explanation of how Superman got his power by being sent to Earth in a rocket when his home planet, Krypton, exploded. When he appeared in a complete title devoted to his adventures only a year later (the first comic book ever devoted to a single character, save one giveaway based on the humorous *Skippy* some four years before), the origin was expanded to two pages, with the explanation of how Superman was adopted by the Kent family. From one or two pages, hundreds of comic book stories, many radio and televison episodes, novels, and multimillion dollar movies (as well as cheaper ones) have been spun.

The first story, published in *Action* and reprinted in the initial issue of *Superman*, tells how Superman saved the life of a man falsely accused of murdering "Jack Kennedy" (long before the U. S. president of that name came on the national scene).

Many of the early stories of Superman are obvious wish-fullfillment fantasies of the readers. Superman could get back at the bully who humiliated him as Clark Kent, effortlessly tossing him into the gutter. He could expose the big money boys who were risking the lives of innocent workers in unsafe mines. And most important, he could cause dictators who were planning death and destruction in war to face their exploding shells, to taste what warfare was really like and change their ways. The attractive idea of one man who could prevent a war or win one singlehanded may have been the main reason for the success of Superman.

When World War II actually came and a fictional character could not change reality, the comic strip hero vowed that although he could win the war singlehanded, dictators like Hitler had to be defeated by ordinary people as a warning to those who would follow in their paths. It was not an entirely convincing explanation, but readers saw that the man of steel did do his part, fighting enemy planes and tanks and submarines. Moreover, even as children, readers probably saw that the war was so immense that not even Superman could win it all by himself.

When Superman first found Robin, Batman's sidekick, in that drifting rowboat in 1945, there had been earlier meetings of the two superheroes in the comics. *All-Star Comics* featured a group of diverse superheroes (or "mystery men" as they were known then, a term inspired by pulp fiction magazine) from features in various DC comic magazines. *The Official Overstreet Comic Book Price Guide*, almost always the last word on comics, says that this group, the Justice Society of America, was "unprecedented in all of literature," but the group may have been inspired in the mind of writer Gardner Fox by Alexander Dumas' *Three Musketeers*, each of whom had a unique ability (as the great strength of Porthos). The Western novels of William Colt McDonald played on this theme, and it was reflected in the movies of his rangeland heroes, the Three Mesquiteers. Fans knew that such stars as Harry Carey, Hoot Gibsonn, Big Boy Williams (these three were the Mesquiteers), Bob Steele and Tom Tyler had distinct and unique qualities when they banded together in the 1935 film *Powdersmoke Range* (second in the series, but the more significant). It may have been these Western pictures teaming together established stars that served as the inspiration (perhaps an unconscious one) for the comics' Justice Society.

It was not until the third issue of *All-Star Comics* in 1941 that the Justice Society first was gaveled to order. The Green Lantern (who could fly like Superman, but only with the aid of a magic ring), the Flash (fast as Superman, but only running on the ground), Hawkman (who could fly, but with giant wings), Dr. Fate and Spectre (whose powers were supernatural, rather than science fictional like Superman's) and others met at a dinner party to regale each other with tales of their adventures. Comic relief Johnny Thunder (who could control a magic Thunderbolt creature) was allowed to listen. He heard Superman and Batman were too busy to attend. The "honorary member" status they were to be given was already implied.

After Johnny Thunder became a member in No. 6, the story in No. 7 had him call on Superman, Batman and the Flash–a former member, now "honorary"–to help him raise his share of a war orphans relief fund the whole Justice Society agreed to finance. The few panels in which Superman and Batman appeared together constituted their first meeting anywhere in a story, years before they met on radio. Although their pictures regularly appeared in the corners of Justice Society title pages, it was not until No. 36 of *All-Star* that Superman and Batman had the four- or five-page individual chapter typically given to members of the group. In this story, the whole group sought to solve the mystery of a group of drowned men who returned to life to become sinister criminals.

On the covers of another pubication, *World's Finest Comics*, Superman, Batman and Robin had appeared together symbolically, sitting astride the guns of a great naval vessel or playing baseball. Only years later when economic factors shrunk the number of pages in the comic book did DC actually put the two characters in one story inside.

It was in No. 76 of the *Superman* title that Superman and Batman officially met for the first time in comics, on board a ship where they saw each other changing from their civilian identities to their famous costumes. Ignored were all those covers, the sequence in *All-Star* and the radio version. Since then, they have crossed into each other's strips and appeared elsewhere together hundreds of times.

In 1960, the two most famous superheroes were part of a new team, the Justice League of America, sprung pheonix-like from the ashes of the Justice Society. In this organization, Superman and Batman met newly costumed (and newly named, in their civilian roles) counterparts of their old allies, the Flash, the Green Lantern and others. (The existence of two Flashes was explained by a complex alternate universe story.) Even that group has been transformed into the Justice League International, with only Batman currently active in it.

A whole mini-world of comic books continues to flow today, featuring team-ups of Superman and Batman and many other characters, following that first time the two most famous superheroes banded together to raise funds for war orphans in *All-Star Comics* and met in a wax museum on the radio.

Premiums

The premiums offered on the *Superman* radio show were as follows, listed alphabetically with sponsor and date (where known) as well as approximate value in 1992 (assuming average condition).

Airplane, Balsa Wood, 33 models ($25 ea.), Airplane, Cardboard, 40 models ($20 ea.), Badge (Gum, Inc., Varies; $500 up), Buckle and Belt ($350), Button (Action Comics; $65), Button, Cello (Action Comics; $45), Button, Superman with White Shirt ($250), Button, Supermen of America ($65), Card, Code (Action Comics; $25), Card, Code, Supermen of America ($65), Card, Member, Defense Club of America ($65), Certificate, Membership (Action Comics; $90), Certificate, Supermen of America ($100), Comic Book (Macy's; $475), Parachute Rocket (H-O Oats; $350), Pennant ($275), Pin, Junior Defense League ($90), Press Cards ($15), Radio Show Recordings (3), Intros by Jim Harmon (Kelloggs, 1975; $20 ea.), Ring, Airplane (Pep; 1948; from SM Sponsor, Not Radio but Collected; $125), Ring, Crusaders ($300), Ring, F87 Jet (Kelloggs; 1948; from SM Sponsor, Not Radio, but Collected; $135), Ring, Secret Compartment, Initial, Paper Picture Inside (Varies, $1000 up), Ring, Secret Compartment, Initial (Varies, $1000 up), Ring, Supermen of America (Varies Widely, $18,000 known), Walky Talky (Kelloggs; $90).

Tom Mix
and His Ralston
Straight Shooters

Began Sept. 25, 1933, on NBC Mon., Wed., Fri. as a 15-minute afternoon serial. Aired Mon–Fri. beginning in 1936. Off the air 1943; resumed June 7, 1944. Became half-hour complete story on Mon., Wed., Fri. in fall 1949; ended June 23, 1950. Revived in 1983 for five-chapter serial (first and last episodes new productions, middle episodes recorded repeats) in a quarter-hour format with one half-hour new complete story, aired on numerous stations on a participation basis. Always sponsored by Ralston-Purina products; references to one season sponsored by Kellogg's are erroneous

Series Creator: Charles Claggett **Producer-Directors:** Clarence L. Menser (1930s-42), Al Chance (1944-47), Mary Afflick (1947-50), Jim Harmon (1983) **Writers:** Roland Martini (1930s), Charles Tazewell (1930s), George Lowther (1944-50), Jim Harmon (1983) **Tom Mix** (the greatest cowboy who ever lived; based on movie star and former officer Tom Mix; one of the classic Western music singers): Artells Dickson (1933), Willard Waterman (first show from Chicago only, 1934), Jack Ross (once, 1935), Jack Holden (1935-37), Russell Thorson (1938-42), Curley Bradley (1944-1950; also 1983) **Wrangler** (Tom's warm, wise, elderly sidekick; called "the Old Wrangler" on earliest shows; a good shot and good rider who can keep up with younger men; originally the narrator of the series): Percy Hemus (1933-42) **Pecos Williams** (Tom's young sidekick; in earliest shows, a strongman who can bend horseshoes but is devoted to children; later until 1942 a singer of Western songs on the show; becoming from 1940 to 1942 and in the 1983 revival a younger version of Tom, not as wise or skilled but learning): Curley Bradley (1935-42), Jim Harmon (1983) **Sheriff Mike Shaw** (Tom's sidekick; always fifty-five years old, portly and with silver hair and mustache; sheriff of Dobie County; a minor character who became the second most important character after the death of "Wrangler" actor Hemus): Hal Peary (1930s), Leo Curley (1944–50), Jack Lester (1983) **Jane** (Tom's ward, who ages from ten to college age): Winifred Toomey (1930s), Jane Webb (1940s–50), Virginia Gregg (1983) **Jimmy** (another ward, who went away to boarding school and was not much heard from in later years): Andy Donnelly, George Gobel (1935), Hugh Rowlands **Wash** (the black cook; originally a minstrel show stereotype but later warm, lovable character, although never totally free of stereotype): Vance McCune (1930s), Forrest Lewis (1940s–50) **Doc Green** (crusty old medical man): Forrest Lewis (1940s–50), Les Tremayne (1983) **Amos Q. Snood** (Scrooge-like comic villain): Sidney Ellstrom **William Snood** (wimpy nephew): Cornelius Peeples **Longbow Billy** (a mountain man): Willard Waterman (1947–48) **Boss of Flying City** (a villain): Lou Krugman (1947) **Capitola** (a maid): Betty Lou Gerson **Sgt. Hank Smith** (young serviceman): Johnathon Hole (1947), Richard Gulla (1983) **Mary** (Hank's sweetheart): Barbara Gratz (1983) **The Great Dane** (movie director): Art Hern (1983) **Guest Star:** Jock Mahoney (1983) **The Ranch Boys** (singing trio, sang theme song/Ralston commercial, played parts in drama): Jack Ross, Shorty Carson (later Ken Carson), Curley Bradley (most prominent) **Announcers:** Don Gordon (1940–50), Franklyn Ferguson, Les Griffith, Les Tremayne (1983) **Others:** Jack Lester, Art Hern, Olan Soule, Bob Jellison, Arthur Peterson, Jess Pugh, Carl Kroenke, DeWitt McBride, Patricia Dunlap, Bruno Wick, Jack Petruzzi.

The *Tom Mix* show created a greater sense of reality in the minds of its youthful listeners than any other, or so the present writer believes. Tom Mix was a real person, a famed movie star and, as one was constantly reassured by mailed brochures and newspaper advertisements, a real hero, a real Texas Ranger, Western Marshal and soldier of fortune. Other actors always portrayed Tom Mix on radio; they were more skilled at the microphone and would do the daily grind of a weekday show for a lot less money than Tom was accustomed to. So even after the death of the real man in a 1940 auto accident, the show continued. Listeners thought it was some mistake, or there was a *new* Tom Mix somehow, maybe a Tom Mix, Jr., like there had been a replacement for his horse, a Tony, Jr. Most of all, listeners thought the show was a real story about real people.

The situations were hardly mundane, but the characters seemed real. One of the earliest episodes, for example, involved Tom Mix being forced down in a faltering airplane and landing in the unburned center of a forest fire, ringed by flames. Tom could radio out his position, but helicopters were

The radio cast of *Tom Mix and his Ralston Straight Shooters*, circa 1940. Back row: Vance McCune in blackface as Wash, Percy Hemus as the Old Wrangler, Jane Webb as Jane, Russell Thorson as Tom Mix, Sid Ellstrom as Amos Q. Snood, announcer Lynn Brandt. Front row: Curley Bradley as Pecos, with other members of the Ranch Boys trio: Ken "Shorty" Carson, and Jack Ross.

not as common in the thirties as they are now, and there was no way to reach him.

Young Jane and Pecos listen to Tom's radioed description of his trouble – a shattered propeller blade. If a new propeller can be brought to him, he can fit it in place and take off, out of the path of the flames. "But there's no way to do that. It looks like I'll have to stay here and see how Providence deals the hand," Tom says (approximately – no scripts or recordings of these early episodes are known to exist). Tom escapes when Pecos rides Tony through the flames with a new propeller.

Once again, the lack of preservation of radio broadcasting history makes itself apparent. Much of radio exists only in fading memory now. Many recordings and scripts have been preserved by dedicated hobbyists, but much more is gone forever. Only about twenty individual episodes of *Tom Mix* are known to exist; the forest fire sequence isn't one of them.

Another incident that survives in memory concerns Tony. In one of the many hazardous stunts he does for Tom, the Wonder Horse breaks his leg. In those days, the only treatment thought possible for a horse with a broken limb was to put it out of its pain. Tom Mix prepares for the unthinkable; he must shoot Tony. Tom takes a silver bullet that he and Tony won together and loads it into his six gun. Before doing the deed, Tom recalls the many things that he and Tony did together, the times Tony saved his life, and now all he can do to repay him is to shoot him.

Meanwhile, Jane and Pecos are in the TM-Bar ranch house sunk in gloom, with the radio droning in the background. As they share their memories of Tony too, the results of a horse race are given over the air. The winner is a horse who once had a broken leg, but who was saved and restored to racing fitness by a certain Eastern doctor with a miraculous new technique. There is hope for Tony! The two Straight Shooters rush for Tony's stable. Before they get there, a shot sounds out.

It is too terrible to think. With hope for Tony in sight, has Tom fired too soon? It was so terrible that the announcer could not keep his listeners in suspense until the next episode. He assured everyone that things were going to be all right and that there was no need to worry. (That happened several times over the years—when things were simply too sad or desperate, the kids were reassured that everything was going to be okay.)

And next show, the announcer was proved correct. Tom had fired, but his love for his horse had been too great, or perhaps some inner instinct had told him there was hope, and for once, Tom Mix's shot had missed.

Tony did get well. He had survived the forest fire and he survived the broken leg, and went on to be Tom's faithful mount in a thousand more fabulous adventures.

In 1932, the real Tom Mix and Tony were still magic names. They hadn't been in a movie for a few years, and that had been an old-fashioned silent. They had yet to debut in a talkie. (That would by *Destry Rides Again* in another year.) But there was not something new on television every week, so fame was not so fleeting. Tom Mix was still touring the country, making appearances in theaters and with the Sells-Floto Circus. He would eventually have his own Tom Mix Circus.

Mix first got into early films when the Selig Company came West and made a movie on a ranch where he worked about 1909. He was a fine rider and helped with the horses and other stock. He was always the center attraction at rodeos with his stunt riding, and he took to acting easily. He had

had a colorful career in the still unsettled West at the turn of the century. Tom Mix has an interesting background, one that didn't really need enhancing, but studio representatives and Tom himself did choose to elaborate on it.

He did not fight in as many wars as was claimed; those included the Spanish-American War, the Boer War and the Boxer Rebellion. One must very carefully fit those dates together to make it possible for anybody to have been in all those places within a few short years, allowing for a lot of fast transfers and discharges. It is known he served in the U. S. Army at the time of the Spanish-American War, but records seem to indicate he never went to Cuba with Teddy Roosevelt and the Rough Riders. But records can be wrong. He was known to be a friend of the first President Roosevelt, and he attended the annual conventions of the Rough Riders.

Much is made of him leaving the Army without official discharge. But the severity of "sins" change with the times. In the peacetime army of the early part of the century "taking French leave" was very common, and was not taken seriously enough to merit pursuit or prosecution.

It is a hard fact that Tom Mix was a peace officer in the last days of the Old West. The town of Dewey, Oklahoma, where Mix served as town marshal for the years around 1908, has a museum dedicated to him and a plaque with the names of Tom's predecessors and successors who were killed in the line of duty. Since the death of a law officer on duty now is actually a pretty rare event, one can safely assume that it was a dangerous job there. When the author visited about 1970, his taxi was driven by an active old gentleman well into his eighties who remembered when "Tom Mix was the law in Dewey." He recalled Tom bringing in a horse thief with both Tom and the prisoner covered in blood from the encounter.

It is also a good bet Tom Mix also served as deputy sheriff and a detective for both the railroad and the oil fields. He was also "sheriff" – and actually functioned more as the mayor – of the boom town of LeHunt, Kansas, in 1905 as living men remember. Some of Tom's titles may have been blown up to grander status. Perhaps he was not a full fledged sheriff or a United States Marshal (just a town marshal). As for his being a Texas Ranger, the museum in Dewey houses, along with Tony's saddle, many of Tom's cowboy outfits, photos and posters, and displays Tom's enlistment papers in the Texas Rangers. But the dates on the papers appear to have been changed. Perhaps they were only an honorary membership given him after he became a movie star. But the papers themselves appear to have been issued around the turn of the century, judging from the style of printing and penmanship. Was the date changed to fit the legend, giving him time to fight in one of those numerous wars? Like so many things about Tom Mix, the answer may never be known.

One thing is certain: Tom Mix was absolutely fearless, an incomparable rider and a miraculous shot. Movie producer Sam Peeples recalled that when he was a boy, Tom Mix shot out his name "SAM" in a fence thirty yards away with a hand gun. Such a man had to have many adventures in his life. If he did not have quite as many as the legend would have it, he had enough to inspire generations of boys and to endure as a subject for big budget movies like *Sunset* in 1988. Bruce Willis, his impersonator there, was really not very much like Tom Mix – but then nobody ever has been. He was one of a kind.

In the mid-seventies, Roy Rogers said he continued to regard Tom Mix very highly and fondly remembered the times he and Tom would go out horseback riding in the early gray of morning. Gene Autry also claimed him as a friend. Pat Buttram said otherwise: "Autry liked Mix, but Mix didn't like Autry. Oh, they were friends, but Mix did not care for the musical Western."

George DeNormand, a stuntman who did some of the stunts (usually credited exclusively to Cliff Lyons) in Mix's last film, the serial *The Miracle Rider* (Mascot, 1935) confirmed Mix's love for the more rugged Western. He joined in the horseplay of the wranglers, which could get hairy at times. DeNormand told of how some cowboys had fastened George's clothes to the mattress of his bed with safety pins while he was asleep, and then set the room on fire, their idea of a good joke on George as he struggles to get free. Mix played the same kind of joke as the other cowboys. One oft-used device was the "bang-board" – two pieces of lumber strapped together, with a nail in one board that struck the primer of a bullet stuck in the hole of the other board. When a man was dozing, feet crossed or on his side, the bang-board applied sharply to backside or sole of foot produced a result hilarious to the rough-hewn characters. One day, Tom Mix whacked the rear end of a snoozing wrangler and found that he had gotten the board backwards so the shot went into his victim, not just exploding outward harmlessly. It was only paper wadding from a blank, but it made a painful intrusion. Mix was apologetic and chagrined.

Patsy Ruth Miller, a Mix leading lady who did publicity for *Sunset*, told movie authority Forrest J Ackerman a Tom Mix anecdote. Tom had to rescue Ms. Miller from a movie forest fire. But as he rode up and tried to untie her, he found the ropes had been tied too tightly. Patsy's hair caught on fire. Worse, Tony's tail burst into flame. Ignoring his own burns, Tom freed Patsy and rode off with her to safety. But others had to tend to Patsy's burning hair; Mix was too busy looking after Tony. The horse had to wear a tail toupe the rest of the film.

Such incidents begin to sketch in the likeness of Tom Mix. He was a friend to half a dozen presidents and a few kings. He was once nominated at the Democratic convention for vice president of the United States. If he didn't always stick to the literal truth, it was because he found reality a bit boring. A good story was worth more than dull detail. He was a showman. A hundred years and more after his birth in 1880, nearly fifty years after his death, he is still a star. With more and more of his films becoming available on videocassette, his star may shine forever. His inspiration was more than sufficient to create a dramatic series.

In 1932, he still had millions of fans—and one of them was William H. Danforth, head of the Ralston-Purina Company, one of the largest packagers of breakfast cereal and animal feed. Danforth's devotion was known to Charles E. Claggett, a copywriter for the St. Louis–based Gardner Advertising Agency. He also knew from a survey of school children in the area that their favorite hero was still Tom Mix. Gardner was on shaky ground with the huge Ralston account, and Claggett suggested a way to win Ralston's approval was to sign up Tom Mix.

The screen actor and circus star was approached, and according to legend he signed an agreement on the back of an envelope (which Ralston still has on file somewhere) permitting use of his name and likeness in advertising, and allowing himself to be impersonated on the radio. One report has it that Mix simply "gave the program to the boys and girls of America," to let them enjoy his adventures on the airwaves. Good business would suggest he got royalties for the use of his name in the huge corporation's advertising, but it is not a matter of public record.

Despite Danforth's personal regard for Mix, a test of his popularity was made. A trial advertisement was prepared for the Sunday comic section, with a *Tom Mix* comic strip and an invitation to join his Straight Shooter Club. Some accounts hold that this advertisement offered a wooden model of Tom's own six-gun. Actually, the first offer may have been for a TM-brand arm patch and a Secret Manual.

Ralston representatives would have been satisfied with 25,000 responses, advertising man Claggett later said. Instead they received half a million. "Boxtops literally buried Ralston's president, William H. Danforth," Claggett continued. "We photographed him at his desk with letters up to his neck."

The radio series began September 25, 1933, three times a week over NBC for a quarter hour. Before long, it would air five days a week, Monday through Friday. Only in the last season would it revert to Monday-Wednesday-Friday, and then it was expanded to a complete half-hour story, following the example of radio's *Lone Ranger*.

The new radio show was first broadcast from New York with a radio performer named Artells Dickson impersonating Mix. No examples of this first version survive, not even accurate memories. The Old Wrangler and Jane were on hand, we know from publicity photos. Dickson, a heavy-browed man, was said to be "much like Tom" in stalwart character, but looked out of place with a Western shirt and vest topping his tweed suit pants.

The broadcast series was moved after the first year from New York City to the Chicago area to be closer to Ralston's St. Louis headquarters, and Willard Waterman did the first show from Chicago. "I had to work on the microphone which was tilted down for Young Jane," Waterman said. "Later, the ad agency told me I didn't 'dominate the scene' well enough to be Tom Mix. I told them I had a contract. They told me if I wanted to continue working in any fashion, I had better forget the contract, and I did."

The part of Mix eventually went to Jack Holden, the announcer on the *National Barn Dance* show (another version of the *Grand Old Opry*). He had a sort of country accent, though not exactly Western.

After several years, Russell Thorson, an announcer in Chicago, replaced Holden in the role of Mix. Thorson had no accent whatsoever, but a great commanding voice. Of course, Tom Mix was becoming on the show more than a cowboy – indeed a universal hero, flying airplanes, sailing the seas, solving crimes in the big city. Only the voices of Tom's sidekicks, the elderly Wrangler and young Pecos, reminded the audience of Tom Mix's Western heritage.

The movie star Tom Mix died in a 1940 auto accident, but the show never missed a broadcast, and Thorson continued in the role until, after a hiatus, Curley Bradley moved up from the role of Pecos to play Tom Mix himself.

It was quite a shock to many children in America to hear of the death of one of their heroes. On his own show Gene Autry announced that Tom Mix had gone to join Buffalo Bill, Kit Carson and other Western legends in that great range in the sky, and dedicated his next song to Tom – "Empty Saddles." Probably there were some sudden conferences around the Ralston offices on exactly what to do. From what one has been able to learn, it was decided to go on with the show for at least the time being to gauge the reaction of the young listeners. When the listenership dropped not a bit, the show continued as before.

After the Second World War started, Tom Mix's radio adventures had him fighting spies and enemy agents. The Master Mind was one of those foes. He sought a secret formula with wartime possibilities.

The formula is given Tom for safekeeping by the daughter of a scientist who pins a flower to his lapel. The spies make an attempt to steal it from Pecos, who had been given the job of looking after the flower. Abducted in their car, Pecos forces the car to run off a bridge into water below rather than let the formula fall into enemy hands. He manages to escape from the sinking car but loses the flower in the stream. At least he has prevented the enemy from getting it.

Since the foreign agents do not know the flower is lost, they make another attempt to get it by kidnapping Tom's old partner, Wrangler, and trying to make Tom deliver the bud as ransom for the old-timer. Of course,

Tom would never sell out his country even for the life of a friend, but he stalls the spies while he conducts a complicated police search for the source of the paper the ransom note was written on, an investigation worthy of the FBI.

Locating the address of the enemy, Tom and the police close in, and the foreign spies learn the hard way that their nasty Lugers are no match for Tom Mix's six-guns.

The formula wasn't lost after all, as Tom finally deduces. It was not secreted in the lost flower at all; instead it was engraved on the head of a pin that had fastened the flower to Tom's jacket. Fortunately, Tom still has the pin in his lapel.

Other wartime adventures had Tom preventing the foe from bombing the Verdi River Powder Plant which manufactured gunpowder for munitions; exposing the bad guys who were using a phantom ship, a Flying Dutchman, to disguise their activities (it was a movie image projected on clouds of fog); and winning out against a mysterious man, the Black Cat, who was dressed in the likeness of that animal and who could scale high buildings with feline skill. This last character seemed more like a comic-book character (and there was a female crusader of the same name in comics) than the more well-drawn and intellectual villains Tom usually fought on the radio show.

The year 1943 was a bleak one for Straight Shooters. After surviving even the loss of the show's real-life inspiration, the series did not return from summer vacation that year. It was widely thought the mortality of the movie great was the reason. Actually, the program was doing well in the ratings (in fact, it ranked first among afternoon thrillers), but Ralston executives foresaw a problem, according to Curley Bradley. Around that time Daylight Savings Time (then called) was being put into effect, and it was thought kids would not come inside from their games while daylight persisted. It did seem to work that way in summer when the lure of sunny afternoons lowered the listenership of the afternoon shows, many of which went off the air to be replaced by less familiar programs. Sometimes the paid advertising was dropped and the network continued the show on a sustaining basis. So Ralston decided to drop the *Tom Mix* series for the duration of the war.

Ralston soon discovered that the shows that did stay on the air retained their listenership. Kids got tired of playing after a while and went inside, longer daylight or not. They often had to come in to eat dinner and to do their homework. Moreover, the kids *wanted* to come inside to hear their favorite shows.

Finally, after Ralston could not find an open time on the NBC network, they brought time on the less prestigious Mutual Broadcasting System and determined to put *Tom Mix* back on the air, and "never take it off again."

The show had to be put back together. Russ Thorson had moved to Hollywood to try his luck there. The Gardner Agency finally gave the role of Tom Mix to Curley Bradley, formerly Pecos. It had been a long time coming.

Agency representatives first spotted Curley Bradley on the West Coast as far back as 1935 and decided he would do well playing Tom Mix. Bradley had been born in Coalgate, Oklahoma, on September 18, 1910, as Raymond George Courtney and had worked as a range cowboy along with his two brothers for his true pioneer parents. As a boy, he watched some of the last of the old time Western gun duels from under the courthouse steps. He went to one of the last places a cowboy could still ride and rope for a living – Hollywood.

In 1926, when he was only sixteen but six feet one and 175 pounds, Bradley had worked in a number of silent films as a stunt rider with Hoot Gibson, Buck Jones and Tom Mix, the movie star. Bradley did chases and horse falls, fights and falls.

When he was asked why he quit stunts, Bradley said, "I didn't like having one arm stuck up in the air, and one leg tied down, while broken bones healed up. I enjoyed singing. I didn't enjoy being busted into bits. Just no accounting for taste."

Bradley was friends with Tom Mix, but like many people, he found Tom Mix aloof and introspective. He could indulge in horseplay with the other riders, but when it was over, he kept them at arms' length.

But according to Bradley, Buck Jones held back little, and it was Buck whom Curley regarded as a close friend, rather than Tom. Buck Jones is generally remembered as a prince of a man who went through life helping others and giving of himself. Those who knew him were not surprised that he gave his life saving others in the disastrous Coconut Grove fire in Boston in 1942. He was in a nightclub in the first place only to raise money for war bonds. No one ever lived the life of the fictional cowboy hero more than Buck Jones. (He even was a successful radio actor, playing himself, in the 1936 radio series *Hoofbeats*.) It was, however, Tom Mix who seemed to symbolize the Western hero for more people.

Curley Bradley preferred to be a Western singer, following his experience as a stuntman and minor player in films. Most of Curley's singing was with the trio, the Ranch Boys, which had been formed while Curley was a stuntman in films. Most of the wranglers were real cowboys, and they did what cowboys do when the work was over for the day. They sat around the campfire and entertained each other with jokes, tall stories and songs. The "doubles" had a quick conference, and with Shorty Carson on guitar, Curley and Jack Ross sang ballads of the west. It was Jack Ross' idea to try the trio professionally, and he became the leader. Shorty, who would eventually be known as Ken Carson, went on to sing on Garry Moore's daytime television show and appear in a number of John Wayne big screen Westerns. The Ranch Boys made many records for Decca. The solo lead on about half of them was by Curley, who also made a smaller number of recordings on his own, including "The Tom Mix Album" of songs supposedly sung on the show by the Tom Mix of radio. (Actually Curley only got to sing anything other than the theme song once every few months.) The Ranch Boys though unbilled can be seen singing in the back of a bus near the opening of the movie *It Happened One Night* and in the Gene Autry feature *In Old Monterey*. It was while Curley was in the Ranch Boys that Ralston representatives spotted him. They thought he would be a good candidate to play Mix from the first, and Curley reported when they offered him that job, they agreed to hire the whole group when Curley would not split up the trio.

In 1938, with time off from the Mix program and others they were doing, the Ranch Boys decided on a great adventure. It may have started as a publicity stunt to further their careers, but Curley recalled it as one of the highlights of his life. The three men determined to ride all the way from Hollywood back to their radio base in Chicago on horseback. To anyone's knowledge no one had done such a thing in fifty years. "I don't know if you could do it now with modern freeways, and no alternate routes in some places," Curley said in the mid-1970s.

The three troubadours started off on the 2,875-mile trip on May 10, 1938. Their route would take them over the old stagecoach trails up to San Francisco, east to Sacramento and on to Carson City, Nevada. Mountains and deserts fell behind them as they came to Salt Lake City, then up into the high country for Denver. Past North Platte, Omaha, Council Bluffs and then across the bridge over the Mississippi River into Chicago.

They started at 4:30 in the morning. The boys cleaned the horses, cooked breakfast, broke up the night's camp and got on the road by 6:30. There was a truck on the trip, carrying relief horses and camp gear, but it generally went on ahead to have the camp set up when the boys rode in. The horses were checked out thoroughly, and although the Humane Society twice investigated, they agreed the animals were well cared for.

Curley's horse at the time was Lucky, who was only two years old. "People keep telling me I couldn't take a two-year-old on a trip like that because he didn't have his teeth," Curley said. "But I took care of him." He would carefully grind up the horses's oats in the feedbag with a little water, kneading it with his fingers, and hand feeding the result to the horse. "Sometimes I just let Lucky suck on my thumb for a long time. It made him feel better."

After the men ate lunch, they would be on the road again, their tired horses riding in the truck as fresh mounts took their places. Curley and his pals could not replace themselves, however.

Even in 1938, it was very much the age of the automobile and the men had to ride at the edge of the highway. Most drivers were interested, curious and polite, but riding down the eastern slopes of the Donner Pass in California, the group met one that wasn't. A truck driver deliberately made his engine backfire to scare the horses, and they reared and sideslipped, nearly going over the rim into the pass below. Death would have been certain. But these men were virtually born in the saddle, and they regained control and reassured the horses.

There were fans and autograph seekers along the way, and the Ranch Boys also managed to do thirty-six broadcasts en route from remote locations before crossing the bridge into Chicago and making a triumphant appearance on the *National Barn Dance* after three months.

Appropriately enough for the Tom Mix of radio, Bradley and his partners were also on a secret mission for the U. S. Government. Just before they left, they were approached by a representative of the U. S. cavalry. Horse cavalry was still an important part of the Army; it was thought horses would always be able to go where no vehicle could. The cavalry officer asked the Ranch Boys to test out a special kind of horseshoe on the trip, one that might be used in the next war. They agreed, and the shoes worked just fine. They may have been used in the early fighting in World War II before the cavalry completely motorized.

In those days, Bradley also knew well the members of another Western group. As Bradley remembered it, it was he who told Leonard Sly (later Roy Rogers) Bob Nolan was looking for people to form a new group, the Sons of the Pioneers. (Rogers' account is different.) Bradley's recollection is that he was on the Sons of the Pioneers' first record, "Way Out There," and he had that record in his personal belongings at the end, one of the relatively few recordings he kept. He was at various times hired to stand by to replace a member of the group for radio broadcasts – particularly Nolan, who admitted to having a drinking problem. Despite his problems, Bradley had an enormous respect for Nolan, "the greatest cowboy songwriter" (and Bradley himself was a good one). He recalled the night that Bob Nolan first wrote "Tumbling Tumbleweeds" on the back of a napkin when he, Curley and others were having a few beers. Originally, he called the song "Falling Leaves" (the same as a later pop song he had nothing to do with). Curley liked the song very much and asked Bob if he could have the napkin it was first written on. Bradley had it for a number of years, but lost it in moving. He did keep a number of letters from members of the Pioneers asking him to join them, offering Bradley at one time a starting salary of $10,000 a year. Since he was making over $30,000 a year in Chicago radio, one can see why he refused although tempted. His best salary as radio's Tom Mix was $550 per week. That would be over $7,000 a week in 1992 dollars.

When the Ranch Boys were first brought to Chicago for the radio show, Bradley was auditioned for the role of Tom Mix, but he reported they decided he was too inexperienced as a radio actor to be given the lead in the show. He was "temporarily" given the second lead to allow him to gain experience. Bradley said the original character description called for Pecos Williams to have a lot of physical strength, to be able to bend iron bars and horseshoes, but to be slavishly devoted to and protective of the two kids, Jimmy and Jane. The part sounds like some sort of hulking idiot, a bit like Lenny in *Of Mice and Men*. On the air Curley Bradley's own personality took over, and Pecos became a good-natured, loyal young cowboy who liked to sing.

During the auditions for the part of Mix, Jack Ross, leader of the Ranch Boys trio, decided he would like to try out for the part too. Nobody else seemed to think him right for it—except Ralston head Danforth, who was in the studio for the important casting. Curley said Ross played the part on the air just once, and new auditions were called. Again, Danforth selected Ross. One reason may have been that was Ross was a dark complected man who rather looked like Tom Mix. Somehow Danforth was bypassed, and the part at that time went to Jack Holden.

Curley Bradley began playing the part of Pecos "temporarily" and singing the theme song with the other Ranch Boys. This went on for seven years, from 1935 to 1942, until the show went off for a year. Bradley kept busy with many other shows in Chicago, working sixteen hours some days, doing everything from the *National Farm and Home Hour* as a singer to playing a cowboy on the *First Nighter* anthology drama. One of his busiest times came when he was substituting for Don McNeill as host of *The Breakfast Club*. When one of the quartet on that show got sick, Bradley also filled in for him (unknown to the home audience). Then when the boy singer took a vacation, Bradley also sang his solos and did some duets with the girl singer. He also had to do some of the commercials. "It was an hour show, and I was talking or singing for just about every minute it was on the air. If you don't think I was tired after that, you'd be wrong!"

He also sang on Garry Moore's *Club Matinee*, a short-lived series about truckers called *Road to Danger* and another brief series called *Ranch-House Jim* that prefigured his taking over as Tom Mix. In the latter series he played a singing cowboy-detective.

In 1944, the Gardner Agency approached him and told him they were going to put *Tom Mix* back on the air, and he was going to be Tom, fulfilling an offer made over a decade before. As Pecos, he had gotten more fan mail than any other character on the show, even Tom Mix. He had star quality. Bradley had nearly the same voice as Pecos when he finally took over as Tom. But he did have a lot of acting ability, and his level of authority went up in the title role.

In the time the show had been off the air, Percy Hemus had died, and with him died his character of the Old Wrangler. Danforth thought no one else could ever do that role as well and decided to retire the part. "Sheriff

Members of a later *Tom Mix* cast arrive in St. Louis for a charity rodeo: Leo Curley as Sheriff Mike Shaw, two young admirers—one held by Curley Bradley, now moved up to play Tom Mix himself—and Forrest Lewis out of Wash's black face, perhaps as Doc Green.

Mike Shaw" had been around in the story for years, but now he was going to be elevated to the role of Tom's chief sidekick. The last actor to do that role had also died, although some others who had done it earlier were available. A new audition was held and one of those trying out was an old vaudeville performer, square-jawed 300-pound Leo Curley. He did a scene on mike with Curley Bradley, and after it was over and the mike shut off, he turned to Bradley. "I've only got five bucks in my pants, but I'll buy the drinks if you could put in a good word for me. I sure need this job." Bradley made some hasty mental calculation and called into the control booth. "Hey, you know, I think this old fellow and I work together pretty good." Leo Curley got the job and became a memorable character on the show.

The agency solicited Bradley's opinion for an announcer, and he told them, "For me there was only one announcer for *Tom Mix*–Don Gordon." Gordon had been doing the show before it went off. Gordon's career had not been going well, and he and his wife were very grateful when he was called back to the show. Bradley said after every show, Don Gordon and some others would stand around and literally and figuratively pat him on the back. "Well, old buddy, we did another one! Yes, sir, another one in the bag!"

They did a lot of them, nearly six years of daily shows, with no summer vacations–five days a week, fifty-two weeks a year. The only slacking off Ralston did was to drop off sponsoring the Tuesday and Thursday shows during the really hot part of summer when kids were outdoors and listenership was down, but the network ran those on a sustaining basis. On those shows Bradley got to sing the real lyrics to "When the Bloom is on the Sage," instead of the Ralston commercial.

Bradley recalled a number of stories about behind the scenes goings-on at the *Tom Mix* shows. One actor read his part so slowly and deliberately that he put Bradley and everybody else off their timing. One day, Bradley set the actor's script on fire so he had to read it very fast. Another time Bradley and some of the others knew the show was going to be preempted by a presidential address, but somehow the producer, Al Chance, had not been told. The cast and crew went ahead with the show as usual, except it was not going out of the studio. On the opening Ralston theme, Bradley's voice broke into a horrible clinker. He turned angrily to the organist, Harold Turner, and said, "Damn it to hell–can't you play that damned thing in the right key?" In the control booth, Chance's face went white.

Don Gordon stepped to the microphone. "Boys and girls, go out and buy a box of Ralston cereal. Some people can actually stand the stuff." By this time, Chance was beginning to see the light.

Actually doing something wrong on the real show was another matter. One young actor who had played the title role on another juvenile series for a time had a part on the *Mix* show and did it so badly, ad-libbing lines and throwing everybody off their cues, that after the show, Curley met him in the hallway, slammed his shoulders to the wall and told him, "Listen, son, if you ever do that bad a job on my show again, I'll punch your ticket from here to San Francisco!"

Of course, sometimes mistakes did happen innocently. On one episode, following the successful conclusion to an adventure, "Sheriff Mike" was saying, "It sure is great, Tom – just to be sitting here on the porch of the TM-Bar ranch-house." But the word "sitting" whooshed out of "Mike's" bridgework sounding more like something they should be doing in the little house behind the house, instead of on the front porch.

"How's that, Mike?" Curley ad-libbed. Occasionally actors would mangle a line and have to be re-cued.

"I said," actor Leo Curley said very distinctly, "it sure is great, Tom – just to be [the word again] here on the porch of the TM-Bar ranch-house."

"Yes, Mike, it sure it."

Ralston didn't receive one letter about it.

The new *Tom Mix* series began June 7, 1944, delayed from its start by one day because of the D-Day invasion of France in World War II. Before long, Curley was singing the theme (without the other Ranch Boys – the group had split by now) in the best-remembered version:

Shredded Ralston for your breakfast,
Starts the day off shining bright,
Gives you lots of cowboy energy
With a flavor that's just right.
It's delicious, And nutritious
Bite size and ready to eat;
Take a tip from Tom
Go and tell your Mom
Shredded Ralston can't be beat!

The ready-to-eat product Shredded Ralston (now know as Wheat Chex) became the usual sponsor of the radio series. Only during the coldest months of winter did "Tom" sing praises of Hot Ralston, the Ralston-Purina Company's founding product. That theme went:

Hot Ralston for your breakfast,
Start the day off shining bright
Gives you lots of cowboy energy
With a flavor that's just right.
It's delicious, And nutritious,
Made of golden Western wheat,
So take a tip from Tom
Go and tell you Mom
Hot Ralston can't be beat!

There were variations in the wording over the years.

On the first episode of the revived series, Tom Mix flew back from helping the war effort in Europe and met his old friends at the TM-Bar. His young ward Jane was glad to see him, but after a bit complained the war was making things hard; she couldn't get a new pair of boots she wanted. Gently Tom told her of the hungry people in Europe, some of whom had no shoes at all, explaining that all real Americans, real Straight Shooters, knew that sacrifices were necessary to bring an end to the tragic war still going on. Jane, who had the real stuff inside, quickly saw the light. The initial episode ended with the arrival of an Englishman who was looking for Winston Churchill and who thought he might be up the fireplace chimney.

The following episode revealed that "Winston Churchill" was only the name of the rather silly Englishman's pet monkey, duly located. More serious trouble comes from "The Mystery of the Vanishing Herd," in which large numbers of cattle needed to feed a hungry nation in wartime are disappearing from the range. It seems that Tom Mix was returned home to solve this problem. Behind the trouble is a Nazi spy and flying ace, the Iron Mask. He is using aircraft to destroy the herds, as Tom discovers.

At one point, the spies capture Jane and the Englishman—who turns out to be an American FBI agent with a fake accent. The FBI man helps Jane escape, at the cost of being shot himself. Jane finds Tom, and justice is swift. In a borrowed Army fighter plane, Tom Mix swoops down on the nest of enemy agents and machine-guns it to pieces. He lands the plane and captures the Iron Mask himself.

This story, like many others, did not seem particularly Western. In a good business move, Ralston had hired the writer of *Dick Tracy*, which had sometimes outdrawn *Mix* in the ratings showdown. The writer was George Lowther, who had also written at times for *Superman* and *Inner Sanctum* and who would go on to write for *Captain Video* on television and for the last network radio drama to date, *CBS Mystery Theatre* in the mid-seventies before his death. He was an exceptional radio writer—perhaps not a creative genius on the level of Carlton E. Morse or Norman Corwin, but terrific at what he did.

He was a exceptional individual to know, as well. He lived in New York but occasionally visited the radio cast and crew in Chicago to be more familiar with them. He once met Curley Bradley and a group from the show at an expensive restaurant, entering with a pet duck on a leash.

Some later episodes of "Vanishing Herd" exist on recording, and some of his style and characterization of Tom Mix can be seen in the aftermath of the capture of the Iron Mask.

Mike: I sure do feel like singin' about those heifers out there bein' all safe on Peterson's range. They wouldn't be there if you hadn't throwed the Iron Mask . . . roped and tied him. . .

Tom: Oh, the breaks were with me, Mike.
Mike: Sure, you would say that—but everybody else is saying what brains it took, and what courage...
Tom: One thing sort of lead to another.
Mike: One thing didn't sort of lead to another before you got back from England, Tom.... It took you to find that gas was killing them steers and ... that gas was spread by an airplane.
Tom: Mike, I'm going to start preening my feathers like a peacock any minute now.
Mike: No, you won't, Tom. You ain't no fancy dude with grand ideas. Sure, you've traveled. I reckon you've seen about all the world there is to see, sat down to chow with dukes and countesses, kings, and all that there sort of thing, but you're just natural and regular—like any other Westerner.
Tom: Let's say like any other American, Mike.
Mike: Sure, Tom, sure... Don't tell me you're going back across the ocean? Don't tell me you're going to get into the invasion?
Tom: I'd like nothing better. I sure was cut up about coming back here when I knew the invasion was to break loose.
Mike: I guess you knowed more about that than you're saying, Tom.
Tom: Well, maybe, Mike...

No loyal Straight Shooter had any doubt Tom Mix had been helping General Eisenhower plan D-Day. He continued to fight wartime enemies, departing on a new "Secret Mission" even on V-E Day (Victory over Europe) because there were still some "hot spots" there.

In real life, Curely Bradley had repeatedly tried to get into the Armed Services, but had been rejected because of his eyesight. Outside of public appearances, he had to wear glasses. But he spent a lot of time putting on USO shows and selling war bonds. He was given an honorary membership in his local Veterans of Foreign Wars chapter.

As the revived *Tom Mix* went on, Tom, Mike, Wash and the rest of the people in Dobie got involved in many problems. In fact, it would be safe to say that Dobie was the most crime-ridden and disaster-prone small town in America.

Tom Mix stayed in the Western United States for most of the rest of the war, although in one of the most improbable stories, the chief Straight Shooter disguised himself as a Japanese and was landed by American submarine on the main island of Japan. Speaking the language well enough to fool the locals, Tom involved himself in vital intelligence work while Sheriff Mike stood by in the U. S. sub off shore to pick him up. Even the most ardent Tom Mix admirer had to question the cowboy's ability to look and sound Japanese enough to fool the Nippon high command.

One of the problems he came up against most often was a menace that seemed to have the power to make himself invisible. One of the earliest of the "Invisible Men" came while Thorson was playing Mix, and the unseen villain was nothing more than a speaker over a hidden microphone. In the Curley Bradley era, "The Man Who Could Work Miracles" had the power to strike down people in the street or in their homes. His weapon turned out to be a ray akin to the present-day laser beam. One of the last examples was a thirty-minute complete story aired during the final season. "The Invisible Rider" seemed to be a transparent horseman, displaying only his gloves on the reins and his hat floating in air. It was done with thin, stiff wires. His voice came from a radio in the saddlebags, and that voice also gave the trained horse instructions on where to trot.

There was a question as to whether "The Man Who Wasn't There" made himself invisible and escaped from locked rooms, or simply walked through walls. After committing a crime, he escaped Tom by disappearing from several such locked rooms. The cowboy detective went over each room, pounding on the floors and walls for secret panels, but they gave not an inch, steady as a rock. There was a contest where Tom phoned listeners for their solution. Several kids suggested that the man got out through the ceiling. But in the next episode, Tom examined the ceiling and there was no excape mechanism there. The answer Tom finally figured out: There was no panel in the wall, but the entire wall could be slid along a rail, providing an opening. The wall, Tom deduced, was *too* solid – a normal wall would shake a bit when pounded.

As always in the Mix series, the premium offers – first for a boxtop, later for a boxtop and ten cents and more later – played a large part in the stories. In one of the earlier serials before the Bradley starring series, a gold ore charm with a sample of the mineral was the clue of the gold mine that could save Tom's beloved TM-Bar ranch from foreclosing. Like many others in the late thirties, Tom was having trouble paying off the mortgage. He had been going on too many missions to help other people, and his own ranch was at risk. Finally, the day the ranch was to be auctioned came. Wrangler expressed no regret over seeing the cuckoo clock Wash had bought go. He hated the noisy contraption. But he convinced the miserly Amos Snood that he loved the clock dearly, so the old skinflint naturally paid a fabulous sum for it. But that was the first item only. A blanket bid on everything else was made by a stranger who wound up with everything. As Tom, Wrangler and Pecos perpared to leave their home, the stranger revealed that he was acting on behalf of Tom's ward, Jane, who had found the gold mine to whose existence the charm was a clue, and since everything she had was Tom's and vice versa, she was buying back the TM Bar for him. Apparently, solid bags of gold dust made people forget about whether a minor could control her own fortune.

One of the early premiums after Curley Bradley became Tom Mix was the Magnet Ring, which on the show contained a secret formula. When the ring was stolen, Tom tracked it by observing such things as a pile of paper clips that old Snood had stacked up in his precise way at the desk of his Dobie House Hotel being tipped over by the power of the passing magnet. Then the thief found out the magnet had no power over lead – not when it was in Tom Mix's six-guns.

Over the years, the premiums played a part in many stories. Tom could use the wooden model of one of his guns to escape a trap when deprived of his working guns. His model Telegraph Set could pound out a message in his hip pocket when he was in danger. (That one worked by radio, apparently – the ones that came in the mail had to be hooked together with wires and batteries.)

His Decoder Badge could send him a warning signal of "Danger Ahead." His Mystery Ring could provide a magnified "look-in" picture of himself to identify Tom to authorities when a fake Tom Mix tried to take over a gold shipment. And in one of the very last offers, his glow-in-the-dark Tiger Eye Ring would provide enough light for rescuers to spot him when he was tied hand and foot and tossed into a river.

One of the best things to come out of the show was marginally a premium – a prize in a contest to name Tony's filly (winner: Dobie Gal). It was a juvenile novel called *Tom Mix and the Mystery of the Flaming Warrior* by the program's writer, George Lowther, and illustrated with photos of Curley Bradley as Tom Mix, Leo Curley as Mike, etc. It was a novelization of one of the radio serials, and since no complete serial of the original show has yet been made available to the public (if such exists), the book is the best example of what a complete serial from this classic series was like.

The story concerned the appearance of a phantom Indian warrior who shot flaming arrows and warned of danger and death. Tom feared that the Indians might be about to go on the warpath again. Even though it was 1947, time was a strange thing around Dobie.

As Tom, Mike and Wash took the trail, their fears were realized. They were taken captive by a renegade Indian band and each man was tied between two trees, his arms and legs stretched out by strands of wet rawhide. The Indians left the wetness to evaporate from the rawhide, as it shrank and pulled their limbs agonizingly outward.

Before the suspense was drawn out to the breaking point, a mysterious arrow sang through the air and cut through one of Tom's bonds. With one hand free, Tom freed himself and shortly his friends.

Eventually, Tom would figure out that the mysterious flaming warrior who appeared in the sky was created by modern mechanical means as another white man's trick to exploit the Indians. He tried to turn back his Indian friends from the folly of resorting to violence.

About 1949, Curley Bradley, Tom Mix of radio (center), and Leo Curley as Sheriff Mike make an appearance before an integrated audience at a store selling Ralston.

"Now hear me!" Tom Mix said to the renegade Indian leader. "Your treachery, whatever the reason for it, will bring about your own downfall, Bear Claw! You seek to lead Gray Eagle's clan into war, when you know there can only be one result, death or imprisonment for them all. And like the jackal, you will stand aside, waiting for the kill, that you may feed! Be warned. Even the wind changes its course. Change yours before it is too late!"

Wise and brave words from a wise and brave man. It seemed Tom Mix could solve any problem. But like all the great characters of radio, he could not solve the problem of television. Kids could now see the old movies of Tom Mix on television, as well as other, newer heroes of the West and outer space. There was a fight put up. The old serial quarter hours were replaced with a fast-moving half-hour story to better compete with the half-hours and even full hour shows on the tube. The radio programs also seemed to be louder – more gunshots, more thundering hooves, something to keep the listeners awake. And actually it worked—*Tom Mix* had its highest ratings ever when it was cancelled.

It was a corporate decision spurred by statistical projections that the show soon would start slipping. If Ralston wanted to quit *Tom Mix*, General Mills, makers of the rival cereal Wheaties and sponsors of another great radio Western, *The Lone Ranger*, wanted to continue it, Bradley said. But Ralston did not want any other company to be identified with *Tom Mix*, and it was possible that Ralston would revive the show sometime.

So there came a final broadcast. Some radio series simply ended with the notice that this was the last of the "current series." Some even told listeners to watch their newspapers for an announcement of a return to the air. But the *Tom Mix* show told it straight. It was the end. "The end—yet only the beginning, Mike," Tom said to his faithful sidekick. "How many times will the figure of big, burly Mike Shaw stride across the imagination of some grown-up child?" How true those words!

Then Tom rode Tony off into an echoing Valhalla. As Don Gordon said, "In the heart and the imagination of the world, Tom Mix rides on, and lives on, forever."

Some fans never forgot. They collected the premiums, the comics, what Tom Mix films were available. Eventually a few Tom Mix radio episodes became available, traded on tape among collectors. Many wrote letters to Ralston, suggesting they do something, anything, with Tom Mix. Ralston was still getting requests for the radio series to be resumed into the 1980s. It looked as if nothing would ever happen.

The present author tried for years to locate Curley Bradley. He had last been heard of in Hollywood, working as an actor on Roy Rogers' radio show and *Wild Bill Hickok* among others. But nobody seemed to know where he was.

Finally, I met Forrest Lewis, Curley's sidekick on the Mix show, playing both the black cook, Wash, and crusty old Doc Green. We met at a bar in Hollywood, and Lewis still seemed quite busy, getting the usual number of Hollywood-type phone calls during the lunch. He told me he had made a television pilot of *Lum and Abner* with him playing Abner. He had been in a lot of big color "A" Western features, and regularly turned up on television shows such as *Perry Mason*. But he complained that he was getting too old; old men weren't wanted even for old men parts. I didn't believe it at the time, but he was right. He didn't work much more after our mid-'60s meeting.

As for Curley, when Forry Lewis had last heard of him, he was working at a small Nevada station, announcing, running the board and "I think sweeping up at night," Forry said regretfully. But he couldn't remember the city or the call letters. And anyway, Bradley might have moved on.

Years passed. I made many other attempts to locate the hero of my childhood favorite. Then one day I was being visited by a Western fan when

I learned he had seen Curley Bradley only a few months before. I was stunned. This man, Bob Wolter, actually knew Curley Bradley and had spoken to him recently. He had met Curley through a chance meeting with Curley's mother. Curley was reluctant to meet people these days, he said, but gave me Curley's phone number.

It was a big moment for me to speak to him on the phone. He did not seem the least bit reclusive. He told me he had dropped out of show business in the early sixties and had devoted himself to taking care of his elderly mother in her last years. Later, I found he had been working in a small steel plant, turning out precision rods and pipes. He suggested I meet him at his favorite place, the bar of a veterans' organization in Norwalk, California. When I walked in, I spotted the man in the cowboy hat at the bar, and he turned to greet me. "Well, hello, Jimmy!" he said as if he had known me all his life. Perhaps he hadn't known me, but I had known him. The round smiling face seemed right for a cowboy star of any medium. He reminded me a bit of Johnny Mack Brown at the time.

We spent a long time in that bar, and at Curley's house he shared with his wife, Margaret. I was with my frequent partner and collaborator, Ron Haydock. I wanted to do some new radio shows with Curley, a lifelong dream. It didn't seem impossible in 1974. There was the *CBS Mystery Theatre* going on radio and there was a new series beginning, *The Sears Radio Theatre*. It looked as if radio drama was finally coming back. So far there had been nothing with continuing characters except the reruns of *The Shadow*, *The Lone Ranger* and others, but I thought a show like *Tom Mix* would be ideal to return to a new age of heroic drama.

Of course, my experience in radio was limited. I had written, produced and appeared in some dramas on FM station KPFK, and some of them were heard on other stations of the Pacifica Network. But I felt with a star like Curley Bradley, anything was possible. Just finding him after so many years of looking filled me with a heady confidence.

Since I assumed Ralston still controlled rights to the Tom Mix name, I decided to do a series of shows where Curley would use his own name but appear in stories much like those of the old *Tom Mix* show. I had one of the best paying jobs I had had in years, so I figured I could afford the production costs on the radio shows, a tiny fraction of what any kind of film would cost.

Curley was a study in contradictions. He wanted to get back into action at the microphone, but he did not want to fail at something again. He rightly doubted that modern radio audiences would be receptive to any drama, and he must have had some doubts about the abilities of a "kid" like me. But through constant cajoling, pleading, begging and listening to hours and hours of his innermost thoughts, I got him to do this series of shows, which finally became known as *Curley Bradley's Trail of Mystery*.

As second lead in the show I got my longtime friend Kirk Alyn, who had played many parts on stage, radio and film, including Superman in two fifteen-chapter serials. Kirk did not like playing second to anybody, but for some reason he did it. Though Kirk Alyn was meant to be a leading man, he had to give Curley credit where credit was due. I wrote a script recalling my fond memories of the *Tom Mix* episode where Curley's horse, Junior (as he often called Tony), is trapped in a forest fire after bringing through the needed part to get Curley's plane off the ground. At this point, Curley gives his horse a tearful goodbye. "He had me crying!" Kirk Alyn admitted later.

Actually being in the studio with Curley, hearing him doing the scene I had written, and after playing the part of the young sidekick who had ridden the horse through the flames, I had a dizzy feeling of living a dream come true, a feeling I would have more than once doing shows with Curley.

And to have with me in the same cast "Superman" Kirk Alyn and character actor and stuntman George DeNormand, and later to have Forrest Lewis join us for one of his last performances ever to play a crusty old doctor – it was heaven on earth.

Of course, the show did not sell.

There was very little call for radio drama, and stations were not prepared to pay even our modest fee. They could run forty-year-old recordings of *The Shadow* and *The Lone Ranger* for less – and sometimes for nothing. Some stations just ran the old shows without paying anyone. *Curley Bradley's Trail of Mystery* was run on the Armed Forces network at least once, thanks to producer-host Frank Bresee, and it was sampled on a few other stations. But it was not a financial success.

Curley took it well, as did the rest of the cast. He and I remained friends, and I continued to visit him over the next ten years.

But dreams die hard, and fate was not through with us.

The *Tom Mix* Revival

For years, letters about *Tom Mix* had been coming into the offices of the Ralston-Purina Company in St. Louis. Customers loyal for decades wanted to know where the actors on the show were – especially Curley Bradley, radio's Tom Mix. Others wanted to know if the company still had some of the old radio premiums. There were even requests to revive the radio show (although there were no other radio dramas in new productions on the air) or to put the show on television. All this over thirty years after the last Ralston-sponsored *Tom Mix* show had left the air.

In the early 1980s, Steve Kendall had become general manager of the Hot Ralston division of Ralston-Purina. The cereal was the founding product of the now vast organization, and the company wanted to keep it going for the sake of tradition. They expected nothing spectacular. But Steve was not a man to sit still and shuffle papers. He noticed the letters still coming in about *Tom Mix*, and for the first time in thirty years, someone at Ralston responded. He phoned back some of the letterwriters and began to make plans with their help.

In 1982, the Ralston cereal box offered a set of Tom Mix Ralston bowls – the first new connection with the famous cowboy in all that time. As a loyal Straight Shooter, the present writer wanted to get his new premium (after a fellow collector sent me a Xerox of the box) but I could not find the old favorite cereal for sale anywhere in the Los Angeles area for the required box-top. I wrote Ralston asking how to get the cereal for the bowls, telling them of my longtime interest in their product and *Tom Mix* and of my writing about their radio show. To my surprise, Steve Kendall phoned me in response to my letter, telling me what market chains carried the product and soliciting my ideas for further promotions.

The next premium was to be the first in a possible series of miniature *Tom Mix* comic books to be included in the Ralston box. The basic idea of the comic books had been sold to Kendall by another dedicated fan, Randall Hornbeck, but since I was a professional writer and editor, I got the job of actually adapting one of the old 1940s premium comic book stories to the new format. Several stories were considered. I finally did the "Taking of Grizzly Grebb" episode with a slight borrowing from another story, adding a cover and a backcover with an ad for Ralston and another premium, a Tom Mix glossy photo. I also added a page about "Famous Straight Shooters" including Tom Mix, Annie Oakley and the famous black cowboy Bill Pickett, who according to legend invented the rodeo sport of bulldogging. Kendall did not care to revive the old stereotype of Wash, the TM-Bar cook. He wanted to introduce a positive black image, without altering the original story too much. This special page featuring a genuine black Western hero (and a friend of the real Tom Mix) was what I came up with to do the task.

The new *Tom Mix* comic book artwork was done well by Alex Toth, from the beloved but antique art of Fred Meagher. Toth was a master of the comic format, but years of working in animated cartoons had given him a free style lacking in detail, a style he loved, but which I thought too loose for this project. I had to ask him for more detail. He complained about having to work from the "crude" 1940s work of artist Meagher (and from the storyboards I designed). I didn't tell him that there were lots of people, including me, who loved the work of Meagher and held it higher than almost any contemporary artist.

I edited a second issue of the *Tom Mix* comic, and did the panel breakdowns again. It was accepted and paid for by Ralston, but never actually put into final art or printed.

In almost daily telephone discussions with Steve Kendall, and several personal meetings when he flew out from St. Louis, I kept suggesting that

Curley Bradley, still alive, still acting, do some more radio shows of *Tom Mix and his Ralston Straight Shooters*. Steve was certainly receptive, and perhaps had been thinking of something along those lines himself.

Finally, for a second album of old *Mix* radio shows "produced" or arranged for recording by promoter George Garabedian, Steve wanted Curley to read a narration telling how the serial ended. (Radio recordings are rare. All episodes of a serial may no longer exist. Sometimes only one episode of a serial story has survived on a disc recording.) In the case of "The Mystery of the Vanishing Village," there were three consecutive episodes from the middle of the story. I suggested to Steve how much better it would be to have other members of the old show join Curley and to have a fully dramatized last chapter of the serial. I could remember pretty well how the story had come out from hearing it on the air years before. Eventually Steve approved my script for the final episode and authorized me to produce and direct it, after hearing my low-budget shows of *Curley Bradley's Trail of Mystery*.

For the first time, I could hire the professional actors I wanted. For the crucial part of Sheriff Mike Shaw, we could no longer use Leo Curley, who had long since departed. At Curley's suggestion I tried Jack Lester, known to me as radio's Sky King, an announcer on *Jack Armstrong* and countless other assignments. Jack had been on the *Mix* show in the 1940s, playing cowhands and crooks, character parts. On the *Tom Mix*-inspired series *Curley Bradley, The Singing Marshal*, he played Curley's fictional brother and took over the lead in the series while Curley recovered from an illness. To establish a continuity from the old shows, Jack had to be recognized as Sheriff Mike. Curley sounded older, but he was still Tom. Jack listened to the old recordings of Leo Curley. A consummate professional, Jack approximated Leo pretty well, but his voice didn't sound quite right. I suggested that Leo really was old at the time of the show, far older the Jack, and that he was having to strain to get the words out forcefully. With the added element of strain, Jack sounded remarkably like the old Sheriff Mike. It was Jack's skill that saved the project.

In the fellowship of radio actors, just as Curley had suggested Jack, Jack suggested Art Hern for the show. Art had done the original *Mix* countless times, and it seemed he would be perfect for the villain of the piece, a movie director called the Great Dane. Like a number of real-life directors, Dane was more a hammy actor than anything else. Art did a sort of send-up of John Barrymore that closely matched the original actor in the role decades before. Art had been prominent in Chicago television, playing Natco the Clown (representative of the National Tea Co.), doing a sailor character called Moby on *The Happy Pirates* with entertainer Two-Ton Baker, and generally being omnipresent in the early days of television – in fact he was dubbed the "Pied Piper of Television." Art still does character roles on the tube, as does his old friend, Jack Lester. (Jack may be best known these days as Neil the Mechanic in a series of commercials for automotive belts.)

For the final continuing character, Doc Green, I asked Les Tremayne, star of seemingly half the shows on radio, including *First Nighter*, *Betty and Bob*, *CBS Mystery Theatre*, and some on television such as *Shazam* (with Captain Marvel). He took over for his late friend Forrest Lewis, the original in the role. While Forry had played it as a cantankerous old Westerner, I couldn't ask Les to disguise his wonderful voice that much and merely suggested he give the role a little age and dignity. The dignity was easy for Les; the other was more difficult, since he is ageless, his voice and face still everywhere on the airwaves.

For the rest of the cast, I used people closer to home. Richard Gulla was an old friend and had been a radio actor in Chicago in the last days of drama there. He and I had done lots of recreations of old radio shows together for fun, and he had worked on my earlier, unsold series with Curley. He doubled as a press agent for the unscrupulous Dane, and as Hank Smith, a young man whose girlfriend has disappeared along with the rest of the "Vanishing Village." He did the two parts okay, but not with the separation I knew he was capable of. I think he was nervous, working with such big guns. It was his last professional work. He had not beaten cancer as we hoped, and in a few years would succumb to it.

For Hank's girl, Mary, I used my wife, Barbara Gratz Kovner Harmon. Barbara liked to work with Dick Gulla and me, and others like Dave Amaral and Lloyd Nesbitt, in our recreations. She did fine.

Our daughter (my stepdaughter), Dawn Kovner, helped out on the sound effects. She was just thirteen. Jack Lester liked her as a child actor, she having worked with him on some things we had tried. But I felt that having her play Jane would perhaps be smacking too much of nepotism.

Finally, I played the young sidekick to Tom, just as I had on the earlier pilot series. Of course, "Tom" – Curley Bradley – was not that high on me as an actor. "You're spreading your talent mighty thin," he told me, suggesting I stick to writing and directing. Steve Kendall heard my audition tape and suggested I make my part bigger, but I tried to keep my character in only one or two important scenes so I could, as Curley suggested, spend most of my time concentrating on the directing. On the earlier pilot series, my character was called Dallas, but since we were now officially sponsored by Ralston, I used the name of Tom's sidekick from the old show – Pecos, the part played by Curley Bradley before he became Tom.

For a time I really felt a part of that wonderful world I so loved and admired from the other side of the speaker. Being part of the cast was a big thrill. Even when we were doing that earlier pilot series, Curley would get to talking and say to me, "Remember that time at the Bull-Mich [the

After some thirty years, Curley Bradley recreated his radio role of Tom Mix, seen here at a prop "Mutual" microphone with producer-actor Jim Harmon. (Photo by Frank Bresee).

Chicago radio actors' favorite bar] when we...", momentarily forgetting that I had not been there, that I had only been a ten-year-old kid listening at home.

With the technical direction of our engineer, Steve Markham, and the general helpfulness of studio owner and all-around radio great Frank Bresee, the first show of our revival of *Tom Mix* – the last episode of "Vanishing

Village" – was a success. We also did the opening episode of the serial (also missing from the original run). The shows were broadcast on many radio stations around the country on a participation basis; that is, Ralston would provide the shows and a station could run them for free, with the only advertising being the short Ralston theme song/commercial (though stations could run their local commercials fore and aft). Frequently, the station would do a phone interview with Curley, or occasionally with me, about the proposed revival.

Our next effort was a half-hour complete story of *Tom Mix* as it had been in the 1949–50 final season for Ralston. I had a hard time convincing Steve Kendall that the half-hour show was the way to go. All the revivals – on old recordings – of such shows as *The Lone Ranger, The Green Hornet, Sgt. Preston of the Yukon,* had been in that format. No old fifteen-minute continued stories had been commercially successful. (There were long runs available of *Jack Armstrong* and *Captain Midnight* in the quarter-hour serial format, but nobody had successfully packaged them for new sponsorship.) Kendall had me do a half-hour pilot, but told me to do it so that it could be broken into a two-part quarter-hour serial for short-term use.

We kept the same cast, and added a guest star in the part of a troubled rancher, Jock Mahoney. Jock told me he had worked in radio years before, but he did not seem to have any longer the radio actor's gift, which I describe as being able to get it right on the first take. Despite that, he was helpful in taking an unpaid day to pose with Curley for publicity pictures, and he is certainly a wonderful part of the entertainment world, playing everything from cowboy heroes to Tarzan, and I was honored to have him in the show.

Virginia Gregg, whom I mentioned before, played Jock's wife in the show and doubled as Jane. While she did a professional job, as she always did (and much more) on countless episodes of radio's *Gunsmoke, Dragnet, et al,* it was quite a stretch for her to play a teenage girl, and perhaps more than I should have asked of her. Once again, Jack suggested I use my daughter, Dawn, but I felt that a radio-trained actress was needed. No one of that description was really a teenager in 1983.

The sponsor, Steve Kendall, who had story-conferenced the script with me, loved the show. And he told me that he would like to do a fifty-two half hours of the new *Tom Mix*. The shows would be heard twice a week, Tuesdays and Thursdays, for twenty-six weeks and then be repeated. If interest was strong enough, the following season we would do another fifty-two. It seemed like my every hope was coming true.

Then, for still unexplained reasons, Steve Kendall was no longer general manager of the Hot Ralston division. He was transferred to the dog food division, and finally left the company. He told me this might happen, almost from the first day. But he said we were going to make the *Tom Mix* revival such a triumph that his successor could not turn his back. In reality his successor never answered a letter or phone call of mine. The big dream was over.

Kendall's problem, I believe, was that he was *too* successful with this *Tom Mix* promotions to advance Ralston sales. The sales did go up. An in-house organ said sales had gone up 20 percent. Other sources tell me sales went up five times or 500 percent. The mammoth organization just wasn't interested. They only wanted the Hot Ralston product kept alive as a token. They did not care about it really prospering.

Even as Steve Kendall had warned me he might not forever be general manager at Ralston, Curley Bradley let me know he might not last as Tom Mix forever. He said he might want to "retire." We both knew what he meant . He suggested Jack Lester could take over for him. After all, Jack had played the similar hero, Sky King, and had replaced Curley as his fictional brother on *The Singing Marshal*. He also said another of our group, Les Tremayne, could do it, but he thought Jack had the more authentic Western background. I concurred.

In the half-hour pilot we did there were warnings of what was ahead. In the very opening of the show, Curley struck some sort of glitch and could not read his opening properly. Thanks to recording, we could try it again and again. Virginia suggested a way in which Curley might try it; he did not appreciate the assistance, but finally he got into the swing of it and did a fine show.

In less than a year, I got a phone call from Curley's wife, Margaret. Curley was in his last illness. The emphysema from his constant smoking had its final grip on him. Barbara and I visited him in the hospital and from out of a near coma he struggled up and gripped my hand in recognition. A few days later, he was dead. Margaret asked me to deliver the funeral oration. That was a dark dream I never had listening to my childhood favorite – my delivering the funeral service for "Tom Mix," Curley Bradley.

Films

There were many movies starring Tom Mix before the radio series began, and one final film shortly after the program started.

The early films of Tom Mix contributed to the image presented on the broadcasts. He was of course a masterfully skilled cowboy, a great rider and terrific shot. That was demonstrated in his earliest films for the Selig company beginning in 1910. *In the Days of the Thundering Herd* demonstrated his riding skills as he delivered the mail via Pony Express and rode down to scoop up the herione from in front of a stampede of real buffalo. *The Man from Texas* displayed his shooting skills as he won a gun duel with the villain who did his sister wrong in the classical sense.

Tom Mix and His Ralston Straight Shooters   249

Tom Mix and Tony, from the 1932 sound film *Destry Rides Again*. This same photo was twice used a a premium, in 1933 and for the 1983 revival.

The radio series also employed some elements from the films beyond the obvious cowboy skills Tom represented in his screen image, basically created by him. He was his own director on a number of films, and even when someone else got the credit line, he still directed himself. His later, bigger budgeted films for Wm. Fox set Tom Mix in the contemporary West. *Sky High* (1922) has Tom going after border smugglers in an airplane, hanging from a rope and dropping into the Colorado river. (Unlike most Tom Mix stunts, this one was mostly early special effects.) In the 1926 feature *The Great A & K Train Robbery*, the trains are contemporary; automobiles and modern communication are in evidence. So when *Tom Mix* came to radio, it was in a modern West where there were planes and cars, not the Old West of *The Lone Ranger* radio series beginning the same year, 1933.

Two of the nine talking pictures Tom made for Universal came out in 1933 after the radio show had begun, but it was too soon for any cross-referencing either way. The year before, several Universal pictures were set in the modern West, including *Flaming Guns* and *Hidden Gold*, the film in which the original Tony was injured and retired (definitely not shot!).

The *Tom Mix* radio show format had been established by 1935, when Tom made his only serial (and last film of any kind), *The Miracle Rider*, for Nat Levine's Mascot Pictures. This chapterplay, written by John Rathmell and directed by Armand Schaeffer and B. Reeves Eason, shows some definite similarities to the radio show. It could have been coincidence, but producer Levine was well aware of the ability of radio to attract a movie audience. The same year, he would make a movie star out of radio singer Gene Autry in the serial that preceded *Miracle Rider* on the schedule, *Phantom Empire*.

Like the radio series, *Miracle Rider* was set in the contemporary West with cars and aircraft. Tom Mix was in the Texas Rangers on screen. An older Ranger in his company played by Jack Rockwell corresponded somewhat to the radio show's Old Wrangler. There was a young girl character, Ruth, who somewhat corresponded to the Jane of radio. Tom's attitude toward her seemed to swing from the romantic to the paternalistic. The paternal seemed to win. This character was an Indian, unlike Jane. Some changes had to be made; Levine would not have wanted to pay Ralston for rights to their format when he was paying Tom Mix himself more than he had ever paid anybody before to star in a serial—$10,000 a week for four weeks (a very sound investment—the serial returned large grosses for years). In contrast, a youthful John Wayne was earning $150 a week for starring in serials for Mascot at around this time.

There was also a similarity in the plots of *Miracle Rider* and the broadcasting series. Tom Mix was up against a seemingly supernatural menace, as he was so often on the air. The Indians were made to believe their god, the Firebird, had returned and was raining death and destruction down on them. Tom found the answer in a science fictional radio-controlled aircraft and associated devices. The same sort of premise was used before and after by the radio series. A similar radio serial was "The Mystery of the Flaming Warrior," mentioned previously.

The one aspect of his screen persona that never was presented on radio was his humor, his sense of fun. Like the Lone Ranger, Tom Mix was always presented as a stern, dedicated symbol of justice.

The only fictional presentation of Tom Mix with a sense of humor came in the movie *Sunset*, starring Bruce Willis as Tom Mix and James Garner as Wyatt Earp. While Willis does not resemble Mix in the least and has few cowboy abilities (he was doubled in almost everything), his sense of ironic fun is not unlike what we know of the real Mix. The element of mystery, somewhat like the radio series, is present but is almost certainly a coincidence. This is all the *screen* Mix. The so-called "fictional" friendship between movie star Tom and Marshal Earp was not really fictional at all. But they were friends when Tom was in his forties and Wyatt in his seventies, so they were not quite the brawling, wench-bedding buddies of this film by writer-director Blake Edwards. The movie has fun moments but is no masterpiece. Still after seeing countless films about Tom Mix being proposed for decades and being shelved before production, it was good to see *any* film about Tom Mix actually on the screen. Perhaps someday there will be a definitive film made about him.

Books

There are a number of books about the real Tom Mix, including *The Fabulous Tom Mix* by one of his ex-wives, Olive Stokes Mix, and *The Life and Legend of Tom Mix* by Paul E. Mix, a cousin. The latter sparked quite a bit of disagreement over its claims of Mix's off-screen adventuring: Paul Mix believes they were at least exaggerated.

There are even novels written about Mix, including Darryl Ponicsan's *Tom Mix Died for Your Sins*, a vision born in hell by a man totally devoid of any romance, and *Tom Mix and Poncho Villa* by Clifford Irving, a man perhaps given to too much romance.

Juvenile fiction about Mix appeared in a number of Big Little Books and one Big Big Book. These small volumes, half pictures and half text, are mostly movie adaptations (*Terror Trail*) or cowboy stories (*Stranger from the South*) not connected with the radio series. One small premium Big Little Book, *Trail of the Terrible Six*, does reflect radio program content, circa 1935.

The juvenile novel, *Radio's Tom Mix and the Mystery of the Flaming Warrior* by George Lowther, which was sold in stores in 1947 and offered as a Ralston contest prize as previously mentioned, offers the best representation of the broadcast series in a novel for young readers, or adults who loved and remember the radio show.

Comics

The *Tom Mix Comics* magazines offered as premiums by Ralston were the first comic books to feature a single Western hero when they appeared in September 1940, shortly ahead of the newsstand title *Red Ryder*. Since 1933, *Tom Mix* Sunday comics had been appearing as advertisements for Ralston cereal and their giveaways. The ads were entertaining in themselves and no doubt inspired further comics about Tom. A few pages of cowboy stories of Tom Mix (much more crudely done than the ads) appeared in such general anthology comic magazines as *The Comics*, beginning in No. 1, 1937. They only foreshadowed the Ralston premium series, which were among the best Western comics, featuring the work of writer-editors Stan Schendel and Ray Bouvert and artist Fred Meagher and his assistant, Bill Allison ("a real cow hand," the comic claimed). A photo page dramatized Schendel swinging from a cross support and kicking catcher-masked Bouvert in the jaw, as Tom Mix did to a badman in the same issue, to prove it could be done. Perhaps more interesting is a photo of Fred Meagher at his drawing board, creating some of the best-loved comics ever. Meagher was still admired decades after leaving the comics industry.

Meagher's comics were cleanly drawn, with lavish detail and subtly shaded colors that have yet to be equaled. The stories were carefully plotted and had genuine characterization. This artistry came at a time when newsstand comic books were often incredibly crude, with characters so roughly drawn they were not recognizable from panel to panel. But these lovingly produced comics did retain the raw vitality that was in the comics at the birth of the industry. The stories, set in the fantasized modern West, often featured science fictional devices and fantastic menaces.

The radio listener sent in a Ralston box-top and got a copy of the comic back through the mail. A few were given away across the store counter with purchase of Ralston. When one got the comic, one saw Tom Mix and Tony bursting through the cover of Book 1 ("Book" was used in place of "Number"). Inside, a cowboy called at the TM-Bar Ranch rants, "Ghost Canyon is haunted! No one's ever come back from there!" Tom Mix is unimpressed. "I have! Scouted it years ago!" It is time to do it again with new trouble reported. Tom goes with his Straight Shooters, Wrangler, Jane and Wash. When the trouble is traced to a walled compound, a rope from Tony's saddle bends a sapling double. Tom rides it and is catapulted through the air into a nest of rustlers who are using a movie projector to show "ghost" images of Indian braves on the canyon sides. The crooks are no match for Tom's fists and six-guns. A second Mix story concerns a train robbery. The rest of the 32-page book (half the size of newsstand comic at the time) contains tricks, puzzles, humor and "Jane at Dream Castle," a continuing feature inspired by the classic strip *Little Nemo*.

Later in the series, Tom Mix singlehandedly stops a Mexican revolution (Book 2), finds the lost treasure of the Toltec Indians (Book 5), battles the Cobra, a costumed super-villain (Book 6), saves a crippled submarine from a sea serpent (Book 8) and prevents the theft of America's gold depository at a Fort Knox–like vault (Book 9). Books 10, 11 and 12 became *Tom Mix Commandos Comics* with Tom leading a World War II Special Forces unit of his usual Straight Shooters against a Japanese submarine, a whole army of invisible men from Japan and finally, Nippon's secret weapon, a squadron of flying dragons.

The Ralston giveaways ended in 1942. It was only in January 1948 that Fawcett Publications began putting out a new *Tom Mix* comic for newsstand distribution. *Tom Mix Western* ran until May 1953; at the same time Tom Mix was also appearing as a single feature in several other Fawcett titles, including *Master Comics* with Captain Marvel, Junior. *Tom Mix Western* comics had photo covers of movie star Tom Mix (and sometimes painted covers of him) but featured the radio cast inside, including occasionally Wash and regularly Sheriff Mike Shaw (whose image was definitely based on radio actor Leo Curley). The stories, now set in the Old West, were much more mundane, dealing with cattle rustlers, bank robbers and the like. The artwork was clean and fluid, done by Carl Pfeufer (pencils) and John Jordon (inks), as identified by researchers Bill and Teresa Harper. These artists have many admirers.

The Ralston books were selling in 1992 for $25 to $100 each (good to mint condition); the Fawcett books go for $10 to $35 (double for first issues of either).

After forty years, Ralston offered a new *Tom Mix* comic in 1983, a 16-page miniature inside the cereal box, unnumbered and called "The Taking of Grizzly Grebb." It was written for this format, edited and designed by the present writer and was illustrated by Alex Toth in a more modern style.

Premiums

The *Tom Mix* radio show offered the most, the best and most representative premiums of all radio series. Perhaps Ralston worked harder to sell their cereal to kids because the stuff was healthy but hardly sweet-tasting, either Hot Ralston or Shredded Ralston. Besides the Ralston premiums, movie star Tom Mix authorized the use of his name on countless other toys, games, clothes, pinbacks and dime store rings. The present work is concerned with radio and will list only those items offered by Ralston as premiums for the radio series. These premiums were as follows, listed alphabetically with date and approximate value in 1992 (assuming average condition). All were sponsored by Ralston.

Arm Patch, TM-Bar Straight Shooters, Cloth (1933; Red, White, Blue; $25), Badge, Sheriff's, Dobie County Siren (1946; $55), Badge, Six-Gun Decoder (1941; $75), Badge, Straight Shooters (1937; offered in silver or gold; $45), Badge, Wrangler (1938; front view head, $50), Badge, Wrangler (1938; 3/4 view Mix head, $50), Badge, Ranch Boss (1938; $75), Blow Gun & Target, Indian (1940; $125), Bracelet, Initial

Identification (1947; $65), Branding Iron and Ink Pad, TM-Bar (1934; $95), Brass, TM-Bar Compass & Magnifying Glass (1940; $65), Buckle and Belt, Championship, TM-Bar (1936; $155 – buckle alone $45), Buttons, Decoder, 5 pcs. (1946; pinbacks of radio cast characters with code word on back; set $125, Curley Bradley $37.50, others $20 ea.), Cast Photo Postcard (1939; variations; $30), Chaps, Cowboy (1935; TM-Bar brand; $150), Chaps, Woolly (1933; 35 box-tops; $90), Compass-Gun & Whistle Arrowhead (1947; $95), Compass & Magnifying Glass, Glow-in-Dark Plastic (1946; $65), Compass/Magnifier (1934; no identification; silver finish with heavy metal case object, 1/8 in. thick with single word "Japan" on back; a known counterfeit is similar but of much lighter metal, 1/16 in., with boxed words "Comet-Japan" on back; $35), Cowboy Hat (1933; 20 box-tops; $65), Cowboy, Plastic Belt, with Secret Compartment Buckle (1950–51; $125), Cowboy Vest, TM-Bar (1935; $125), Cowgirl, TM-Bar Skirt (1935; none now known to still exist; $300), Cuffs, Leather (1933; 8 box-tops; $50), Dangle Bracelet with charms (1936; Tom on Tony, TM-Bar brand, six-shooter, steer head; $200), Face Mask of Tom Mix (1933; $45), Films for Toy Television Set film viewer (1949; packet of 5 discs minature mysteries, cartoons, movie stars; 5 packets known; $35), Flashlight, Bullet (1938; $35), Flashlight, Three-Color Lens ($55), Fountain Pen (1938; $40), Gold Ore Charm & Assay Certificate (1940; $75), Gold Ore Watch Fob & Certificate (1940; $75), Good Luck Spinner (1933; $35), Gun, Wooden (1933; opens, cylinder spins; $85), Gun, Wooden (1936; second model, with revolving cylinder, does not break open, cardboard "Ivory" grips with TM-Bar markings: $75), Gun, Wooden (1939; third model, no moving parts, smaller size; $95), Holster and Cartridge Belt, TM-Bar (1933; $250), Horseshoe Medal & Checkerboard Ribbon, Glow-in-Dark Plastic (1945; $45), Leather Cuffs, TM-Bar ($75), Lucky Charm, Horseshoe (1934; $35), Lucky Wrist Band (1935; $50), Make-Up Kit, Movie (1937; included false beard, mustache, four make-up tins with TM-Bar markings; $150; tins alone; $22.50 ea.), Make-Up Kit, Movie (1940; second version, with eyeglasses, mustache, 2 make-up tins saying "Ralston Straight Shooters"; $175), Manual, "Life of Tom Mix" (1933; First Edition cover showed Tom sitting on fence; $65), Manual, "Life of Tom Mix" (1933; "New Enlarged Edition" cover showed classic semi-profile of Tom in black hat; $50), Manual, Secret (1945; TM-Bar brand & covered wagon on cover; originals have blank inside front & back covers; $55; Reprints; $7.50), Manual, Secret (1944; Tom on rearing horse; came with Siren Ring; $70), Manual, Straight Shooters (1941; Tom in Tony's saddle; $80), Medal, Captain Spur (1941; rare "bounceback"; $95), Membership Kit, Straight Shooters, complete (first) (1933; contains manual, TM-Bar cloth patch, halftone photo of Tom beside Tony, letter, advisory to mother, original mailing envelope, and Horseshoe Nail Ring; $175), Model Kit, Airplane (1936; balsa wood with TM-Bar brand; $80), Parachute Airplane ($105), Parachute, Rocket (1947; $95), Pen and Pencil Set ($40), Periscope (1939; cardboard tube with mirrors; $75), Photo Set "A" (1933; halftone 8 x 10, text stories on obverse, 4 count; $60), Photo Set "B" (1933; as above, different contents; $60)*, Photo, Tom Mix, in silver color frame (1938; autographed to each Straight Shooter by name from "Tom Mix" – not an authentic autograph; $45), Pocketknife, Checkerboard, TM-Bar Brand (1939; $95), Premium Catalog (1933; $25), Premium Catalog (1936; $30), Premium Catalog (1937; $22.50), Premium Catalog (1938; $25), Premium

*Individual photos from a set are worth about $10.

Catalog (1939; $30), Premium Catalog (1940; $30), Premium Sheet (1941; $18.50), *Radio's Tom Mix and the Mystery of the Flaming Warrior* (1947; hardcover book used as contest prize and also sold in stores; $40), Ring, Horseshoe Nail (1933; difficult to authenticate alone – same as real horseshoe nails today for about 3 cents; $35), Ring, Look-Around (1946; $75), Ring, Magic Tiger-Eye (1950; last *Mix* ring – rare; $125), Ring, Magnet (1947; $75), Ring, Mystery (1938; magnified look-in picture of Tom and Tony; $150), Ring, Siren (1944; $65), Ring, Slide Whistle (1949; $65), Ring, Straight Shooters (1934; only displays TM-Bar brand against Ralston checkerboard – first *Tom Mix* ring with identifying insignia; $65), Ring, Tom Mix Signature ($95), Rocket Parachute (1936; cardboard/balsa wood "rocket" contains parachute and metal man, all launched by rubber band; $105), Signal Arrowhead (1949; clear plastic containing 4-tube whistle, 2-tone siren, magnifying lens, "smallifying" lens; does not glow; $75), Signet Ring (1937; single initial; $65), Skull Cap, TM-Bar (1936; $45), Spurs, Glow-in-the-Dark (1949; plastic glow rowels, alumnium sides; $105), Spurs (1933; TM-Bar leather straps; 8 box-tops; $150), Stationery, Straight Shooters (1935; $35), "Straight Shooters News" newsletter (1940; $45), Sun Watch (1935; circular band, looks like bracelet; $95), Sweat Shirt, TM-Bar (1935; $90), Telegraph Set (1940; red; battery operated; works with second set; $150), Telegraph Set, Postal (1938; blue with mechanical clicker; $65), Telephone Set (1938; two metal cups and string; $95), Telescope (1938; $60), Television Set, Toy (3 models known 1949–50, including chocolate brown, reddish brown and rare gold version, after RCA Victor; $85), *Tom Mix Comics* (1940–42; series of giveaway comics magazines): (Book 1; $250, Book 2; $150, Book 3; $145, Book 4; $145, Book 5; $145, Book 6; $140, Book 7; $135, Book 8; $135, Book 9; $135, Book 10; (becomes *Tom Mix Commandos Comics*); $145, Book 11; $145, Book 12; $145), T-Shirt, Tom Mix and Tony (1950–51; from photo of Curley Bradley and his horse; none known collected; $150), "Trail of the Terrible Six" by Tom Mix (1935; miniature Big Little Book, 3 x 3½ in., 176 pages; $30), Turtle, baby, live, TM-Bar Branded (1937; none known to be alive or preserved; mailing box and feeding instructions valued at $30), Vest, Sheepskin (1933; 15 box-tops; $50), Western Movie Reel (1935; cardboard box with wood dowels to unroll paper strip with 30 still frame & captions in cut-out center viewer; different movie titles offered including "Rustlers' Round-Up" and "The Miracle Rider"; $175), Writing Kit, Secret Ink (1938; included ink, developer, decoder, instructions; $75), Zyp Gun (1933; no markings if in original mailer; $40).

The plastic cowboy belt and Tom Mix and Tony T-shirt continued to be offered on the backs of Ralston cereal boxes and in magazine ads after the radio series left the air; it is the present writer's opinion, based on his personal memories, that these items were never advertised on the radio itself. Others disagree.

During the long span of the series, a number of radio cast picture postcards, cast photos, letters on Straight Shooter stationery, advertisements and other show-related items were sent out. Any paper item with the TM-Bar brand, the words "Ralston Straight Shooters" or pictures of Tom Mix or the cast is worth something; the average value is about $15.

Sunday comics had miniature adventures and offers for virtually all the premiums listed (some ads listed several different premiums). They appeared for over seventeen years. Fifty-two ads are known, and each is worth about $15.

There was also a Tom Mix Coloring Book given out in doctors' offices ($35) and a Tom Mix Green Cross Safety Poster (original, $50; reprint $15). These items were not offered on the air or on cereal boxes.

APPENDIX

The following is the author's version of the "Temple of Vampires" sequence from *I Love a Mystery*. Printed with the permission of writer-producer Carlton E. Morse and the Morse Family Trust, owners of the copyrighted story and characters, it is included here to provide an impression of the flavor of one of the classic series.

Jack Packard dropped the map of Central America back into his lap and glanced out the window of the cabin plane to look at some of the real terrain far below the wings of the twin-motored craft. The tropical sun was intense at four o'clock in the afternoon. The foliage flashed up with a greener-than-green look in the strong light, like some mammoth Broadway neon sign. He listened to the sound of the new engines, seemingly running perfectly. In the seat beside him, Reggie York was intent on the controls.

Reggie was all business for somebody of his tender years, Jack thought. Reggie was several years younger than either Jack or their other partner, Doc Long, who was stirring restlessly in the left rear seat. Ordinarily Doc would be paying too much attention to the beautiful, golden-haired girl beside him to show impatience. But the long-legged, red-haired Texan had the scent of adventure in his nostrils, and that—and probably only that—could take his mind off a girl like that even momentarily.

Jack gave a thin smile, and chuckled inwardly over Doc. Doc was always good for a little cheering up. Maybe that was why they had stuck together this long. The leader of the group dropped his eyes back to the map. "Let's see now, Reggie—how long ago did we leave Metagalpa?"

The fair-haired Briton kept his eyes on the gauges. "Was that the last big jungle town we passed over?"

Jack nodded. "Yeah, Metagalpa."

Reggie checked a read-out. "Fifty-five minutes ago, Jack."

Doc stirred, running a large hand through his unruly crop of red hair. "Then we should ought to be gettin' pretty close to . . . un, Boa-co."

Sunny Richards flashed a smile that lived up to her name. "Bo-AC-o, Doc!"

"What's this?" Doc demanded.

Sunny seemed amused. "Bo-AC-o. . . Not BO-a-co."

Doc did not seem overly concerned. "You don't say? Well, anyway, ain't we almost there, Jack?"

Jack nodded. "Reggie," he said, "we ought to be sighting Boaco any moment now."

"Righto."

"After we leave Boaco, there's nothing between us and five hundred miles of jungle but the town of Juigalopa. And there's no airport there."

"Mmm, jungles..." Sunny said dreamily. "Five hundred miles of them."

Not every girl would consider it a vacation to go flying off over one of the wildest regions left on Earth with three strapping male specimens. But during that business about the Richard's Curse, Sunny had learned that she could trust not only her honor but her life to these three modern knights.

Jack indicated the route on the map for Reggie. "We fly between the Huapi Mountains and Lake Nicagaragua."

"Lake Nicararagua..." Doc repeated, almost pronouncing it right. "Is it much of a lake?"

"Only fifty miles long," Jack said.

"Fifty miles?" Doc exclaimed in his unusual sate of wonder at what the world offered. "Why, that's an infant ocean!"

"Lots of Indians all along the lake, I understand... from the lower end of the lake to San Jose, Costa Rica is another hundred and fifty miles."

"And that's our destination? For tonight? San Jose, Costa Rica," Sunny said.

"Eight or nine o'clock tonight," Doc said. "Sunny, then's about the time and place I'll start lookin' for trouble..."

"Doc, you don't mean something tall, dark and lovely?"

Doc Long was not often serious. But if there was anything he didn't joke around about, it was beautiful women. His sunburned face took on the expression of a temple priest at his devotions. "Sunny, the girls down in this part of the world have the biggest black eyes and the longest eyelashes of any girls in the whole wide world."

"My, my. How can you bear to wait?" Sunny asked.

Doc shook his head. "I can't – hardly."

The girl leaned closer to the quiet leader. "What sort of trouble are you going to look for, Jack?"

"I'm reserving my right to pick and choose my brand of trouble when we get there."

Doc excitedly tried to stand up in the cabin plane – impossible even for a short man, much less one as tall as the Texan. "And man, oh man, is there plenty of trouble to pick and choose from. Anything you want from an ordinary gamblin' house brawl with cuttin' knives to black magic and native voodoo rites."

Sunny was not quite sure of all this. "Really?"

"You never saw the like of it," Doc assured her. "Why, Sunny, last time we was down this way, Reggie almost got hisself skinned alive trying to save a half-breed girl from an Indian sacrifice."

Sunny was beginning to half-believe. "Did you save her, Reggie?"

"No," Reggie said.

Sunny returned to the airplane from their stopover at Boaco with a little more sense of the reality of Central America.

Doc took the controls. "Everybody relax and try to digest them beans."

"I liked that stop best of all," Sunny mused. "I really got the feel of the jungle tropics – lazy, dreamy and just a little bit rotten and dangerous."

Jack nodded. The girl kept her eyes open and was no fool. "Yep, that's life in the tropics as she is lived. Our first real taste of – "

"*Hello, everybody!*"

Packard broke off his sentence with an expletive. He and his two partners, as well as Sunny, turned in their seats to see a small, round face staring at them from behind the last pair of seats, the loose leather flap of the luggage compartment draped around his thin shoulders like a cloak.

Reggie, aghast, searched for words. "Jack, I say – a bally infant!"

Sunny was more accurate about the child's age. "Why, Jack, it's a little boy."

Infant, small boy or trained ape, Jack Packard was not overly fond of any creature who threw a monkey wrench into his carefully laid plans. There was little kindness in his voice as he asked, "Where did you come from?"

The boy waved a surprisingly clean hand vaguely towards the rear. "Back in there..."

"Back in the luggage compartment?" Reggie blurted. "Oh look here, we've got a blooming stowaway."

After hearing the boy's story, everybody but Jack had to admit it wasn't the boy's fault, becoming a stowaway. His father had put him in the plane in San Diego and told him to stay there until he got hungry. The boy only knew that his name was Hermie, and that his father's name was Hermie too, and that he now *was* hungry. As the others looked after the seven-year-old's needs, Jack began to check on the altitude of the ship and their exact location, and then told Reggie to stick the maps into his pocket. If the plane crashed and burned and they got out, the maps would be a handy thing to have.

Sunny saw a new side to these three who ordinarily did not seem to worry about anything. She couldn't quite take it seriously. She drew Doc's attention away from his watchful gaze out the window. (She usually didn't have so much trouble getting him to look at her.) "I'll bet you five dollars we land in San Jose on schedule, and no trouble..."

Doc looked as if he didn't like the odds. "Hey, Sugar, don't say that."

"Why not?"

"Haven't we got enough trouble without you throwing up a challenge like that?"

Sunny saw Doc's usual good-natured face take on a grim mask that looked out of place on him. "Honest to goodness, Doc – you and your Texas superstitions."

He shook his head. "You don't get it, Sunny... It isn't superstition. That's how a soldier of fortune stays alive, being one jump ahead. It's part of our job to see what's coming. We've all been doing it so long, it's about like a ... well, a sixth sense or second nature to us."

She felt a certain tingle of apprehension beginning to come over her. She sought some reassurance. "Reggie, are you as obsessed with this 'evil eye' rubbish as Doc is?"

"But what's so unnatural or out of the world about a premonition?" Reggie was calm, but as serious as the others. "Something in Jack is simply tuned a bit finer than in the rest of us... Or put it this way, his unconscious has picked up something that isn't apparent to the rest of us... The rhythm of the engines.. the vibration of the propellers... Or the wings... Something so slightly off normal that even his conscious mind doesn't get it... And yet it's registered in that subconscious instinct that warns of impending danger."

Sunny still wasn't certain. "Well, as least that make *some* sense."

Sunny couldn't remember much about the crash. Jack had insisted they strap themselves in and get ready for anything. The motors had faltered one time before they quit completely. Jack had taken the ship in to its jungle landing. There had been a horrible noise, and all her fears seemed to have been realized. The little boy had enjoyed the roller coaster ride, and Doc even complimented Jack on "about the prettiest piece of landing an airship as anybody's going to see." But they had crash landed in the middle of a jungle, and Sunny did not like it.

Doc and Reggie crowded to the window to get bearings, and suddenly Doc yelled, "Holy jumpin' catfish!"

"What is it, Doc?" Sunny asked.

"A doggone *cathedral*..."

"Cathedral..." Sunny repeated.

"Good Lord," Reggie said in amazement. "A New York skyscraper rising right up out of the jungle!"

The plane had not caught fire, so they had time to round up what meager food and supplies they had on board. They couldn't stay in the metal oven the plane would become in the sun, so they headed toward the only apparent shelter – the towering ancient temple they had seen. The three men tried to keep the young woman and the boy on the path, away from what snakes and animals might be in the bush and one very dead Indian they encountered. Then abruptly they were through the jungle growth and in the courtyard of the temple.

Trees and shrubs grew up through the cracked paving blocks of the courtyard, and across the front of the building, some twenty great stone steps marched up to looming arched doorways.

"Somebody put a lot of back-breaking work into this, centuries ago," Jack observed.

The group climbed the steps and went through the open doorways – any doors would have rotted away centuries before.

Doc grabbed Jack's shoulder. "Jack – Jack, did you see what I just saw?"

"What, Doc?"

"Something just flew from one side of the temple to the other – 'way up yonder..."

"Probably an owl," Jack said.

"Owl my grandma... It was big as a man, it didn't have no wings – and what's more it was wearing a human skin *and that's all!*"

Jack's logical, pragmatic mind had a dozen answers for what Doc thought he saw – anything but admitting that the Texan had seen a human being flying through the air on his own power. Considering the matter closed, Jack Packard assigned everybody tasks for exploring the ancient ruin and setting up their camp. With the little boy in the doorway, almost within arm's reach, Sunny stayed behind with Doc as the other two climbed an interior stairway and examined tiers of monks' cells.

Then Doc saw the flying creature again, and this time Sunny saw it too. It was threateningly close to his two partners, and Doc felt he had to go warn them. Shouting was no good in this huge place. Almost as soon as he was gone, Sunny noticed the boy was nowhere in sight.

The girl raced to the doorway and into the sunlight, calling frantically for the missing boy. "Hermie darling, are you out here?"

"Who is Hermie?"

Sunny gasped at hearing the soft, seductive, Spanish-accented voice. And then framed in the doorway of the great, ancient place she saw the man who went with the voice—a tall, delicately handsome Latin man in long black robes.

"You are afraid?" he asked.

"Who are you? Where did you come from?"

A smile revealed very white teeth that gleamed in the light. "I have always been here."

"But... there is no one here."

"Oh yes, I am here."

"But who are you?"

"I am Manuel."

Sunny felt weak, dizzy. She tried to hold on to reality, to the important matters at hand. "Have... have you seen Hermie?"

"Who is Hermie?"

"A little boy."

The dark man looked startled, his thin red lips drawing down in disbelief. "A little boy?"

"Yes, seven years old. He was with me just a minute ago—he just disappeared."

"If I may say so this is very bad place for little boys... and not a good place for a beautiful girl."

"Don't come any closer!"

"I have not moved since I spoke to you. You should never have entered the Temple of Vampires. Why did you?"

"Temple of Vampires!" Sunny gasped. The world was growing darker around her. "There aren't any such things... just fairy stories to... to chill people's blood."

"*Aaaah, blood!*"

"Don't! Don't... look at me like that."

"You are mistaken. This temple belongs to the Vampires and it is not given to many people to leave this temple once they have entered."

Sunny was trying to hang on. She couldn't see the dark man very clearly anymore. "But Hermie... I've got to find Hermie."

"You are outside the temple now. If you are wise you will not enter again, ever."

"But Hermie..."

"I don't think you will ever see the boy Hermie again. I don't think you will ever *want* to see Hermie again."

She could hold on no longer. Sunny slipped to the ground, fainting, falling into protective darkness.

The man looked down at her. He murmured "She falls to the floor to forget. She sleeps... a beautiful woman asleep..."

When Jack, Doc and Reggie found Sunny, she was unhurt but as she came out of her sleep state, she could only babble about the Temple of the Vampires and the man she had seen who told her he had always been here.

"Hello, everybody!"

Hermie was back. He told of being led away by a lovely, dark-haired girl who took him to a secret place and gave him figs to eat. She told him that her name was Angelina and that she was High Priestess of the Temple. She brought him back, but she would see him again. "She had the whitest teeth and about the reddest lips I ever did see," the little boy told them.

Angelina was as beautiful as Hermie said. Doc found that out when she came back for the little boy. Doc tried to get her mind off the boy with some adult admiration, but the dark-robed priestess didn't seem to care much for lovemaking, Texas style. The woman grabbed Hermie and jumped off a high ledge, disappearing into thin air. The trio of adventurers would see Manuel perform the same trick, coming and going off the high ledges of the old temple as if he had the wings of a giant bird – or a bat.

Of course, Manuel had no interest in Hermie, and perhaps to gain the group's confidence and put them off their guard, he brought the boy back, although without any clothes except a native loincloth. Hermie was unharmed, but he had had enough of Angelina. Manuel dismissed his good deed returning Hermie. "It is the girl I want," he said.

Experienced as he was with the rooms and passageways of the ancient ruin, with his secret of coming and going invisibly from the ledges, Manuel got Sunny.

It didn't take some of the smartest private detectives in the business to find out the secret of Manuel's and Angelina's seeming ability to fly from ledge to ledge. There was a network of ropes spider-webbing the ancient place. With these the priests could swing from one stone walkway to another. In the darkness, they had seemed to fly.

With Reggie guarding the rescued Hermie and the captured Angelina (who had come around after Hermie just once too often), Jack and Doc used the ropes to swing through the still air of the ancient place, hundreds of feet above the stone floor below. Doc liked the experience – it was exhilarating.

Landing on the opposite ledge, the boys didn't find Manuel's private chambers immediately. First they opened the sacred room of the temple vampires themselves, huge winged beasts as tall as a man, selectively bred for size and blood-lust over the centuries by the brotherhood of the temple. The creatures shuffled nearer to Jack and Doc, making sucking noises.

Jack and Doc each had a forty-five in either hand, ready to blast the vampire bats straight to hell where they belonged. Only there were too many vampires and not enough bullets to get all the beasts before a tide of the hairy-bodied blood-seekers, would overcome Jack and Doc, covering them with membraned wings and eager sharp-toothed mouths, sucking, sucking.

Then the door to the Sacred Chamber swung shut solidly, holding back the anxious creatures, the beloved of the jungle religion.

It was Manuel who had shut the door, and now he led them to his private chambers, where they found Sunny, tied up by the high priest for his protection. He sported a black eye delivered by one of Sunny's quick fists.

The high priest had a gun on the two men, demonstrating that he had somewhere learned more of the outside world than just the English language. Now that Jack and Doc had actually seen the Sacred Vampires, they could not be allowed to live. There was another entrance to the giants bats' den from Manuel's quarters. Doc was to go first. He would feed the vampires' hunger, and then it would be Jack's turn. Doc gave Jack a signal, and Manuel was abruptly relieved of his gun and his consiousness, downed by Doc and put out by a solid right from Jack.

They untied Sunny, and even though walking was painful after being tied, they got her out of Manuel's rooms and onto the outer ledge. Faced with the prospect of having to swing on the end of a rope across an empty void far above the stone floor, and still reeling from all she had endured, Sunny fainted as when she had first encountered Manuel. Now Jack and Doc faced the problem of getting an unconscious girl across the open gulf to the monk's cell where they had left Reggie with Hermie and the captive priestess. It wasn't their only problem, however. Somehow the Sacred Vampires had gotten loose and were coming along the ledge in the darkness toward them... real vampire bats, as large as men, bloated and grisly with a vicious sort of rapaciousness.

Ignoring the approaching creatures, Doc helped Jack get Sunny on his back. He would swing across on one rope, carrying double, and Doc would follow on a second rope.

"Well, here I go," Jack said.

"'Luck, Jack."

"Yeah," Jack said. "Be seeing you," Jack called to Doc behind on the ledge as the air whipped past his face and the rope burned against his hands, his grip sliding a bit in spite of himself with the weight of the girl whose limp, warm arms circled his neck.

Back on the ledge, Doc muttered to himself, "Man, that's high-diving into space. Well, come on, Doc , me lad, we're next." He unfastened a rope from the stone niche carved out to hold it. Then there was a movement in the darkness, a whisper of sound. "Hey, what's that... Look out!" Doc felt himself falling over the edge, into the open void. "Hey, hey... Jack... Jack!" he called instinctively to his partner.

On the opposite ledge, Jack safely deposited Sunny, who was still thankfully unaware of her swift but perilous crossing. Reggie was watching over Hermie and the captive Angelina. Reggie had no trouble to report, but Hermie wanted his clothes back, particularly before Sunny woke up and saw him. As the minutes wore on and Doc did not show up, Jack knew that something was wrong and that he would have to try those crazy acrobatics again.

Leaving the others in the cell, Reggie and Jack stepped out on the ledge and Jack took hold of the swinging rope again. "Oh, Reggie... keep a close guard on the door of the monk's cell. I think those creatures finished off Manuel, but he disappeared. He just may have gotten away."

"I imagine he'll be a pretty dangerous customer by now," Reggie said.
"He won't stop at anything. So watch out."
"I'll be watching."
Jack firmed his grip on the swinging rope. "So long. Here goes..."
With more of the rush of air but less strain on his hands with only his weight to support, Jack was again moving through the empty nothingness of the old ruin. Then, incredibly, he was stopping in mid-air, as if he had run into a wall. He gave an exclamation.
"Hey, wat's that?" It was Doc's voice, not far off.
"Doc, is that you?"
"Jack," Doc said in realization.
"What's happened?"
"Well, feller, looks like we met out here in mid-air."
Holding on to the rope was getting harder for Jack–for them both, he knew. "Our ropes are all tangled up."
"Yeah, What you doing out here?"
"I was just going back across to find you," Jack said.
"Well, here I am," Doc said. "Out here swinging fifty feet from the floor and anyway that far from the ceiling."
"You think it's funny?" Jack said in exasperation.
"I don't think it's one blamed bit funny. Hey, we're spinning. Our ropes are coming untangled.
"Hang onto each other's ropes. Let's keep together for a minute."
"Yeah," Doc said.
"What happened, Doc? We shouldn't have met out here. Our ropes are ten or fifteen feet apart."
"Yeah, I know. I was swinging in a circle."
"That's a big help."
"I couldn't help it, Jack. Just as I got a hold of my rope something pushed me off the ledge."
"Pushed you off?"
"Yeah, a minute sooner and I wouldn't have had the rope in my hands."
"You didn't see what did it?"
"No," Doc admitted. "Anyway, I went off the ledge sideways and that threw me in a circle. I never even come close to our ledge."
Jack let out a sigh of exasperation. "Well, we're in one swell pickle."
In a moment, though, Jack had a plan. The two of them would climb up their ropes to where they had been fastened to the roof. There had to be some way down from there; how else could the ropes have been fastened? Ropes would rot away in a few years in this tropical climate, and they would have to be changed regularly.
Jack and Doc climbed and climbed, their hands burning and their arms and chests aching. It didn't seem that they could be in much more trouble, but as they neared the ceiling, a low rumbling began to build and an earthquake shook the old ruin as other earthquakes had over the centuries. This time, another huge section of the roof gave way and rushed by Jack and Doc to crash below. "And here we are hanging to the rest of the ceiling like a couple of flies!" Doc observed.
These two were not the kind to passively hang on. They climbed. It took them

all night to do it, but as dawn was breaking through the holes in the roof, Jack and Doc made it to the girder to which the ropes were tied. Only... they were too tired to lift themselves up onto the girder. But Jack reasoned that his legs were less tired than his arms. All he had to do was hang head down, a hundred feet in the air, holding on with his legs while he threw the rope over the beam to haul himself up. He had to let go of the rope to have the slack to throw it over. And he had one try.

"Got my feet locked over the girder," Jack said.

Doc noticed something strange in Jack's voice. "Jack, you be careful. If the blood goes to your head..."

Hanging head down by his legs, Jack threw the slacked rope over the bracing beam. "Here she goes..."

"Jack, Jack, your legs are slippin'... Hang on to that rope – Look out Jack!"

"I got it, I got it," Jack gasped.

"Jack, don't ever do that to me again," Doc said.

Already recovering his breath, Jack said, "I'm all right and the slack went over the beam. Look – I've got a loop to stand in."

"Jack, you were so near to heaven I could hear the angel's wings flappin'."

Jack waved it aside. "Never mind that. Now I can get up on the girder. And I'm not wasting any time."

Packard did not waste time. In a moment he was on top of the ancient crossbeam.

"You made it, Jack, you made it!"

Jack nodded. "Let me get my breath a minute and I'll crawl along the beam and give you a hand."

"I never seen such a guy," Doc marveled in his Texas boy way. "I'd' a stayed right there and starved to death before I'd' atried what you did."

The worst was over. The two men figured out that if they tied the two sixty-foot swinging ropes together they would have more than enough rope to slide to the floor a hundred feet below.

Jack and Doc made their way to the floor and found their partner, Reggie, with Sunny and Hermie. Reggie told them Manuel had reappeared, but he had been outpunched by the Englishman.

Jack asked, "Where are our two captives?"

"Manuel and Angelina?" Reggie asked. "I turned them free during the earthquake. Thought the whole temple was falling in."

Doc was disgusted at the idea of letting the unsavory pair loose. "Well, ain't that a sweet-smelling kettle of fish."

Ever chivalrous, Reggie said, "Really, there wasn't anything else to do."

Then the second earthquake struck – no mere aftershock, but a second and even more thunderous temblor.

"Oh, what's that?" Sunny asked, but really suspecting the worst.

"It's another earthquake," Jack announced. "Come on – get away from the temple."

"*Earthquake, earthquake, earthquake!*" Hermie babbled in childish terror.

Doc grabbed the boy as Jack and Reggie each took one of Sunny's arms and all rushed toward the collapsing doorway, which showed bright sunlight beyond.

"Look out," Doc yelled. "The whole blessed temple is falling in!"

Sunny could not hold back a piercing scream, drowned by the rumble of a tormented earth and grinding and crashing stones of the once proud temple half as old as eternity.

"If you ask me, this is a day for celebration," Reggie said to the other four members of his party.

All of them had made it, but the temple was a complete ruin. Manuel and Angelina and all the other priests must have perished. The plane looked as if it could make a take off if a way could be found to filter the watered gasoline that had downed it. Was that watering an attempt on their lives, or just the locals trying to make as much money off the gas as possible? They would never know. One of the problems was what to filter the gas into before returning the purified product to the plane tanks. Sunny suggested the waterproof air mattresses.

"Well, doggone," Doc said. "Who says the female of the species ain't worth her weight in salt?"

Then, as everything seemed to be winding up successfully, Manuel reappeared, walking out of the jungle into their circle. "The religion is no more," he told them. "With the fall of the Temple of Vampires, all is ended. The Indian's medicine men say it is a sign. The medicine men have roused the Indians against me, the High Priest."

The group agreed to give Manuel sancturary, but before long a native arrow from the shadowy trees put an end to the life of the last resident of the temple, a wooden shaft through the heart of the vampire priest.

Later, the plane lifted into the air, powered by the filtered gasoline. Hermie and Sunny announced their intentions to adopt one another. "Just think," Sunny said. "Eight hours from now we'll be back in the United States. Aren't airplanes wonderful!"

Hermie nodded. "Yeah, especially when they don't come down kerflop in the jungle like this one did!"

Sunny laughed brightly, "Oh, yes!"

Jack exchanged looks with Doc and Reggie that said it all. He headed the plane's nose northward, toward Texas and the states beyond.

ANNOTATED BIBLIOGRAPHY

Every radio show I ever heard, every conversation I have had with a radio listener or a radio creative person, every line I have ever read about radio has helped me write this book. But often the help was pretty small – a line of dialog, the title of some particular story, the name of the actor on some particular show.

Before the pubication of my book *The Great Radio Heroes* (Doubleday, 1967), there was *no* book that dealt at any length with the popular drama forms of radio that most people listened to – the soap opera, the children's adventure serial, the half-hour mystery or detective show. Earlier books dealt with the technical history of broadcasting – the innovations of David Sarnoff, the engineering devices of Lee DeForrest, and so on. Others dealt with only the "best" of radio: the patriotic blank verse plays of Norman Corwin, innovative drama on the *CBS Workshop*, the broadcasts of the Metropolitian Opera, the great news analysts like H. V. Kaltenborn and Elmer Davis. Great stuff, but 90 percent of the audience was listening to *The Lone Ranger, Ma Perkins*, Jack Benny and *Amos 'n' Andy*.

The following books contributed information of some substance to me on specifically my subject, radio mystery and adventure.

Books

Barnouw, Erik. *Handbook of Radio Writing*. New York, Little, Brown, 1939 and later editions. Mr. Barnouw does use quotes from the less intellectual fare of the ordinary listener and offers good advice in general for the writer.

Buxton, Frank, and Bill Owen. *Radio's Golden Age*. New York, Viking, 1966, 1972. (Later editions: *The Big Broadcast*.) This encyclopedic reference work contained cast lists of virtually every well-known drama, comedy or variety program on the air, 1920–1950, and sometimes a paragraph of information. But the book offered nothing of depth. It was popular with people who played the party game Trivia, and commercially successful. It was a great help to the present writer in matching some actors with the roles they played.

Correll, Charles J., and Freeman F. Gosden. *All about Amos 'n' Andy*. Skokie, Ill., Rand McNally, 1929. The actor-writers of one of radio's earliest hits give background and story content. The modern controversy over the way in which whites played black men in a comical light obscures the overwhelming influence this program had on the structure of radio and television broadcasting. The original Monday-Friday format of stories involving comedy, romance and often danger and suspense was the seed not only of other dialect comedy like the "rube" *Lum and Abner* and the Jewish *Goldbergs* but of the soap opera (*Just Plain Bill*) and the adventure serial (*Jack Armstrong*). It was the most important single program in the history of broadcasting.

Corwin, Norman. *Thirteen by Corwin.* New York, Henry Holt, 1942. In this and his other books, Corwin offered his own unique plays but also revealed much about the technique and style of radio drama in general.

Dunning, John. *Tune in Yesterday.* Englewood Cliffs, N. J., Prentice Hall, 1976. This enclopedic work lists programs alphabetically and gives background information ranging from one paragraph to several pages. It is very popular with the dedicated hobbyists, but it owes much to the pioneering works of Buxton & Owen and Harmon, who are not listed in any bibliography (there is none) or acknowledgments (some are made to tape collectors).

Gibson, Walter B., with Anthony Tollin. *The Shadow Scrapbook*, San Diego, Harcourt Brace Jovanovich, 1979. This is the kind of book usually done long after the creator is dead and unable to provide the answers to questions; this time, however, it was done by creator Gibson and number one Shadow fan Tollin. A fine effort.

Harmon, Jim. *The Great Radio Heroes.* New York, Doubleday, 1967.

———. *The Great Radio Comedians.* New York, Doubleday, 1970.

———. *The Nostalgia Catalogue.* Los Angeles, Tarcher, 1973.

——— with Donald F. Glut. *The Great Movie Serials.* New York, Doubleday, 1975.

———. *The Great Television Heroes.* New York, Doubleday, 1975. These five books, the present author's own contributions to the subject, are out of print. I consult them to refresh my memory and to access the many pieces of information contributed by others.

Higby, Mary Jane. *Tune in Tomorrow.* New York, Cowles, 1968. The soap opera star gives information on the real lives of the actors in the soaps, mystery and adventure shows. The book had a limited appeal, since the listener knew the fictional roles better than the actors (unlike Hollywood movie stars).

Holland, Dave. *From Out of the Past: A Pictorial History of the Lone Ranger.* Granada Hills, Calif., Holland House, 1988. Great pictures from all media, but a fine text as well. The best book ever done on a single popular fiction character.

Lowther, George. *Tom Mix and the Mystery of the Flaming Warrior.* Declan X. McMullen, 1947.

Mix, Olive Stokes, and Eric Heath. *The Fabulous Tom Mix.* New York, Prentice Hall, 1957.

Mix, Paul E. *The Life and Legend of Tom Mix.* New York, A. S. Barnes, 1972.

Morse, Carlton E. *Stuff the Lady's Hatbox.* Seven Stones Press, 1988.

Norris, M. G. "Bud." *The Tom Mix Book.* World of Yesterday, 1989.

Oboler, Arch. *Oboler Omnibus.* New York, Duell, Sloan and Pierce, 1945. In this and his other books, the writer of the horror series "Lights Out" (created by the ignored but perhaps more talented Willis Cooper) presents his plays of horror based on endless repetition of words and suggestive sound effects, but never the script of his most famous story, "The Chicken Heart." Oboler doggedly tried to revive radio drama in the sixties, seventies and eighties, and did succeed in presenting new productions of some of his old stories.

O'Brien, Richard. *Collecting Toys.* Florence, Ala., Books Americana, annual editions. Includes "Premiums" guide by Jim Harmon.

Osgood, Dick. *WYXIE Wonderland.* Bowling Green, Ohio, Bowling Green University Popular Press, 1981. A fascinating book on one of the great radio stations, WXYZ Detroit, home of *The Lone Ranger* and compatriots, by a man who was there to see it all.

Overstreet, Robert. *The Official Overstreet Comic Book Price Guide*, 19th ed. New York, Ballantine, 1989.

Seiverling, Richard F. *Tom Mix: Portrait of a Superstar.* Keystone Enterprises, 1991.

Wylie, Max. *Best Broadcasts of 1938-39.* Whittley House, 1938, and later editions.

_____. *Radio Writing.* New York, Farrar and Rhinehart, 1939, and later editions. Wylie was the most liberated of the early critics, and was bold enough to include a *Lone Ranger* episode as one of the best plays of the current year.

Periodicals

Radio Mirror. New York, MacFadden, 1930s to 1950s. This publication in particular, and a few other similar to it, offered some help – but again, not much. It was primarily aimed at women and what the publisher thought women wanted, so it was about 90 percent dedicated to soap operas, picture stories of the cast in costume and character and serializations of soap opera plotlines. Occasionally, there would be a picture or paragraph (or very occasionally a whole feature) on some mystery or adventure program.

Privately Published Works

Bennett, Jack, *Review of the Circus*. Privately printed, 1992. Reprints on circus life, including the shows of Tom Mix, "Lone Ranger" appearances by Lee Powell and Brace Beemer. Long a circus man, Jack Bennett has the distinction of probably being the only stunt double for a *radio* actor. He doubled Felix Valu as old-timer Buckskin from the *Red Ryder* radio series, appearing with "Red," Brooke Temple, in the Johnny Strong Circus. Bennett did a bullwhip act.

Harmon, Jim, editor. *Radiohero Magazine*. Harmon, 1963. Three issues. Many contributors, including Redd Boggs, Ron Haydock and Don Glut, offered memories of early adventure series, still being drawn upon by various writers on the subject. Out of print.

King, Fred. *The Jack Armstrong Enclopedia*. Privately printed, various editions. Practically everything on Jack.

SPERDVAC (Society for the Preservation and Encouragement of Radio Drama, Variety and Comedy). *SPERDVAC Radiogram*. Los Angeles, 1980s to date. This radio club bulletin is probably the best of the current group, often offering accounts of talks delivered at meetings by radio pioneers and publishing priceless old photos from the collections of pioneers. Staff: Dan Haefly, Bobb Lines, Barbara Watkins, Chris Lembesis, John and Larry Gassman.

INDEX

Note: (p) after a page number indicates a photograph

Abbott, John 181
ABC 18, 41, 50, 79, 106, 121–126, 169, 183, 197, 204, 214
Ackerman, Forrest J 224
Action Comics 214–216
Adams, Mason 206
Adams, Neil 215
Adreon, Franklyn 139
"Adventure of the Empty House" 175
Adventures by Morse 55
Adventures of Captain Marvel 212
Adventures of Sherlock Holmes 179–180
Afflick, Mary 219
"African Jungle Mystery" 62
The Air Adventures of Jimmie Allen 1–7, 8, 183, 201
Alamo 126
Albert, Elaine 106
Aldrich Family 21
Alexander, Joan 197–198
Alger, Horatio 163
All-Star Comics 216–218
Allen, Hoyt 99
Allen, Judith 149
Allison, Bill 252
Allman, Lee 41, 48
Alter-Ego 215
Alyn, Kirk 14, 209–212, 214, 241–242
Amaral, Dave 245
"Ambassador Ricardo Santos Affair" 63

Ameche, Don 79, 82
Ameche, Jim 79, 82
America's Great Comic-Strip Artists 99
Anderson, Marjorie 149
André, Mike 183
André, Pierre 2, 7, 10, 99–101, 102, 183
Andrews, Clark 149, 152
Andrews, Robert Hardy 79, 149
Andrews, Stanley 99–100
Aplon, Boris 7–9, 99
Archer, John 149, 153, 161
Archie Comics 162
"Arctic Mystery" 94
Armstrong of the S.B.I. 92
"Assignment with a Displaced Person" 63
Atom Man Vs. Superman 212
"Atomic Footprints" 91
Atwill, Lionel 179–180
Autry, Gene 138, 140, 229

Bad Man of the Border 192
Baer, Parley 50
Bailes, Jerry 215
Bailey, Mel 50
Baker, "Two-Ton" 244
Bank Dick 93
Bannon, Jim 22, 51, 72, 74(p), 75(p)
Bantam Books 166

Barker, Brad 99, 101
Barnes, Paul 7-8
Barron, Robert 79
Barrymore, John 17, 176, 179
Bartel, Harry 169
Bates, Cary 145
Batman 14, 43, 49, 76; television 210, 214
"Battle of the Century" 56, 61
BBC 175, 182
Beals, Dick 106
Beat the Clock 198
Beatty, Dan 106
Beatty, Ned 214
Beck, C.C. 14
Beck, Jackson 197, 203, 206
Beebe, Ford 47
Beemer, Brace 18, 20, 106, 109, 116-122, 133, 139, 140, 144
Beetleware 102
Beggs, Hegan 76
Behind the Mask 160
Bell, Dr. Joseph 170
Bell, Joseph 169, 171
Bell, Shirley 99-100
Bellamy, Ralph 73
Bellem, Robert 213
Belmont Paperbacks 166
Bennet, Spencer 14, 92, 210-211
Bennett, Bruce (*see* Brix, Herman)
Benton, Robert 214
Berwick, Viola 183
Bester, Alfred 149
Better Little Books 96
Betty and Bob 245
Beyond the Blue Horizon 117
Bierstadt, Edward Hale 149, 151, 152
Big Big Books 15
Big Broadcast 130
Big Little Books 5, 12, 15, 86, 95, 145, 215
Big Town 151
Billsbury, Rye 79
Billy the Kid 129
"Billy Throws a Boomerang" 91

Binder, Jack 162
Bivens, Jack 7, 9(p), 10, 183, 185(p)
Black Beauty 42
Black Museum 175
Blackstone 163
Blane, Sally 157
Blazing the Overland Trail 92, 211
Bletcher, Billy 132
Blondell, Gloria 51-53
"Blood of the Cat" 62
"Blood on the Border" 61
Blue Coal Co. 155, 167
Blue Coal Radio Revue 149
Blue Network 122, 124
"Blue Phantom Murders" 61
"Blue Water and Black Gold" 91
Blummer, Jon 144
Bobby Benson 59
Bobby Benson & his B-Bar B Riders 186
Bobby Benson and his H-Bar-O Rangers 109
Boggs, Redd 125,
Bold Caballero 137
Boles, Jim 50, 58-59
Bond, Tommy 210
Book of Monetti 78
Borg, Veda Ann 158
Boston Blackie 205
Boteler, Wade 48
Boucher, Anthony 170, 173
Bouchey, Bill 7-8
Bourbon Street Shadows 161
Bourdon, Rosario 117
Bouvert, Ray 252
Bowie, Jim 126
Bradley, Curley 57-59, 120-121, 219-256, (221, 232, 239, 246 p)
Bradley, Truman 79, 101
"Brahms' Lullabye" 65
Brando, Marlon 214
Breakfast Club 231
Bresee, Frank 57, 242, 247
"Bride of the Werewolf" 62, 65
Bridges at Toko-Ri 117
British Broadcasting Corporation 175, 182

Britt, Jeremy 182
Brix, Herman 127, 133
Broadcast Corned Beef Hash 122
Bromo Quinine Cold Tablets 171, 173
Brook, Clive 169, 171, 176, 177
Brooke, Walter 49
"Brooks Kidnapping" 62
Brown, Joe 93–94
Brownlow, Kevin 176
Bruce, Nigel 169–172, 179–180
"Bruce-Partington Plans" 173
Buck Rogers 215; radio, 85, 100, 205
Buffalo Bill 128, 143, 226
Buffalo, N.Y. 107
"Burglar to the Rescue" 157
Burtt, Robert M. 1, 5, 7–8, 183–184
"Bury Your Dead, Arizona" 55, 59, 61, 67
"But Grandma, What Big Teeth You Have" 63
Butterfield, Herb 79
Butterfield, Roland 79
Buttram, Pat 224
Buxton, Frank 130
Byrd, Commander 1

Call of the Wild 19
Campbell Playhouse 175
Canniff, Milton 95
Cannutt, Yakima 134, 137
Cansdale, Harry 99
Capone, Al 192
Capra, Frank 54
Captain America 11
Captain Marvel 15, 43, 95, 132, 212
Captain Midnight: comics magazine 15; film 10; radio 2, 4, 8–17, 102–103, 183; television 13
Captain Midnight's Adventure Theatre television 13,
Captain Video 44
Carey, Harry 137, 138, 217
Carey Salt 167
Carpenter, Laura Mae 149
Carradine, John 179

Carson, Ken "Shorty" 220, 221(p), 228
Carson, Kit 226
Carson, Paul 50
Cartier, Edd 163
"Case of the Nevada Man Killer" 61
"Case of the Roxy Mob" 61
"Case of the Terrified Comedian" 62
Casebook of Gregory Hood 174
"Caverns of Death" 152
Cavett, Dick 116
CBN 194
CBS 50, 56, 62, 79, 149
CBS Mystery Theatre 235, 240, 245
CBS Workshop 267
Challenge of the Yukon (Sgt. Preston) 18–25, 44–120
Chance, Al 219, 233
Chandler, Lane 127, 133
"Charity Takes It on the Chin" 44
Charlie Chan 48
Charlot, Harry Engman 149, 150
Charteris, Leslie 169, 170, 173
Cheerios 106, 122
Cherri-Oats 122
Chertok, Jack 191
"China Coast Incident" 63
"Circus Show-up" 157
"City of the Dead" 55
"City of the Sun God" 90
Claggett, Charles 219, 225
"Clear the Tracks" 91
Cleveland, George 135
Club Matinee 231
Coast to Coast on a Bus 100
Coates, Phyllis 212
Cobra 165
"Cobra King Strikes Back" 55
"Cobweb Castle" 91
Collier, Clayton (Bud) 197–199, 204–205, 209, 214
Collins, Ray 149
Collins, Tom 50, 63
Columbia Pictures 10, 12, 72, 158, 160, 209, 212
Columbo, Alberto 117
The Comics (magazine) 252
"Commuter to the Grave" 92

Conan Doyle, Sir Arthur 51, 54, 169–177, 180–181
Conway, Tom 169, 174
Coons, Johnny 7, 10, 183, 187
Copeland, Maurice 7
Corey, Rex 50
"Corpse in Compartment C, Car 76" 62
"Corpse of the Year" 49
Corwin, Norman 235
Country Beyond 19
Courtley, Steve 149
Courtney, Margaret 241, 248
Courtney, Raymond George *see* Bradley, Curley
Covered Wagon Days 107–111
Crane, Les 76
Craven, James 10
Crawford, H. Marion 182
Crime Circus 165
Crime Does Not Pay 157
Crime Files of Flammond 120
Crime Master 165
Crockett, Davy 126
Crosby, Bing 173
Crowley, Matt 197, 205
Curley, Leo 220, 232(p), 233, 239(p)
Curley Bradley, the Singing Marshal 244, 248
Curley Bradley's Trail of Mystery 211, 241, 242, 244
Curley Edwards and His Cowboys 109–111
Curwood, James Oliver 19
Cushing, Peter 181–182
Custer, General George 129, 143
Cutts, Graham 177
Dahlsted, Dresser 51
Dane, Frankie 79
Danforth, William H. 225, 231
"Danger-North of Singapore" 91
"Danger Under the Sea" 91
Daniel, Henry 181
Daniels, Leslie N. 95
Daniels, Mark 161
David Harding, Counterspy 92, 205
Davidson, Ronald 139
Dawn Patrol 2

DC Comic Magazines 162, 209, 211, 213, 215–217
"Deadliest of the Species" 92
"Deadly Sin of Sir Richard Coyle" 62
Deadwood Dick 107
Dean, Basil 176
"Death and the Dollar Sign" 92
"Death from the Deep" 152
"Death House Rescue" 152
"Death Prowls at Night" 152
"Death Rides High" 151
Death Valley Days 100
"Decapitation of Jefferson Monk" 62, 73
Deeds, Jack 106, 117, 119
Deerstalker 176
Dell Publishing 15
Delmar, Kenny 149
DeMille, Katherine 5
DeNormand, George 47, 134, 158, 224, 242
Dent, Lester 163
Derr, Richard 161
Destry Rides Again (film, 1932) 222, 249
Detective Comics 214, 215
Detective in Film 176
Detective Story Hour 151
Detective Story Magazine 151, 157
Detroit Evening Times 117
"Devil and the Pumpkin" 91
"Devil's Castle" 90
Devil's Mask 75
"Devil's Sanctuary" 63
Devine, Jerry 149, 152
Dick Tracy 1, 4, 14, 26–40, 64, 235
Dickens, Charles 150
Dickey, Basil 47
Dickson, Artells 219, 225
Diller, Phyllis 117
Disney, Walt 142
Doc Savage 43, 162
Dr. Dragonette 108
"Donna Diana Overture" 19
Donnelly, Andy 220
Donner, Richard 213
Doty, Jack 79
Doubleday Crime Club 166

Dougall, Tom 106
Douglas, Don 51
Douglas, Paul 101
Dover Books 166
Dozier, William 48
Dracula 70
"Dragon's Teeth" 203
Dressed to Kill 181
Dru, Joanne 49
Dryden, Robert 59, 197
DuBois, Gaylord 146
Ducovy, Allen 197
Dumas, Alexander 60, 217
Dunlap, Patricia 79, 220

Earp, Wyatt 250, 251
Eason, B. Reeves "Breezy" 141, 250
Eastwood, Clint 57, 142
Eby, Lois 139
E.C. Publishers 95
Edwards, Blake 251
Edwards, Jack 50
"Eight Kinds of Murder" 62
Eisenhower, Dwight D. "Ike" 236
Elders, Harry 7
Eldredge, Tom 109
Elizabeth the Queen 118
Ellery Queen 63
Elliot, Bruce 163
Ellstrom, Sidney 220, 221(p)
Engel, Roy 183, 187
English, John 132, 139
"Enter the Lone Ranger" 140
Erhlich, Max 149
Erskine, Laurie York 21
"Escapade of the Desert Hag" 61
Evans, Mitch 197

Fabulous Tom Mix 251,
Fairbanks, Douglas 109
"Faith, Hope and Charity" 66
Falken, Jinx 139
Famous Funnies 214
Farrington, Feilden 41
Fatima cigarettes 174
Faust, Donovan 41
Fawcett Publications 15

F.B.I. 89-90, 92
"Fear That Creeps Like a Cat" 61-62, 76
Ferguson, Franklyn 220
Fields, W.C. 93
"Final Hour" 154
"Final Problem" 175
"Find Elsa Holberg, Dead or Alive" 62
First Nighter 59, 231, 245
Fiske, Robert 1, 3, 5
Fitzmaurice, Michael 197, 204
"The Five Hundred Hitter" 91
Flaming Guns 250
Flanders, Charles 144
Flash Gordon: comics magazine 95; radio 117
Fleisher, Dave 209
Fleisher, Max 209
Fleishmann's Yeast 55
Fleming, Ian 177
Fletcher, Tex 186
"Flight of the Bumble Bee" 42, 49
"Flight to Death" 61
Floweraday, Fred 18, 106, 122
Flynn, Charles 79, 81(p), 82, 93
"Fog Island" 91
Ford, Glenn 214
Ford, John 54
Forman, Carol 212
Foster, Hal 145
Fox, Gardner 217
Fox, Gibson Scott 106
Fox, William 249
Foy, Fred 18, 20, 82, 106, 116
Fran Striker Continuities 111
Frank, Carl 149
Frank Merriwell 161
Fraser, Ferrin N. 99
From Out of the Past: A Pictorial History of the Lone Ranger 107
Frost, Alice 149
The Funnies (magazine) 15
Fussel, Sarah 51

Gangbusters 10, 41, 111, 155
Gannon, John 79, 85(p), 85
Garabedian, George 244

Gardner Agency 228, 231
Gargan, William 5
Garner, James 251
Garrett, Sheriff Pat 125, 129
Gielgud, John 169, 175
Gene Autry Western Heritage Museum 139
General Mills 95-96, 98, 106, 122, 240
Genghis Khan 165
George, Earl 7
George Washington Coffee 171, 182
Gerson, Betty Lou 220
Getty, Estelle 13
Gettysburg Address 204
Ghost of Frankenstein 73
Ghost of Zorro 139
"Ghost Riders of Cripple Creek" 91
"Giant Rat of Sumatra" 173
Gibson, Hoot 217
Gibson, John 51
Gibson, Walter 149-151, 158, 160-167
Gilbert, Janice 99
Gill, Tom 144
Gillette, William 169, 171
Gillman, Page 51
Gingham Bread 122
Girard, Joe 13
"Girl in the Gilded Cage" 62, 67
"Girl in the Street" 63-64
"Girl to Aid" 126
"Girl's Finishing School Kidnapping" 63
Gladney, Graves 163
Glut, Donald F. 45
Gobel, George 220
Golden Days of Radio 58
Golden Girls 13
"Golden Master" 166
Golder, Harry 106, 116
Goldwyn, Samuel 176
Gomez, Thomas 180
Gordon, Don 7, 220, 233
Gordon, Mary 169, 181
Gordon, Richard 169, 171, 182
Gordon, Stanley 183
Gordon Bakery's Silver Cup Bread 122

Gosden, Freeman 267
Goss, Jim 84(p), 85
Gottchak, Norman 183, 189
Gough, Lloyd 48
Grainer, Sharon 7
Grand Central Station 41
Grand National Studio 157-158
Grand Ole Opry 226
"Grandma, What Big Teeth You Have!" 64
Grant, Kirby 192, 193(p), 195
Grant, Maxwell *see* Gibson, Walter
Grant, Ulysses S. 143
Graser, Earle W. 20, 106, 118-121, 133
Gratz, Barbara 220
"Graves of Whamperjaw, Texas" 62
Gray, Harold 99-103
Gray Seal 43
Grayson, Mitchell 197
"Great Air Mail Robbery" 63
Great Detectives 167
Great K&A Train Robbery 249
"Great Lunar Rocket" 91
Green, Bob 106
Green, Dennis 169, 170, 173
The Green Hornet: radio 41-49, 120, 130-131, 155, 205, 247; film 47
The Green Hornet Strikes Again 49
Green Mansions 69
Greene, Richard 179
Greene, Vernon 162
Greenwald, Ken 170
Gregg, Virginia 247-248
Grey, Zane 21, 107, 110
Grey Fist 165
Griffith, Les 220
Grosset and Dunlap, publishers 146, 166
Grossman, Gary H. 22
Guiou, Milt 79
Gulla, Richard 195, 220, 245
Gunsmoke (television) 57

Haggerty, Ron 193-195
Hall, Bob 41, 45(p)
Halliday, Brett 167

Hammett, Dashiel 144
Hang 'Em High 57
Happy Days 141
Harcourt Brace Jovanovich 164
Harding, Lyn 177
Harper, Bill and Teresa 253
Harris, Graham 169
Harris, Paul 107
Harris, Stacy 197, 205
Hart, John 92-94, 141
Hartman, David 76
Hartzel, Clarence 183, 190
Hatton, Rhondo 181
"Haunted Lighthouse" 213
Hawkes, Kirby 7, 9(p)
Hawkins Falls 188
Hayashi, Raymond 41
Haydock, Ron 176, 240
Hearn, Lou 158
"Hearse on the Highway" 63
Hearst, George 43
Hearst, William Randolph 43
Heath, Russ 145
Hector, Louis 169, 171
Hemus, Percy 219, 221(p), 231
"Hermit of San Felipe Atabapo" 62, 69
Hern, Art 7, 9, 13, 183, 220, 244
Hess, Erwin 15
Hickock, Wild Bill 125, 129
Hidden Gold 250
"High Heels" 140
His Typewriter Wore Spurs 126
Hitchcock, Alfred 54
Hite, Bob 18, 41, 106
Hodge, Al 18, 41, 44, 47-48, 106, 120, 205
Hodiak, John 106
Hoey, Dennis 181
Hoffman, Bill 169
Holden, Jack 219, 226
Hole, Jonathan 220
Holland, Dave 107, 109, 113, 114, 116, 130, 144
"Hollywood Cherry" 66
Holmes, Wendell 169, 175
Holt, Felix 106
Holt, Jack 10
Hoover, J. Edgar 90, 92

Hop Harrigan 1, 144
Horne, James V. 12, 160
Horse, Michael 142
Houdini, Harry 163
Houdini Escapes 163
Hound of the Baskervilles 171, 174, 176-178, 179, 182
House of Fear 181
"House of Mystery" 157
Household Finance 182
Howard, Ronald 182
Howard, William K. 176
Hudson, W.H. 69
Hughes, Floy Margaret 99, 100
Hughes, Paul 106
Hugo, Victor 164
Hull, Warren 49
"Hundred Million Dollar Manhunt" 63
Hunter, Ian 177
"Hurricane Destroyer" 91
"Hypnotized Audience" 152

"I Am the Destroyer of Women" 62
I Love a Mystery: film 72, radio 1, 41, 50-78, 173, 257-266; television 76
I Love Adventure 50, 63-64
"I Remember Comic Books" 215
"I Remember Flash Gordon" 215
In Old Monterey 229
In the Days of the Thundering Herd 248
"Incident Concerning Death" 61
Ingram, Jack 159
Inner Sanctum 150, 235
International Crime 158
"Invincible Shiwan Khan" 166
Invisible Avenger 161
"Invisible Rider" 237
Irving, Clifford 251
Irwin, Jim 41, 44
"Island of Skulls" 55

Jack Armstrong 4, 10, 79-98, 100, 120, 183-186, 189, 191, 200-201, 205

Jack Armstrong & the Ivory Treasure 95
Jack Armstrong & the Mystery of Iron Key 96
"Jack Armstrong in South America" 90
Jackson, Thomas 158
Jacobs, Amos 106
Jameson, House 21
Jefferson studios 125
Jellison, Bob 220
Jet Jackson 14
Jewell, James 41, 79, 90–91, 106–109, 111–124
Jimmie Allen in Sky Parade 5
Johnstone, Bill 149, 152, 161
Johnstone, Jack 197, 200
Johnstone, Ted 106
Jones, Buck 187, 228
Jones, Gerard 162
Jones, Gordon 46(p), 47, 48
Jones, Reginald 117
Jordan, Miriam 176
Jordon, John 253
Jory, Victor 158–159
Joyce of the Secret Squadron 15
Jungle Jim 117
"Jungle Shadows" 91
Just Plain Bill 80

KaDell, Carlton 187
Kalish, Scheindel 70
Kaluta, Mike 162
Kamp Kee-Mo Sah-Bee 114
Kane, Bob 150
Kane, Frank 151
Katzman, Sam 92, 209–212
Kaufman, Phil 160
Keach, Jim 142
Keane, Jack 197
Keene, Day 99
Kellogg's Pep 203
Kendall, Steve 242–244, 247–248
Kennedy, Edgar 157
Killer at the Wheel 77
"Killer of the Circle M" 62
King, Fred L. 94, 96, 270
King, John 125

King Features 144
King of the Rocket Men 212
King of the Royal Mounted 21, 22
Kirby, Jack 11
Kix 106
Knight, Frank 197
Kolmar, Richard 205
Komach, James 49
Kosleck, Martin 181
Kovner, Dawn 70, 245
Kramer, Mandel 197
Kressy, Ed 143
Kressy, Maryland 144
Kroneke, Carl 220
Krugman, Lou 220
KTTV 180
Ku Klux Klan 127
Kunsky *see* King, John
"Kwan-Moon Dagger" 63–64

La Planche, Rosemary 93–94
La Rocque, Rod 157–158
LaCurto, James 149
"Lake of Mystery" 90
Lanfield, Sidney 179
Laurel and Hardy 12, 160
Lava, William 117
A Lavish of Sin 77
Lee, Bruce 49
Lee, Christopher 182
Lee, Don 122
"Legion of Old Timers" 140
Leone, Serge 142
Lester, Jack 79, 90, 183, 187, 188(p), 190, 194, 245, 247
Lester, Warner 108
Let's Pretend 100
Letz, George *see* Montgomery, George
Levin, Henry 74
Levine, Nat 250
Lewis, Cathy 51
Lewis, Elliot 51
Lewis, Forrest 51, 73, 189, 220, 232(p), 240, 245
Lincoln, Abraham 128, 177, 204
Lincoln, Elmo 135
Lindbergh, Charles 1–2, 5

"Lingo" 162
Lipton, James 106
Liss, Ron 197, 205
Little, Brown 167
Little Orphan Annie 4, 99–105, 144, 203
Living Shadow (novel) 163, 166
Livingston, Robert 136, 137(p)
Livingstone, Charles D. 18, 41, 106, 120, 124
Lockridge, Richard 167
London, Jack 19
The Lone Ranger: radio 18–21, 41, 42, 44, 80, 82, 86–87, 90–92, 98, 106–148, 155, 161, 185, 239, 240, 241–242, 247, 249; film 142; film serial 117, 132; magazine 146; novel 146
The Lone Ranger & His Horse, Silver 146
The Lone Ranger & the Lost City of Gold 142
The Lone Ranger & the Menace of Murder Valley 146
The Lone Ranger & the Mystery Ranch 146
The Lone Ranger & the Red Renegades 146
The Lone Ranger & the Secret Killer 146
The Lone Ranger & the Vanishing Herd 146
"The Lone Ranger Fights On" 140
"The Lone Ranger Follows Through" 145
The Lone Ranger on the Barbary Coast 145
The Lone Ranger Rides Again 137, 146
Lone Ranger Television/Palladium 122
"The Lone Ranger's Triumph" 140
Lone Star Ranger 107
Lord, Athena 51, 59
Lord, Phillips H. 111
"Lost Moon" 14
Loughrane, Basil 169
Lovell, Leigh 169, 171, 182
Lowther, George 152, 197, 219, 235, 251

Lucky (horse) 229
Luke, Keye 49
Lum and Abner 190
Lupino, Ida 179
Lupoff, Richard 215
Lux Radio Theatre 173
Lynds, Denis 166
Lyons, Cliff 134, 164, 224

Ma Perkins 80, 108, 267
McBride, DeWitt 220
Maccabees Building 124
McCambridge, Mercedes 51, 55
McCarthy, Frank 51
McCarthy, Jack 41, 44
McCarthy, John 191
MacCormack, Franklyn 79, 101
McCoy, Tim 187
MacCready, George 74
McCullough, Dan 203
McCune, Vance 220, 221(p)
MacDonald, Ross 167
MacDonald, Wallace 74
McDonald, William Colt 217
McGill, Jerry 154
McIntire, John 50
McKee, Bob 79
McKinnell, Norman 177
McKnight, Tom 169
McLaughlin, Don 197, 205
McLean, Murray 1, 3(p), 5, 8, 79
McNeill, Don 231
Mad magazine 77
Magyar, Rich 162
Mahoney, Jock 220, 247
"Man Who Could Work Miracles" 237
"Man Who Hated to Shave" 62
"Man Who Wasn't There" 236
"Man with a Million Faces" 94
"Man with the Third Green Eye" 63
Manhunters 108, 111
Manning, Knox 169, 171, 172
Margolies, Lyonel 47
"Mark of El Diablo" 190
Mark Trail 205
Markham, Steve 246
Marks, Sherman 7

Marschall, Richard 99
Martin, Ian 169
Martini, Roland 99, 219
Martinson, Leslie H. 48
Marvel Comics Publishers 162
Mascot Pictures 250
Massey, Raymond 177
Master Comics 253
Master of Death 166
Mathews, Grace 149
Maxwell, Jessica 197
Maxwell, Robert 106, 197, 213
May, Naomi 79
Mayal, Herschel 106
Maynard, Ken 187
Meagher, Fred 243, 252
"Medicine Men of the Everglades" 91
Meiser, Edith 169-173
Melton, Sid 13
Mendelssohn mansion 125
Menser, Clarence L. 219
Merita Bread 122
Merrill, Gary 197
Merrill, Howard 169
Metropolitan Opera of the Air 267
MGM 157, 179
Michael, Jay 18, 106, 120
Michaelson, Charles 122, 155
Michigan Radio Network 117 121
Miller, Marvin 7, 79
Miller, Ruth 224
Miller, Walter 157
"Million Dollar Mystery" 59, 61
Miracle Rider 224, 250
Missing Lady 160
Missing Rembrandt 177
Mr. District Attorney 151
Mr. Mercury 92
Mr. Peepers 58
Mix, Olive Stokes 251
Mix, Paul 251
Mix, Tom 1, 109, 187, 218-256, 249(p)
Monks, James 99
Monogram Pictures 160
"Monster in the Mansion" 62, 64

Montgomery, George 127, 133
Moon Mullins 203
Moore, Clayton 5, 8, 139, 141, 161, 184
Moore, Garry 228, 231
Moore, Roger 159
Moore, Tom 7
Moore, Willfred G. 1, 7, 183
Moore, William 158
Moorehead, Agnes 149, 169
Morell, André 182
Morgot Stevenson 149
Morison, Patricia 181
Morrison, Bret 149, 152-154, 161, 197, 205
Morse, Carlton E. 50-78, 164, 235, 257-266
Morse, Ed 85
Mowry, Jean 183
Mox 165
Munday, Talbot 79, 95
Murder at the Baskervilles 177
"Murder Hollywood Style" 61
"Murder in E Flat" 152
"Murder in the Dope Racket" 45
"Murder in Turquoise Pass" 62
"Murder Is the Word for It" 62
"Murder on February Island" 62
"Murders in Wax" 152
Murphy, Pat 79
Mutual Broadcasting System 8, 18, 41, 56, 62, 99, 106, 122, 127, 149, 155, 169, 197, 204, 227
"My Beloved Is a Vampire" 62
Mysterious Pilot (film) 12
Mysterious Rider 107
"Mystery of Holiday Lodge" 92
"Mystery of the Flaming Warrior" 250
"Mystery of the Iron Key" 87
Mystery of the Masked Man's Music 117
"Mystery of the Trans-Coast Limited" 91
"Mystery of the Vanishing Herd" 235
"Mystery of the Vanishing Village" 244

Nabisco Products 194
Nagel, Anne 49
Nanovic, John 165
Natco the Clown 244
National Airways 2
National Barn Dance 226, 230
National Farm and Home Hour 231
NBC 50, 55-56, 62, 99-100, 122, 169, 219; NBC Blue 79, 106; NBC Red 79
Neal, Hal 41
Neil, Noel 210, 214
Neill, Roy William 180
Neily, Rev. Robert E. 82
Nesbitt, Lloyd 245
Neumeyer, Marilou 7, 10
Neville, Harry 169
New Fun Comics 215
Newman, David 214
Newman, Leslie 214
Newman, Paul S. 144
Nick Carter, Master Detective 161
"Night Marauders" 152
"Night Rider" 90
"Night Without End" 152
Nightingale, Earl 183, 187, 195
Noa, Julian 197
Nolan, Bob 230
Nolan, Jeanette 63, 169, 181
Nolan, Lloyd 73
Nordine, Ken 183
Northern Patrol 192
Northwest Mounted Police 18
Norwood, Eille 176
Novello, Jay 50

Oakley, Annie 243
O'Brien, Dave 10, 11(p)
Odd Couple 59
Of Mice and Men 231
Official Overstreet Comic Book Price Guide 217
Olivier, Laurence 76
O'Mera, Jerry 99
"On the High Seas" 90

One Man's Family 54-55, 57, 61, 78, 190
O'Neal, Charles 74
Orban, Paul 163
Orr, Angeline 7
Ovaltine Products 12, 99-103
Owen, Bill 130
Owen, Reginald 176, 177
Owens, David 79

Packard, Frank 43
Paramount on Parade 176
Parker, Rollon 41, 106
Parmount Pictures 212
Patterson, Walter 50, 54, 63
Payne, Virginia 108
Pearl Harbor, Dec. 1, 1941 202
Pearl of Death 181
"Pearl of Great Price" 63
Peary, Hal 220
Peeples, Cornelius 220
Peeples, Sam 224
Penzler, Otto 167
Peon 215
Pep cereal 197, 203
Perils of Pauline 12, 92
"Perils of Superman" 213
Pete Smith Specialties 10
Peter Pan Peanut Butter 91, 196
Peterson, Arthur 220
Petri wine 175
Petrie, George 197
Petruzzi, Jack 41, 106, 220
Pettus, Ken 48-49
Pfeufer, Carl 253
"Phantom of the Sawdust Trail" 90
Pickett, Bill 243
Pickford, Mary 101
Pierce, Holward 109
Pistol Packin' Mama 209
Plympton, George H. 47, 136, 212
Ponicsan, Darryl 251
Poppe, Harry H. 141
Portia Faces Life 211
"Portrait of a Murderer" 62
Powell, Bob 162
Powell, Lee 127, 133
Powersmoke Range 217

Prentiss, Ed 1, 7-8, 9(p)
Public Broadcasting System 76
Pugh, Jess 7, 220
Pursuit to Algiers 181
Puzo, Mario 214
Pynton, Loretta 79
Pyramid/Jove Paperbacks 166

Quaker Puffed Wheat Sparkies 102

Raboy, Mac 15
Radio Guide 78
Radio Mirror 78, 124
Radio's Golden Age 130
Raffetto, Michael 50, 52, 60, 63, 72-73
Ralston-Purina products 4, 219-256
Ranch Boys Trio 220, 221(p), 229
Ranch-House Jim 231
Randall, Tony 58-59, 63
Rashomon 110
Rathbone, Basil 169-174, 179-180
Rathmell, John 250
Rathrauff, Bourne 149
Rawlings, John 180
Raymond, Alex 95, 144, 145
RCA Black Seal 117
Reader's Digest 116
Readick, Frank 149, 157
Red Ryder 57, 73
"Red Scare" 157
Red Skelton Show (television) 10
Reed, Alan 149
Reed, Barbara 160
Reeve, Christopher 210, 214
Reeves, George 210, 212-214
Reeves-Smith, H. 176
Renaldo, Duncan 138
Rendell, Robert 178
Renfrew of the Mounted 21-22
Republic Pictures 11, 117, 124, 138, 160-161, 212
"Return of Carnation Charlie" 152
Return of Sherlock Holmes 176
Rhinehart, Mary Roberts 150
Richardson, Ralph 175
Richmond, Kane 160

Riders of Durango Valley 150
The Right Stuff 160
Rimsky-Korsakov 42
Rin Tin Tin 19
Rio, Rosa 149
Ritter, Tex 10
Road to Danger 231
Rockwell, Jack 250
Rodier, Rene 7-8
Rogers, Roy 224, 230, 240
Roland, Gilbert 138
Roosevelt, Franklin D. 138, 223
Rose, Bill 7
Ross, Jack 219-220, 221(p), 228
Ross, Stanley Ralph 161
Rothel, David 114
Rough Riders 223
Rowlands, Hugh 220
Rozen, George 163
Russell, Frank 106
Rye, Michael 79

Saint, Eva Marie 57
St. John, Al "Fuzzy" 137
St. Louis Post-Dispatch 143
Salkind, Alexander 213
Salkind, Ilya 213
Sam Spade 63
San Francisco Examiner 43
Sanders, George 174
Saturday Evening Post 107
Saxe, Henry 99
"Scandal in Bohemia" 173
Scarlet Claw 181
Scarlet Pimpernell 175
Scattergood Baines 190
Schaefer, Armand 250
Schendel, Stan 252
Scott, Randolph 73
"Sealed Lips" 157
Sears Radio Theatre 241
Seaton, George *see* Stenius, George
"Secret Base" 90
"Secret Loot of the Island of Skulls" 62
"Secret Mission" 236
"Secret Passage to Death" 56, 62, 67
Seldon, George 169-175

Selig Films 248
Sells-Floto Circus 222
Sergeant Preston of the Yukon 18–25, 87, 155, 192, 247
Serling, Rod 150
Service, Robert W. 19
Seven Doors to Death 72
Sewell, Anne 42
Seyfferitz, Gustav 176
The Shadow 8, 41, 43, 63, 149–168, 241–242
Shadow Comics 161
Shadow Detective Series 157
Shadow Magazine 163–166
The Shadow Returns 160
The Shadow Scrapbook 164
The Shadow Strikes 157; comic 162
The Shadow Unmasks 164
Shaw, Bob 106
Shazam (television) 245
Shea, Gil 41
Shelley, Bill 169
"Shells of Evil" 12
Sherlock Holmes 155, 169–181; film 176
Sherlock Holmes and the Secret Weapon 180
Sherlock Holmes Baffled 176
Sherlock Holmes Faces Death 180
Sherlock Holmes in Washington 180
Sherlock Holmes Stories 182
Sherlock Holmes' Fatal Hour 177
Sherwood, Don 77
Shipman, Barry 139
Shirley, Alfred 169
Shirley, Tom 79
"Shiwan Khan Returns" 166
"Shooting of Dan McGrew" 19
Short, Dorothy 10
Shuster, Joe 215
Sibelius 51
Siegel, Jerry 215
Sign of Four 177
"Silent Gun" 48
Silver Blaze 177
Silvercup Bread 106
Silverheels, Jay 140, 141
Simcox, Tom 49
Simmons, Richard 22

Sitting Bull 129
Six Shooter 173
60 Minutes 189
Skelly Oil Company 4
Skippy 216
Sky King 1, 4, 14, 91, 120, 183–196, 244
Sky King & the Runaway Train 195
Sloan, Everett 149
Slobb, Kermit 79
Sly, Leonard *see* Rogers, Roy
Smart, J. Scott 169–173
Smythe, J. Anthony 61
Sneary, Rick 215
Snowden, Eric 169, 175
Sondergaard, Gale 180
Sons of the Pioneers 230
Sorel, Guy 197
Soubier, Cliff 183–184
Soule, Olan 7, 13, 79, 99, 220
Spear, William 54
Speckled Band 177
Spell of the Yukon 19
The Spider Magazine 43
The Spider Returns (film) 12
Spider Woman Strikes Back 181
The Spider's Web (film) 12, 160
Spillsbury, Klinton 142
"The Spook Train" 91
Spy Smasher 160
"Stairway to the Sun" 56, 62
Stanley, Ernie 106
Stanley, John 169, 175
Star Wars 142
Stark, Sheldon 106, 115
Starr, Leonard 99, 103
Steele, Bob 22, 217
Stenius, George 106, 114–119
Stevenson, Margot 151
Stevenson, Robert Louis 51, 164, 202
Stewart, James 173
Stoker, Bram 70
"Stolen Costume" 213
Straight Arrow 115, 187
Strange, Glenn 140
Stranger from the South 251
Street & Smith 151, 157, 161, 163

Street & Smith's Detective Hour 149-150, 149
Striker, Fran 18, 41, 44, 47, 106-108, 110-146
Strong, Col. Pascal 79, 88
Studebaker, Hugh 7
A Study in Scarlet 177
Stuff the Lady's Hatbox 77
Sully, Frank 160
Sunset 251
Superman 1, 14, 43, 93, 95, 197-218, 235, 241, 242; serial 212
Superman and the Mole Men 212
Superman V 214
Superman, the Movie 213
"Superman Week" 213
"Superman's Wife" 213
Suspense 54, 173
"Sussex Vampire" 173
Sutton, Paul 18, 20, 23
Swanson, Gloria 173

Tailspin Tommy 1
Talbot, Lyle 212
Tales of Fatima 174
Taliaferro, Hal 127, 133
Taylor, Bruce 169, 170
Taylor, Glenhall 169, 174
Taylor, Ray 47
Tazewell, Charles 219
Tedro, Henrietta 99
"Temple Bells of Neban" 152
"Temple of Vampires" 61-62, 70
Tempo 166
Tennessee Jed 59
"Tenor with the Broken Voice" 152
Terrell, St. John 79, 82, 99
Terror by Night 181
"Terror of Frozen Corpse Lodge" 62
Terror Trail 251
Terry and the Pirates 95
Texas Rangers 223
Thailing, Bill 125
Thin Man 59
"Thing That Cries in the Night" 55, 61, 65, 76
"Thing Wouldn't Die" 62

Third Man 175
Thomas, Frank 171
Thomas, Roy 215
Thorne, Richard 183
Thorson, Russell 57-59, 63, 219, 221(p), 228
Three Mesquiteers 137, 217
Three Musketeers 60, 217
Three Stooges 157
Thundercloud, Chief 132, 133, 137(p), 138, 140
Tinsley, Theodore 150, 163
To Tell the Truth 198
Todd, John 18, 20, 41, 44, 106, 116-117
Tolan, Mickey 41
Tollin, Anthony 151
Tom Mix Album (records) 229
Tom Mix and His Ralston Straight Shooters 57, 58, 80, 86, 130, 183-184, 188-189, 219-256
Tom Mix and Poncho Villa 251
Tom Mix & the Mystery of the Flaming Warrior 238
Tom Mix Circus 222
Tom Mix Comics 251
Tom Mix Commandos Comics 252
Tom Mix Died for Your Sins 251
Tom Mix Western 253
Tony (horse) 219-256
Tony Jr. (horse) 220
Toomey, Winifred 220
"Top Secret Weapon" 14
Toth, Alex 243
Tracy, Spencer 158
Trader Horn 138
Trail of the Terrible Six 251
Trail of the Yukon 192
"Trapped" 157
Treasure Island 51, 89, 101, 202
Tremayne, Les 51, 59, 68(p), 69, 79, 220, 244, 248
Trendle, George W. 18, 42, 49, 106-109, 113-146
Triumph of Sherlock Holmes 177
"Tropics Don't Call it Murder" 62
"Trouble at Sea" 61
True, Harold 106, 109-111, 116
True Comics 94

"Turn of the Wheel" 61
Turner, Harold 233
TV Guide 206
Twentieth Century Fox 179
"Twenty Traitors of Timbuktu" 62
Tyler, Tom 137, 217

Ultra Violet 108
"Undertaker's Funeral" 92
Union Pacific Railroad 128
Universal Pictures 49, 157, 179–181, 249
The Unknown 74

Vallee, Rudy 179
Vallely, Henry E. 95–96, 145
"Valley of Fear" 177
"Valley of Silent Men" 19
"Valse Triste" 51
Van Rooten, Luis 51
Van Slyke, Arthur 79
Vaughn, Beryl 183, 185(p), 189
Vic and Sade 190
Victor Symphony 117
Vigilantes Are Coming 137
Vinton, Arthur 149
"Voice Machine" 204
Voice of Terror 180
"Voice of Treason" 92

Wagner, Wende 49
Wales, Wally *see* Taliaferro, Hal
Wall, Lucille 169
Wallace, Alan 7, 99
Wallace, Mike 41, 120, 183, 189
Wander Co. 14, 102
Warden Lawes of Sing Sing 151
Warner, Gertrude 149
Warner Communications 216
Washburn, Bryant 10
Waterman, Willard 219–220, 226
Watkin, Pierre 93–94
Way Out There 230
Wayne, John 132, 137, 192, 229, 250
Wayne State University 119

WDET 124
Webb, Jane 220, 221(p)
Webb, Richard 13
WEBR 107, 111
"Wedding of Superman" 213
Welles, Orson 54–55, 149, 152, 161, 169–170
Wells, H. G. 54
Wells, Sarajane 79, 84(p), 85
West, Adam 210
West, Harold 169, 171
Western Union 128
Wever, Ned 197
WGN, Chicago 155
Wheaties 4, 81, 92, 96, 106
"When the Bloom Is on the Sage" 233
"Whispering Eyes" 163
White, Pearl 12
"White God" 152
Whiting, Barbara 193
Whitman Publishing 12, 15, 95–96
"Whose Body Got Buried" 61
Wick, Bruno 220
Widmark, Richard 149
"A Wife for Judas" 92
Wild Bill Hickok 240
Wilding Pictures 194
Wilkerson, Guy 10
"William Tell Overture" 42, 110, 117
Williams, Big Boy 217
Williams, Van 49
Windsor, Roy 183, 187, 191
Wings 2
Winterbothom, Russ 15
Winters, Gloria 194–195
"Wise Guy" 92
Witch's Tale 150
Wither's Grant 5
Witney, William 132, 139
Wolter, Bob 241
Woman in Green 181
Woman in My House 59
Wonder Woman 161
Wong, Barbara Jean 51, 53, 63
Wontner, Arthur 177
Wood, Morrison C. 47
Woods, Charles 41, 106
Woods, Lesley 149

World Broadcasting 1–2
World's Finest Comics 217
Wrather, Jack 142
Wright, Ben 50, 169, 175
Wright, Peter 152
Wright Brothers 13
WXYZ 18, 21, 41–42, 44, 106–109, 113, 117, 120, 122, 124–129, 144
Wyatt Earp 194

XERO 215

Yarborough, Barton 50, 54, 60, 63, 73, 74(p), 75(p)
Yates, George Washington 139
Yates, Herbert J. 138
York, Dick 79
Young, Polly Ann 157
Young, Roland 176
Young, Russ 7
Younger, Beverly 183
Yrigoyen, Joe 134

Zatara the Magician 214
Zucco, George 179–180

www.ingramcontent.com/pod-product-compliance
Ingram Content Group UK Ltd.
Pitfield, Milton Keynes, MK11 3LW, UK
UKHW041926140426
5217IPUK00014B/335